THE NEW
PALGRAVE

ECONOMETRICS

THE NEW
PALGRAVE

ECONOMETRICS

EDITED BY

JOHN EATWELL · MURRAY MILGATE · PETER NEWMAN

W.W. NORTON & COMPANY

NEW YORK · LONDON

© The Macmillan Press Limited, 1987, 1990

First published in
The New Palgrave: A Dictionary of Economics
Edited by John Eatwell, Murray Milgate and Peter Newman
in four volumes, 1987

The New Palgrave is a trademark of
The Macmillan Press Limited

First American Edition, 1990
All rights reserved.

ISBN 0-393-02731-7

ISBN 0-393-95856-6   PBK

W. W. Norton & Company, Inc.
500 Fifth Avenue
New York, NY 10110

W. W. Norton & Company, Ltd.
37 Great Russell Street
London WC1B 3NU

Printed in Hong Kong

1   2   3   4   5   6   7   8   9   0

Contents

Contents

General Preface

The books in this series are the offspring of *The New Palgrave: A Dictionary of Economics*. Published in late 1987, the *Dictionary* has rapidly become a standard reference work in economics. However, its four heavy tomes containing over four million words on the whole range of economic thought is not a form convenient to every potential user. For many students and teachers it is simply too bulky, too comprehensive and too expensive for everyday use.

By developing the present series of compact volumes of reprints from the original work, we hope that some of the intellectual wealth of *The New Palgrave* will become accessible to much wider groups of readers. Each of the volumes is devoted to a particular branch of economics, such as econometrics or general equilibrium or money, with a scope corresponding roughly to a university course on that subject. Apart from correction of misprints, etc. the content of each of its reprinted articles is exactly the same as that of the original. In addition, a few brand new entries have been commissioned especially for the series, either to fill an apparent gap or more commonly to include topics that have risen to prominence since the dictionary was originally commissioned.

As *The New Palgrave* is the sole parent of the present series, it may be helpful to explain that it is the modern successor to the excellent *Dictionary of Political Economy* edited by R.H. Inglis Palgrave and published in three volumes in 1894, 1896 and 1899. A second and slightly modified version, edited by Henry Higgs, appeared during the mid-1920s. These two editions each contained almost 4,000 entries, but many of those were simply brief definitions and many of the others were devoted to peripheral topics such as foreign coinage, maritime commerce, and Scottish law. To make room for the spectacular growth in economics over the last 60 years while keeping still to a manageable length, *The New Palgrave* concentrated instead on economic theory, its originators, and its closely cognate disciplines. Its nearly 2,000 entries (commissioned from over 900 scholars) are all self-contained essays, sometimes brief but never mere definitions.

Apart from its biographical entries, *The New Palgrave* is concerned chiefly with theory rather than fact, doctrine rather than data; and it is not at all clear how theory and doctrine, as distinct from facts and figures, *should* be treated in an encyclopaedia. One way is to treat everything from a particular point of view. Broadly speaking, that was the way of Diderot's classic *Encyclopédie raisonée* (1751–1772), as it was also of Léon Say's *Nouveau dictionnaire d'économie politique* (1891–2). Sometimes, as in articles by Quesnay and Turgot in the *Encyclopédie*, this approach has yielded entries of surpassing brilliance. Too often, however, both the range of subjects covered and the quality of the coverage itself are seriously reduced by such a self-limiting perspective. Thus the entry called '*Méthode*' in the first edition of Say's *Dictionnaire* asserted that the use of mathematics in economics 'will only ever be in the hands of a few', and the dictionary backed up that claim by choosing not to have any entry on Cournot.

Another approach is to have each entry take care to reflect within itself varying points of view. This may help the student temporarily, as when preparing for an examination. But in a subject like economics, the Olympian detachment which this approach requires often places a heavy burden on the author, asking for a scrupulous account of doctrines he or she believes to be at best wrong-headed. Even when an especially able author does produce a judicious survey article, it is surely too much to ask that it also convey just as much enthusiasm for those theories thought misguided as for those found congenial. Lacking an enthusiastic exposition, however, the disfavoured theories may then be studied less closely than they deserve.

The New Palgrave did not ask its authors to treat economic theory from any particular point of view, except in one respect to be discussed below. Nor did it call for surveys. Instead, each author was asked to make clear his or her own views of the subject under discussion, and for the rest to be as fair and accurate as possible, without striving to be 'judicious'. A balanced perspective on each topic was always the aim, the ideal. But it was to be sought not *internally*, within each article, but *externally*, between articles, with the reader rather than the writer handed the task of achieving a personal balance between differing views.

For a controversial topic, a set of several more or less synonymous headwords, matched by a broad diversity of contributors, was designed to produce enough variety of opinion to help form the reader's own synthesis; indeed, such diversity will be found in most of the individual volumes in this series.

This approach was not without its problems. Thus, the prevalence of uncertainty in the process of commissioning entries sometimes produced a less diverse outcome than we had planned. 'I can call spirits from the vasty deep,' said Owen Glendower. 'Why, so can I,' replied Hotspur, 'or so can any man;/ But will they come when you do call for them?' In our experience, not quite as often as we would have liked.

The one point of view we did urge upon every one of *Palgrave*'s authors was to write from an historical perspective. For each subject its contributor was asked to discuss not only present problems but also past growth and future prospects. This request was made in the belief that knowledge of the historical development of any theory enriches our present understanding of it, and so helps to construct better theories for the future. The authors' response to the request was generally so positive that, as the reader of any of these volumes will discover, the resulting contributions amply justified that belief.

John Eatwell
Murray Milgate
Peter Newman

Preface

When the Econometric Society was founded 60 years ago it proclaimed itself 'An International Society for the Advancement of Economic Theory in its Relation to Statistics and Mathematics'. That programmatic description still flies proudly at the masthead of its journal *Econometrica*, but it does not fit what 'econometrics' means now. In modern economic theory and statistical inference, for example, the use of mathematics is now so standard that it no longer calls for comment. Much more importantly, the proclaimed goal of the advancement of economic theory has gradually withered away over time, as econometrics has evolved to be part of *applied* economics. Indeed, this evolution has proceeded so far that many economists have come to regard the scope of 'empirical work' in economics as coextensive with applied econometrics.

One important stage in this evolution was Tinbergen's *Statistical Testing of Business-Cycle Theories* (1939), part of a League of Nations project which included Haberler's famous survey of cycle theories, *Prosperity and Depression* (1937). Building on his earlier work on the Dutch economy, Tinbergen carried out his tests in the context of a complete model of the U.S. economy. Once designed and estimated, however, the models developed by this 'macro-economic approach' (as he called it) seemed to cry out to be used for purposes other than the difficult one of theory-testing. In particular, they suggested ways to assess economic consequences of proposed changes in public policy, and to predict macro-economic performance. A great volume of econometric research in the next decades followed up these suggestions, at least until the coming of the Lucas critique in 1976.

Statistical testing of economic theories can be frustrating for many reasons, not least of which is their usually low specific content. For example, elementary theory says that equilibrium price in a market is determined by the intersection of the schedules of demand and supply. But because there is seldom any satisfactory theory of how prices are formed away from equilibrium, testing the theory by market data usually requires an auxiliary assumption to the effect that the observations are all generated as equilibrium positions. But then the test is of the original theory *plus* the supplementary assumption, not of that theory alone.

A further difficulty in the empirical analysis of supply and demand was recognized quite early in the history of econometrics. Even assuming that the available price-quantity data are generated by various intersections of market supply and demand schedules, still there is a problem of identifying and estimating those schedules as separate entities. This problem of *identification* was probably the first to be recognised as one of 'pure econometrics', rather than as a problem of either economic theory or statistical inference. In such problems the two parent disciplines combine in such a way as to produce a new species, partaking of the nature of each but with qualities all its own.

Since that early discovery, many more members of the species have been found. A few important examples are the bias inherent in least-squares estimates of the coefficients of behavioural equations that form part of a simultaneous system; the problems of estimation that arise when economically natural non-negativity restrictions are taken seriously; and the difficulties in studies of labour supply caused by the phenomenon of self-selection.

Most of this purely econometric theory has developed from the increasing realisation by econometricians that they usually deal with a complete economic model composed of optimising agents. More recently, however, there has developed what might be called meta-econometric theory, which turns on the realisation by the econometrician that the model's agents themselves realise that they are living in a complete model, whose economic and probabilistic structures they believe they know. It is not quite clear where in this regress such theorizing will stop, or even (as Arrow has remarked) that it logically *can* stop; but it makes for some interesting theory meanwhile.

The data which econometricians use are seldom generated by experiment, and although that disadvantage is by no means unique to them (think of astronomers and meteorologists), it does tend to make them especially wary of the data to which they do have access. The difficulties thrown up by pure econometric theory, and especially such recently perceived problems as self-selection bias and the Lucas critique of macro-econometric models, have only reinforced this occupational wariness. Thus to be a modern econometrician is to possess, among other worthy qualities, a solid scepticism about mere appearance; and that is no bad thing, in a world where economic and scientific credulity seem to be in infinitely elastic supply.

The Editors

Econometrics

M. HASHEM PESARAN

1 WHAT IS ECONOMETRICS? Econometrics is a rapidly developing branch of economics which, broadly speaking, aims to give empirical content to economic relations. The term 'econometrics' appears to have been first used by Pawel Ciompa as early as 1910; although it is Ragnar Frisch, one of the founders of the Econometric Society, who should be given the credit for coining the term, and for establishing it as a subject in the sense in which it is known today (see Frisch, 1936, p. 95). Econometrics can be defined generally as 'the application of mathematics and statistical methods to the analysis of economic data', or more precisely in the words of Samuelson, Koopmans and Stone (1954),

> ...as the quantitative analysis of actual economic phenomena based on the concurrent development of theory and observation, related by appropriate methods of inference (p. 142).

Other similar descriptions of what econometrics entails can be found in the preface or the introduction to most texts in econometrics. Malinvaud (1966), for example interprets econometrics broadly to include 'every application of mathematics or of statistical methods to the study of economic phenomena'. Christ (1966) takes the objective of econometrics to be 'the production of quantitative economic statements that either *explain* the behaviour of variables we have already seen, or *forecast* (i.e. predict) behaviour that we have not yet seen, or both'. Chow (1983) in a more recent textbook succinctly defines econometrics 'as the art and science of using statistical methods for the measurement of economic relations'.

By emphasizing the quantitative aspects of economic problems, econometrics calls for a 'unification' of measurement and theory in economics. Theory without measurement, being primarily a branch of logic, can only have limited relevance for the analysis of actual economic problems. While measurement without theory, being devoid of a framework necessary for the interpretation of the statistical observations, is unlikely to result in a satisfactory explanation of the way economic forces interact with each other. Neither 'theory' nor 'measurement' on their own is sufficient to further our understanding of economic phenomena. Frisch was fully aware of the importance of such a unification for the future development of economics as a whole, and it is the recognition of this fact that lies at the heart of econometrics. This view of econometrics is expounded most eloquently by Frisch (1933a) in his editorial statement and is worth quoting in full:

> ...econometrics is by no means the same as economic statistics. Nor is it identical with what we call general economic theory, although a considerable portion of this theory has a definitely quantitative character. Nor should econometrics be taken as synonymous with the application of mathematics to economics. Experience has shown that each of these three view-points, that of statistics, economic theory, and mathematics, is a necessary, but not by itself a sufficient, condition for a real understanding of the quantitative relations in modern economic life. It is the *unification* of all three that is powerful. And it is this unification that constitutes econometrics.
>
> This unification is more necessary today than at any previous stage in economics. Statistical information is currently accumulating at an unprecedented rate. But no amount of statistical information, however complete and exact, can by itself explain economic phenomena. If we are not to get lost in the overwhelming, bewildering mass of statistical data that are now becoming available, we need the guidance and help of a powerful theoretical framework. Without this no significant interpretation and coordination of our observations will be possible.
>
> The theoretical structure that shall help us out in this situation must, however, be more precise, more realistic, and in many respects, more complex, than any heretofore available. Theory, in formulating its abstract quantitative notions, must be inspired to a larger extent by the technique of observation. And fresh statistical and other factual studies must be the healthy element of disturbance that constantly threatens and disquiets the theorist and prevents him from coming to rest on some inherited, obsolete set of assumptions.
>
> This mutual penetration of quantitative economic theory and statistical observation is the essence of econometrics (p. 2).

Whether other founding members of the Econometric Society shared Frisch's viewpoint with the same degree of conviction is, however, debatable, and even today there are no doubt economists who regard such a viewpoint as either ill-conceived or impractical. Nevertheless, in this survey I shall follow Frisch and consider the evolution of econometrics from the unification viewpoint.

2 EARLY ATTEMPTS AT QUANTITATIVE RESEARCH IN ECONOMICS. Empirical analysis in economics has had a long and fertile history, the origins of which can be traced at least as far back as the work of the 16th-century Political Arithmeticians such as William Petty, Gregory King and Charles Davenant. The political arithmeticians, led by Sir William Petty, were the first group to make systematic use of facts and figures in their studies. (See, for example, Stone (1984) on the origins of

national income accounting.) They were primarily interested in the practical issues of their time, ranging from problems of taxation and money to those of international trade and finance. The hallmark of their approach was undoubtedly quantitative and it was this which distinguished them from the rest of their contemporaries. Political arithmetic, according to Davenant (1698, Part I, p. 2) was 'the art of reasoning, by figures, upon things relating to government', which has a striking resemblance to what might be offered today as a description of econometric policy analysis. Although the political arithmeticians were primarily and understandably preoccupied with statistical measurement of economic phenomena, the work of Petty, and that of King in particular, represented perhaps the first examples of a unified quantitative/theoretical approach to economics. Indeed Schumpeter in his *History of Economic Analysis* (1954) goes as far as to say that the works of the political arithmeticians 'illustrate to perfection, what Econometrics is and what Econometricians are trying to do' (p. 209).

The first attempt at quantitative economic analysis is attributed to Gregory King, who is credited with a price–quantity schedule representing the relationship between deficiencies in the corn harvest and the associated changes in corn prices. This demand schedule, commonly known as 'Gregory King's law', was published by Charles Davenant in 1699. The King data are remarkable not only because they are the first of their kind, but also because they yield a perfectly fitting cubic regression of price changes on quantity changes, as was subsequently discovered independently by Whewell (1850), Wicksteed (1889) and by Yule (1915). An interesting account of the origins and nature of 'King's law' is given in Creedy (1986).

One important consideration in the empirical work of King and others in this early period seems to have been the discovery of 'laws' in economics, very much like those in physics and other natural sciences. This quest for economic laws was, and to a large extent still is, rooted in the desire to give economics the status that Newton had achieved for physics. This was in turn reflected in the conscious adoption of the method of the physical sciences as the dominant mode of empirical enquiry in economics. The Newtonian revolution in physics, and the philosophy of 'physical determinism' that came to be generally accepted in its aftermath, had far-reaching consequences for the method as well as the objectives of research in economics. The uncertain nature of economic relations only began to be fully appreciated with the birth of modern statistics in the late 19th century and as more statistical observations on economic variables started to become available. King's law, for example, was viewed favourably for almost two centuries before it was questioned by Ernest Engel in 1861 in his study of the demand for rye in Prussia (see Stigler, 1954, p. 104).

The development of statistical theory at the hands of Galton, Edgeworth and Pearson was taken up in economics with speed and diligence. The earliest applications of simple correlation analysis in economics appear to have been carried out by Yule (1895, 1896) on the relationship between pauperism and the method of providing relief, and by Hooker (1901) on the relationship between the marriage-rate and the general level of prosperity in the United Kingdom,

3

measured by a variety of economic indicators such as imports, exports and the movement in corn prices. In his applications Hooker is clearly aware of the limitations of the method of correlation analysis, especially when economic time series are involved and begins his contribution by an important warning which continues to have direct bearing on the way econometrics is practised today:

> The application of the theory of correlation to economic phenomena frequently presents many difficulties, more especially where the element of time is involved; and it by no means follows as a matter of course that a high correlation coefficient is a proof of causal connection between any two variables, or that a low coefficient is to be interpreted as demonstrating the absence of such connection (p. 485).

It is also worth noting that Hooker seems to have been the first to use time lags and de-trending methods in economics for the specific purpose of avoiding the time-series problems of spurious or hidden correlation that were later emphasized and discussed formally by Yule (1926).

Benini (1907), the Italian statistician, according to Stigler (1954) was the first to make use of the method of multiple regression in economics. He estimated a demand function for coffee in Italy as a function of coffee and sugar prices. But as argued in Stigler (1954, 1962) and more recently detailed in Christ (1985), it is Henry Moore (1914, 1917) who was the first to place the statistical estimation of economic relations at the centre of quantitative analysis in economics. Through his relentless efforts, and those of his disciples and followers Paul Douglas, Henry Schultz, Holbrook Working, Fred Waugh and others, Moore in effect laid the foundations of 'statistical economics', the precursor of econometrics. Moore's own work was, however, marred by his rather cavalier treatment of the theoretical basis of his regressions, and it was therefore left to others to provide a more satisfactory theoretical and statistical framework for the analysis of economic data. The monumental work of Schultz, *The Theory and the Measurement of Demand* (1938), in the United States and that of Allen and Bowley, *Family Expenditure* (1935), in the United Kingdom, and the pioneering works of Lenoir (1913), Wright (1915, 1928), Working (1927), Tinbergen (1930) and Frisch (1933b) on the problem of 'identification' represented major steps towards this objective. The work of Schultz was exemplary in the way it attempted a unification of theory and measurement in demand analysis; whilst the work on identification highlighted the importance of 'structural estimation' in econometrics and was a crucial factor in the subsequent developments of econometric methods under the auspices of the Cowles Commission for Research in Economics.

Early empirical research in economics was by no means confined to demand analysis. Another important area was research on business cycles, which in effect provided the basis of the later development in time-series analysis and macroeconometric model building and forecasting. Although through the work of Sir William Petty and other early writers economists had been aware of the existence of cycles in economic time series, it was not until the early 19th century that the phenomenon of business cycles began to attract the attention that it deserved. (An interesting account of the early developments in the analysis of economic time series is given in Nerlove and others, 1979.) Clement Juglar (1819–1905), the French physician turned economist, was the first to make systematic use of time-series data for the specific purpose of studying business cycles and is credited with the discovery of an investment cycle of about 7–11 years duration, commonly known as the Juglar cycle. Other economists such as Kitchin, Kuznets and Kondratieff followed Juglar's lead and discovered the inventory cycle (3–5 years duration), the building cycle (15–25 years duration) and the long wave (45–60 years duration), respectively. The emphasis of this early research was on the morphology of cycles and the identification of periodicities. Little attention was paid to the quantification of the relationships that may have underlain the cycles. Indeed, economists working in the National Bureau of Economic Research under the direction of Wesley Mitchell regarded each business cycle as a unique phenomenon and were therefore reluctant to use statistical methods except in a non-parametric manner and for purely descriptive purposes (see, for example, Mitchell, 1928 and Burns and Mitchell, 1947). This view of business cycle research stood in sharp contrast to the econometric approach of Frisch and Tinbergen and culminated in the famous methodological interchange between Tjalling Koopmans and Rutledge Vining about the roles of theory and measurement in applied economics in general and business cycle research in particular. (This interchange appeared in the August 1947 and May 1949 issues of *The Review of Economics and Statistics.*)

3 THE BIRTH OF ECONOMETRICS. Although, as I have argued above, quantitative economic analysis is a good three centuries old, econometrics as a recognized branch of economics only began to emerge in the 1930s and the 1940s with the foundation of the Econometric Society, the Cowles Commission in the United States and the Department of Applied Economics (DAE) under the directorship of Richard Stone in the United Kingdom. (A highly readable blow-by-blow account of the founding of the first two organizations can be found in Christ (1952, 1983), while the history of the DAE is covered in Stone, 1978.) The reasons for the lapse of more than two centuries between the pioneering work of Petty and the recognition of econometrics as a branch of economics are complex, and are best understood in conjunction with, and in the light of, histories of the development of theoretical economics, national income accounting, mathematical statistics, and computing. Such a task is clearly beyond the scope of the present paper. However, one thing is clear: given the multi-disciplinary nature of econometrics, it would have been extremely unlikely that it would have emerged as a serious branch of economics had it not been for the almost synchronous development of mathematical economics and the theories of estimation and statistical inference in the late 19th century and the early part of the 20th century. (An interesting account of the history of statistical methods can be found in Kendall, 1968.)

Of the four components of econometrics, namely *a priori* theory, data, econometric methods and computing techniques, it was, and to a large extent still is, the problem of econometric method which has attracted most attention. The first major debate over econometric method concerned the applicability of the probability calculus and the newly developed sampling theory of R.A. Fisher to the analysis of economic data. As Morgan (1986) argues in some detail, prior to the 1930s the application of mathematical theories of probability to economic data was rejected by the majority in the profession, irrespective of whether they were involved in research on demand analysis or on business cycles. Even Frisch was highly sceptical of the value of sampling theory and significance tests in econometrics. His objection to the use of significance tests was not, however, based on the epistemological reasons that lay behind Robbins's and Keynes's criticisms of econometrics. He was more concerned with the problems of multicollinearity and measurement errors which he believed, along with many others, afflicted all economic variables observed under non-controlled experimental conditions. By drawing attention in the *fictitious determinateness created by random errors* of observations, Frisch (1934) launched a severe attack on regression and correlation analysis which remains as valid now as it was then. With characteristic clarity and boldness Frisch stated:

> As a matter of fact I believe that a substantial part of the regression and correlation analyses which have been made on economic data in recent years is nonsense for this very reason [the random errors of measurement] (1934, p. 6).

In order to deal with the measurement error problem Frisch developed his confluence analysis and the method of 'bunch maps'. Although his method was used by some econometricians, notably Tinbergen (1939) and Stone (1945), it did not find much favour with the profession at large. This was due, firstly, to the indeterminate nature of confluence analysis and secondly, to the alternative probabilistic rationalizations of regression analysis which were advanced by Koopmans (1937) and Haavelmo (1944). Koopmans proposed a synthesis of the two approaches to the estimation of economic relations, namely the error-in-variables approach of Frisch and the error-in-equation approach of Fisher, using the likelihood framework; thus rejecting the view prevalent at the time that the presence of measurement errors *per se* invalidates the application of the 'sampling theory' to the analysis of economic data. In his words:

> It is the conviction of the author that the essentials of Frisch's criticism of the use of Fisher's specification in economic analysis may also be formulated and illustrated from the conceptual scheme and in the terminology of the sampling theory, and the present investigation is an attempt to do so (p. 30).

The formulation of the error-in-variables model in terms of a probability model did not, however, mean that Frisch's criticisms of regression analysis were unimportant, or that they could be ignored. Just the opposite was the case. The probabilistic formulation helped to focus attention on the reasons for the indeterminacy of Frisch's proposed solution to the problem. It showed also that without some *a priori* information, for example on the relative importance of the measurement errors in different variables, a determinate solution to the estimation problem would not be possible. What was important and with hindsight path-breaking, about Koopmans's contribution was the fact that it demonstrated the possibility of the probabilistic characterization of economic relations, even in circumstances where important deviations from the classical regression framework were necessitated by the nature of the economic data.

Koopmans did not, however, emphasize the wider issue of the use of stochastic models in econometrics. It was Haavelmo who exploited the idea to the full and argued forcefully for an explicit probability approach to the estimation and testing of economic relations. In his classic paper published as a supplement to *Econometrica* in 1944, Haavelmo defended the probability approach on two grounds: firstly, he argued that the use of statistical measures such as means, standard errors and correlation coefficients for inferential purposes is justified only if the process generating the data can be cast in terms of a probability model: 'For *no tool developed in the theory of statistics has any meaning* – except, perhaps, for descriptive purposes – *without being referred to some stochastic scheme'* (p. iii). Secondly, he argued that the probability approach, far from being limited in its application to economic data, because of its generality, is in fact particularly suited for the analysis of 'dependent' and 'non-homogeneous' observations often encountered in economic research. He believed what is needed is

> to assume that the *whole set* of, say n, observations may be considered as *one* observation of n variables (or a 'sample point') following an n-dimensional *joint* probability law, the 'existence' of which may be purely hypothetical. Then, one can test hypotheses regarding this joint probability law, and draw inference as to its possible form, by means of *one* sample point (in n dimensions) (p. iii).

Here Haavelmo uses the concept of joint probability distribution as a tool of analysis and not necessarily as a characterization of 'reality'. The probability model is seen as a convenient *abstraction* for the purpose of understanding, or explaining or predicting events in the real world. But it is not claimed that the model represents reality in all its minute details. To proceed with quantitative research in any subject, economics included, some degree of formalization is inevitable, and the probability model is one such formalization. This view, of course, does not avoid many of the epistemological problems that surround the concept of 'probability' in all the various senses (subjective, frequentist, logical, etc.) in which the term has been used, nor is it intended to do so. As Haavelmo himself put it:

> The question is not whether probabilities *exist* or not, but whether – if we proceed as *if* they existed – we are able to make statements about real phenomena that are 'correct for practical purposes' (1944, p. 43).

The attraction of the probability model as a method of abstraction derives from its generality and flexibility, and the fact that no viable alternative seems to be available.

Haavelmo's contribution was also important as it constituted the first systematic defence against Keynes's (1939) influential criticisms of Tinbergen's pioneering research on business cycles and macroeconometric modelling. The objective of Tinbergen's research was twofold. Firstly, to show how a macro-econometric model may be constructed and then used for simulation and policy analysis (Tinbergen, 1937). Secondly, 'to submit to statistical test some of the theories which have been put forward regarding the character and causes of cyclic fluctuations in business activity' (Tinbergen, 1939, p. 11). Tinbergen assumed a rather limited role for the econometrician in the process of testing economic theories, and argued that it was the responsibility of the 'economist' to specify the theories to be tested. He saw the role of the econometrician as a passive one of estimating the parameters of an economic relation already specified on *a priori* grounds by an economist. As far as statistical methods were concerned he employed the regression method and Frisch's method of confluence analysis in a complementary fashion. Although Tinbergen discussed the problems of the determination of time lags, trends, structural stability and the choice of functional forms, hd did not propose any systematic methodology for dealing with them. In short, Tinbergen approached the problem of testing theories from a rather weak methodological position. Keynes saw these weaknesses and attacked them with characteristic insight (Keynes, 1939). A large part of Keynes's review was in fact concerned with technical difficulties associated with the application of statistical methods to economic data. Apart from the problems of the 'dependent' and 'non-homogeneous' observations mentioned above, Keynes also emphasized the problems of misspecification, multi-collinearity, functional form, dynamic specification, structural stability and the difficulties associated with the measurement of theoretical variables. In view of these technical difficulties and Keynes's earlier warnings against 'inductive generalisation' in his *Treatise on Probability* (1921), it was not surprising that he focussed his attack on Tinbergen's attempt at *testing* economic theories of business cycles and almost totally ignored the practical significance of Tinbergen's work on econometric model building and policy analysis (for more details, see Pesaran and Smith, 1985a).

In his own review of Tinbergen's work, Haavelmo (1943) recognized the main burden of the criticisms of Tinbergen's work by Keynes and others, and argued the need for a general statistical framework to deal with these criticisms. As we have seen, Haavelmo's response, despite the views expressed by Keynes and others, was to rely more, rather than less, on the probability model as the basis of econometric methodology. The technical problems raised by Keynes and others could now be dealt with in a systematic manner by means of formal probabilistic models. Once the probability model was specified, a solution to the problems of estimation and inference could be obtained by means of either classical or of Bayesian methods. There was little that could now stand in the way of a rapid development of econometric methods.

4 EARLY ADVANCES IN ECONOMETRIC METHODS. Haavelmo's contribution marked the beginning of a new era in econometrics, and paved the way for the rapid

development of econometrics on both sides of the Atlantic. The likelihood method soon became an important tool of estimation and inference, although initially it was used primarily at the Cowles Commission where Haavelmo himself had spent a short period as a research associate.

The first important breakthrough came with a formal solution to the identification problem which had been formulated earlier by E. Working (1927). By defining the concept of 'structure' in terms of the joint probability distribution of observations, Haavelmo (1944) presented a very general concept of identification and derived the necessary and sufficient conditions for identification of the entire system of equations, including the parameters of the probability distribution of the disturbances. His solution, although general, was rather difficult to apply in practice. Koopmans, Rubin and Leipnik, in a paper presented at a conference organized by the Cowles Commission in 1945 and published later in 1950, used the term 'identification' for the first time in econometrics, and gave the now familiar rank and order conditions for the identification of a single equation in a system of simultaneous *linear* equations. The solution of the identification problem by Koopmans (1949) and Koopmans, Rubin and Leipnik (1950), was obtained in the case where there are *a priori* linear restrictions on the structural parameters. They derived rank and order conditions for identifiability of a single equation from a complete system of equations without reference to how the variables of the model are classified as endogenous or exogenous. Other solutions to the identification problem, also allowing for restrictions on the elements of the variance–covariance matrix of the structural disturbances, were later offered by Wegge (1965) and Fisher (1966). A comprehensive survey of some of the more recent developments of the subject can be found in Hsiao (1983).

Broadly speaking, a model is said to be identified if all its structural parameters can be obtained from the knowledge of its underlying joint probability distribution. In the case of simultaneous equations models prevalent in econometrics the solution to the identification problem depends on whether there exists a sufficient number of *a priori* restrictions for the derivative of the structural parameters from the reduced-form parameters. Although the purpose of the model and the focus of the analysis explaining the variations of some variables in terms of the unexplained variations of other variables is an important consideration, in the final analysis the specification of a minimum number of identifying restrictions was seen by researchers at the Cowles Commission to be the function and the responsibility of 'economic theory'. This attitude was very much reminiscent of the approach adopted earlier by Tinbergen in his business cycle research: the function of economic theory was to provide the specification of the econometric model, and that of econometrics to furnish statistically optimal methods of estimation and inference. More specifically, at the Cowles Commission the primary task of econometrics was seen to be the development of statistically efficient methods for the estimation of structural parameters of an *a priori* specified system of simultaneous stochastic equations.

Initially, under the influence of Haavelmo's contribution, the maximum likelihood (ML) estimation method was emphasized as it yielded consistent estimates. Koopmans and others (1950) proposed the 'information-preserving maximum-likelihood method', more commonly known as the Full Information Maximum Likelihood (FIML) method, and Anderson and Rubin (1949), on a suggestion by M.A. Girshick, developed the Limited Information Maximum Likelihood (LIML) method. Both methods are based on the joint probability distribution of the endogenous variables and yield consistent estimates, with the former utilizing all the available *a priori* restrictions and the latter only those which related to the equation being estimated. Soon other computationally less demanding estimation methods followed, both for a fully efficient estimation of an entire system of equations and for a consistent estimation of a single equation from a system of equations. The Two-Stage Least Squares (2SLS) procedure, which involves a similar order of magnitude of computations at the least squares method, was independently proposed by Theil (1954, 1958) and Basmann (1957). At about the same time the instrumental variable (IV) method, which had been developed over a decade earlier by Reiersol (1941, 1945) and Geary (1949) for the estimation of errors-in-variables models, was applied by Sargan (1958) to the estimation of simultaneous equation models. Sargan's main contribution consisted in providing an asymptotically efficient technique for using surplus instruments in the application of the IV method to econometric problems. A related class of estimators, known as k-class estimators, was also proposed by Theil (1961). Methods of estimating the entire system of equations which were computationally less demanding than the FIML method also started to emerge in the literature. These included the Three-Stage Least Squares method due to Zellner and Theil (1962), the iterated instrumental variables method based on the work of Lyttkens (1970), Brundy and Jorgenson (1971), Dhrymes (1971); and the system k-class estimators due to Srivastava (1971) and Savin (1973). An interesting synthesis of different estimators of the simultaneous equations model is given by Hendry (1976). The literature on estimation of simultaneous equation models is vast and is still growing. Important contributions have been made in the areas of estimation of simultaneous non-linear models, the seemingly unrelated regression model proposed by Zellner (1962), and the simultaneous rational expectations models which will be discussed in more detail below. Recent studies have also focused on the finite sample properties of the alternative estimators in the simultaneous equation model. Interested readers should consult the relevant entries in *The New Palgrave*, or refer to the excellent survey articles by Hausman (1983), by Amemiya (1983) and by Phillips (1983).

While the initiative taken at the Cowles Commission led to a rapid expansion of econometric techniques, the application of these techniques to economic problems was rather slow. This was partly due to a lack of adequate computing facilities at the time. A more fundamental reason was the emphasis of all the Cowles Commission on the simultaneity problem almost to the exclusion of other problems that were known to afflict regression analysis. Since the early applications of the correlation analysis to economic data by Yule and Hooker, the serial dependence of economic time series and the problem of spurious correlation that it could give rise to, had been the single most important factor explaining the profession's scepticism concerning the value of regression analysis in economics. A satisfactory solution to the spurious correlation problem was therefore needed before regression analysis of economic time series could be taken seriously. Research on this important topic began in the mid-1940s under the direction of Richard Stone at the Department of Applied Economics (DAE) in Cambridge, England, as a part of a major investigation into the measurement and analysis of consumers' expenditure in the United Kingdom (see Stone and others, 1954a). Stone had started this work during the 1939–45 war at the National Institute of Economic and Social Research. Although the first steps towards the resolution of the spurious correlation problem had been taken by Aitken (1934/35) and Champernowne (1948), the research in the DAE introduced the problem and its possible solution to the attention of applied economists. Orcutt (1948) studied the autocorrelation pattern of economic time series and showed that most economic time series can be represented by simple autoregressive processes with similar autoregressive coefficients, a result which was an important precursor to the work of Zellner and Palm (1974) discussed below. Subsequently in their classic paper, Cochrane and Orcutt (1949) made the important point that the major consideration in the analysis of stationary time series was the autocorrelation of the error term in the regression equation and not the autocorrelation of the economic time series themselves. In this way they shifted the focus of attention to the autocorrelation of disturbances as the main source of concern. Secondly, they put forward their well-known iterative method for the computation of regression coefficients under the assumption that the errors followed a first order autoregressive process.

Another important and related development at the DAE was the work of Durbin and Watson (1950, 1951) on the method of testing for residual autocorrelation in the classical regression model. The inferential breakthrough for testing serial correlation in the case of observed time-series data had already been achieved by von Neumann (1941, 1942) and by Hart and von Neumann (1942). The contribution of Durbin and Watson was, however, important from a practical viewpoint as it led to a bounds test for residual autocorrelation which could be applied irrespective of the actual values of the regressors. The independence of the critical bounds of the Durbin–Watson statistic from the matrix of the regressors allowed the application of the statistic as a general diagnostic test, the first of its type in econometrics. The contributions of Cochrane and Orcutt and of Durbin and Watson under the leadership of Stone marked the beginning of a new era in the analysis of economic time-series data and laid down the basis of what is now known as the 'time-series econometrics' approach.

The significance of the research at the DAE was not confined to the development of econometric methods. The work of Stone on linear expenditure systems represented one of the first attempts to use theory *directly* and *explicitly* in applied econometric research. This was an important breakthrough. Previously, economic theory had by and large been used in applied research only indirectly and as a general method for deciding on the list of the variables to be included in the regression model and, occasionally, for assigning signs to the parameters of the model. (For an important exception, see Marschak and Andrews, 1944.) In his seminal paper in the *Economic Journal*, Stone (1954b) made a significant break with this tradition and used theory not as a substitute for common sense, but as a formal framework for deriving 'testable' restrictions on the parameters of the empirical model. This was an important move towards the formal unification of theory and measurement that Frisch had called for and Schultz earlier had striven towards.

5 CONSOLIDATION AND FURTHER DEVELOPMENTS. The work at the Cowles Commission on identification and estimation of the simultaneous equation model and the development of appropriate techniques in dealing with the problem of spurious regression at the DAE paved the way for its widespread application to economic problems. This was helped significantly by the rapid expansion of computing facilities, the general acceptance of Keynesian theory and the increased availability of time-series data on national income accounts. As Klein (1971) put it, 'The Keynesian theory was simply "asking" to be case in an empirical mold' (p. 416). The IS–LM version of the Keynesian theory provided a convenient and flexible framework for the construction of macroeconomic models for a variety of purposes ranging from pedagogic to short- and medium-term forecasting and policy analysis. In view of Keynes's criticisms of econometrics, it is perhaps ironic that his macroeconomic theory came to play such a central role in the advancement of econometrics in general and that of macroeconometric modelling in particular.

Inspired by the Keynesian theory and the pioneering work of Tinbergen, Klein (1947, 1950) was the first to construct a macroeconometric model in the tradition of the Cowles Commission. Soon others followed Klein's lead: prominent examples of early macroeconometric models included the Klein–Goldberger and the Brookings–SSRC models of the US economy, and the London Business School and the Cambridge Growth Project models of the UK economy. Over a short space of time macroeconometric models were built for almost every industrialized country, and even for some developing and centrally planned economies. Macroeconometric models became an important tool of *ex ante* forecasting and economic policy analysis, and started to grow both in size and sophistication. The relatively stable economic environment of the 1950s and 1960s was an important factor in the initial success enjoyed by macroeconometric models. Whether the use of macroeconometric models in policy formulation contributed towards the economic stability over this period is, of course, a different matter.

The construction and use of large-scale models presented a number of important computational problems, the solution of which was of fundamental significance not only for the development of macroeconometric modelling, but also for econometric practice in general. In this respect advances in computer technology were clearing instrumental, and without them it is difficult to imagine how the complicated computational problems involved in the estimation and simulation of large-scale models could have been solved. The increasing availability of better and faster computers was also instrumental as far as the types of problems studied and the types of solutions offered in the literature were concerned. For example, recent developments in the area of microeconometrics (see section 6.3 below) could hardly have been possible if it were not for the very important recent advances in computing facilities.

The development of economic models for policy analysis, however, was not confined to macroeconometric models. The inter-industry input–output models originating from the seminal work of Leontief (1936, 1941, 1951), and the microanalytic simulation models pioneered by Orcutt and his colleagues (1961), were amongst the other influential approaches which should be mentioned here. But it was the surge of interest in macroeconometric modelling which provided the single most important impetus to the further development of econometric methods. I have already mentioned some of the advances that took place in the field of estimation of the simultaneous equation model. Other areas where econometrics witnessed significant developments included dynamic specification, latent variables, expectations formation, limited dependent variables, discrete choice models, random coefficient models, disequilibrium models and non-linear estimation. The Bayesian approach to econometrics was also developed more vigorously, thanks to the relentless efforts of Zellner, Drèze and their colleagues. (See Drèze and Richard (1983) and Zellner (1984, 1985) for the relevant references to theoretical and applied Bayesian econometric studies.) It was, however, the problem of dynamic specification that initially received the greatest attention. In an important paper, Brown (1952) modelled the hypothesis of habit persistence in consumer behaviour by introducing lagged values of consumption expenditures into an otherwise static Keynesian consumption function. This was a significant step towards the incorporation of dynamics in applied econometric research and allowed the important distinction to be made between the short-run and the long-run impacts of changes in income on consumption. Soon other researchers followed Brown's lead and employed his autoregressive specification in their empirical work.

The next notable development in the area of dynamic specification was the distributed lag model. Although the idea of distributed lags had been familiar to economists through the pioneering work of Irving Fisher (1930) on the relationship between the nominal interest rate and the expected inflation rate, its application in econometrics was not seriously considered until the mid 1950s. The geometric distributed lag model was used for the first time by Koyck (1954) in a study of investment. Koyck arrived at the geometric distributed lag model *via* the adaptive expectations hypothesis. This same hypothesis was employed later by Cagan (1956) in a study of demand for money in conditions of hyperinflation, by Friedman (1957) in a study of consumption behaviour and by Nerlove (1958a) in a study of the cobweb phenomenon. The geometric distributed lag model was subsequently generalized by Solow (1960), Jorgenson (1966) and others, and was extensively applied in empirical studies of investment and consumption behaviour. At about the same time Almon (1965) provided a polynomial generalization of Fisher's (1937) arithmetic lag distribution which

13

was later extended further by Shiller (1973). Other forms of dynamic specification considered in the literature included the partial adjustment model (Nerlove, 1958b; Eisner and Strotz, 1963) and the multivariate flexible accelerator model (Treadway, 1971) and Sargan's (1964) work on econometric time series analysis which we discuss below in more detail. An excellent survey of this early literature on distributed lag and partial adjustment models is given in Griliches (1967).

Concurrent with the development of dynamic modelling in econometrics there was also a resurgence of interest in time-series methods, used primarily in short-term business forecasting. The dominant work in this field was that of Box and Jenkins (1970), who, building on the pioneering works of Yule (1921, 1926), Slutsky (1927), Wold (1938), Whittle (1963) and others, proposed computationally manageable and asymptotically efficient methods for the estimation and forecasting of univariate autoregressive-moving average (ARMA) processes. Time-series models provided an important and relatively cheap benchmark for the evaluation of the forecasting accuracy of econometric models, and further highlighted the significance of dynamic specification in the construction of time-series econometric models. Initially univariate time-series models were viewed as mechanical 'black box' models with little or no basis in economic theory. Their use was seen primarily to be in short-term forecasting. The potential value of modern time-series methods in econometric research was, however, underlined in the work of Cooper (1972) and Nelson (1972) who demonstrated the good forecasting performance of univariate Box–Jenkins models relative to that of large econometric models. These results raised an important question mark over the adequacy of large econometric models for forecasting as well as for policy analysis. It was argued that a properly specified structural econometric model should, at least in theory, yield more accurate forecasts than a univariate time-series model. Theoretical justification for this view was provided by Zellner and Palm (1974), followed by Trivedi (1975), Prothero and Wallis (1976), Wallis (1977) and others. These studies showed that Box–Jenkins models could in fact be derived as univariate final form solutions of linear structural econometric models so long as the latter were allowed to have a rich enough dynamic specification. In theory, the pure time-series model could always be embodied within the structure of an econometric model and in this sense it did not present a 'rival' alternative to econometric modelling. This literature further highlighted the importance of dynamic specification in econometric models and in particular showed that econometric models that are out-performed by simple univariate time-series models most probably suffer from serious specification errors.

The response of the econometrics profession to this time-series critique was rather mixed and has taken different forms. On the one hand, a full integration of time-series methods and traditional econometric analysis has been advocated by Zellner and Palm, Wallis and others. This blending of the econometric methods which Zellner has called the SEMTSA (structural econometric modelling times-series analysis) approach is discussed in some detail in Zellner (1979). The SEMTSA approach emphasizes that dynamic linear structural econometric models are a special case of multivariate time-series processes, and argues that time-series methods should be utilized to check the empirical adequacy of the final equation forms and the distributed lag (or transfer function) forms implicit in the assumed structural model. The modelling process is continued until the implicit estimates of the final equation forms and the distributed lag forms of the structural model are empirically compatible with the direct time-series estimates of these equations.

An alternative 'marriage' of econometric and time-series techniques has been developed by Sargan, Hendry and others largely at the London School of Economics (LSE). This marriage is based on the following two premises:

(i) Theoretical economic considerations can at best provide the specification of equilibrium or long-run relationships between variables. Little can be inferred from *a priori* reasoning about the time lags and dynamic specification of econometric relations.

(ii) The best approach to identification of lags in econometric models lies in the utilization of time-series methods, appropriately modified to allow for the existence of long-run relations among economic variables implied by economic theory.

Although the approach is general and in principle can be applied to systems of equations, in practice it has been primarily applied to modelling one variable at a time. The origins of this approach can be found in the two highly influential papers by Sargan (1964) on the modelling of money wages, and by Davidson and others (1978) on the modelling of non-durable consumption expenditures. By focusing on the modelling of one endogenous variable at a time, the LSE approach represents a partial break with the structural approach advocated by the Cowles Commission. But in an important sense the LSE approach continues to share with the Cowles Commission the emphasis it places on *a priori* economic reasoning, albeit in the form of equilibrium or long-period relationships.

6 RECENT DEVELOPMENTS. With the significant changes taking place in the world economic environment in the 1970s, arising largely from the breakdown of the Bretton Woods system and the quadrupling of oil prices, econometrics entered a new phase of its development. Mainstream macroeconometric models built during the 1950s and 1960s, in an era of relative economic stability with stable energy prices and fixed exchange rates, were no longer capable of adequately capturing the economic realities of the 1970s. As a result, not surprisingly, macroeconometric models and the Keynesian theory that underlay them came under severe attack from theoretical as well as from practical viewpoints. While criticisms of Tinbergen's pioneering attempt at macroeconometric modelling were received with great optimism and led to the development of new and sophisticated estimation techniques and larger and more complicated models, the more recent bout of disenchantment with macroeconometric models prompted a much more fundamental reappraisal of quantitative modelling as a tool of forecasting and policy analysis. At a theoretical level it is argued that econometric

relations invariably lack the necessary 'microfoundations', in the sense that they cannot be consistently derived from the optimizing behaviour of economic agents. At a practical level the Cowles Commission approach to the identification and estimation of simultaneous macroeconometric models has been questioned by Lucas and Sargent and by Sims, although from different viewpoints. There has also been a move away from macroeconometric models and towards micro-econometric research where it is hoped that some of the pitfalls of the macroeconometric time-series analysis can be avoided. The response of the econometric profession as a whole to the recent criticism has been to emphasize the development of more appropriate techniques, to use new data sets and to call for a better quality control of econometric research with special emphasis on model validation and diagnostic testing.

What follows is a brief overview of some of the important developments of the past two decades. Given space limitations and my own interests there are inevitably significant gaps. These include the important contributions of Granger (1969), Sims (1972) and Engle and others (1983) on different concepts of 'causality' and 'exogeneity', and the vast literature on disequilibrium models (Quandt, 1982; Maddala, 1983, 1986), random coefficient models (Chow, 1984), continuous time models (Bergstrom, 1984), non-stationary time series and testing for unit roots (Dickey and Fuller, 1979, 1981; Evans and Savin, 1981, 1984; Phillips, 1986, 1987; Phillips and Durlauf, 1986) and small sample theory (Phillips, 1983; Rothenberg, 1984), not to mention the developments in the area of policy analysis and the application of control theory of econometric models (Chow, 1975, 1981; Aoki, 1976).

6.1 Rational expectations and the Lucas critique. Although the Rational Expectations Hypothesis (REH) was advanced by Muth in 1961, it was not until the early 1970s that it started to have a significant impact on time-series econometrics and on dynamic economic theory in general. What brought the REH into prominence was the work of Lucas (1972, 1973), Sargent (1973), Sargent and Wallace (1975) and others on the new classical explanation of the apparent breakdown of the Phillips curve. The message of the REH for econometrics was clear. By postulating that economic agents form their expectations *endogenously* on the basis of the *true* model of the economy and a *correct* understanding of the processes generating exogenous variables of the model, including government policy, the REH raised serious doubts about the invariance of the structural parameters of the mainstream macroeconometric models in the face of changes in government policy. This was highlighted in Lucas's critique of macroeconometric policy evaluation. By means of simple examples Lucas (1976) showed that in models with rational expectations the parameters of the decision rules of economic agents, such as consumption or investment functions, are usually a mixture of the parameters of the agents' objective functions and of the stochastic processes they face as historically given. Therefore, Lucas argued, there is no reason to believe that the 'structure' of the decision rules (or economic relations) would remain invariant under a policy intervention. The implication of the Lucas critique for econometric research was not, however, that policy evaluation could not be done, but rather than the traditional econometric models and methods were not suitable for this purpose. What was required was a separation of the parameters of the policy rule from those of the economic model. Only when these parameters could be identified separately given the knowledge of the joint probability distribution of the variables (both policy and non-policy variables) would it be possible to carry out an econometric analysis of alternative policy options.

There have been a number of reactions to the advent of the rational expectations hypothesis and the Lucas critique that accompanied it. The least controversial has been the adoption of the REH as *one* of several possible expectations formation hypotheses in an otherwise conventional macroeconometric model containing expectational variables. In this context the REH, by imposing the appropriate cross-equation parametric restrictions, ensures that 'expectations' and 'forecasts' generated by the model are consistent. The underlying economic model is in no way constrained to have particular Keynesian or monetarist features, nor are there any presumptions that the relations of the economic model should necessarily correspond to the decision rules of economic agents. In this approach the REH is regarded as a convenient and effective method of imposing cross-equation parametric restrictions on time series econometric models, and is best viewed as the 'model-consistent' expectations hypothesis. The econometric implications of such a model-consistent expectations mechanism have been extensively analysed in the literature. The problems of identification and estimation of linear RE models have been discussed in detail, for example, by Wallis (1980), Wickens (1982) and Pesaran (1987). These studies show how the standard econometric methods can in principle be adapted to the econometric analysis of rational (or consistent) expectations models.

Another reaction to the Lucas critique has been to treat the problem of 'structural change' emphasized by Lucas as one more potential econometric 'problem' (on this see Lawson, 1981). It is argued that the problem of structural change resulting from intended or expected changes in policy is not new and had been known to the economists at the Cowles Commission (Marschak, 1953), and can be readily dealt with by a more careful monitoring of econometric models for possible changes in their structure. This view is, however, rejected by Lucas and Sargent and other proponents of the rational expectations school who argue for a more fundamental break with the traditional approach to macroeconometric modelling.

The optimization approach of Lucas and Sargent is based on the premise that the 'true' structural relations contained in the economic model and the policy rules of the government can be obtained *directly* as solutions to well-defined dynamic optimization problems faced by economic agents and by the government. The task of the econometrician is then seen to be the disentanglement of the parameters of the stochastic processes that agents face from the parameters of their objective functions. As Hansen and Sargent (1980) put it,

Accomplishing this task [the separate identification of parameters of the exogenous process and those of taste and technology functions] is an absolute prerequisite of reliable econometric policy evaluation. The execution of this strategy involves estimating agents' decision rules jointly with models for the stochastic processes they face, subject to the cross-equation restrictions implied by the hypothesis of rational expectations (p. 8).

So far this approach has been applied only to relatively simple set-ups involving aggregate data at the level of a 'representive' firm or a 'representive' household. One important reason for this lies in the rather restrictive and inflexible econometric models which emerge from the strict adherence to the optimization framework and the REH. For analytical tractability it has often been necessary to confine the econometric analysis to quadratic objective functions and linear stochastic processes. This problem to some extent has been mitigated by recent developments in the area of the estimation of the Euler equations (see Hansen and Singleton, 1982). But there are still important technical difficulties that have to be resolved before the optimization approach can be employed in econometrics in a flexible manner. In addition to these technical difficulties, there are fundamental issues concerning the problem of aggregation across agents, information heteogeneity, the learning process and the effect that these complications have for the implementation of the Lucas–Sargent research programme (cf. Pesaran, 1987).

6.2 Atheoretical macroeconometrics. The Lucas critique of mainstream macro-econometric modelling has also led some econometricians, notably Sims (1980, 1982), to doubt the validity of the Cowles Commission style of achieving identification in econometric models. The view that economic theory cannot be relied on to yield identification of structural models is not new and has been emphasized in the past, for example, by Liu (1960). The more recent disenchantment with the Cowles Commission's approach has its origins in the REH, and the unease with *a priori* restrictions on lag lengths that are needed if rational expectations models are to be identified (see Pesaran, 1981). Sims (1980, p. 7) writes: 'It is my view, however, that rational expectations is more deeply subversive of identification than has yet been recognized.' He then goes on to say that 'In the presence of expectations, it turns out that the crutch of *a priori* knowledge of lag lengths is indispensable, even when we have distinct strictly exogenous variables shifting supply and demand schedules' (ibid.). While it is true that the REH complicates the necessary conditions for the identification of structural models, the basic issue in the debate over identification still centres on the validity of the classical dichotomy between exogenous and endogenous variables. Whether it is possible to test the 'exogeneity' assumptions of macroeconometric models is a controversial matter and is very much bound up with what is in fact meant by exogeneity. In certain applications exogeneity is viewed as a property of a proposed model (*à la* Koopmans, 1950), and in other situations it is defined in terms of a group of variables for purposes of inference about 'parameters of interest' (Engle and others, 1983). In the Cowles Commission approach exogeneity was assumed to be the property of the structural model, obtained from *a priori* theory and testable *only* in the presence of maintained restrictions. Thus it was not possible to test the identifying restrictions themselves. They had to be assumed *a priori* and accepted as a matter of belief or on the basis of knowledge extraneous to the model under consideration.

The approach advocated by Sims and his co-researchers departs from the Cowles Commission methodology in two important respects. It denies that *a priori* theory can ever yield the restrictions necessary for identification of structural models, and argues that for forecasting and policy analysis, structural identification is not needed (Sims, 1980, p. 11). Accordingly, this approach, termed by Cooley and LeRoy (1985) 'atheoretical macroeconometrics', maintains that only unrestricted vector-autoregressive (VAR) systems which *do not* allow for *a priori* classification of the variables into endogenous and exogenous are admissible for macroeconometric analysis. The VAR approach represents an important alternative to conventional large-scale macroeconometric models and has been employed with some success in the area of forecasting (Litterman, 1985). Whether such unrestricted VAR systems can also be used in policy evaluation and policy formulation exercises remains a controversial matter. Cooley and LeRoy (1985) in their critique of this literature argue that even if it can be successfully implemented, it will still be of limited relevance except as a tool for *ex ante* forecasting and data description (on this also see Leamer, 1985a). They argue that it does not permit direct testing of economic theories, it is of little use for policy analysis and, above all, it does not provide a structural understanding of the economic system it purports to represent. Sims and others (Doan, Litterman and Sims, 1984; Sims, 1986), however, maintain that VAR models can be used for policy analysis, and the type of identifying assumptions needed for this purpose are no less credible than those assumed in conventional or RE macroeconometric models.

6.3 Microeconometrics. Emphasis on the use of micro-data in the analysis of economic problems is not, of course, new and dates back to the pioneering work of Ruggles and Ruggles (1956) on the development of a micro-based social accounting framework and the work of Orcutt and his colleagues already referred to above, and the influential contribution of Prais and Houthakker (1955) on the analysis of family expenditure surveys. But it is only recently, partly as a response to the dissatisfaction with macroeconometric time-series research and partly in view of the increasing availability of micro-data and computing facilities, that the analysis of micro-data has started to be considered seriously in the econometric literature. Important micro-data sets have become available especially in the United States in such areas as housing, transportation, labour markets and energy. These data sets include various longitudinal surveys (e.g. University of Michigan Panel Study of Income Dynamics and Ohio State NLS Surveys), cross-sectional surveys of family expenditures, and the population and labour force surveys. This increasing availability of micro-data, while opening up new possibilities for analysis, has also raised a number of new and interesting econometric issues primarily originating from the nature of the data. The errors of measurement are more likely to be serious in the case of micro- than macro-data. The problem of the heterogeneity of economic agents at the micro level cannot be assumed away as readily as is usually done in the case of macro-data by appealing to the idea of a 'representative' firm or a 'representative' household. As Griliches (1986) put it

> Variables such as age, land quality, or the occupational structure of an enterprise, are much less variable in the aggregate. Ignoring them at the micro level can be quite costly, however. Similarly, measurement errors which tend to cancel out when averaged over thousands or even millions of respondents, loom much larger when the individual is the unit of analysis (p. 1469).

The nature of micro-data, often being qualitative or limited to a particular range of variation, has also called for new econometric models and techniques. The models and issues considered in the micro-econometric literature are wide-ranging and include fixed and random effect models (e.g. Mundlak, 1961, 1978), discrete choice or quantal response models (Manski and McFadden, 1981), continuous time duration models (Heckman and Singer, 1984) and microeconometric models of count data (Hausman and others, 1984 and Cameron and Trivedi, 1986). The fixed or random effect models provide the basic statistical framework. Discrete choice models are based on an explicit characterization of the choice process and arise when individual decision makers are faced with a finite number of alternatives to choose from. Examples of discrete choice models include transportation mode choice (Domenich and McFadden, 1975), labour force participation (Heckman and Willis, 1977), occupation choice (Boskin, 1974), job or firm location (Duncan, 1980), etc. Limited-dependent variables models are commonly encountered in the analysis of survey data and are usually categorized into truncated regression models and censored regression models. If all observations on the dependent as well as on the exogenous variables are lost when the dependent variable falls outside a specified range, the model is called *truncated*, and, if only observations on the dependent variable are lost, it is called *censored*. The literature on censored and truncated regression models is vast and overlaps with developments in other disciplines, particularly in biometrics and engineering. The censored regression model was first introduced into econometrics by Tobin (1958) in his pioneering study of household expenditure on durable goods where he explicitly allowed for the fact that the dependent variable, namely the expenditure on durables, cannot be negative. The model suggested by Tobin and its various generalizations are known in economics as Tobit models and are surveyed in detail by Amemiya (1984).

Continuous time duration models, also known as survival models, have been used in analysis of unemployment duration, the period of time spent between jobs, durability of marriage, etc. Application of survival models to analyse economic data raises a number of important issues resulting primarily from the non-controlled experimental nature of economic observations, limited sample sizes (i.e. time periods) and the heterogeneous nature of the economic environment within which agents operate. These issues are clearly not confined to duration models and are also present in the case of other microeconometric investigations that are based on time series or cross section or panel data. (For early literature on the analysis of panel data, see the error components model developed by Kuh, 1959 and Balestra and Nerlove, 1966.) A satisfactory resolution of these problems is of crucial importance for the success of the microeconometric research programme. As aptly put by Hsiao (1985) in his recent review of the literature:

> Although panel data has opened up avenues of research that simply could not have been pursued otherwise, it is not a panacea for econometric researchers. The power of panel data depends on the extent and reliability of the information it contains as well as on the validity of the restrictions upon which the statistical methods have been built (p. 163).

Partly in response to the uncertainties inherent in econometric results based on non-experimental data, there has also been a significant move towards 'social experimentation', especially in the United States, as a possible method of reducing these uncertainties. This has led to a considerable literature analysing 'experimental' data, some of which has been recently reviewed in Hausman and Wise (1985). Although it is still too early to arrive at a definite judgement about the value of social experimentation as a whole, from an econometric viewpoint the results have not been all that encouraging. Evaluation of the Residential Electricity Time-of-Use Experiments (Aigner, 1985, the Housing-Allowance Program Experiments (Rosen, 1985) and the Negative-Income-Tax Experiments (Stafford, 1985) all point to the fact that the experimental results could have been equally predicted by the earlier econometric estimates. The advent of social experimentation in economics has nevertheless posed a number of interesting problems in the areas of experimental design, statistical methods (e.g. see Hausman and Wise (1979) on the problem of attrition bias) and policy analysis that are likely to have important consequences for the future development of micro-econometrics. (A highly readable account of social experimentation in economics is given by Ferber and Hirsch, 1982.)

Another important aspect of recent developments in microeconometric literature relates to the use of microanalytic simulation models for policy analysis and evaluation to reform packages in areas such as health care, taxation, social security systems and transportation networks. Some of the literature is covered in Orcutt and others (1986).

6.4 Model evaluation. While in the 1950s and 1960s research in econometrics was primarily concerned with the identification and estimation of econometric models, the dissatisfaction with econometrics during the 1970s caused a shift of focus from problems of estimation to those of model evaluation and testing. This shift has been part of a concerted effort to restore confidence in econometrics, and has received attention from Bayesian as well as classical viewpoints. Both these views reject the 'axiom of correct specification' which lies at the basis of

21

most traditional econometric practices, but differ markedly as how best to proceed.

Bayesians, like Leamer (1978), point to the wide disparity that exists between econometric method and the econometric practice that it is supposed to underlie, and advocate the use of 'informal' Bayesian procedures such as the 'extreme bounds analysis' (EBA), or more generally, the 'global sensitivity analysis'. The basic idea behind the EBA is spelt out in Leamer and Leonard (1983) and Leamer (1983) and has been the subject of critical analysis in McAleer, Pagan and Volker (1985). In its most general form, the research strategy put forward by Leamer involves a kind of grand Bayesian sensitivity analysis. The empirical results, or in Bayesian terminology the posterior distributions, are evaluated for 'fragility' or 'sturdiness' by checking how sensitive the results are to changes in prior distributions. As Leamer (1985b) explains:

> Because no prior distribution can be taken to be an exact representation of opinion, a global sensitivity analysis is carried out to determine which inferences are fragile and which are sturdy (p. 311).

The aim of the sensitivity analysis in Leamer's approach is, in his words, 'to combat the arbitrariness associated with the choice of prior distribution' (Leamer, 1986, p. 74).

It is generally agreed, by Bayesians as well as by non-Bayesians, that model evaluation involves considerations other than the examination of the statistical properties of the models, and personal judgements inevitably enter the evaluation process. Models must meet multiple criteria which are often in conflict. They should be relevant in the sense that they ought to be capable of answering the questions for which they are constructed. They should be consistent with the accounting and/or theoretical structure within which they operate. Finally, they should provide adequate representations of the aspects of reality with which they are concerned. These criteria and their interaction are discussed in Pesaran and Smith (1985b). More detailed breakdowns of the criteria of model evaluation can be found in Hendry and Richard (1982) and McAleer and others (1985). In econometrics it is, however, the criterion of 'adequacy' which is emphasized, often at the expense of relevance and consistency.

The issue of model adequacy in mainstream econometrics is approached either as a model selection problem or as a problem in statistical inference whereby the hypothesis of interest is tested against general or specific alternatives. The use of absolute criteria such as measures of fit/parsimony or formal Bayesian analysis based on posterior odds are notable examples of model selection procedures, while likelihood ratio, Wald and Lagrange multiplier tests of nested hypotheses and Cox's centred log-likelihood ratio tests of non-nested hypotheses are examples of the latter approach. The distinction between these two general approaches basically stems from the way alternative models are treated. In the case of model selection (or model discrimination) all the models under consideration enjoy the same status and the investigator is not committed *a priori* to any one of the alternatives. The aim is to choose the model which is likely to perform best with respect to a particular loss function. By contrast, in the hypothesis-testing framework, the null hypothesis (or the maintained model) is treated differently from the remaining hypotheses (or models). One important feature of the model-selection strategy is that its application always leads to one model being chosen in preference to other models. But in the case of hypothesis testing, rejection of all the models under consideration is not ruled out when the models are non-nested. A more detailed discussion of this point is given in Pesaran and Deaton (1978).

While the model-selection approach has received some attention in the literature, it is the hypothesis-testing framework which has been primarily relied on to derive suitable statistical procedures for judging the adequacy of an estimated model. In this latter framework, broadly speaking, three different strands can be identified, depending on how specific the alternative hypotheses are. These are the *general specification tests*, the *diagnostic tests* and the *non-nested tests*. The first of these, introduced in econometrics by Ramsey (1969) and Hausman (1978), and more recently developed by White (1981, 1982) and Hansen (1982), are designed for circumstances where the nature of the alternative hypothesis is kept (sometimes intentionally) rather vague, the purpose being to test the null against a *broad* class of alternatives. Important examples of general specification tests are Ramsey's regression specification error test (RESET) for omitted variables and/or misspecified functional forms, and the Hausman–Wu test of misspecification in the context of measurement error models, and/or simultaneous equation models. Such general specification tests are particularly useful in the preliminary stages of the modelling exercise.

In the case of diagnostic tests, the model under consideration (viewed as the null hypothesis) is tested against more specific alternatives by embedding it within a general model. Diagnostic tests can then be constructed using the likelihood ratio, Wald or Lagrange multiplier (LM) principles to test for parametric restrictions imposed on the general model. The application of the LM principle to econometric problems is reviewed in the papers by Breusch and Pagan (1980), Godfrey and Wickens (1982) and Engle (1984). Examples of the restrictions that may be of interest as diagnostic checks of model adequacy include zero restrictions, parameter stability, serial correlation, heteroskedasticity, functional forms and normality of errors. As shown in Pagan and Hall (1983), most existing diagnostic tests can be computed by means of auxiliary regressions involving the estimated residuals. In this sense diagnostic tests can also be viewed as a kind of residual analysis where residuals computed under the null are checked to see whether they can be explained further in terms of the hypothesized sources of misspecification. The distinction made here between diagnostic tests and general specification tests is more apparent than real. In practice some diagnostic tests such as tests for serial correlation can also be viewed as a general test of specification. Nevertheless, the distinction helps to focus attention on the purpose behind the tests and the direction along which high power is sought.

The need for non-nested tests arises when the models under consideration belong to separate parametric families in the sense that no single model can be obtained from the others by means of a suitable limiting process. This situation, which is particularly prevalent in econometric research, may arise when models differ with respect to their theoretical underpinnings and/or their auxiliary assumptions. Unlike the general specification tests and diagnostic tests, the application of non-nested tests is appropriate when *specific* but rival hypotheses for the explanation of the same economic phenomenon have been advanced. Although non-nested tests can also be used as general specification tests, they are designed primarily to have high power against specific models that are seriously entertained in the literature. Building on the pioneering work of Cox (1961, 1962), a number of such tests for single equation models and systems of simultaneous equations have been proposed (see the entry on NON-NESTED HYPOTHESES in this volume for further details and references).

The use of statistical tests in econometrics, however, is not a straightforward matter and in most applications does not admit of a clear-cut interpretation. This is especially so in circumstances where test statistics are used not only for checking the adequacy of a *given* model but also as guides to model construction. Such a process of model construction involves specification searches of the type emphasized by Leamer and presents insurmountable pre-test problems which in general tend to produce econometric models whose 'adequacy' is more apparent than real. As a result, in evaluating econometric models less reliance should be placed on those indices of model adequacy that are used as guides to model construction, and more emphasis should be given to the performance of models over other data sets and against rival models. The evaluation of econometric models is a complicated process involving practical, theoretical and econometric considerations. Econometric methods clearly have an important contribution to make to this process. But they should not be confused with the whole activity of econometric modelling which, in addition to econometric and computing skills, requires data, considerable intuition, institutional knowledge and, above all, economic understanding.

7 APPRAISALS AND FUTURE PROSPECTS. Econometrics has come a long way over a relatively short period. Important advances have been made in the compilation of economic data and in the development of concepts, theories and tools for the construction and evaluation of a wide variety of econometric models. Applications of econometric methods can be found in almost every field of economics. Econometric models have been used extensively by government agencies, international organizations and commercial enterprises. Macroeconometric models of differing complexity and size have been constructed for almost every country in the world. Both in theory and practice econometrics has already gone well beyond what its founders envisaged. Time and experience, however, have brought out a number of difficulties that were not apparent at the start.

Econometrics emerged in the 1930s and 1940s in a climate of optimism, in the belief that economic theory could be relied on to identify most, if not all, of the important factors involved in modelling economic reality, and that methods of classical statistical inference could be adapted readily for the purpose of giving empirical content to the received economic theory. This early view of the interaction of theory and measurement in econometrics, however, proved rather illusory. Economic theory, be it neoclassical, Keynesian or Marxian, is invariably formulated with *ceteris paribus* clauses, and involves unobservable latent variables and general functional forms; it has little to say about adjustment processes and lag lengths. Even in the choice of variables to be included in econometric relations, the role of economic theory is far more limited than was at first recognized. In a Walrasian general equilibrium model, for example, where everything depends on everything else, there is very little scope for *a priori* exclusion of variables from equations in an econometric model. There are also institutional features and accounting conventions that have to be allowed for in econometric models but which are either ignored or are only partially dealt with at the theoretical level. All this means that the specification of econometric models inevitably involves important auxiliary assumptions about functional forms, dynamic specifications, latent variables, etc. with respect to which economic theory is silent or gives only an incomplete guide.

The recognition that economic theory on its own cannot be expected to provide a complete model specification has important consequences both for testing economic theories and for the evaluation of econometric models. The incompleteness of economic theories makes the task of testing them a formidable undertaking. In general it will not be possible to say whether the results of the statistical tests have a bearing on the economic theory or the auxiliary assumptions. This ambiguity in testing theories, known as the Duhem–Quine thesis, is not confined to econometrics and arises whenever theories are conjunctions of hypotheses (on this, see for example Cross, 1982). The problem is, however, especially serious in econometrics because theory is far less developed in economics than it is in the natural sciences. There are, of course, other difficulties that surround the use of econometric methods for the purpose of testing economic theories. As a rule economic statistics are not the results of designed experiments, but are obtained as by-products of business and government activities often with legal rather than economic considerations in mind. The statistical methods available are generally suitable for large samples while the economic data (especially economic time-series) have a rather limited coverage. There are also problems of aggregation over time, commodities and individuals that further complicate the testing of economic theories that are micro-based.

The incompleteness of economic theories also introduces an important and unavoidable element of data-instigated searches into the process of model construction, which creates important methodological difficulties for the established econometric methods of model evaluation. Clearly, this whole area of specification searches deserves far greater attention, especially from non-Bayesians, than it has so far attracted.

There is no doubt that econometrics is subject to important limitations, which stem largely from the incompleteness of the economic theory and the non-experimental nature of economic data. But these limitations should not distract us from recognizing the fundamental role that econometrics has come to play in

25

the development of economics as a scientific discipline. It may not be possible conclusively to reject economic theories by means of econometric methods, but it does not mean that nothing useful can be learned from attempts at testing particular formulations of a given theory against (possible) rival alternatives. Similarly, the fact that econometric modelling is inevitably subject to the problem of specification searches does not mean that the whole activity is pointless. Econometric models are important tools of forecasting and policy analysis, and it is unlikely that they will be discarded in the future. The challenge is to recognize their limitations and to work towards turning them into more reliable and effective tools. There seem to be no viable alternatives.

BIBLIOGRAPHY

Aigner, D.J. 1985. The residential electricity time-of-use pricing experiments: what have we learned? In *Social Experimentation*, ed. J.A. Hausman and D.A. Wise, Chicago: University of Chicago Press.

Aitken, A.C. 1934–5. On least squares and linear combinations of observations. *Proceedings of the Royal Society of Edinburgh* 55, 42–8.

Allen, R.G.D. and Bowley, A.L. 1935. *Family Expenditure*. London: P.S. King.

Almon, S. 1965. The distributed lag between capital appropriations and net expenditures. *Econometrica* 33, 178–96.

Amemiya, T. 1983. Nonlinear regression models. In *Handbook of Econometrica*, ed. Z. Griliches and M.D. Intriligator, Vol. 1, Amsterdam: North-Holland.

Amemiya, T. 1984. Tobit models: a survey. *Journal of Econometrics* 24, 3–61.

Anderson, T.W. and Rubin, H. 1949. Estimation of the parameters of a single equation in a complete system of stochastic equations. *Annals of Mathematical Statistics* 20, 46–63.

Aoki, M. 1976. *Dynamic Economic Theory and Control in Economics*. New York: American Elsevier.

Balestra, P. and Nerlove, M. 1966. Pooling cross section and time series data in the estimation of a dynamic model: the demand for natural gas. *Econometrica* 34, 585–612.

Basmann, R.L. 1957. A generalized classical method of linear estimation of coefficients in a structural equation. *Econometrica* 25, 77–83.

Benini, R. 1907. Sull'uso delle formole empiriche a nell'economia applicata. *Giornale degli economisti*, 2nd series, 35, 1053–63.

Bergstrom, A.R. 1984. Continuous time stochastic models and issues of aggregation over time. In *Handbook of Econometrics*, ed. Z. Griliches and M.D. Intriligator, Vol. 2, Amsterdam: North-Holland.

Boskin, M.J. 1974. A conditional logit model of occupational choice. *Journal of Political Economy* 82, 389–98.

Box, G.E.P. and Jenkins, G.M. 1970. *Time Series Analysis: Forecasting and Control*. San Francisco: Holden-Day.

Breusch, T.S. and Pagan, A.R. 1980. The Lagrange multiplier test and its applications to model specification in econometrics. *Review of Economic Studies* 47, 239–53.

Brown, T.M. 1952. Habit persistence and lags in consumer behaviour. *Econometrica* 20, 355–71.

Brundy, J.M. and Jorgenson, D.N. 1971. Efficient estimation of simultaneous equations by instrumental variables. *Review of Economics and Statistics* 53, 207–24.

Burns, A.F. and Mitchell, W.C. 1947. *Measuring Business Cycles*. New York: Columbia University Press for the National Bureau of Economic Research.

Cagan, P. 1956. The monetary dynamics of hyperinflation. In *Studies in the Quantity Theory of Money*, ed. M. Friedman, Chicago: University of Chicago Press.

Cameron, A.C. and Trivedi, P.K. 1986. Econometric models based on count data: comparisons and applications of some estimators and tests. *Journal of Applied Econometrics* 1, 29–53.

Champernowne, D.G. 1948. Sampling theory applied to autoregressive sequences. *Journal of the Royal Statistical Society* Series B, 10, 204–31.

Chow, G.C. 1975. *Analysis and Control of Dynamic Economic Systems*. New York: John Wiley.

Chow, G.C. 1981. *Econometric Analysis by Control Methods*. New York: John Wiley.

Chow, G.C. 1983. *Econometrics*. New York: McGraw-Hill.

Chow, G.C. 1984. Random and changing coefficient models. In *Handbook of Economics*, ed. Z. Griliches and M.D. Intriligator, Vol. 2, Amsterdam: North-Holland.

Christ, C.F. 1952. *Economic Theory and Measurement: a twenty year research report, 1932–52*. Chicago: Cowles Commission for Research in Economics.

Christ, C.F. 1966. *Econometric Models and Methods*. New York: John Wiley.

Christ, C.F. 1983. The founding of the Econometric Society and Econometrica. *Econometrica* 51, 3–6.

Christ, C.F. 1985. Early progress in estimating quantitative economic relations in America. *American Economic Review*, December, 39–52 (supplementary information and statistical summaries).

Cochrane, P. and Orcutt, G.H. 1949. Application of least squares regression to relationships containing autocorrelated error terms. *Journal of the American Statistical Association* 44, 32–61.

Cooley, T.F. and Leroy, S.F. 1985. Atheoretical macroeconometrics: a critique. *Journal of Monetary Economics* 16, 283–368.

Cooper, R.L. 1972. The predictive performance of quarterly econometric models of the United States. In *Econometric Models of Cyclical Behaviour*, ed. B.G. Hickman, Studies in Income and Wealth 36, Vol. 2, Cambridge, Mass.: Harvard University Press, 813–925.

Cox, D.R. 1961. Tests of separate families of hypotheses. *Proceedings of the Fourth Berkeley Symposium on Mathematical Statistics and Probability*, Vol. 1, Berkeley: University of California Press, 105–23.

Cox, D.R. 1962. Further results of tests of separate families of hypotheses. *Journal of the Royal Statistical Society*, Series B, 24, 406–24.

Creedy, J. 1986. On the King–Davenant 'law' of demand. *Scottish Journal of Political Economy* 33, August, 193–212.

Cross, R. 1982. The Duhem–Quine thesis, Lakatos and the appraisal of theories in macroeconomics. *Economic Journal* 92, 320–40.

Davenant, C. 1968. *Discourses on the Publick Revenues and on the Trade of England*, Vol. 1, London.

Davidson, J.E.H., Hendry, D.F., Srba, F. and Yeo, S. 1978. Econometric modelling of the aggregate time-series relationship between consumers' expenditure and income in the United Kingdom. *Economic Journal* 88, 661–92.

Dhrymes, P. 1971. A simplified estimator for large-scale econometric models. *Australian Journal of Statistics* 13, 168–75.

Dickey, D.A. and Fuller, W.A. 1979. Distribution of the estimators for autoregressive time series with a unit root. *Journal of the American Statistical Association* 74, 427–31.

Dickey, D.A. and Fuller, W.A. 1981. The likelihood ratio statistics for autoregressive time series with a unit root. *Econometrica* 49, 1057–72.

Doan, T., Litterman, R. and Sims, C.A. 1984. Forecasting and conditional projection using realistic prior distributions. *Econometric Reviews* 3, 1–100.

Domenich, T. and McFadden, D. 1975. *Urban Travel Demand: A Behavioural Analysis.* Amsterdam: North-Holland.

Drèze, J.H. and Richard, J.-F. 1983. Bayesian analysis of simultaneous equation systems. In *Handbook of Econometrics*, ed. Z. Griliches and M.D. Intriligator, Vol. 1, Amsterdam: North-Holland.

Duncan, G. 1980. Formulation and statistical analysis of the mixed continuous/discrete variable model in classical production theory. *Econometrica* 48, 839–52.

Durbin, J. and Watson, G.S. 1950. Testing for serial correlation in least squares regression I. *Biometrika* 37, 409–28.

Durbin, J. and Watson, G.S. 1951. Testing for serial correlation in least squares regression II. *Biometrika* 38, 159–78.

Eisner, R. and Strotz, R.H. 1963. Determinants of business investment. In Commission on Money and Credit, *Impacts of Monetary Policy*, Englewood Cliffs, NJ: Prentice-Hall, 59–337.

Engle, R.F. 1984. Wald likelihood ratio and Lagrange multiplier tests in econometrics. In *Handbook of Econometrics*, Vol. 2, ed. Z. Griliches and M.D. Intriligator, Amsterdam: North-Holland.

Engle, R.F., Hendry, D.F. and Richard, J.-F. 1983. Exogeneity. *Econometrica* 15, 277–304.

Evans, G.B.A. and Savin, N.E. 1981. Testing for unit roots I. *Econometrica* 49, 753–77.

Evans, G.B.A. and Savin, N.E. 1984. Testing for unit roots II. *Econometrica* 52, 1241–70.

Ferber, R. and Hirsch, W.Z. 1982. *Social Experimentation and Economic Policy.* Cambridge: Cambridge University Press.

Fisher, F.M. 1966. *The Identification Problem in Econometrics.* New York: McGraw-Hill.

Fisher, I. 1930. *The Theory of Interest.* New York: Macmillan. Reprinted, Philadelphia: Porcupine Press, 1977.

Fisher, I. 1937. Note on a short-cut method for calculating distributed lags. *Bulletin de l'Institut International de Statistique* 29, 323–7.

Friedman, M. 1957. *A Theory of the Consumption Function.* Princeton: Princeton University Press.

Frisch, R. 1933a. Editorial. *Econometrica* 1, 1–4.

Frisch, R. 1933b. *Pitfalls in the Statistical Construction of Demand and Supply Curves.* Leipzig: Hans Buske Verlag.

Frisch, R. 1934. *Statistical Confluence Analysis by Means of Complete Regression Systems.* Oslo: University Institute of Economics.

Frisch, R. 1936. Note on the term 'Econometrics'. *Econometrica* 4, 95.

Geary, R.C. 1949. Studies in relations between economic time series. *Journal of the Royal Statistical Society*, Series B 10, 140–58.

Godfrey, L.G. and Wickens, M.R. 1982. Tests of misspecification using locally equivalent alternative models. In *Evaluation and Reliability of Macro-economic Models*, ed. G.C. Chow and P. Corsi, New York: John Wiley.

Granger, C.W.J. 1969. Investigating causal relations by econometric models and cross-spectral methods. *Econometrica* 37, 424–38.

Griliches, Z. 1967. Distributed lags: a survey. *Econometrica* 35, 16–49.

Grilichez, Z. 1986. Economic data issues. In *Handbook of Econometrics*, ed. Z. Griliches and M.D. Intriligator, Vol. 3, Amsterdam: North-Holland.

Haavelmo, T. 1943. Statistical testing of business cycle theories. *Review of Economics and Statistics* 25, 13–18.

Haavelmo, T. 1944. The probability approach in econometrics. *Econometrica* 12, Supplement 1–118.

Hansen, L.P. 1982. Large sample properties of generalized method of moments. *Econometrica* 50, 1029–54.

Hansen, L.P. and Sargent, T.J. 1980. Formulating and estimating dynamic linear rational expectations models. *Journal of Economic Dynamics and Control* 2, 7–46.

Hansen, L.P. and Singleton, K.J. 1982. Generalized instrumental variables estimation of non-linear rational expectations models. *Econometrica* 50, 1269–86.

Hart, B.S. and von Neumann, J. 1942. Tabulation of the probabilities for the ratio of mean square successive difference to the variance. *Annals of Mathematical Statistics* 13, 207–14.

Hausman, J.Z. 1978. Specification tests in econometrics. *Econometrica* 46, 1251–72.

Hausman, J.A. 1983. Specification and estimation of simultaneous equation models. In *Handbook of Econometrics*, Vol. 1, ed. Z. Griliches and M.D. Intriligator, Amsterdam: North-Holland.

Hausman, J. and Wise, D.A. 1979. Attrition bias in experimental and panel data: the Gary income maintenance experiment. *Econometrica* 47, 455–73.

Hausman, J.A. and Wise, D.A. 1985. *Social Experimentation.* Chicago: University of Chicago Press for the National Bureau of Economic Research.

Hausman, J.A., Hall, B.H. and Griliches, Z. 1984. Econometric models for count data with application to the patents – R & D relationship. *Econometrica* 52, 909–1038.

Heckman, J.J. and Singer, B. 1984. Econometric duration analysis. *Journal of Econometrics* 24, 63–132.

Heckman, J.J. and Willis, R. 1977. A beta-logistic model for the analysis of sequential labour force participation by married women. *Journal of Political Economy* 85, 27–58.

Hendry, D.F. 1976. The structure of simultaneous equations estimators. *Journal of Econometrics* 4, 51–88.

Hendry, D.F. and Richard, J.-F. 1982. On the formulation of empirical models in dynamic econometrics. *Journal of Econometrics* 20, 3–33.

Hooker, R.H. 1901. Correlation of the marriage rate with trade. *Journal of the Royal Statistical Society* 44, 485–92.

Hsiao, C. 1983. Identification. In *Handbook of Econometrics*, Vol. 1, ed. Z. Griliches and M.D. Intriligator, Amsterdam: North-Holland.

Hsiao, C. 1985. Benefits and limitations of panel data. *Econometric Reviews* 4, 121–74.

Jorgenson, D.W. 1966. Rational distributed lag functions. *Econometrica* 34, 135–49.

Kendall, M.G. 1968. The history of statistical methods. In *International Encyclopedia of the Social Sciences*, ed. D.L. Sills, Vol. 15, New York: Macmillan and The Free Press, 224–32.

Keynes, J.M. 1921. *A Treatise on Probability.* London: Macmillan; New York: Harper & Row, 1962.

Keynes, J.M. 1939. The statistical testing of business cycle theories. *Economic Journal* 49, 558–68.

Klein, L.R. 1947. The use of econometric models as a guide to economic policy. *Econometrica* 15, 111–51.

Klein, L.R. 1950. *Economic Fluctuations in the United States 1921–1941.* Cowles Commission Monograph No. 11, New York: John Wiley.

Klein, L.R. 1971. Whither econometrics? *Journal of the American Statistical Society* 66, 415–21.

Klein, L.R. and Goldberger, A.S. 1955. *An Econometric Model of the United States, 1929–1952.* Amsterdam: North-Holland.

Koopmans, T.C. 1937. *Linear Regression Analysis of Economic Time Series.* Haarlem: De Erven F. Bohn for the Netherlands Economic Institute.

Koopmans, T.C. 1949. Identification problems in economic model construction. *Econometrica* 17, 125–44.

Koopmans, T.C. 1950. When is an equation system complete for statistical purposes? In *Statistical Inference in Dynamic Economic Models,* ed. T.C. Koopmans, Cowles Commission Monograph No. 10, New York: John Wiley.

Koopmans, T.C., Rubin, H. and Leipnik, R.B. 1950. Measuring the equation systems of dynamic economics. In *Statistical Inference in Dynamic Economic Models,* ed. T.C. Koopmans, Cowles Commission Monograph No. 10, New York: John Wiley.

Koyck, L.M. 1954. *Distributed Lags and Investment Analysis.* Amsterdam: North-Holland.

Kuh, E. 1959. The validity of cross-sectionally estimated behaviour equations in time series applications. *Econometrica* 27, 197–214.

Lawson, T. 1981. Keynesian model building and the rational expectations critique. *Cambridge Journal of Economics* 5, 311–26.

Leamer, E.E. 1978. *Specification Searches: Ad Hoc Inference with Non-experimental Data.* New York: John Wiley.

Leamer, E.E. 1983. Let's take the con out of Econometrics. *American Economic Review* 73, 31–43.

Leamer, E.E. 1985a. Vector autoregressions for causal inference. In *Carnegie-Rochester Conference Series on Public Policy* 22, ed. K. Brunner and A.H. Meltzer, Amsterdam: North-Holland, 255–304.

Leamer, E.E. 1985b. Sensitivity analyses would help. *American Economic Review* 85, 308–13.

Leamer, E.E. 1986. A Bayesian analysis of the determinants of inflation. In *Model Reliability,* ed. D.A. Belsley and E. Kuh, Cambridge, Mass: MIT Press.

Leamer, E.E. and Leonard, H. 1983. Reporting the fragility of regression estimates. *Review of Economics and Statistics* 65, 306–17.

Lenoir, M. 1913. *Etudes sur la formation et le mouvement des prix.* Paris: Giard et Brière.

Leontief, W.W. 1936. Quantitative input–output relations in the economic system of the United States. *Review of Economic Statistics* 18, 105–25.

Leontief, W.W. 1941. *The Structure of American Economy, 1919–1929.* Cambridge, Mass: Harvard University Press.

Leontief, W.W. 1951. *The Structure of American Economy, 1919–1939,* 2nd edn, Oxford: Oxford University Press; New York: Oxford University Press, 1960.

Litterman, R.B. 1985. Forecasting with Bayesian vector autoregressions: five years of experience. *Journal of Business and Economic Statistics* 4, 25–38.

Liu, T.C. 1960. Underidentification, structural estimation and forecasting. *Econometrica* 28, 855–65.

Lucas, R.E. 1972. Expectations and the neutrality of money. *Journal of Economic Theory* 4, 103–24.

Lucas, R.E. 1973. Some international evidence on output-inflation tradeoffs. *American Economic Review* 63, 326–34.

Lucas, R.E. 1976. Econometric policy evaluation: a critique. In *The Phillips Curve and Labor Markets,* ed. K. Brunner and A.M. Meltzer, Carnegie-Rochester Conferences on Public Policy, Vol. 1, Amsterdam: North-Holland, 19–46.

Lyttkens, E. 1970. Symmetric and asymmetric estimation methods. In *Interdependent Systems*, ed. E. Mosback and H. Wold, Amsterdam: North-Holland.

McAleer, M., Pagan, A.R. and Volker, P.A. 1985. What will take the con out of econometrics? *American Economic Review* 75, 293–307.

Maddala, G.S. 1983. *Limited Dependent and Qualitative Variables in Econometrics*, Cambridge: Cambridge University Press.

Maddala, G.S. 1986. Disequilibrium, self-selection, and switching models. In *Handbook of Econometrics*, Vol. 3, ed. Z. Griliches and M.D. Intriligator, Amsterdam: North-Holland.

Malinvaud, E. 1966. *Statistical Methods of Econometrics*. Amsterdam: North-Holland.

Manski, C.F. and McFadden, D. 1981. *Structural Analysis of Discrete Data with Econometric Applications*. Cambridge, Mass: MIT Press.

Marschak, J. 1953. Economic measurements for policy and prediction. In *Studies in Econometric Method*, ed. W.C. Hood and T.C. Koopmans, Cowles Commission for Research in Economics Monograph No. 14, New York: John Wiley.

Marschak, J. and Andrews, W.H. 1944. Random simultaneous equations and the theory of production. *Econometrica* 12, 143–205.

Mitchell, W.C. 1928. *Business Cycles: the Problem in its Setting*. New York: National Bureau of Economic Research.

Moore, H.L. 1914. *Economic Cycles: Their Law and Cause*. New York: Macmillan Press.

Moore, H.L. 1917. *Forecasting the Yield and the Price of Cotton*. New York: Macmillan Press.

Morgan, M.S. 1986. Statistics without probability and Haavelmo's revolution in econometrics. In *The Probabilistic Revolution: Ideas in the Social Sciences*, ed. L. Kruger, G. Gigerenzer and M. Morgan, Cambridge, Mass: MIT Press.

Mundlak, Y. 1961. Empirical production function free of management bias. *Journal of Farm Economics* 43, 44–56.

Mundlak, Y. 1978. On the pooling of time series and cross section data. *Econometrica* 46, 69–85.

Muth, J.F. 1961. Rational expectations and the theory of price movements. *Econometrica* 29, 315–35.

Nelson, C.R. 1972. The prediction performance of the FRB–MIT–Penn model of the US economy. *American Economic Review* 62, 902–17.

Nerlove, M. 1958a. Adaptive expectations and the cobweb phenomena. *Quarterly Journal of Economics* 72, 227–40.

Nerlove, M. 1958b. *Distributed Lags and Demand Analysis*. USDA, Agriculture Handbook No. 141, Washington, DC.

Nerlove, M., Grether, D.M. and Carvalho, J.L. 1979. *Analysis of Economic Time Series: A Synthesis*. New York: Academic Press.

Neumann, J. von. 1941. Distribution of the ratio of the mean square successive difference to the variance. *Annals of Mathematical Statistics* 12, 367–95.

Neumann, J. von. 1942. A further remark on the distribution of the ratio of the mean square successive difference to the variance. *Annals of Mathematical Statistics* 13, 86–8.

Orcutt, G.H. 1948. A study of the autoregressive nature of the time series used for Tinbergen's model of the economic system of the United States, 1919–1932. *Journal of the Royal Statistical Society*, Series B 10, 1–45 (Discussion, 46–53).

Orcutt, G.H., Greenberger, M., Korbel, J. and Rivlin, A.M. 1961. *Microanalysis of Socioeconomic Systems: A Simulation Study*. New York; Harper & Row.

Orcutt, G.H., Merz, J. and Quinke, H. (eds) 1986. *Microanalytic Simulation Models to Support Social and Financial Policy*. Amsterdam: North-Holland.

Pagan, A.R. and Hall, A.D. 1983. Diagnostic tests as residual analysis. *Econometric Reviews* 2, 159–218.

Paris, S.J. and Houthakker, H.S. 1955. *The Analysis of Family Budgets*. Cambridge: Cambridge University Press.

Pesaran, M.H. 1981. Identification of rational expectations models. *Journal of Econometrics* 16, 375–98.

Pesaran, M.H. 1987. *The Limits to Rational Expectations*. Oxford: Basil Blackwell.

Pesaran, M.H. and Deaton, A.S. 1978. Testing non-nested nonlinear regression models. *Econometrica* 46, 677–94.

Pesaran, M.H. and Smith, R.P. 1985a. Keynes on econometrics. In *Keynes' Economics: methodological issues*, ed. T. Lawson and M.H. Pesaran, London: Croom Helm.

Pesaran, M.H. and Smith, R.P. 1985b. Evaluation of macroeconometric models. *Economic Modelling*, April, 125–34.

Phillips, P.C.B. 1983. Exact small sample theory in the simultaneous equations model. In *Handbook of Econometrics*, ed. Z. Griliches and M.D. Intriligator, Vol. 1, Amsterdam: North-Holland.

Phillips, P.C.B. 1986. Understanding spurious regressions in econometrics. *Journal of Econometrics* 33, 311–40.

Phillips, P.C.B. and Durlauf, S.N. 1986. Multiple time series regression with integrated processes. *Review of Economic Studies* 53, 473–95.

Phillips, P.C.B. 1987. Time series regression with unit roots. *Econometrica* (forthcoming).

Prothero, D.L. and Wallis, K.F. 1976. Modelling macroeconomic time series. *Journal of the Royal Statistical Society*, Series A 139, 468–86.

Quandt, R.E. 1982. Econometric disequilibrium models. *Econometric Reviews* 1, 1–63.

Ramsey, J.B. 1969. Tests for specification errors in classical linear least squares regression analysis. *Journal of the Royal Statistical Society*, Series B 31, 350–71.

Reiersol, O. 1941. Confluence analysis by means of lag moments and other methods of confluence analysis. *Econometrica* 9, 1–24.

Reiersol, O. 1945. *Confluence Analysis by Means of Instrumental Sets of Variables*. Stockholm.

Rosen, H.S. 1985. Housing behaviour and the experimental housing-allowance program: what have we learned? In *Social Experimentation*, ed. J.A. Hausman and D.A. Wise, Chicago: University of Chicago Press.

Rothenberg, T.J. 1984. Approximating the distributions of econometric estimators and test statistics. In *Handbook of Econometrics*, ed. Z. Griliches and M.D. Intriligator, Vol. 2, Amsterdam: North-Holland.

Ruggles, R. and Ruggles, N. 1956. *National Income Account and Income Analysis*. 2nd edn, New York: McGraw-Hill.

Samuelson, P.A., Koopmans, T.C. and Stone, J.R.N. 1954. Report of the evaluative committee for Econometrica. *Econometrica* 22, 141–6.

Sargan, J.D. 1958. The estimation of economic relationships using instrumental variables. *Econometrica* 26, 393–415.

Sargan, J.D. 1964. Wages and prices in the United Kingdom: a study in econometric methodology. In *Econometric Analysis for National Economic Planning*, ed. P.E. Hart, G. Mills and J.K. Whitaker, London: Butterworths.

Sargent, T.J. 1973. Rational expectations, the real rate of interest and the natural rate of unemployment. *Brookings Papers on Economic Activity* No. 2, 429–72.

Sargent, T.J. and Wallace, N. 1976. Rational expectations and the theory of economic policy. *Journal of Monetary Economics* 2, 169–84.

Savin, N.E. 1973. Systems k-class estimators. *Econometrica* 41, 1125–36.

Schultz, M. 1938. *The Theory and Measurement of Demand.* Chicago: University of Chicago Press.

Schumpeter, J.A. 1954. *History of Economic Analysis.* London: George Allen & Unwin; New York: Oxford University Press.

Shiller, R.J. 1973. A distributed lag estimator derived from smoothness priors. *Econometrica* 41, 775–88.

Sims, C.A. 1972. Money, income and causality. *American Economic Review* 62, 540–52.

Sims, C.A. 1980. Macroeconomics and reality. *Econometrica* 48, 1–48.

Sims, C.A. 1982. Policy analysis with economic models. *Brookings Papers on Economic Activity* No. 1, 107–64.

Sims, C.A. 1986. Are forecasting models usable for policy analysis? *Federal Reserve Bank of Minneapolis Review* 10, 2–16.

Slutsky, E. 1927. The summation of random causes as the source of cyclic processes. In *Problems of Economic Conditions*, Vol. 3, Moscow. English trans. in *Econometrica* 5, (1937), 105–46.

Solow, R.M. 1960. On a family of lag distributions. *Econometrica* 28, 393–406.

Srivastava, V.K. 1971. Three-stage least-squares and generalized double k-class estimators: a mathematical relationship. *International Economic Review* 12, 312–16.

Stafford, F.P. 1985. Income-maintenance policy and work effort: learning from experiments and labour-market studies. In *Social Experimentation*, ed. J.A. Hausman and D.A. Wise, Chicago: University of Chicago Press.

Stigler, G.J. 1954. The early history of empirical studies of consumer behaviour. *Journal of Political Economy* 62, 95–113.

Stigler, G.J. 1962. Henry L. Moore and statistical economics. *Econometrica* 30, 1–21.

Stone, J.R.N. 1945. The analysis of market demand. *Journal of the Royal Statistical Society* Series A 108, 286–382.

Stone, J.R.N. et al. 1954a. *Measurement of Consumers' Expenditures and Behaviour in the United Kingdom, 1920–38*, Vols. 1 and 2. London: Cambridge University Press.

Stone, J.R.N. 1954b. Linear expenditure systems and demand analysis: an application to the pattern of British demand. *Economic Journal* 64, 511–27.

Stone, J.R.N. 1978. *Keynes, Political Arithmetic and Econometrics.* British Academy, Seventh Keynes Lecture in Economics.

Stone, J.R.N. 1984. The accounts of society. Nobel Memorial lecture. Reprinted in *Journal of Applied Econometrics* 1, (1986), 5–28.

Theil, H. 1954. Estimation of parameters of econometric models. *Bulletin of International Statistics Institute* 34, 122–8.

Theil, H. 1958. *Economic Forecasts and Policy.* Amsterdam: North-Holland; 2nd edn, 1961.

Tinbergen, J. 1929–30. Bestimmung und Deutung von Angebotskurven: ein Beispiel. *Zeitschrift für Nationalökonomie* 1, 669–79.

Tinbergen, J. 1937. *An Econometric Approach to Business Cycle Problems.* Paris: Herman & Cie Editeurs.

Tinbergen, J. 1939. *Statistical Testing of Business Cycle Theories.* Vol. 1: *A Method and its Application to Investment activity*; Vol. 2: *Business Cycles in the United States of America, 1919–1932.* Geneva: League of Nations.

Tobin, J. 1958. Estimation of relationships for limited dependent variables. *Econometrica* 26, 24–36.

Treadway, A.B. 1971. On the multivariate flexible accelerator. *Econometrica* 39, 845–55.

Trivedi, P.K. 1975. Time series analysis versus structural models: a case study of Canadian manufacturing behaviour. *International Economic Review* 16, 587–608.

Wallis, K.F. 1977. Multiple time series analysis and the final form of econometric models. *Econometrica* 45, 1481–97.

Wallis, K. 1980. Econometric implications of the Rational Expectations Hypothesis. *Econometrica* 48, 49–73.

Wegge, L.L. 1965. Identifiability criteria for a system of equations as a whole. *Australian Journal of Statistics* 3, 67–77.

Whewell, W. 1850. *Mathematical Exposition of some Doctrines of Political Economy: Second Memoir.* Cambridge: Cambridge Philosophical Society, 1856, Transaction 9, Pt. I. *Philosophical Society.*

White, H. 1981. Consequences and detection of misspecified nonlinear regression models. *Journal of the American Statistical Association* 76, 419–33.

White, H. 1982. Maximum likelihood estimation of misspecified models. *Econometrica* 50, 1–26.

Whittle, P. 1963. *Prediction and Regulation by Linear Least-squares Methods.* London: English Universities Press; Princeton, N.J.: Van Nostrand.

Wickens, M. 1982. The efficient estimation of econometric models with rational expectations. *Review of Economic Studies* 49, 55–68.

Wicksteed, P.H. 1889. On certain passages in Jevons's theory of political economy. *The Quarterly Journal of Economics* 3, 293–314.

Wold, H. 1938. *A Study in the Analysis of Stationary Time Series.* Stockholm: Almqvist and Wiksell.

Working, E.J. 1927. What do statistical 'demand curves' show? *Quarterly Journal of Economics* 41, 212–35.

Wright, P.G. 1915. Review of economic cycles by Henry Moore. *Quarterly Journal of Economics* 29, 631–41.

Wright, P.G. 1928. *The Tariff on Animal and Vegetable Oils.* London: Macmillan for the Institute of Economics.

Yule, G.U. 1895, 1896. On the correlation of total pauperism with proportion of out-relief. *Economic Journal* 5, 603–11; 6, 613–23.

Yule, G.U. 1915. Crop production and price: a note on Gregory King's law. *Journal of the Royal Statistical Society* 78, March, 296–8.

Yule, G.U. 1921. On the time-correlation problem, with special reference to the variate-difference correlation method. *Journal of the Royal Statistical Society* 84, 497–526.

Yule, G.U. 1926. Why do we sometimes get nonsense correlations between time-series? A study in sampling and the nature of time-series. *Journal of the Royal Statistical Society* 89, 1–64.

Zellner, A. 1962. An efficient method of estimating seemingly unrelated regressions and tests for aggregation bias. *Journal of the American Statistical Association* 57, 348–68.

Zellner, A. 1979. Statistical analysis of econometric models. *Journal of the American Statistical Association* 74, 628–43.

Zellner, A. 1984. *Basic Issues in Econometrics.* Chicago: University of Chicago Press.

Zellner, A. 1985. Bayesian econometrics. *Econometrica* 53, 253–70.

Zellner, A. and Palm, F. 1974. Time series analysis and simultaneous equation econometric models. *Journal of Econometrics* 2, 17–54.

Zellner, A. and Theil, H. 1962. Three-stage least squares: simultaneous estimation of simultaneous equations. *Econometrica* 30, 54–78.

Aggregation of Economic Relations

WALTER D. FISHER

A simplification or aggregation problem is faced by a research worker whenever he finds that his data are too numerous or in too much detail to be manageable and he feels the need to reduce or combine the detailed data in some manner. He will want to use aggregative measures for his new groups. But what will be the effect of this procedure on his results? How can he choose among alternative procedures? In grouping his data and/or relations he must also decide how many groups to use; a smaller number is more manageable but will cause more of the original information to be lost. The research worker seeks a solution to this problem that will best serve his objectives, or those of some decision-maker who will use his results.

For example, say that a true micro-model is

$$y = Px + v \qquad (1)$$

where y is a vector of g endogenous variables and x is a vector of h predetermined variables. It is desired to work with a macro-model

$$\bar{y} = \bar{P}\bar{x} + \bar{v} \qquad (2)$$

where $\bar{y}$ is a reduced *vector* of f aggregated endogenous variables, and $\bar{x}$ is a reduced vector of j predetermined variables, where $f < g$, and $j < h$. The reduction is to be made in such a manner that when predictions are made with the macro-model, results will be as close as possible to those that could have been obtained with the micro-model.

General reviews of the aggregation problem in the various stages of its development may be found in Malinvaud (1956), Theil (1962), Fisher (1969) and Chipman (1976).

It is not surprising that the aggregation problem in economics began to attract attention with the development of econometrics since the task of inferring realistic models becomes particularly acute when only limited empirical data are available. It was only a dozen years or so after the founding of the Econometric Society that there occurred an early methodological discussion of the problem in Klein (1946), May (1946, 1947) and Shou Shan Pu (1946). This discussion related specifically to simultaneous equation macro-models.

The important and pioneering work of Theil (1954) treated the question of the consequences of aggregation in a stochastic model of simultaneous equations. Theil derived relationships between estimated parameters in detailed and aggregated models when the parameters are estimated by linear unbiased methods.

The approach of Theil, that of measuring the consequences of aggregation in terms of the discrepancies from a true micro-model, leads directly to the goal of optimal aggregation – that is, selecting a mode of aggregation resulting in a macro-model based on the data at hand and a given degree of detail, such that the expected discrepancies are minimized. To pursue this goal it is necessary to postulate a loss function in terms of the discrepancies and to have available a procedure for minimizing expected loss from a very large number of alternatives. Say that it is desired to predict y in (1) with small error, but that it is also desired to use a simplified model, $\tilde{P}$, of the same size as P, so the prediction will be

$$\tilde{y} = \tilde{P}x. \tag{3}$$

The simplified model $\tilde{P}$ is considered to be subject to certain a priori restrictions. For example, it may be assumed to be of a rank lower than that of P, or to be expressible in the form

$$\tilde{P} = T'\bar{P} \tag{4}$$

where $\bar{P}$ is an *aggregated matrix* of smaller order than P, and T' is given a priori.

Say that the cost of this procedure to the investigator is

$$c = E(\tilde{y} - y)'C(\tilde{y} - y), \tag{5}$$

where C is a known positive-definite matrix that weights the relative importance of forecast errors in the various endogenous variables and their interactions. It has been shown that

$$c = \operatorname{tr} C(\tilde{P} - P)M(\tilde{P} - P)' + \text{constant}, \tag{6}$$

where $M = E(xx')$. The problem of choosing $\tilde{P}$ so as to minimize c may be called a *simplification problem*.

The lower the rank of $\tilde{P}$, or the smaller the dimensions of $\bar{P}$, the more severe is the aggregation and simplification. To find the matrix $\bar{P}$, or $\tilde{P}$, that minimizes the cost c subject to a given level of severity of aggregation, is a well defined but not a trivial problem. It may be accomplished in two steps: first, finding the optimal $\bar{P}$ conditional on a partition and second, searching for the partition that gives a minimum minimorum c. For the second step a computer is necessary. First suggested by Hurwicz (1952) and Malinvaud (1956), the optimal aggregation approach has been extended and applied to a number of econometric problems by Fisher (1953, 1962, 1969) and Chipman (1975a, 1975b, 1976).

One of the most frequent applications and most strongly felt needs of aggregation is to Leontief inter-industry (intput–output) models. We can make our equation (1) above into an input–output model by setting $g = h$, defining y as the set of outputs, x the set of final demands and defining $P = (I - A)^{-1}$, where A is the matrix of technical coefficients. Here it is natural to require that the aggregation over both rows and columns of the matrix A involve the same partition, that is, that the combination of 'small industries' into 'large industries' implied by the row partition be the same as for the column partition. Some excellent preliminary discussion of the model is given by Leontief (1947). Conditions for obtaining perfect (without error) aggregation in this system were given by Hatanaka (1952).

Since the input–output model may be considered a special case of the simultaneous equations model, the same principles of optimal aggregation may be applied to find an aggregated or a simplified model. This approach is used in McCarthy (1956), Fisher (1958, 1969) and Neudecker (1970).

There is a well known correspondence between such concepts as distance, variance, and scatter, on the one hand, and entropy and information content on the other. If an m by n rectangular table contains a set X of numbers that sum to unity, the *entropy* of the table may be defined as

$$E(X) = - \sum_{i,j=1}^{n} x_{ij} \log x_{ij}. \tag{7}$$

This may be considered a measure of the degree of sameness or homogeneity of the elements of the matrix X.

If X is aggregated by rows and by columns, an aggregated entropy may be found from the aggregated cells of the smaller matrix. This entropy will be larger than that of X. The difference may be regarded as a loss of information from the aggregation. The problem may be posed: to find the mode of aggregation (to a specified degree of detail) that minimizes this loss.

Skolka (1964) and Theil (1967) have applied this idea to input–output tables. Fisher (1969, ch. 6) has shown an exact correspondence between this problem and the minimization of his objective function (5). Recent insights into the aggregation problem in input–output analysis are found in Tintner and Sondermann (1977) and Laisney (1982).

Practically all of the work reviewed so far has proceeded on the assumption that the micro-model is true, or at least that the microdata with which the investigator works form an unbiased estimate of the truth. Thus, the expected loss from using an aggregated artefact can never be negative, and can be tolerated only if there is a compensating gain from aggregation, owing to increased manageability, understanding, etc., of a smaller model.

But in Grunfeld and Griliches (1960) an example was presented where the errors were *less* after aggregation. The monograph of Ringwald (1980) made the point that this situation is probably very frequent in economics, especially as

37

so-called microdata have in reality undergone much processing and are a pre-aggregation of unobserved, yet more detailed data, probably subject to bias. Ringwald's critique has been followed by Chipman (1985), who has developed formulae expressing the relationship between stage 1 and stage 2 models, where stage 1 is the result of some previous aggregation. The issue is obviously of considerable importance and it is evident that more work needs to be done.

BIBLIOGRAPHY

Chipman, J.S. 1975a. The aggregation problem in econometrics. *Advances in Applied Probability*, September.

Chipman, J.S. 1975b. Optimal aggregation in large-scale economic models. *Sankhya* 37(4), 121–59.

Chipman, J.S. 1976. Estimation and aggregation in economics: an application of the theory of generalized inverses. In *Generalized Inverses and Applications*, ed. M.Z. Nashed, New York: Academic Press.

Chipman, J.S. 1985. Testing for reduction of mean-square error by aggregation in dynamic econometric models. In *Multivariate Analysis VI: Proceedings of the Sixth International Symposium on Multivariate Analysis*, Amsterdam: North-Holland.

Day, R.H. 1963. On aggregating linear programming models of production. *Journal of Farm Economics* 45, November, 797–813.

Fei, J.C.H. 1956. A fundamental theorem for the aggregation problem of input–output analysis. *Econometrica* 24(4), October, 400–412.

Fisher, W.D. 1953. On a pooling problem from the statistical decision viewpoint. *Econometrica* 21(4), October, 567–85.

Fisher, W.D. 1958. Criteria for aggregation in input–output analysis. *Review of Economics and Statistics* 40(3), August, 250–60.

Fisher, W.D. 1962. Optimal aggregation in multi-equation prediction models. *Econometrica* 30(4), October, 744–69.

Fisher, W.D. 1969. *Clustering and Aggregation in Economics*. Baltimore: The Johns Hopkins Press.

Fisher, W.D. 1979. A note on aggregation and disaggregation. *Econometrica* 47(3), May, 739–46.

Fisher, W.D. and Kelley, P.L. 1968. Selecting representative firms in linear programming. Ch. 13 in *Economic Analysis and Agricultural Policy*, ed. R.H. Day, Ames: Iowa State University Press, 1982.

Gorman, W.M. 1968. The structure of utility functions. *Review of Economic Studies* 35, October, 367–90.

Grunfeld, Y. and Griliches, Z. 1960. Is aggregation necessarily bad? *Review of Economics and Statistics* 42(1), February, 1–13.

Hatanaka, M. 1952. Note on consolidation within a Leontief system. *Econometrica* 20(2), April, 301–3.

Hurwicz, L. 1952. Aggregation in macroeconomic models [abstract]. *Econometrica* 20(3), July, 489–91.

Ijiri, Y. 1971. Fundamental queries in aggregation theory. *Journal of the American Statistical Association* 66, December, 766–82.

Klein, L.R. 1946. Remarks on the theory of aggregation. *Econometrica* 14(4), October, 303–12.

Laisney, F. 1984. Theory and practice in optimal aggregation of linear models. *Economic Letters*, 315–24.

Leontief, W. 1947. Introduction to a theory of the internal structure of functional relationships. *Econometrica* 15(4), October, 361–73.

Malinvaud, E. 1956. L'agrégation dans les modèles économiques. *Cahiers du Seminaire d'Econométrie* No. 4, Paris: Centre National de la Recherche Scientifique.

May, K. 1946. The aggregation problem for a one-industry model. *Econometrica* 14(4), October, 285–98.

May, K. 1947. Technological change and aggregation. *Econometrica* 15(1), January, 51–63.

McCarthy, J. 1956. Aggregation in the Leontief model. Joint Allied Social Science Association meeting in Cleveland, Ohio, 27 December.

Nataf, A. 1960. Résultats et directions de recherche dans la théorie de l'agrégation. *Logic, Methodology and Philosophy of Science. Proceedings of the 1960 International Congress*, ed. E. Nagel, P. Suppes and A. Tarski, Stanford, California: Stanford University Press, 1962.

Neudecker, H. 1970. Aggregation in input–output analysis: an extension of Fisher's method. *Econometrica* 38(6), November, 921–26.

Ringwald, K. 1980. *A Critique of Models in Linear Aggregation Structures*. Boston: Oelgeschlager, Gunn & Hain.

Schneeweiss, H. 1965. Das Aggregationsproblem. *Statistische Hefte*.

Shou Shan Pu. 1946. A note on macroeconomics. *Econometrica* 14(4), October, 299–302.

Skolka, J. 1964. *The Aggregation Problem in Input–Output Analysis*. Prague: Czechoslovakian Academy of Sciences.

Sondermann, D. 1973. Optimale Aggregation von grossen linearen Gleichungssystemen. *Zeitschrift für Nationalökonomie* 33(3–4), 235–50.

Theil, H. 1954. *Linear Aggregation of Economic Relations*. Amsterdam: North-Holland.

Theil, H. 1962. Alternative approaches to the aggregation problem. *Logic, methodology and philosophy of science. Proceedings of the 1960 International Congress*, ed. E. Nagel, P. Suppes and A. Tarski, Stanford, California: Stanford University Press.

Theil, H. 1967. *Economics and Information Theory*. Chicago: Rand McNally.

Tintner, G. and Sondermann, D. 1977. Statistical aspects of economic aggregation. In *Mathematical Economics and Game Theory*, ed. Henn and Moeschlin, Berlin: Springer.

Almon Lag

ROGER N. WAUD

The Almon distributed lag, due to Shirley Almon (1965), is a technique for estimating the weights of a distributed lag by means of a polynomial specification.

Consider the distributed lag model,

$$y_t = w_0 x_t + \cdots + w_n x_{t-n} + \varepsilon_t \tag{1}$$

where y_t is the value of the dependent variable at time t; $x_t, x_{t-1}, \ldots, x_{t-n}$ are the values of the regressor x at times, $t, t-1, \ldots, t-n$; and ε_t is the value of the disturbance ε at time t. The dependent variable y is influenced by the regressor x both contemporaneously and with a lag of up to n time periods. If the lag length, n, is finite and less than the number of observations, the regression coefficients w_i can be estimated by ordinary least squares (OLS).

It is often the case, however, that there is a high degree of multicollinearity among the regressors $x_t, \ldots, x_{t-n}$ so that most or all of the estimated regression coefficients are statistically insignificant, and powerful inferences about the true weights are impossible. This problem can be circumvented by introducing *a priori* information into the estimation procedure, typically by imposing restrictions on the true weights. If the restrictions are valid, the estimates of the weights will be unbiased, consistent *and* more efficient than the OLS estimates. Similarly, the tests of hypotheses about the true weights will be valid *and* more powerful than the tests based on OLS estimation.

The Almon lag technique introduces *a priori* information by estimating the distributed lag model (1) subject to the restriction that the weights lie on a polynomial of degree p,

$$w_i = \lambda_0 + \lambda_1 i + \lambda_2 i^2 + \cdots + \lambda_p i^p, \tag{2}$$

$i = 0, 1, \ldots, n; p \leqslant n$. This reduces the number of parameters from $n+1$ $(w_0, w_1, \ldots, w_n)$ to $p+1$ $(\lambda_0, \lambda_1, \ldots, \lambda_p)$. (A very readable description of the procedure for estimating the 'new' parameters $(\lambda_0, \lambda_1, \ldots, \lambda_p)$ and transforming these into estimates of the original weights $(w_1, w_2, \ldots, w_n)$ is provided by Kmenta

(1971, pp. 492–3).) As with any *a priori* restriction, the restriction that the weights lie on a polynomial will lead to more efficient and more powerful tests if the restriction is valid, but will give biased and inconsistent and invalid tests if the restriction is false. Following are some important caveats to be borne in mind when using the Almon technique.

1. *The presence or absence of a lag is not a testable proposition when the Almon lag technique is used.* Suppose no lag is present so that x affects y only instantaneously; $w_0 \neq 0$ but $w_1 = w_2 = \cdots = w_n = 0$. Since a polynomial of degree p can equal zero in only p places (unless it is identically zero), any choice of $p < n$ involves a specification error; the n zeros $w_1, w_2, \ldots, w_n$ cannot lie on a polynomial of degree $p < n$. Therefore if the Almon lag technique is used in this case, the results will suggest the presence of a lag even though there is none.

2. *The use of end-point constraints.* It has been a rather common practice among users of the Almon technique to impose one or both end-point constraints

$$w_{-1} = 0; \quad w_{n+1} = 0 \tag{3}$$

in estimation. In terms of (2) this involves the following restrictions on the λs:

$$\lambda_0 - \lambda_1 + \lambda_2 - \cdots \pm \lambda_p = 0 \tag{4}$$

$$\lambda_0 + (n+1)\lambda_1 + (n+1)^2\lambda_2 + \cdots + (n+1)^p\lambda_p = 0. \tag{5}$$

The imposition of (4) and (5) increases the efficiency of estimation if the restrictions are true, but gives biased and inconsistent estimates if they are false. In general, however, there are no convincing reasons for imposing these constraints. For example, it is tempting to argue that $w_{-1} = 0$ because it is the coefficient on x_{t+1} and x_{t+1} does not affect y_t. By the same logic one would conclude $0 = w_{-2} = w_{-3} = w_{-4} = \cdots$. However, this is not possible. If the weights w_i do in fact lie on a polynomial of degree p, no more than p of them can equal zero. This illustrates why one should be concerned only with the weights $w_0, w_1, \ldots, w_n$ – the behaviour of the polynomial outside this range is irrelevant.

3. *Choosing the lag length and polynomial degree.* Understating the length (choosing n less than the true lag length) is a specification error which results in biased and inconsistent estimates and invalid tests. A specification error is also committed by overstating the lag length. This occurs whenever the lag length is overstated by more than p minus the number of endpoint constraints because a p-degree polynomial can have only p zeros. Choosing a small value of p increases the possible efficiency gain from use of the Almon technique, but also makes specification error more likely. However, if p is not considerably less than n, using the technique may be pointless since the results will strongly resemble the OLS results; when $p = n$ the estimates are the same as OLS. A discussion of the procedures for testing for appropriate lag length and degree of polynomial, along with relevant literature citations, can be found in Judge et al. (1980, pp. 645–51).

BIBLIOGRAPHY

Almon, S. 1965. The distributed lag between capital appropriations and expenditures. *Econometrica* 33(1), January, 178–96.

Judge, G., Griffiths, W., Hill, R. and Lee, T. 1980. *The Theory and Practice of Econometrics.* New York: Wiley.

Kmenta, J. 1971. *Elements of Econometrics.* New York: Macmillan.

Bunch Maps

WILFRED CORLETT

Bunch maps were developed by Ragnar Frisch (1934) to deal with the problems of confluence analysis. By 'confluence analysis' he meant the study of several variables in some sets of which a regression equation might have a meaning, while in others it might not because of the existence of more than one relation between the variables. Frisch's exposition of bunch maps was based on a situation where each variable in a set could be split into two components: one, the systematic component, was connected with the other variables; the other, the disturbance, was not so connected. The method was used to try to determine sets of variables in which one, and only one, exact linear relation held between the systematic components of the variables. Examples of the use of the method were given for constructed data where exact relations did exist. It is less clear whether they were assumed to exist in examples of applications to actual economic data. The other major applications of bunch maps were in Richard Stone's work on consumers' expenditure (Stone, 1945, 1954), but he did not consider an assumption of exact linear relations between systematic components as satisfactory.

In a full analysis of a number of variables, the bunch map was based on regressions calculated for every possible subset of two or more variables with minimization in the direction of every member of the subset. Each variable was normalized to give a unit sum of squares over observations of deviations from means. For any pair of variables, x_i and x_j (ij), in the subset, if the regression with minimization in the direction of x_k were written to express x_i in terms of the other variables, the coefficient of x_j would be minus the ratio of the cofactors of r_{jk} and r_{ik} in the correlation matrix of the variables in the subset. These cofactors were used as ordinate and abscissa respectively, but with one sign changed in such a way that the abscissa was positive, to obtain a point in a diagram. Similar points were plotted in the same diagram for all possible x_k in the subset and labelled with k. The points were joined to the origin to give the individual bunch with its beams. There was a separate bunch for every pair of variables in every subset. Together they formed the bunch map.

The bunch map was used mainly for comparing bunches of two subsets where the second contained the variables in the first plus an additional one. Attempts were made to classify the added variable as useful, superfluous or detrimental. Criteria which suggested that a variable was useful included the tightening of the bunch, a change in its general slope and the beam associated with the new variable being inside the bunch. The length of the beams and changes in length were also considered. An explosion of the bunch showed that the new variable was detrimental; that is, it introduced multiple relations.

The complexity of the procedure and the apparent subjectivity of combining different criteria in classifying variables may have contributed to the relatively small impact of bunch maps on applied econometrics, despite frequent references in textbooks and other works on econometric techniques. Frisch's analysis did, however, draw more attention to the dangers of errors of measurement in multicollinear situations than is common in more recent discussions of multicollinearity.

BIBLIOGRAPHY

Frisch, R. 1934. *Statistical Confluence Analysis by Means of Complete Regression Systems.* Oslo: University Institute of Economics.

Stone, J.R.N. 1945. The analysis of market demand. *Journal of the Royal Statistical Society* 108, parts 3 and 4, 286–382.

Stone, J.R.N. 1954. *The Measurement of Consumers' Expenditure and Behaviour in the United Kingdom, 1920–1938*, Vol. 1, Cambridge: Cambridge University Press.

Causal Inference

C.W.J. GRANGER

When a particular event is observed, such as an economic variable taking a value in some region of the set of all possible values, it is natural to ask why that event occurred rather than some other. If, just earlier, some other event was observed to occur, it is also natural to ask if the joint observation of the two events indicates a relationship and possibly one that could be called an influence of one event by another, or even a causation. For a unique, or very rare event, such as the start of a world war, it will be very difficult to present more than sensible and suggestive statistical evidence about causation. However, in economics, values for many variables are observed with great regularity, such as daily stock market prices or monthly production figures and so a generating mechanism can be postulated that produces these values and the investigation and understanding of this mechanism is obviously one of the main tasks for the economist. In such studies, ideas such as theories, laws and causation arise very naturally, and economists in their workings use such words very frequently. It is unfortunately true that not all writers give the same meanings to these words. The understanding of causality is not the same for all economists, but this is hardly surprising as statisticians and philosophers are also not in agreement among themselves.

Economists who have attempted to discuss the meaning of causation in economics include Herbert Simon (1953), Herman Wold (1954), Julian Simon (1970), Sir John Hicks (1979) and Arnold Zellner (1979). Most of the writers emphasize the difference between a mere association and the deeper sub-class of associations that might be called causal relationships. To distinguish these, some statisticians have emphasized the use of experimental studies, but these are rarely available in economics and so this aspect of causation will not be further considered.

One can either discuss causation in very general, abstract terms or the discussion can be focused on the specific question of whether it is possible to test for causation using the data available. The latter requires an operational

45

procedure and definition. There are basically two types of causal testing situations. In the first, a population of economic agents is observed and some variables measured for each, for example, the amount of electricity used by a household. The totality of these measurements gives a distribution. A question can then be asked – why does this household use more electricity than that one? This is a cross-sectional causality question. It is also possible to measure parameters of the distribution, such as the mean or the variance, and to ask why these parameters are changing through time. Thus, the question is asked, why is electricity demand higher this year than last? This could be called a temporal causality question. The definitions of causality and their interpretations may differ between these two cases.

It is convenient to assume the existence of a quantity called the 'degree of belief' held by an individual about the correctness of some causal theory or proposition and to assume further that this quantity can be represented as a probability. The objective of any causal analysis, such as a statistical test, might be to try to influence the degree of belief of oneself or of others. For this purpose, the analysis need not be complete or perfect, but merely to have enough value to make one reconsider one's beliefs.

A mere association between a pair of economic variables, such as a correlation or a non-independent joint distribution, is insufficient to determine a causation, partly because such associations are symmetric between the variables, the extent to which X is correlated to Y, or can be explained by Y, is exactly the same as Y is correlated, or explained, by X. It is generally thought that causation is a non-symmetric relationship, and there are various ways in which asymmetry can be introduced, the most important of which are controllability, a relevant theory, outside knowledge, and temporal priority. Amongst the economic writers, each has its advocates and detractors.

Concerning controllability, Strotz and Wold (1960) write:

> z is a cause of y if, by hypothesis, it is or 'would be possible' by controlling z indirectly to control y, at least stochastically. But it may or may not be possible by controlling y indirectly to control z this way.

Essentially this idea is from their experimental background and uses hypothetical experiments. By utilizing enough knowledge about lack of controllability in a system, so that some possible causal links are put to zero, tests can be constructed on the remaining links. This would obviously be the case if a system of variables, all measured at the same time, could be displayed recursively, so that the jth equation involved only the first j variables. However, by redefining variables as linear combinations of the original set, such a recursive system can always be achieved and not uniquely, unless there are sufficient identifying qualifications on the system. J. Simon suggests that controllability is required to make causal analysis useful for policy-makers. The equivalence of causation and controllability is not generally accepted, the latter being perhaps a deeper relationship. If a causal link were found and was not previously used for control, the action of attempting to control with it may destroy the causal link.

Hicks, Zellner and J. Simon, in discussing causal links, all emphasize the relevance of a sound economic theory. Hicks (1979) accepts static or equilibrium theory as sufficient for use, while J. Simon (1970) suggests that a statement that is 'logically connected to the general framework of systematic economics is much more likely to be considered causal than one that stands alone'. Thus, the theory is used to increase the degree of belief, and these writers suggest that a strong degree of belief cannot be achieved without a convincing theory. Zellner (1979) takes a much stronger view, leaning heavily on the work of the philosopher H. Feigl who says that 'the clarified (or purified) concept of causation is defined in terms of *predictability according to a law* (or more adequately, according to a set of laws)'. In his work, Zellner appears to be saying that for him a degree of belief cannot be anything but very small unless the causal analysis is based on some generally acceptable economic theory. He gives no examples of such economic laws and it is interesting to note that Hicks (1979, p. 2) says that 'there are few economic laws that are at all firmly based'.

Concerning temporal priority, it is generally, although not universally, accepted that the cause cannot occur after the effect. It is also frequently assumed that the cause will occur before the effect, providing a convenient asymmetry, but this view is certainly more controversial. Both Zellner and Hicks firmly reject it and Hicks maintains that instantaneous and contemporaneous causality is the 'characteristic form of the causal relation in modern economics'. It is certainly true that much economic theory is written as though causation is instantaneous. However, as Hicks also points out, all economic variables are accumulations of the outcomes of economic decisions and it is difficult to present a sensible decision mechanism in which there is an instantaneous relationship between the observed inputs to the decision (the causes) and the observed outputs (the effects). Thus, for statistical testing purposes, which has to use just observed variables, the temporal priority assumption appears to be more reasonable. It is also clear that if any part of the cause cannot occur later than any part of the variable being effected, instantaneous causation cannot occur between some pairs of stock and flow variables. For example, production of steel in a month could not instantaneously cause production of automobiles in the month, as part of one variable occurs after part of the other. There is always the possibility of apparent instantaneous causation occurring because of temporal aggregation or missing common causes.

Occasionally other outside information is used to break the symmetry of association. One variable may be thought to be generated outside the economic system, such as a weather variable, so that causation can only flow from it to part of the economy. This idea is the classical one of exogeneity. For a discussion of this topic with generalizations concerned with estimation problems, see Engle et al. (1983). A particular case is when a variable is thought to be completely controlled, such as tax rates or possibly money supply, so that controlled money could cause price changes but not vice versa. In all these cases, the outside information may be useful, if it is correct.

Although many important economic questions can be phrased in the cross-section causal situation, they have received little causal testing in that context, except under the 'outside information' assumption. However, many tests have been conducted for economic questions that can be stated as temporal causation. These tests have been conducted using the concepts known in the literature as 'Granger-causation'. This approach is based on two axioms – that the cause will occur before the effect (strict temporal priority) and that the cause contains unique information about the effect. The second can be stated more formally as follows. Let A_t represent all the observable information available at time t and $A_t - Y_t$ represent all this information except that contained in the series $Y_{t-j}, j \geqslant 0$. Then Y_t will be said to cause X_{t+1} if

$$\text{Prob}(X_{t+1} \text{ in } C | A_t) \neq \text{Prob}(X_{t+1} \text{ in } C | A_t - Y_t)$$

for any region C. The two axioms have the simple consequence that any well-behaved function $f(X_{t+1})$ will be generally better forecast using any cost function as a criterion. Thus, tests of this type of causation potentially can be based on forecastability but to be operational some simplifications are required. If one has a belief about a temporal causation then it could be called a prima facie causality. If a test is based on the above definition, but with the unuseful universal information-set replaced by a restricted but practical information set I_t, and if the test finds evidence for causation, then the relationship remains a prima facie cause. The set I_t will consist of a group of time series and the larger and more relevant it is, the more stringent will be the test; it is then more likely that degrees of belief will change. The choice of the causation to investigate and the choice of I_t will probably depend on some theory, but this could be a low-level theory and, if the tests so suggest, may be worth further development. In practice, tests are rarely based on distributions but on parameters of the distributions such as means. This could be stated as 'Y_t is a prima facie cause in mean of X_{t+1}' with respect to I_t,' if

$$E[X_{t+1} | I_t] \neq E[X_{t+1} | I_t - Y_t].$$

It will follow that X_{t+1} is better forecast, using a least squares criterion, if Y_t is used than if it is not used. Standard time-series modelling techniques will provide models of X_{t+1} based on I_t and on $I_t - Y_t$ and the post-sample forecasting ability of the two models can then be used to test this particular form of causation. Some of these tests are described in Pierce and Haugh (1977) and evaluated in Nelson and Schwert (1982). They are generally linear in data, although do not have to be, and, if misapplied, can of course lead to incorrect results. To correspond strictly to the definition, tests should be based on the post-sample forecasting abilities of the alternative models.

The definition has both some advances and some problems, and these are discussed in Granger (1980). In theory, the tests are not altered if backward filters are applied to the data, but some kinds of seasonal adjustments or measurement errors can give problems. If Y_t causes X_{t+1} the X_t may, but need not cause Y_{t+1}, so that feedback can occur but need not. Similarly, if Y_t causes X_{t+1} and X_t causes Z_{t+1} then Y_t may, but need not, cause Z_{t+2}. It has to be remembered when interpreting results based on tests that missing common causal variables can always alter the interpretation, that causation may be lost if one variable is controlled so as to reduce the strength of the causal link, and that temporal aggregation or using data measured over intervals much wider than actual causal lags can also destroy causal interpretation.

BIBLIOGRAPHY

Engle, R.F., Hendry, D.F. and Richard, J.F. 1983. Exogeneity. *Econometrica* 51, 277–304.

Granger, C.W.J. 1980. Tests for causation – a personal viewpoint. *Journal of Economic Dynamics and Control* 2, 329–52.

Hicks, Sir J. 1979. *Causality in Economics*. New York: Basic Books.

Nelson, C.R. and Schwert, G.W. 1982. Tests for predictive relationships between time series variables. *Journal of the American Statistical Association* 77, 11–18.

Pierce, D.A. and Haugh, L.D. 1977. Causality in temporal systems. *Journal of Econometrics* 5, 265–93.

Simon, H. 1953. Causal ordering and identifiability. *Studies in Econometric Method*, Cowles Commission Monograph No. 14, ed. W.C. Hood and T.C. Koopmans. New York: John Wiley.

Simon, J.L. 1970. The concept of causality in economics. *Kyklos* 23, 226–52.

Strotz, R.H. and Wold, H. 1960. Recursive versus nonrecursive systems: an attempt at synthesis. *Econometrica* 28, April, 417–27.

Wold, H. 1954. Causality and econometrics. *Econometrica* 22, 162–77.

Zellner, A. 1979. Causality and econometrics, policy and policy making. *Carnegie-Rochester Conference Series on Public Policy* 10, 9–54.

Causality in Economic Models

HERBERT A. SIMON

Causal notions arise when we week to understand the workings of a complex system by analysing it into component subsystems and mechanisms. Thus, if we wish to understand the quantities of strawberries that are produced and consumed and the prices at which they are exchanged, we may consider a number of mechanisms that affect quantity and price. What mechanisms we will include depends on how widely we draw the boundaries of the system to be examined.

For example, we may include (1) a weather mechanism that determines the amount of rainfall; (2) a productivity mechanism that determines the yield of strawberries per acre; (3) a supply mechanism that determines the acreage sowed in strawberries; and (4) a demand mechanism that determines the quantity of strawberries purchased. In this formulation, each mechanism, which might be represented by an equation, determines the value of a particular variable as a function of some other variables (not specified in the account above). The variable whose value is so determined (dependent variable) may be called the *effect* of the working of that particular mechanism, while the values of other variables entering into the mechanism (independent variables) are the *causes* of that effect.

In the example before us, we might write:

$$R = r \tag{1}$$

$$Y = f_1(R, F, T) \tag{2}$$

$$A = f_2(p) \tag{3}$$

$$Q = YA \tag{D}$$

$$p = f_3(Q). \tag{4}$$

Here R is rainfall, and r a positive constant; Y is the yield per acre, F the amount of fertilization, and T the amount of tillage; A is the acreage sowed, and p the market price; Q is the total yield. Equation (D) represents a definition, not a separate mechanism. In equation (4), p is taken as the dependent variable, since Q is assumed already to be determined by (2) and (3) (cobweb assumption).

CAUSAL ORDERING. The system of equations defines a *causal ordering* among the variables. The value of R is determined exogenously, as are the values of F and T. That is to say, they are determined in some larger system of which the mechanisms described in the equations are only a subset. The value of Y follows from those of R, F, and T. The values of A, Q, and p are determined simultaneously. Thus, the equations determine a partial ordering:

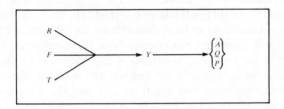

Figure 1

Notice that the asymmetry that underlies this ordering cannot be interpreted as the asymmetry of logical implication, for from 'A implies B' we can infer that 'not-B implies not-A', while from, 'Heavy rainfall causes the yield to be large' we cannot conclude that 'A small yield causes a scanty rainfall.' The most accurate mode of expression is: 'The amount of rainfall determines (causes) the amount of yield' – large or small in both cases. The asymmetry reflects a distinction between exogeneity and endogeneity of variables, based, in turn, upon controllability (in the case of variables that can be manipulated directly), or time precedence. Thus R is exogenous to mechanism (2) on the assumption that the weather is unaffected by changes in the yield of strawberries. (That this is an empirical assumption is clear from the fact that widespread cultivation *can* cause changes in climate.)

If we wish to remove the ambiguity from the causal relations among A, Q and p, we may assume (as in the classical cobweb theory) a time lag, replacing p in equation (3) by the exogenous and predetermined variable, p_{-1}. Then the causal ordering becomes:

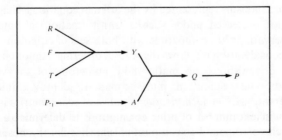

Figure 2

Now it is clear why we took p as the dependent variable in equation (4). Introducing the time lag requires making an empirical assumption – specifically an assumption about how farmers form expectations about future prices. In a rational expectations model, for example, this lag would not be admissible.

FORMALIZATION. To formalize these ideas, consider a system of n simultaneous linear equations in n variables (*linear structure*). We assume that each equation represents a mechanism. In some linear structures, certain subsets of equations can be solved independently of the remaining equations (*self-contained subsets*). Consider the *minimal self-contained subsets* of a system (those that do not themselves contain smaller self-contained subsets). With each such subset, associate the variables that can be evaluated from the subset alone (endogenous variables), and call them *variables of order zero*. Next, substitute the values of these variables in the remaining equations of the system, and repeat the whole process, obtaining the variables of order one, two, and so on, and the corresponding minimal self-contained subsets of equations. If a variable of some order occurs with non-zero coefficient in an equation belonging to a subsystem of higher order, then that variable is one of the causes of the values of the endogenous variables of the latter set.

Thus, in our original example, equation (1) is the minimal self-contained subset of zero order, and R is its variable; (2) is the minimal subset of first order, and Y its variable; while (3), (D) and (4) constitute the minimal self-contained subset of second order, and A, Q and p are their variables. The exogenous variables, F and T, can be regarded as parameters of the system, or equations parallel to (1) can be added for them, so that each belongs to a separate minimal self-contained subset of order zero.

IDENTIFIABILITY OF CAUSAL ORDERING. The causal ordering among variables in a linear self-contained structure depends on which variables appear with non-zero coefficients in which equations. Consider a set of observations of the variables satisfying the equations of such a structure. Clearly these observations will also satisfy a new structure made up of equations that are arbitrary linear combinations of equations drawn from the original set. But different combinations of variables will generally appear in the equations of the new structure than appeared in the equations of the original structure. Taking these linear combinations 'blends' the separate mechanisms represented by the original equations. Hence, the causal ordering is not preserved under such a transformation, although the same empirical observations are compatible with both sets of equations.

From this consideration it follows that causal ordering cannot be inferred from simultaneous observations, no matter how numerous, of the variables of a structure. Additional assumptions must be made to identify a unique structure from the observations. The *identification problem* of econometrics is the problem of finding a sufficient number of prior assumptions to determine a unique set of equations, each corresponding to a mechanism, that fits the observations. The equations thus determined are usually called *structural equations*, while algebraically equivalent equations derived from them by linear combination are called *reduced form* equations.

The assumptions needed to identify structural equations may be derived from prior knowledge about mechanisms (e.g., our knowledge that the weather affects crops, but crops do not usually affect the weather). Where experimentation is possible, holding particular variables constant while varying others, experimental findings are a powerful source of empirically valid identifying assumptions. Sometimes, there is prior knowledge, also, that particular mechanisms are independent of each other (that farmers make their decisions independently of consumers, and vice versa). Whatever their source, the identifying assumptions are genuine empirical assertions, and cannot be made arbitrarily or for reasons of statistical convenience if the correct causal inferences are to be drawn. So-called 'spurious' correlation is best interpreted as a relation between variables that does not have causal force because it was estimated from equations that did not correspond to independent mechanisms.

BIBLIOGRAPHY
Goldberger, A.S. and Duncan, O.D. 1973. *Structural Equation Models in the Social Sciences.* New York: Academic Press.
Hood, W.C. and Koopmans, T.C. 1953. *Studies in Econometric Method.* New York: Wiley.
Simon, H.A. 1977. Causes and possible worlds. Section 2, in H.A. Simon, *Models of Discovery*, Dordrecht: D. Reidel.

Censored Data Models

G.S. MADDALA

The *censored* normal regression model considered by Tobin (1958), also commonly known as the 'tobit' model, is the following:

$$y_i^* = \beta x_i + u_i. \quad u_i \sim \text{IN}(0, \sigma^2)$$

The observed y_i are related to y_i^* according to the relationship

$$\begin{aligned} y_i &= y_i^* \quad \text{if } y_i^* > y_0 \\ &= y_0 \quad \text{otherwise} \end{aligned} \tag{1}$$

where y_0 is a prespecified constant (usually zero). The y_i^* could take values $< y_0$. The only thing is that they are not observed. Thus, y_i is set equal to y_0 because of *non-observability*. The values x_i are observed for all the observations. If *both* y_i and x_i are unobserved for $y_i \leqslant y_0$ then we have what is known as a *truncated* regression model.

The problem is essentially one of missing data. Data on y are missing for some observations. Hence, we have to ask why data are missing. In some cases this is due to the design of the experiment, as in the case of the data from the negative income tax experiment. These data have been analysed by Hausman and Wise (1977), who consider a truncated regression model. In almost all other cases y_0 is the outcome of choices of individuals. In this case the model is incomplete unless the determinants of y_0 are studied.

SOME EARLY DEVELOPMENTS. The first application of the censored regression model (1) is that of Tobin (1958) who studied the expenditures on durable goods by 735 non-farm households. y_i^* is the ratio of total durable expenditures to disposable income and $y_0 = 0$. However, y_i is not equal to zero here because of non-observability, but because of individuals' choices. Thus, the censored regression model (1) is inappropriate for this problem. In fact, the tobit model is inappropriate for almost all the applications in which it has been used (including that by Tobin).

The model by Cragg (1971) considers this as a sequential decision problem. For the case of demand for automobiles, the decisions are whether or not to buy a car and how much to spend if the decision to buy a car is made. In this model we have the latent variable:

$$I_i = x_i \delta_1 + \eta_{1i} \qquad \eta_{1i} \sim IN(0, 1) \tag{2}$$

The subscript i denotes the ith individual. We observe the dummy variable D_i which is defined as

$$D_i = 1 \text{ if } I_i > 0 \qquad \text{(buyers)}$$
$$= 0 \text{ otherwise} \qquad \text{(non-buyers)} \tag{3}$$

For those who purchased a car, Cragg specifies a log normal model. Thus, denoting expenditures by y_i, we have

$$\log y_i = x_i \delta_2 + \eta_{2i} \qquad \eta_{2i} \sim IN(0, \sigma^2) \tag{4}$$

The equation is defined only for the individuals for which $D_i = 1$.

In practice, however, it is questionable whether individuals make their decisions this way. The decision of whether or not to buy a car and how much to spend if a car is bought are often joint decisions. One can formulate this model in terms of two latent variables. Though there are several variants of this that one can think of, one formulation is the following:

$y_1 =$ the cost of the car the individual wants to buy.
$y_2 =$ the maximum expenditure the individual can afford.

The actual expenditure y is given by

$$y = y_1 \qquad \text{if } y_1 \leqslant y_2$$
$$= 0 \qquad \text{if } y_1 > y_2 \tag{5}$$

We can, in fact, consider y_1 and y_2 both to be log normal. This model is discussed in Nelson (1977), though not with reference to the example of automobile expenditures.

It is tempting to use the simple tobit model (1) every time that one has a bunch of zero (or other limit) observations on y. However, this is inappropriate. For instance, if hours worked for a number of individuals in a sample are zero, it does not mean that one can apply the tobit model to explain hours worked. One has to construct a model where hours worked are zero because of some decisions about labour force participation, in terms of reservation and market wages, as done by Heckman (1974). Estimation of this model from censored as well as truncated samples is discussed in Wales and Woodland (1980).

SELECTION MODELS. In the estimation of censored regression models we often have to formulate the censoring function that incorporates individual decisions. This function is also called a *selection criterion*. Usually the selection criterion

55

involves the choice of variables and other explanatory variables. Thus, the model is formulated as:

$$y_1 = \beta_1 x_1 + u_1 \qquad \text{Choice 1} \qquad (6)$$

$$y_2 = \beta_2 x_2 + u_2 \qquad \text{Choice 2} \qquad (7)$$

and

$$I^* = \gamma_1 y_1 + \gamma_2 y_2 + \beta_3 x_3 + u \qquad \text{Selection criterion} \qquad (8)$$

The observed y is defined as

$$y = y_1 \qquad \text{if } I^* > 0$$
$$= y_2 \qquad \text{if } I^* \leqslant 0.$$

Interest centres on the determinants of γ_1 and γ_2 (see Lee, 1978; Willis and Rosen, 1979). One can substitute y_1 and y_2 in (8) and get a reduced form for the selection criterion. In this approach interest mainly centres on the so-called 'selectivity bias' in the estimation of (6) and (7) by OLS. Since both y_1 and y_2 are censored, we have to estimate the parameters in (6) and (7) by the use of ML methods. Heckman (1979) suggests a simple correction to the OLS, which involves the addition of an extra explanatory variable to each of (6) and (7) obtained from the estimation of the criterion function (8) in its reduced form. This criterion is based on the assumption of normality. Goldberger (1983) made some calculations with alternative error distributions and showed that this adjustment for selection bias is quite sensitive to departures from normality.

There have been two solutions to this problem. One is the extension of the analysis of selectivity to general error distributions. This is the approach considered in Lee (1982, 1983), a summary of which is also given in Maddala (1983, pp. 272–5) along with earlier suggestions by Olsen. The other alternative approach is to consider distribution-free estimates (see Cosslett, 1984), though this methodology is in early stages of development. Thus, there are computationally feasible alternatives available to explore the selectivity problem without assuming normality and there are procedures available to test the assumption of normality as well (see Lee and Maddala, 1985).

The 'Heckman correction' for selectivity bias is very popular, mainly because it is easy to apply. But for this same reason it has also been applied in cases where it is not applicable, such cases are cited in Maddala (1985).

SOME OTHER PROBLEMS. Many of the problems connected with the estimation of the censored regression model, assuming parametric distributions, are discussed in Maddala (1983, chs 6 and 9) and Amemiya (1984). For distribution-free methods one can refer to Miller and Halpern (1982), Cosslett (1984) and Powell (1984). It is now well known that the properties of the estimators change with the violation of some basic assumptions. For instance, heteroskedasticity and errors in the dependent variable do not affect the consistency property of OLS estimators in the normal regression model. With the censored regression model, the ML estimators are no longer consistent under these assumptions. Stapleton and Young (1984) suggest that with errors in the dependent variable, the 'correct' ML estimation appears computationally difficult but find some alternative estimators promising.

There has been some progress made in the development of distribution free estimation and estimation when the standard assumptions are violated. For tests of some of the standard assumptions, see Lee and Maddala (1985).

BIBLIOGRAPHY

Amemiya, T. 1984. Tobit models: a survey. *Journal of Econometrics* 24, 3–61.

Cosslett, S.R. 1984. Distribution-free estimator of a regression model with sample selectivity. Discussion Paper, CEDS, University of Florida.

Cragg, J.G. 1971. Some statistical models for limited dependent variables with application to the demand for durable goods. *Econometrica* 39, 829–44.

Goldberger, A.S. 1983. Abnormal selection bias. In *Studies in Econometrics, Time-Series and Multivariate Analysis*, ed. S. Karlin, T. Amemiya and L.A. Goodman, New York: Academic Press.

Hausman, J.A. and Wise, D.A. 1977. Social experimentation, truncated distributions, and efficient estimation. *Econometrica* 45, 919–38.

Heckman, J.J. 1974. Shadow prices, market wages, and labor supply. *Econometrica* 42, 679–93.

Heckman, J.J. 1979. Sample selection bias as a specification error. *Econometrica* 47, 153–61.

Lee, L.F. 1978. Unionism and wage rates: a simultaneous equations mode with qualitative and limited dependent variables. *International Economic Review* 19, 415–33.

Lee, L.F. 1982. Some approaches to the correction of selectivity bias. *Review of Economic Studies* 49, 355–72.

Lee, L.F. 1983. Generalized econometric models with selectivity. *Econometrica* 51, 507–12.

Lee, L.F. and Maddala, G.S. 1985. The common structure of tests for selectivity bias, serial correlation, heteroscedasticity, and non-normality in the tobit model. *International Economic Review* 26, 1–20.

Maddala, G.S. 1983. *Limited Dependent and Qualitative Variables in Econometrics*. New York: Cambridge University Press.

Maddala, G.S. 1985. A survey of the literature on selectivity bias as it pertains to health-care markets. In *Advances in Health Economics*, ed. R.M. Scheffler and L.F. Rossiter, Greenwich, Conn.: JAI Press.

Miller, R. and Halpern, J. 1982. Regression with censored data. *Biometrika* 69, 521–31.

Nelson, F.D. 1977. Censored regression models with unobserved stochastic censoring thresholds. *Journal of Econometrics* 6, 309–27.

Powell, J.L. 1984. Least absolute deviations estimation for censored regression models. *Journal of Econometrics* 25, 303–26.

Stapleton, D.C. and Young, D.J. 1984. Censored normal regression with measurement error on the dependent variable. *Econometrica* 52, 737–60.

Tobin, J. 1958. Estimation of relationships for limited dependent variables. *Econometrica* 26, 24–36.

Wales, T.J. and Woodland, A.D. 1980. Sample selectivity and the estimation of labor supply functions. *International Economic Review* 21, 437–68.

Willis, R.J. and Rosen, S. 1979. Education and self-selection. *Journal of Political Economy* 87, S5–S36.

Discrete Choice Models

TAKESHI AMEMIYA

These are those statistical models which specify the probability distribution of discrete dependent variables as a function of independent variables and unknown parameters. They are sometimes called *qualitative response models*, and are relevant in economics because the decision of an economic unit frequently involves discrete choice: for example, the decision regarding whether a person joins the labour force or not, the decision as to the number of cars to own, the choice of occupation, the choice of the mode of transportation, etc.

Despite their relevance, however, it is only recently (approximately in the last twenty years) that economists have started using them extensively. There seem to be three reasons for a recent surge of interest in such models: (1) Economists have realized that econometric models using only aggregate data cannot accurately explain economic phenomena nor predict the future values of economic variables well. (2) Large scale disaggregated data on consumers and producers have become available. (3) The rapid development of computer technology has made possible estimation of realistic models of this kind.

Note that when aggregated over many individuals, discrete variables behave almost like continuous variables and therefore can be subjected to standard regression analysis. A discrete choice model becomes necessary when we want to model the behaviour of an individual economic unit.

As econometric applications of these models have increased, we have also seen an increase of theoretical papers which address the problem of their specification and estimation. Biometricians have in fact used such models longer than have econometricians, using them, for example, to analyse the effect of an insecticide or the effect of a medical treatment. However, since the versions that econometricians use are generally more complex than those used by biometricians, it has been necessary for the former to develop new models and new methods of statistical inference.

There are cases where a discrete decision of an economic unit is closely interrelated with the determination of the value of a continuous variable. For

58

example, a decision to join the labour force necessitates the decision of how many hours to work and at what wage rate. A decision to buy a car cannot be separated from the decision of how much to spend on a car. The joint determination of the values of discrete variables and continuous variables belongs to the topic of *limited dependent* variables.

Other closely related topics are *Markov chain models* and *duration* (or survival) *models*. These models introduce the time domain into discrete choice models thereby making the models dynamic. In Markov chain models time changes discretely, whereas in duration models time moves continuously.

Those who wish to study the subject in more detail than the present essay are referred to Amemiya (1981 and 1985), Maddala (1983), and McFadden (1984).

1 UNIVARIATE BINARY MODELS

1.1 *Model specification*. The simplest type of a discrete choice model is a univariate binary model which specifies the binary (1 or 0) outcome of a single dependent variable. Let y_i be the ith observation on the binary dependent variable and x_i the ith observation on the vector of independent variables. Then a general univariate binary model is defined by

$$P(y_i = 1) = F(x_i'\beta) \qquad i = 1, 2, \dots, n, \tag{I}$$

where P stands for probability, F is a particular distribution function, and β is a vector of unknown parameters. For example, the event $y_i = 1$ may signify that the ith individual buys a car and the elements of the vector x_i may include the income of the ith individual and the price of the car the individual must pay if he decides to buy a car.

Note that we have assumed the argument of F in (I) to be a linear function of the independent variables. As in the linear regression model, this linearity assumption is more general than appears at first, because x_i need not be the original economic variables like income and price, but instead could contain various transformations of the original variables. However, the model in which the function F depends on a nonlinear function of the independent variables and unknown parameters can be handled with only a slight modification of the subsequent analysis.

A variety of models arises so we choose different distribution functions for F. The most commonly used functions are the standard normal distribution function Φ and the logistic distribution function Λ. These functions are defined by

$$\Phi(x) = \int_{-\infty}^{x} (2\pi)^{-1/2} \exp(-2^{-1}t^2) \, dt$$

and

$$\Lambda(x) = (1 + e^{-x})^{-1}.$$

When $F = \Phi$, the model is called the *probit* model, and when $F = \Lambda$, it is called the *logit* model.

The decision regarding which function to use should be based both on theoretical considerations and on how well a model fits the data. However, as long as a researcher experiments with various independent variables and with various ways in which the independent variables appear in the argument of F, the particular choice of F is not crucial.

Let us consider by way of an example how this model arises as the result of an individual maximizing a utility function. Consider the decision of a person regarding whether he drives a car to work or travels by public transport. We suppose that a level of utility is associated with each alternative and the person is to choose the alternative for which the utility is greater. Let U_{i1} and U_{i0} be the ith person's utilities associated with driving a car and travelling by public transport respectively. We assume that they are linear functions of independent variables with additive error terms as follows:

$$U_{i1} = x'_{i1}\beta_1 + \varepsilon_{i1},$$

and

$$U_{i0} = x'_{i0}\beta_0 + \varepsilon_{i0}.$$

Here, the vector x_{i1} may be thought of as consisting of the time and the cost which would be incurred if the ith person were to drive a car, plus his socio-economic characteristics. The error term may be regarded as the sum of all the unobserved independent variables. Defining $y_i = 1$ if the ith person travels by car and $y_i = 0$ if he travels otherwise, we have

$$P(y_i = 1) = P(U_{i1} > U_{i0}) = F(x'_{i1}\beta_1 - x'_{i0}\beta_0),$$

where F is the distribution function of $\varepsilon_{i0} - \varepsilon_{i1}$. Thus, a probit model will result from the normality of $\varepsilon_{i0} - \varepsilon_{i1}$. The normality may be justified on the ground of a central limit theorem.

If a probit model fits the data well, so will a logit model because the logistic distribution function is similar to the standard normal distribution function.

1.2 *Estimation.* Let us consider the estimation of the parameter vector β in the model (I). We shall first discuss the maximum likelihood (ML) estimator and second, the minimum chi-square (MIN χ^2) estimator.

The likelihood function based on n independent binary observations $y_1, y_2, \ldots, y_n$ is given by

$$L = \prod_{i=1}^{n} F(x'_i\beta)^{y_i}[1 - F(x'_i\beta)]^{1-y_i}.$$

The ML estimator $\hat{\beta}$ is obtained by maximizing $\ln L$. Under general conditions $\hat{\beta}$ is consistent and asymptotically normal with the asymptotic variance–covariance matrix given by

$$V\hat{\beta} = \left\{ \sum_{i=1}^{n} \left[\frac{f^2(x'_i\beta)}{F(x'_i\beta)[1 - F(x'_i\beta)]} x_i x'_i \right] \right\}^{-1},$$

where f is the derivative of F.

Since an explicit formula for the ML estimator cannot be obtained for this model, the calculation of the estimator must be done by an iterative method. The log likelihood function can be shown to be globally concave in the probit and logit models. In these models, therefore, a standard iterative algorithm such as the Newton–Raphson method will generally converge to the global maximum.

The MIN χ^2 estimator, first proposed by Berkson (1944) for the logit model, works only if there are many observations on y for each of the values taken by the vector x. Let us suppose that x_i takes T vector values $x_1, x_2, \ldots, x_T$ and classify integers $1, 2, \ldots, n$ into T disjoint sets $I_1, I_2, \ldots, I_T$ by rule: $i \in I_t$ if $x_i = x_t$. Define n_t = number of integers contained in I_i and $P_t = n_t^{-1} \Sigma_{i \in I_t} y_i$. Then, by a Taylor expansion, we have approximately

$$F^{-1}(\hat{P}_t) \simeq x_t'\beta + \{f[F^{-1}(P_t)]\}^{-1}(\hat{P}_t - P_t),$$

where F^{-1} denotes the inverse function of F. The MIN χ^2 estimator $\tilde{\beta}$ is the weighted least squares estimator applied to this last heteroscedastic regression equation; that is,

$$\tilde{\beta} = \left[\sum_{t=1}^{T} w_t x_t x_t' \right]^{-1} \sum_{t=1}^{T} w_t x_t F^{-1}(\hat{P}_t),$$

where

$$w_t = n_t f_t^2 [F^{-1}(\hat{P}_t)] / [\hat{P}_t (1 - \hat{P}_t)].$$

The MIN χ^2 estimator has the same asymptotic distribution as the ML estimator. Its advantage over the latter is computational simplicity, while its weakness is that it requires many observations for each value of the independent variables. The required number of observations increases with the number of the independent variables. If an independent variable takes many values it may be necessary to group the values into a small number of groups in order to define the MIN χ^2 estimator. But such a procedure will introduce a certain bias to the estimator.

2 MULTINOMIAL MODELS

A multinomial model is a statistical model for independent discrete variables, some of which take more than two values: Supposing that y_i takes $m_i + 1$ integer values $0, 1, \ldots, m_i$, the model is defined by specifying the $\Sigma_{i=1}^{n} m_i$ probabilities:

$$P(y_i = j) = F_{ij}(x, \beta), \qquad i = 1, 2, \ldots, n$$
$$j = 1, 2, \ldots, m_i. \tag{II}$$

Note that $P(y_i = 0)$ need not be specified because the sum of the $m_i + 1$ probabilities is one for each i. It is important to let m depend on i because the number of alternatives available to different individuals may differ.

Defining $\Sigma_{i=1}^{n}(m_i + 1)$ binary variables

$$y_{ij} = 1 \quad \text{if} \quad y_i = j$$
$$= 0 \quad \text{if} \quad y_i \neq j, \qquad i = 1, 2, \ldots, n$$
$$j = 0, 1, \ldots, m_j,$$

the likelihood function of the model can be written as

$$L = \prod_{i=1}^{n} \prod_{j=0}^{m_i} F_{ij}(x, \beta)^{y_{ij}}.$$

Note that this reduces to the L equation of Section 1 if $m_i = 1$ for all i.

The ML estimator of β is consistent and asymptotically normal with its asymptotic variance–covariance matrix given by

$$V\hat{\beta} = -\left[E\frac{\partial^2 \log L}{\partial\beta\,\partial\beta'} \right]^{-1},$$

which will be equal to $V\hat{\beta}$ equation in Section 1 in the binary case. The MIN χ^2 estimator can be also defined for the multinomial model, although the definition will not be given here.

2.1 *Ordered models.* An ordered multinomial model arises when there is an unobserved continuous random variable y_i^* which determines the outcome of y_i by the rule

$$y_i = j \quad \text{if and only if} \quad \alpha_j < y_i^* < \alpha_{j+1},$$

$$j = 0, 1, \ldots, m, \quad \alpha_0 = -\infty, \quad \alpha_{m+1} = \infty.$$

Such a rule may be appropriate, for example, if $y_i = j$ signifies the event that the ith individual owns j cars and y_i^* refers to a measure of the intensity of the ith individual's desire to own cars. If the distribution function of $y_i^* - x_i'\beta$ is F, the last equation leads to an ordered model defined by

$$P(y_i = j) = F(\alpha_{j+1} - x_i'\beta) - F(\alpha_j - x_i'\beta).$$

As in the binary case, the choice of Φ and Λ for F is most frequently used.

An ordered model is attractive because of its simplicity. However, in many economic applications it may be an oversimplification to assume that the outcome of a multinomial variable can be completely determined by the outcome of a simple continuous variable. For example, for owning cars it is probably more realistic to assume that the ith person owns j cars if $U_{ij} > U_{ik}$ for all $k \neq j$, where U_{ij} is the utility that accrues to the ith person if he owns j cars. In this case m continuous variables $U_{ij} - U_{i,j+1}$, $j = 0, 1, \ldots, m$, determine the outcome of the discrete variable.

A multinomial model which is not an ordered model is called an unordered model. The models discussed in the next parts of this section are all unordered.

2.2 *Multinomial logit model.* A multinomial logit model is described below by defining the probabilities of the ith individual who faces three alternatives $j = 0$, 1, and 2. A generalization to the case of more alternatives can be easily inferred.

The three probabilities are given by

$$P(y_i = 2) = D^{-1} \exp(x'_{i2}\beta),$$
$$P(y_i = 1) = D^{-1} \exp(x'_{i1}\beta),$$
$$P(y_i = 0) = D^{-1},$$

where $D = 1 + \exp(x'_{i1}\beta) + \exp(x'_{i2}\beta)$.

McFadden (1974) showed how a multinomial logit model can be derived from the maximization of stochastic utilities. Suppose that the ith individual's utility U_{ij} associated with the jth alternative is the sum of the nonstochastic part μ_{ij} and the stochastic part ε_{ij} and that the individual chooses the alternative for which the utility is a maximum. Suppose further that ε_{i0}, ε_{i1} and ε_{i2} are independent and identically distributed according to the distribution function $\exp[\exp(-\varepsilon)]$ – called the *type I extreme value distribution*. Then we can show

$$P(y_i = 2) = P(U_{i2} > U_{i1}, U_{i2} > U_{i0})$$
$$= \exp(\mu_{i2})/[\exp(\mu_{i0}) + \exp(\mu_{i1}) + \exp(\mu_{i2})],$$

and similarly for $P(y_i = 1)$ and $P(y_i = 0)$. Thus, the model defined by the three equations above follows from putting $\mu_{i2} - \mu_{i0} = x'_{i2}\beta$ and $\mu_{i1} - \mu_{i0} = x'_{i1}\beta$.

The multinomial logit model has been extensively used in economic applications, such as the choice of modes of transportation, the choice of occupations, and the choice of types of appliances. The likelihood function of the model can be shown to be globally concave; consequently, the ML estimator can be computed with relative ease.

A major limitation of the multinomial logit model lies in its independence assumption. Consider the choice of transportation modes and suppose first that the alternatives consist of car, bus, and train. Then the assumption of independent utilities may be reasonable. Next, to use McFadden's famous example, suppose instead that the choice is among a car, a red bus, and a blue bus. Then it is clearly unreasonable to assume that the utilities associated with the red bus and the blue bus are independent. In the next subsection we shall consider a multinomial model which corrects this deficiency.

2.3 *Nested logit model.* We continue the last example. Let $U_j = \mu_j + \varepsilon_j, j = 0, 1,$ and 2, be the utilities associated with car, red bus, and blue bus, respectively. (The subscript i is suppressed to simplify notation.) Following McFadden (1977), suppose that ε_0 is distributed according to the type I extreme value distribution and independent of ε_1 and ε_2 and that the joint distribution of ε_1 and ε_2 is given by

$$F(\varepsilon_1, \varepsilon_2) = \exp\{-[\exp(-\rho^{-1}\varepsilon_1) + [\exp(-\rho^{-1}\varepsilon_2)]^\rho\}, \qquad 0 \leqslant \rho \leqslant 1.$$

This distribution is called *Gumbel's type B bivariate extreme value distribution.* The correlation coefficient is $1 - \rho^2$, and if $\rho = 1$ (the case of independence), $F(\varepsilon_1, \varepsilon_2)$ becomes the product of two type I extreme value distributions.

63

Under these assumptions it can be shown that

$$P(y = 0) = \exp(\mu_0)/\{\exp(\mu_0) + \exp(\rho^{-1}\mu_1) + \exp(\rho^{-1}\mu_2)]^\rho\}$$

and

$$P(y = 1 | y \neq 0) = \exp(\rho^{-1}\mu_1)/[\exp(\rho^{-1}\mu_1) + \exp(\rho^{-1}\mu_2)].$$

The other probabilities can be deduced from the above. Note that the last equation shows that the choice between red bus and blue bus is made according to a binary logit model, while the previous equation shows that the choice between car and noncar is also like a logit model except that a certain weighted average of $\exp(\mu_1)$ and $\exp(\mu_2)$ is involved.

2.4 *Multinomial probit model.* A multinomial probit model is derived from the assumption that the utilities $U_{i0}, U_{i1}, \ldots, U_{im_i}$ are multivariate normal for every i. Its advantage is that general assumptions about the correlations among the utilities are allowed. Its major disadvantage is that the calculation of the choice probability requires the evaluation of multiple integrals of joint normal densities, which is feasible only for a small number of alternatives.

3 MULTIVARIATE MODELS

A multivariate discrete choice model specifies the joint probability distribution of two or more discrete dependent variables. For example, the joint distribution of two binary variables y_1 and y_2 each of which takes values 1 or 0 is determined by the four probabilities $P_{jk} = P(y_1 = j, y_2 = k), j, k = 0, 1$. (Of course, the sum of the probabilities must be equal to 1.)

A multivariate model is a special case of a multinomial model. For example, the model of two binary variables mentioned in the preceding paragraph may be regarded as a multinomial model for a single discrete variable which takes four values with probabilities $P_{11}, P_{10}, P_{01},$ and P_{00}. Therefore, all the results given in section 2 apply to multivariate models as well. In this section we shall discuss three types of models which specifically take into account the multivariate feature of the model.

3.1 *Log-linear model.* A log-linear model refers to a particular parameterization of a multivariate discrete choice model. In the previous bivariate binary model, the log-linear parameterization of the four probabilities is given as follows:

$$P_{11} = D^{-1} \exp(\alpha_1 + \alpha_2 + \alpha_{12}),$$
$$P_{10} = D^{-1} \exp(\alpha_1),$$
$$P_{01} = D^{-1} \exp(\alpha_2)$$

and

$$P_{00} = D^{-1}, \tag{III}$$

where $D = 1 + \exp(\alpha_1) + \exp(\alpha_2) + \exp(\alpha_1 + \alpha_2 + \alpha_{12})$.

There is a one-to-one correspondence between any three probabilities and the three α parameters of the log-linear model; thus, the two parameterizations are equivalent. An advantage of the log-linear parameterization lies in its feature that $\alpha_{12} = 0$ if and only if y_1 and y_2 are independent.

Equations (III) may be represented by the following single equation:

$$P(y_1, y_2) \propto \exp(\alpha_1 y_1 + \alpha_2 y_2 + \alpha_1 \alpha_2 y_1 y_2).$$

Each equation of (III) is obtained by inserting values 1 or 0 into y_1 and y_2 in this equation. This formulation can be generalized to a log-linear model of more than two binary variables. The case of three variables is given below:

$$P(y_1, y_2, y_3) \propto \exp(\alpha_1 y_1 + \alpha_2 y_2 + \alpha_3 y_3 + \alpha_{12} y_1 y_2$$
$$+ \alpha_{13} y_1 y_3 + \alpha_{23} y_2 y_3 + \alpha_{123} y_1 y_2 y_3).$$

The first three terms in the exponential function are called the main effects. Terms involving the product of two variables are called second-order interaction terms, the product of three variables third-order interaction terms, and so on.

Note that the last equation has seven parameters, which can be put into one-to-one correspondence with the seven probabilities that completely determine the distribution of y_1, y_2 and y_3. Such a model, without any constraint among the parameters, is called a *saturated* model. Researchers often use a constrained log-linear model, called an *unsaturated* model, which is obtained by setting some of the higher-order interaction terms to zero; e.g. Goodman (1972). See also Nerlove and Press (1973) for an example of a log-linear model in which some of the α parameters are specified to be functions of independent variables and unknown parameters.

3.2 *Multivariate nested logit model.* The multivariate nested logit model is a special case of the nested logit model discussed in section 2.3, which is useful whenever a set of alternatives can be classified into classes each of which contains similar alternatives. It is useful in a multivariate situation because the alternatives can be naturally classified according to the outcome of one or more of the variables.

For example, in the bivariate binary case, the four alternatives can be classified according to whether $y_1 = 1$ or 0. Let U_{jk} be the utility associated with the choice $y_1 = j$ and $y_2 = k$, $j, k = 0, 1$ and assume as before that $U_{jk} = \mu_{jk} + \varepsilon_{jk}$, where μ's are nonstochastic and ε's are random. As a slight generalization of the Gumbel distribution in section 2.3 assume that

$$F(\varepsilon_{j1}, \varepsilon_{j0}) = a_j \exp\{ -[\exp(-\rho_j^{-1}\varepsilon_{j1}) + \exp(-\rho_j^{-1}\varepsilon_{j2})]^{\rho_j}\}, \quad j = 1, 0$$

and that $(\varepsilon_{11}, \varepsilon_{10})$ are independent of $(\varepsilon_{01}, \varepsilon_{00})$. Then the resulting multivariate nested logit model is characterized by the following probabilities:

$$P(y_1 = 1) = a_1 [\exp(\rho_1^{-1}\mu_{11}) + \exp(\rho_1^{-1}\mu_{10})]^{\rho_1}$$
$$\div \{a_1 [\exp(\rho_1^{-1}\mu_{11}) + \exp(\rho_1^{-1}\mu_{10})]^{\rho_1}$$
$$+ a_0 [\exp(\rho_0^{-1}\mu_{01}) + \exp(\rho_0^{-1}\mu_{00})]^{\rho_0}\},$$

$$P(y_2 = 1 | y_1 = 1)$$
$$= \exp(\rho_1^{-1} \mu_{11})/[\exp(\rho_1^{-1} \mu_{11}) + \exp(\rho_1^{-1} \mu_{10})],$$
$$P(y_2 = 1 | y_1 = 0)$$
$$= \exp(\rho_0^{-1} \mu_{01})/[\exp(\rho_0^{-1} \mu_{01}) + \exp(\rho_0^{-1} \mu_{00})].$$

We may further specify $\mu_{jk} = x'_{jk} \beta$.

3.3 *Multivariate probit model.* This model is conceptually different from the models of the preceding two sections in that here the marginal probabilities are specified first and the joint probabilities are then defined in a certain natural way.

As an example of a bivariate binary probit model, let us suppose $y_j^* \sim N(\mu_j, 1)$, $j = 1$ and 2, and y_j^* is unobservable and its value determines the value of the observable binary variable y_j by the rule

$$y_j = 1 \quad \text{if } y_j^* > 0$$
$$= 0 \text{ otherwise.}$$

This rule determines the marginal probabilities

$$P(y_j = 1) = \Phi(\mu_j), \qquad j = 1 \text{ and } 2.$$

Thus, the model will be complete when we specify the joint probability $P(y_1 = 1, y_2 = 1)$. A natural way to specify it would be to assume that y_1^* and y_2^* are jointly normal with a correlation coefficient ρ and define

$$P(y_1 = 1, y_2 = 1) = P(y_1^* > \mu_1, y_2^* > \mu_2).$$

Usually, a researcher will further specify $\mu_1 = x'_1 \beta$ and $\mu_2 = x'_2 \beta$ and estimate the unknown parameters β and ρ; see Morimune (1979) for an econometric example of this model.

A bivariate logit model may be defined similarly. But, unlike the probit case, there is no natural choice among many bivariate logistic distributions with the same marginal univariate logistic distributions.

4 CHOICE-BASED SAMPLING

In models (I) or (II), the independent variables x_i were treated as known constants. This is equivalent to considering the conditional distribution of y_i and given x_i. This practice was valid because it was implicitly assumed that y_i and x_i were generated according to either *random sampling* or *exogenous sampling*.

Under random sampling, y and x are sampled according to their true joint distribution $P(y|x)f(x)$. Thus the likelihood function denoted L_R, is given by

$$L_R = \prod_{i=1}^{n} P(y_i | x_i) f(x_i).$$

Under exogenous sampling, a researcher samples x according to a certain distribution $g(x)$, which may not be equal to the true distribution $f(x)$ of x in the total population, and then samples y according to its true conditional probability $P(y|x)$. Thus the likelihood function, denoted L_E, is given by

$$L_E = \prod_{i=1}^{n} P(y_i|x_i)g(x_i).$$

In either case, as long as the parameters that characterize $P(y|x)$ are not related to the parameters that characterize $f(x)$ or $g(x)$, the maximization of L_R or L_E is equivalent to the maximization of

$$L = \prod_{i=1}^{n} P(y_i|x_i),$$

which is equivalent to the L of Section 2.

Under choice-based sampling, a researcher samples y according to fixed proportions $H(y)$, and then, given y, samples x according to the conditional density $f(x|y)$. By the formula of conditional density,

$$f(x|y) = P(y|x)f(x)/Q(y),$$

where $Q(y) = E_x P(y|x)$, and E_x denotes the expectation taken with respect to the random vector x. Thus, the likelihood function under choice-based sampling, denoted L_c, is

$$L_c = \prod_{i=1}^{n} Q(y_i)^{-1} P(y_i|x_i)f(x_i)H(y_i).$$

Unlike random sampling or exogenous sampling, choice-based sampling requires new analysis because the maximization of L_c is not equivalent to the maximization of L on account of the fact that $Q(y)$ depends on the same parameters that characterize $P(y|x)$.

In particular, it means that the standard ML estimator which maximizes L is not even consistent under choice-based sampling. The reader should consult Amemiya (1985) or Manski and McFadden (1981) for the properties of the choice-based sampling ML estimator which maximizes L_c in various situations.

Choice-based sampling is useful when only a small number of people sampled according to random sampling are likely to choose a particular alternative. For example, in a transportation study, random sampling of individual households in a community with a small proportion of bus riders may produce an extremely small number of bus riders. In such a case a researcher may be able to attain a higher efficiency of estimation by sampling bus riders at a bus depot to augment the data gathered by random sampling.

An interesting problem in choice-based sampling is how to determine $H(y)$ to maximize the efficiency of estimation. Although there is no clear-cut solution to this problem in general, it is expected that if $Q(j)$ is small for some j then the value of $H(j)$ which is larger than $Q(j)$ will yield a more efficient estimator than the value of $H(j)$ which is equal to $Q(j)$. Note that if in the formula for L_c, $H(j) = Q(j)$ for every j, then L_c is reduced to L_R.

67

5 DISTRIBUTION-FREE METHODS

Consider the univariate binary model (I). There, we assumed that the function $F(\cdot)$ is completely specified and known. Recently, Manski (1975) and Cosslett (1983) have shown how to estimate β consistently (subject to a certain normalization) without specifying $F(\cdot)$.

Manski's estimator is based on the idea that as long as F satisfies the condition $F(0) = 0.5$, one can predict y_i to be 1 or 0 depending on whether $x_i'\beta$ is positive or negative. His estimator of β is chosen so as to maximize the number of correct predictions. If we define the characteristic function χ of the event E by

$$\chi(E) = 1 \text{ if } E \text{ occurs}$$

$$= 0 \text{ otherwise,}$$

the number of correct predictions can be mathematically expressed as

$$S(\beta) = \sum_{i=1}^{n} [y_i \chi(x_i'\beta \geq 0) + (1 - y_i)\chi(x_i'\beta < 0)].$$

Manski calls this the score function – and hence his estimator the maximum score estimator. The estimator has been shown to be consistent, but its asymptotic distribution is unknown.

Cosslett proposed maximizing the likelihood function L in Section 1.2 with respect to both β and F, and called his estimator the generalized ML estimator. For a given value of β, the value of F which maximizes that L is a step function, and Cosslett showed a simple method of determining it. Finding the optimal value of β, however, is the computationally difficult part. Like the maximum score estimator, the generalized ML estimator of β is consistent but its asymptotic distribution is unknown.

BIBLIOGRAPHY

Amemiya, T. 1981. Qualitative response models: a survey. *Journal of Economic Literature* 19, 1483–1536.

Amemiya, T. 1985. *Advanced Econometrics*. Cambridge, Mass.: Harvard University Press.

Berkson, J. 1944. Application of the logistic function to bioassay. *Journal of the American Statistical Association* 39, 357–65.

Cosslett, S.R. 1983. Distribution-free maximum likelihood estimator of the binary choice model. *Econometrica* 51, 765–82.

Goodman, L.A. 1972. A modified multiple regression approach to the analysis of dichotomous variables. *American Sociological Review* 37, 28–46.

McFadden, D. 1974. Conditional logit analysis of qualitative choice behavior. In *Frontiers in Econometrics*, ed. P. Zarembka, New York: Academic Press, 105–42.

McFadden, D. 1977. Qualitative methods for analyzing travel behavior of individuals: some recent developments. Cowles Foundation Discussion Paper No. 474.

McFadden, D. 1984. Econometric analysis of qualitative response models. In *Handbook of Econometrics*, ed. Z. Griliches and M.D. Intriligator, Vol. 2, Amsterdam: North-Holland, 1385–1457.

Maddala, G.S. 1983. *Limited-Dependent and Qualitative Variables in Econometrics.* Cambridge: Cambridge University Press.

Manski, C.F. 1975. The maximum score estimation of the stochastic utility model of choice. *Journal of Econometrics* 3, 205–28.

Manski, C.F. and McFadden, D. (eds) 1981. *Structural Analysis of Discrete Data with Econometric Applications.* Cambridge, Mass.: MIT Press.

Morimune, K. 1979. Comparisons of normal and logistic models in the bivariate dichotomous analysis. *Econometrica* 47, 957–76.

Nerlove, M. and Press, S.J. 1973. Univariate and multivariate log-linear and logistic models. R-1306-EDA/NIH, Santa Monica: Rand Corporation.

Dummy Variables

PIETRO BALESTRA

In economics, as well as in other disciplines, qualitative factors often play an important role. For instance, the achievement of a student in school may be determined, among other factors, by his father's profession, which is a qualitative variable having as many attributes (characteristics) as there are professions. In medicine, to take another example, the response of a patient to a drug may be influenced by the patient's sex and the patient's smoking habits, which may be represented by two qualitative variables, each one having two attributes. The dummy-variable method is a simple and useful device for introducing, into a regression analysis, information contained in qualitative or categorical variables; that is, in variables that are not conventionally measured on a numerical scale. Such qualitative variables may include race, sex, marital status, occupation, level of education, region, seasonal effects and so on. In some applications, the dummy-variable procedure may also be fruitfully applied to a quantitative variable such as age, the influence of which is frequently U-shaped. A system of dummy variables defined by age classes conforms to any curvature and consequently may lead to more significant results.

The working of the dummy-variable method is best illustrated by an example. Suppose we wish to fit an Engel curve for travel expenditure, based on a sample of n individuals. For each individual i, we have quantitative information on his travel expenditures (y_i) and on his disposable income (x_i), both variables being expressed in logarithms. A natural specification of the Engel curve is:

$$y_i = a + bx_i + u_i,$$

where a and b are unknown regression parameters and u_i is a non-observable random term. Under the usual classical assumptions (which we shall adopt throughout this presentation), ordinary least-squares produce the best estimates for a and b.

Suppose now that we have additional information concerning the education level of each individual in the sample (presence or absence of college education). If we believe that the education level affects the travel habits of individuals, we should explicitly account for such an effect in the regression equation. Here, the education level is a qualitative variable with two attributes: college education; no college education. To each attribute, we can associate a dummy variable which takes the following form:

$$d_{1i} = \begin{cases} 1 \text{ if college education} \\ 0 \text{ if no college education} \end{cases}$$

$$d_{2i} = \begin{cases} 1 \text{ if no college education} \\ 0 \text{ if college education.} \end{cases}$$

Inserting these two dummy variables in the Engel curve, we obtain the following expanded regression:

Specification I:

$$y_i = a_1 d_{1i} + a_2 d_{2i} + bx_i + u_i,$$

which may be estimated by ordinary least-squares. Alternatively, noting that $d_{1i} + d_{2i} = 1$ for all i, we can write:

Specification II:

$$y_i = a_2 + (a_1 - a_2)d_{1i} + bx_i + u_i,$$

which, again, may be estimated by ordinary least-squares.

It is easy to see how the procedure can be extended to take care of a finer classification of education levels. Suppose, for instance, that we actually have s education levels (s attributes). All we require is that the attributes be exhaustive and mutually exclusive. We then have the two following equivalent specifications:

Specification I:

$$y_i = a_1 d_{1i} + a_2 d_{2i} + \cdots + a_2 d_{si} + bx_i + u_i.$$

Specification II:

$$y_i = a_s + (a_1 - a_s)d_{1i} + \cdots + (a_{s-1} - a_s)d_{s-1,i} + bx_i + u_i.$$

Obviously, the two specifications produce the same results but give rise to different interpretations. Specification I includes all the s dummy variables but no constant term. In this case, the coefficient of d_{ji} gives the specific effect of attribute j. Specification II includes $s-1$ dummy variables and an overall constant term. The constant term represents the specific effect of the omitted attribute, and the coefficients of the different d_{ji} represent the contrast (difference) of the effect of the jth attribute with respect to the effect of the omitted attribute. (Note that it is not possible to indicate all dummy variables plus an overall constant term, because of perfect collinearity.)

It is important to stress that by the introduction of additive dummy variables, it is implicitly assumed that the qualitative variable affects only the intercept but not the slope of the regression equation. In our example, the elasticity parameter, b, is the same for all individuals; only the intercepts differ from individual to individual depending on their education level. If we are interested in individual variation in slope, we can apply the same technique, as long as at least one explanatory variable has a constant coefficient over all individuals. Take the initial case of only two attributes. If the elasticity parameter varies according to the level of education, we have the following specification:

$$y_i = a_1 d_{1i} + a_2 d_{2i} + b_1 d_{1i} x_i + b_2 d_{2i} x_i + u_i.$$

Simple algebra shows that ordinary least-squares estimation of this model amounts to performing two separate regressions, one for each class of individuals. If, however, the model contained an additional explanatory variable, say z_i, with constant coefficient c, by simply adding the term cz_i to the above equation, we would simultaneously allow for variation in the intercept and variation in the slope (for x).

The dummy variable model also provides a conceptual framework for testing the significance of the qualitative variable in an easy way. Suppose we wish to test the hypothesis of no influence of the level of education on travel expenditures. The hypothesis is true if the s coefficients a_i are all equal; that is, if the $s - 1$ differences $a_j - a_s, j = 1, \ldots, s - 1$, are all zero. The test therefore boils down to a simple test of significance of the $s - 1$ coefficients of the dummy variables in Specification II. If $s = 2$, the t-test applied to the single coefficient of d_{1i} is appropriate. If $s > 2$, we may conveniently compute the following quantity:

$$\frac{(SS_c - SS)/(s - 1)}{SS/(n - s - 1)}$$

which is distributed as an F-variable with $s - 1$ and $n - s - 1$ degrees of freedom. In the above expression, SS is the sum of squared residuals for the model with the dummy variables (either Specification I or II), and SS_c is the sum of squared residuals for the model with no dummy variables but with an overall constant term.

In some economic applications the main parameter of interest is the slope parameter, the coefficients of the dummy variables being nuisance parameters. When, as in the present context, only one qualitative variable (with s attributes) appears in the regression equation, an easy computational device is available which eliminates the problem of estimating the coefficients of the dummy variables. To this end, it suffices to estimate, by ordinary least-squares, the simple regression equation:

Specification III:

$$y_i^* = bx_i^* + u_i^*,$$

where the quantitative variables (both explained and explanatory) for each individual are expressed as deviations from the mean over all individuals possessing the same attribute. For the dichotomous case presented in the beginning, for an individual with college education, we subtract the mean over all individuals with college education and likewise for an individual with no college education. Note, however, that the true number of degrees of freedom is not $n-1$ but $n-1-s$. The same procedure also applies when the model contains other quantitative explanatory variables. The interested reader may consult Balestra (1982) for the conditions under which this simple transformation is valid in the context of generalized regression.

The case of multiple qualitative variables (of the explanatory type) can be handled in a similar fashion. However, some precaution must be taken to avoid perfect collinearity of the dummy variables. The easiest and most informative way to do this is to include, in the regression equation, an overall constant term and to add for each qualitative variable as many dummy variables as there are attributes minus one. Take the case of our Engel curve and suppose that, in addition to the education level (only two levels for simplicity), the place of residence also plays a role. Let us distinguish two types of place of residence: urban and rural. Again, we associate to these two attributes two dummy variables, say e_{1i} and e_{2i}. A correct specification of the model which allows for both qualitative effects is:

$$y_i = a_1 + a_2 d_{1i} + a_3 e_{1i} + b x_i + u_i.$$

Given the individual's characteristics, the measure of the qualitative effects is straightforward, as shown in the following table.

	Urban	Rural
College education	$a_1 + a_2 + a_3$	$a_1 + a_2$
No college education	$a_1 + a_3$	a_1

The specification given above for the multiple qualitative variable model corresponds to Specification II of the single qualitative variable model. Unfortunately, when there are two or more qualitative variables there is no easy transformation analogous to the one incorporated in Specification III, except under certain extraordinary circumstances (Balestra, 1982).

One such circumstance arises in connection with cross-section time-series models. Suppose that we have n individuals observed over t periods of time. If we believe in the presence of both an individual effect and a time effect, we may add to our model two sets of dummy variables, one corresponding to the individual effects and the other corresponding to the time effects. This is the so-called covariance model. The number of parameters to be estimated is possibly quite large when n or t or both are big. To avoid this, we may estimate a transformed model (with no dummies and no constant term) in which each quantitative variable (both explained and explanatory) for individual i and time period j is transformed by subtracting from it both the mean of the ith individual and the mean of the jth time period and by adding to it the overall mean. Note that, by this transformation, we lose $n + t - 1$ degrees of freedom.

To conclude, the purpose of the preceding expository presentation has been to show that the dummy-variable method is a powerful and, at the same time, simple tool for the introduction of qualitative effects in regression analysis. It has found and will undoubtedly find numerous applications in empirical economic research. Broadly speaking, it may be viewed as a means for considering a specific scheme of parameter variation, in which the variability of the coefficients is linked to the causal effect of some precisely identified qualitative variable. But it is not, by any means, the only scheme available. For instance, when the qualitative effects are generic, as in the cross-section time-series model, one may question the validity of representing such effects by fixed parameters. An interpretation in terms of random effects may seem more appealing. This type of consideration has led to the development of other schemes of parameter variation such as the error component model and the random coefficient model.

A final remark is in order. In the present discussion, only qualitative variables of the explanatory type have been considered. When the qualitative variable is the explained (or dependent) variable, the problem of these *limited* dependent variables is far more complex, both conceptually and computationally.

BIBLIOGRAPHY

Balestra, P. 1982. Dummy variables in regression analysis. In *Advances in Economic Theory*. ed. Mauro Baranzini, Oxford: Blackwell, 273–92; New York: St. Martin's Press.
Goldberger, A.S. 1960. *Econometric Theory*. New York: John Wiley, 218–27.
Maddala, G.S. 1977. *Econometrics*. New York: McGraw-Hill, ch. 9.
Suits, D.B. 1957. Use of dummy variables in regression equations. *Journal of the American Statistical Association* 52, 548–51.

Endogeneity and Exogeneity

JOHN GEWEKE

Endogeneity and exogeneity are properties of variables in economic or econometric models. The specification of these properties for respective variables is an essential component of the entire process of model specification. The words have an ambiguous meaning, for they have been applied in closely related but conceptually distinct ways, particularly in the specification of stochastic models. We consider in turn the case of deterministic and stochastic models, concentrating mainly on the latter.

A deterministic economic model typically specifies restrictions to be satisfied by a vector of variables $\mathbf{y}$. These restrictions often incorporate a second vector of variables $\mathbf{x}$, and the restrictions themselves may hold only if $\mathbf{x}$ itself satisfies certain restrictions. The model asserts

$$\forall \mathbf{x} \in R, \qquad G(\mathbf{x}, \mathbf{y}) = 0.$$

The variables $\mathbf{x}$ are exogenous and the variables $\mathbf{y}$ are endogenous. The defining distinction between $\mathbf{x}$ and $\mathbf{y}$ is that $\mathbf{y}$ may be (and generally is) restricted by $\mathbf{x}$, but not conversely. This distinction is an essential part of the specification of the functioning of the model, as may be seen from the trivial model,

$$\forall \mathbf{x} \in R^1, \qquad x + y = 0.$$

The condition $x + y = 0$ is symmetric in x and y; the further stipulation that x is exogenous and y is endogenous specifies that in the model x restricts y and not conversely, a property that cannot be derived from $x + y = 0$. In many instances the restrictions on $\mathbf{y}$ may *determine* $\mathbf{y}$, at least for $\mathbf{x} \in R^* \subset R$, but the existence of a *unique* solution has no bearing on the endogeneity and exogeneity of the variables.

The formal distinction between endogeneity and exogeneity in econometric models was emphasized by the Cowles Commission in their pathbreaking work on the estimation of simultaneous economic relationships. The class of models

75

they considered is contained in the specification

$$\mathbf{B}(L)\mathbf{y}(t) + \boldsymbol{\Gamma}(L)\mathbf{x}(t) = \mathbf{u}(t);$$

$$\mathbf{A}(L)\mathbf{u}(t) = \boldsymbol{\varepsilon}(t);$$

$$\mathrm{cov}[\boldsymbol{\varepsilon}(t), \mathbf{y}(t-s)] = \mathbf{O}, s > 0;$$

$$\mathrm{cov}[\boldsymbol{\varepsilon}(t), \mathbf{x}(t-s)] = \mathbf{O}, \text{ all } s;$$

$$\boldsymbol{\varepsilon}(t) \sim \mathrm{IIDN}(\mathbf{O}, \boldsymbol{\Sigma}).$$

The vectors $\mathbf{x}(t)$ and $\mathbf{y}(t)$ are observed, whereas $\mathbf{u}(t)$ and $\boldsymbol{\varepsilon}(t)$ are underlying disturbances not observed but affecting $\mathbf{y}(t)$. The lag operator L is defined by $L\mathbf{x}(t) = \mathbf{x}(t-1)$; the roots of $|\mathbf{B}(L)|$ and $|\mathbf{A}(L)|$ are assumed to have modulus greater than 1, a stability condition guaranteeing the nonexplosive behaviour of $\mathbf{y}$ given any stable path for $\mathbf{x}$. The Cowles Commission definition of exogeneity in this model (Koopmans and Hood, 1953, pp. 117–120) as set forth in Christ (1966, p. 156) is

> An exogenous variable in a stochastic model is a variable whose value in each period is statistically independent of the values of all the random disturbances in the model in all periods.

All other variables are endogenous. In the prototypical model set forth above $\mathbf{x}$ is exogenous and $\mathbf{y}$ is endogenous.

The Cowles Commission distinction between endogeneity and exogeneity applied to a specific class of models, with linear relationships and normally distributed disturbances. The exogenous variables $\mathbf{x}$ in the prototypical model have two important but quite distinct properties. First, the model may be solved to yield an expression for $\mathbf{y}(t)$ in terms of current and past values of $\mathbf{x}$ and ε,

$$\mathbf{y}(t) = \mathbf{B}(L)^{-1}\boldsymbol{\Gamma}(L)\mathbf{x}(t) + \mathbf{B}(L)^{-1}\mathbf{A}(L)\boldsymbol{\varepsilon}(t).$$

Given suitably restricted $\mathbf{x}(t)$ (e.g. all $\mathbf{x}$ uniformly bounded, or being realizations of a stationary stochastic process with finite variance) it is natural to complete the model by specifying that it is valid for all $\mathbf{x}$ meeting the restrictions, and this is often done. The variables $\mathbf{x}$ are therefore exogenous here as $\mathbf{x}$ is exogenous in a deterministic economic model. A second, distinct property of these variables is that in estimation $\mathbf{x}(t)$ ($-\infty < t < \infty$) may be regarded as fixed, thus extending to the environment of simultaneous equation models methods of statistical inference initially designed for experimental settings. It was generally recognized that exogeneity in the prototypical model was a sufficient but not a necessary condition to justify treating variables as fixed for purposes of inference. If $\mathbf{u}(t)$ in the model is serially independent (i.e. $\mathbf{A}(L) = \mathbf{I}$) then lagged values of $\mathbf{y}$ may also be treated as fixed for purposes of the model, this leads to the definition of 'predetermined variables' (Christ, 1966, p. 227) following Koopmans and Hood (1953, pp. 117–121):

A variable is predetermined at time t if all its current and past values are independent of the vector of current disturbances in the model, and these disturbances are serially independent.

These two properties were not explicitly distinguished in the prototypical model (Koopmans, 1950; Koopmans and Hood, 1953) and tended to remain merged in the literature over the next quarter-century (e.g. Christ, 1966; Theil, 1971; Geweke, 1978). By the late 1970s there had developed a tension between the two, due to the increasing sophistication of estimation procedures in nonlinear models, treatment of rational expectations, and the explicit consideration of the respective dynamic properties of endogenous and exogenous variables (Sims, 1972, 1977; Geweke, 1982). Engle, Hendry and Richard (1983), drawing on this literature and discussions at the 1979 Warwick Summer Workshop, formalized the distinction of the two properties we have discussed. Drawing on their definitions 2.3 and 2.5 and the discussions in Sims (1977) and Geweke (1982), $\mathbf{x}$ is *model exogenous* if given $\{\mathbf{x}(t), t \leqslant T\} \in R(T)$ the model may restrict $\{\mathbf{y}(t), t \leqslant T\}$, but given

$$\{\mathbf{x}(t), t \leqslant T + J\} \in R(T + J)$$

there are no further restrictions on $\{\mathbf{y}(t), t \leqslant T\}$, for any $J > 0$. If the model in fact does restrict $\{\mathbf{y}(t), t \leqslant T\}$, then $\mathbf{y}$ is model endogenous. As examples consider

Model 1:

$$y(t) = ay(t-1) + bx(t) + u(t),$$

$$x(t) = cx(t-1) + v(t);$$

Model 2:

$$y(t) = ay(t-1) + bx(t) + u(t),$$

$$x(t) = cx(t-1) + dy(t) + v(t);$$

Model 3:

$$y(t) = ay(t-1) + b\{x(t) + E[x(t)|x(t-s), s > 0]\} + u(t),$$

$$x(t) = cx(t-1) + v(t).$$

In each case $u(t)$ and $v(t)$ are mutually and serially independent, and normally distributed. The parameters are assumed to satisfy the usual stability restrictions guaranteeing that x and y have normal distributions with finite variances. In all three models y is model endogenous, and x is model exogenous in Models 1 and 3 but not 2. For estimation the situation is different. In Model 1, treating $x(t), x(t-1)$ and $y(t-1)$ as fixed simplifies inference at no cost; $y(t-1)$ is a classic predetermined variable in the sense of Koopmans and Hood (1953) and Christ (1966). Similarly in Model 2, $x(t-1)$ and $y(t-1)$ may be regarded as fixed for purposes of inference despite the fact that x and y are both model endogenous. When Model 3 is re-expressed

$$y(t) = ay(t-1) + bx(t) + bcx(t-1) + u(t), \qquad x(t) = cx(t-1) + v(t),$$

it is clear that $x(t)$ cannot be treated as fixed if the parameters are to be estimated efficiently since there are cross-equation restrictions involving the parameter c. Model exogeneity of a variable is thus neither a necessary nor a sufficient condition for treating that variable as fixed for purposes of inference.

The condition that a set of variables can be regarded as fixed for inference can be formalized, following Engle, Hendry and Richard (1983) along the lines given in Geweke (1984). Let

$$\mathbf{X} \equiv [\mathbf{x}(1), \ldots, \mathbf{x}(n)] \quad \text{and} \quad \mathbf{Y} \equiv [\mathbf{y}(1), \ldots, \mathbf{y}(n)]$$

be matrices of n observations on the variables $\mathbf{x}$ and $\mathbf{y}$ respectively. Suppose the likelihood function $L(\mathbf{X}, \mathbf{Y} | \boldsymbol{\Theta})$ can be reparametrized by $\lambda = F(\boldsymbol{\Theta})$ where F is a one-to-one transformation; $\lambda' = (\lambda_1, \lambda_2)', (\lambda_1, \lambda_2) \in \Lambda_1 X \Lambda_2$; and the investigator's loss function depends on parameters of interest λ_1 but not nuisance parameters λ_2. Then $\mathbf{x}$ is *weakly exogenous* if

$$L(\mathbf{X}, \mathbf{Y} | \lambda_1, \lambda_2) = L_1(\mathbf{Y} | \mathbf{X}, \lambda, \lambda_1) \cdot L_2(\mathbf{X} | \lambda_2),$$

and in this case $\mathbf{y}$ is *weakly endogenous*. When this condition is met the expected loss function may be expressed using only $L_1(\mathbf{Y} | \mathbf{X}, \lambda_1)$, i.e. $\mathbf{x}$ may be regarded as fixed for purposes of inference.

The concepts of model exogeneity and weak exogeneity play important but distinct roles in the construction, estimation, and evaluation of econometric models. The dichotomy between variables that are model exogenous and model endogenous is a global property of a model, drawing in effect a logical distinction between the inputs of the model $\{\mathbf{x}(t), t \leqslant T\} \in R(T)$ and the set of variables restricted by the model $\{\mathbf{y}(t), t \leqslant T\}$. Since model exogeneity stipulates that $\{\mathbf{x}(t), t \leqslant T + J\}$ places no more restrictions on $\{\mathbf{y}(t), t \leqslant T\}$ than does $\{\mathbf{x}(t), t \leqslant T\}$, the global property of model exogeneity is in principle testable, either in the presence or absence of other restrictions imposed by the model. When conducted in the absence of most other restrictions this test is often termed a 'causality test' and its use as a test of specification was introduced by Sims (1972). The distinction between weakly exogenous and weakly endogenous variables permits a simplification of the likelihood function that depends on the subset of the model's parameters that are of interest to the investigator. It is a logical property of the model: the same results would be obtained using $L(\mathbf{X}, \mathbf{Y} | \lambda_1, \lambda_2)$ as using $L(\mathbf{Y} | \mathbf{X}, \lambda_1)$. The stipulation of weak exogeneity is therefore not, by itself, testable.

BIBLIOGRAPHY

Christ, C.F. 1966. *Econometric Models and Methods*. New York: Wiley.

Engle, R.F., Hendry, D.F. and Richard, J.-F. 1983. Exogeneity. *Econometrica* 51(2), March, 277–304.

Geweke, J. 1978. Testing the exogeneity specification in the complete dynamic simultaneous equation model. *Journal of Econometrics* 7(2), April, 163–85.

Geweke, J. 1982. Causality, exogeneity, and inference. Ch. 7 in *Advances in Econometrics*, ed. W. Hildenbrand, Cambridge: Cambridge University Press.

Geweke, J. 1984. Inference and causality. Ch. 19 in *Handbook of Econometrics*, Vol. 2, ed. Z. Griliches and M.D. Intriligator, Amsterdam: North-Holland.

Koopmans, T.C. 1950. When is an equation system complete for statistical purposes? In *Statistical Inference in Dynamic Economic Models*, ed. T.C. Koopmans, New York: Wiley.

Koopmans, T.C. and Hood, W.C. 1953. The estimation of simultaneous economic relationships. In *Studies in Econometric Method*, ed. W.C. Hood and T.C. Koopmans, New York: Wiley.

Sims, C.A. 1972. Money, income, and causality. *American Economic Review* 62(4), September, 540–52.

Sims, C.A. 1977. Exogeneity and causal ordering in macroeconomic models. In *New Methods in Business Cycle Research*, ed. C.A. Sims, Minneapolis: Federal Reserve Bank of Minneapolis.

Theil, H. 1971. *Principles of Econometrics*. New York: Wiley.

Errors in Variables

VINCENT J. GERACI

1. THE HISTORICAL AMBIVALENCE

This essay surveys the history and recent developments on economic models with errors in variables. These errors may arise from the use of substantive unobservables, such as permanent income, or from ordinary measurement problems in data collection and processing. The point of departure is the classical regression equation with random errors in variables:

$$y = X^*\beta + u,$$

where y is a $n \times 1$ vector of observations on the dependent variable, X^* is a $n \times k$ matrix of unobserved (latent) values on the k independent variables, β is a $k \times 1$ vector of unknown coefficients, and u is a $n \times 1$ vector of random disturbances. The matrix of observed values on X^* is

$$X = X^* + V,$$

where V is the $n \times k$ matrix of measurement errors. If some variables are measured without error, the appropriate columns of V are zero vectors. In the conventional case the errors are uncorrelated in the limit with the latent values X^* and the disturbances u; and the errors have zero means, constant variances, and zero autocorrelation. In observed variables the model becomes

$$y = X\beta + (u - V\beta).$$

Since the disturbance $(u - V\beta)$ is correlated with X, ordinary least squares estimates of β are biased and inconsistent. The errors thus pose a potentially serious estimation problem. In regard to systematic errors in variables, they will not be discussed, since they raise complex issues of model misspecification which lie outside the scope of this essay.

Errors in variables have a curious history in economics, in that economists have shown an ambivalent attitude toward them despite the universal awareness that economic variables are often measured with error and despite the commitment to economics as a science. Griliches (1974) suggested that much of the ambivalence stems from the separation in economics between data producers and data analysers. If so, why have not economists made a greater effort to cross the breach? Griliches (p. 975) further suggested that 'another good reason for ignoring errors in variables was the absence of any good cure for this disease'. If so, why have not economists made greater use of the econometric techniques developed since Griliches wrote his survey?

We propose an alternative explanation: the way of economic thinking, epitomized by utility theory and consumer maximization, has promoted a neglect of measurement errors. Bentham (1789, ch. IV) was a pioneer of measurement theory in the social sciences in his attempt to provide a theory for the measurement of utility. He went so far as to recommend that the social welfare of a given policy be computed by summing up *numbers* expressive of the 'degrees of good tendency' across individuals. Bentham's notion of cardinal utility met rightfully with great resistance. Pareto (1927, ch. III) pressed the dominant view; the economic equilibrium approach, by producing empirical propositions about consumer demand in terms of observables (quantities, prices, incomes), is to be favoured over theories connecting prices to utility, a metaphysical entity. Thus, theory – here optimization by rational consumers in a competitive market – overcame a fundamental measurement problem.

We do not wish to quarrel with the neoclassical equilibrium approach to the study of demand, although some economists wonder whether the assumptions of the theory have sufficient validity to warrant their acceptance (as part of the maintained hypothesis) in so many empirical demand studies. Rather, our point is that the great successes of this theory, and analogous successes of similar theories about other economic behaviour, have implanted a subconscious bias toward the substitution of economic theory (assumptions) for difficult measurement. In consequence, many economic models do not have an adequate empirical basis, cf. Leontief (1971) and Koopmans (1979).

Whatever the reasons for their neglect, errors in variables have been hard to keep down. Substantive unobservables such as permanent income, expected price and human capital continue to work their way into economic models and raise measurement issues. Friedman's (1957) permanent income model has served as a prototype for the errors-in-variables setup:

$$c_p = k y_p$$

$$y = y_p + y_t$$

$$c = c_p + c_t,$$

where c = consumption, y = income, subscript 'p' = permanent, subscript 't' = transitory, and k is a behavioural parameter. Friedman (p. 36) clearly recognized the connection of the model expressed in observed c and y to the errors-in-variables setup; in his words, 'The estimation problem is the classical one of "mutual regression" or regression "when both variables are subject to error"'.

In the next two sections, early and recent developments on economic models with random errors in variables will be surveyed. Then, we will speculate on the future use of errors-in-variables methods.

2. EARLY ECONOMETRIC DEVELOPMENTS

Frisch (1934) was the first econometrician to face squarely the problem of errors in variables. In a brave book addressing model search, multicollinearity, simultaneity and errors in variables, he decomposed the observed variables into a systematic (latent) part and a random disturbance part. His complicated correlation approach sometimes resembling common factor analysis, did not satisfactorily resolve the errors-in-variables problem, but he raised fruitful questions. While Koopmans (1937), Geary (1942), Hurwicz and Anderson (1946), Reiersöl (1950) and a few others followed up on Frisch's endeavour, interest in the problem waned by the start of the 1950s. The famous Cowles Commission may have unintentionally buried the errors-in-variables problem when the chief investigators put it aside in order to make progress on the simultaneity problem. Applied economists, in their zeal to employ the new simultaneous equations model, ignored the limitations in their data despite the warning cry of Morgenstern (1950). Sargan (1958), Liviatan (1961), Madansky (1959) and a few others made contributions in the 1950s and 1960s, but for the most part errors in variables lay dormant. Widely used econometrics textbooks aggravated matters by highlighting the lack of identification of the classical regression equation in the absence of strong prior information such as known ratios of error variances. Neglect by the theorists led to the widespread use of *ad hoc* proxies in practice.

3. RECENT ECONOMETRIC DEVELOPMENTS

Zellner (1970) sparked a revival of interest in errors in variables. He attained identification of the permanent income prototype by appending a measurement relation that predicted unobservable permanent income in terms of *multiple causes* (e.g. education, age, housing value), to accompany the natural *indicator* relation in which observed current income is a formal proxy for permanent income. Goldberger (1971, 1972b) stimulated the revival by showing how models with substantive unobservables could be identified and estimated by combining all of the measurement information in a set of multiple equations that arise from multiple indicators or multiple causes. He also drew out the connections among the errors-in-variables model of econometrics, the confirmatory factor analysis model of psychometrics, and the path analysis model of sociometrics. On the applications side, Griliches and Mason (1972) and Chamberlain and Griliches (1975) studied the important socioeconomic problem of estimating the economic returns to schooling, with allowance for unobservable 'ability'. With Goldberger and Griliches leading the way, the econometric literature on errors in variables flourished in the 1970s.

Multiple equations. For the permanent income prototype, Zellner's multiple cause relation and indicator relation formed a two-equation measurement system that could be appended to the structural consumption equation. For this three-equation model, Zellner (1970) provided an efficient generalized least squares estimator, and Goldberger (1972a) added a maximum likelihood estimator. This errors-in-variables framework, which can be applied to many situations in which an unobservable appears as an independent variable in an otherwise classical regression equation, has been very useful. Example applications have included Aigner's (1974) study of labour supply in which the wage is an unobservable, Lahiri's (1977) study of the Phillips curve in which price expectations is an unobservable, and Geraci and Prewo's (1977) study of international trade in which transport costs is an unobservable.

Jöreskog and Goldberger (1975) generalized the framework to situations in which there are more than two observed dependent variables. Their model combined prior constraints on the reduced-form coefficients (of the type that arise in econometric simultaneous equations models) with prior constraints on the reduced-form disturbance covariance matrix (of the type that arise in psychometric factor analysis models). For this model which contains multiple indicators and multiple causes (MIMIC) for a single unobservable, they developed a maximum likelihood estimator. Applications of the MIMIC framework have included Kadane et al's (1977) study of the effects of environmental factors on changes in unobservable intelligence over time, and Robins and West's (1977) study of unobservable home value. The framework could be extended to endogenous causes, as Robinson and Ferrara (1977) demonstrated.

Simultaneity. The MIMIC model assumes unidirectional causation. Suppose instead that unobservables appear in a simultaneous equations model. This case calls for less 'outside information' than the single-equation case, since coefficient overidentification, as it would exist in the hypothetical absence of measurement errors, may compensate for the underidentification associated with errors. This idea had appeared in early unpublished works by Hurwicz and Anderson (1946); Goldberger resurrected it in 1971. Geraci (1974), Hausman (1977) and Hsiao (1976) subsequently developed identification analyses and estimators for the simultaneous equations model with errors, taking account of the 'disturbance' covariance restrictions induced by the error structure as well as the usual coefficient restrictions. Many of their results have an instrumental variables interpretation. For illustration, an indicator for an unobservable in a simultaneous equations system is a valid instrumental variable for a given structural equation if the unobservable either (a) does not appear in that equation or (b) appears but has an associated error variance that is identified using information from some other part of the system. Once the latter linkage is recognized, the model may well be identifiable and hence estimable. A notable application has been Griliches and Chamberlain's series of studies on the economic returns to schooling. They employed a triangular model with structural disturbances specified as a function of unobservables (common factors). In various ways their models incorporated simultaneity, multiple indicators, and multiple causes.

Dynamics. Maravall and Aigner (1977), Hsiao (1977), and Hsiao and Robinson (1978) extended the errors-in-variables analysis to dynamic economic models. Among their findings, dynamics are a 'blessing' for identification in that autocorrelation of exogenous variables may provide additional information; and, upon taking a discrete Fourier transform of the data, many of the results for the contemporaneous model can be carried over to the dynamic model. In the same vein, Geweke (1977) developed a maximum likelihood estimator for the dynamic factor analysis model by reprogramming, in complex arithmetic, Jöreskog's (1970) maximum likelihood algorithm which had developed into the widely used LISREL software package. Geweke applied this estimator to investigate manufacturing sector adjustments to unobservable product demand. Singleton (1977) extended this factor analysis approach to study the cyclical behaviour of the term structure of interest rates. His framework allowed estimation of the model without specifying the causes of the unobservable real rate of interest and price expectations, thus isolating the classic Fisher hypothesis for testing.

As the preceding survey indicates, the recent econometric literature contains many theoretical results on the identification and estimation of structural models that contain substantive unobservables and measurement errors. (For a further survey, see Aigner et al., 1984.) The literature also contains some interesting applications, but not many. Are more forthcoming?

4. PROSPECTS

We have an uneasy feeling about the state of empirical economics. The development of formal economic theory and associated econometric technique has proceeded at an extraordinary pace. At the same time, what do economists know empirically? Many reported inferences hinge upon model assumptions whose validity remains to be assessed, and the gap between econometric technique and available data seems to be growing. None the less, there are grounds for some optimism.

Although few in number, the applications of errors-in-variables methods in the 1980s have been striking in their relevance to central economic issues. For example, Attfield (1980) has made the permanent income model a more complete explanation of consumption by incorporating unobservable liquid assets, rateable value, and windfall income. His model is a special simultaneous equations model with errors, in which identification of the individual structural equations can be established on a recursive basis. Geweke and Singleton (1981) also have taken up the permanent income model, adapting the classical latent variables model to this time series context and thereby generating some new tests of the permanent income hypothesis. As another example, Garber and Klepper (1980) have defended the competitive model of short-run pricing in concentrated industries through an explicit accounting for errors in measuring cost and output changes.

They concluded that short-run price behaviour may appear to be related to market structure primarily because of estimation biases due to the measurement errors. As a final example, Stapleton (1984) has shown that the symmetry restrictions on structural parameters imposed by demand theory can be used to identify a linear model's parameters when measurement errors in price perceptions exist. This study is noteworthy in two respects. First, it shows how price, that bedrock of economic theory, may be measured erroneously. Second, economic theory is used to permit the explicit treatment of errors in variables.

These recent empirical works indicate the potential of errors-in-variables methods to lend fresh insights into important economic issues, and should stimulate more use of these methods. There are other encouraging signs as well. Recent studies using micro data have shown increasing attention to measurement error problems. In the macro area the rational expectations hypothesis has raised economists' consciousness of the difference between key conceptual variables of economic theory (i.e. permanent income, expected price, ex ante real rate of interest) and the available measurements. With respect to applications of errors-in-variables methods in economics, the stock is not great but the flow is encouraging.

BIBLIOGRAPHY

Aigner, D.J. 1974. An appropriate econometric framework for estimating a labor-supply function from the SEO file. *International Economic Review* 15(1) February, 59–68.

Aigner, D.J., Hsiao, C., Kapteyn, A. and Wansbeek, T. 1984. Latent variable models in econometrics. In *Handbook of Econometrics*, ed. Z. Griliches and M.D. Intriligator. Amsterdam: Elsevier Science, ch. 23.

Attfield, C.L.G. 1980. Testing the assumptions of the permanent-income model. *Journal of the American Statistical Association* 75, March, 32–8.

Bentham, J. 1789. *An Introduction to the Principles of Morals and Legislation*. London: Clarendon Press, 1907; New York: Hafner Publishing Company, 1948.

Chamberlain, G. and Griliches, Z. 1975. Unobservables with a variance-components structure: ability, schooling, and the economic success of brothers. *International Economic Review* 16(2), June, 422–49.

Friedman, M. 1957. *A Theory of the Consumption Function*. Princeton: Princeton University Press.

Frisch, R. 1934. *Statistical Confluence Analysis by Means of Complete Regression Systems*. Oslo: University Institute of Economics.

Garber, S. and Klepper, S. 1980. Administered pricing, or competition coupled with errors of measurement. *International Economic Review* 21(2), June, 413–35.

Geary, R.C. 1942. Inherent relationships between random variables. *Proceedings of the Royal Irish Academy* 47, 63–76.

Geraci, V.J. 1974. *Simultaneous Equation Models with Measurement Error*. PhD dissertation. New York: Garland, 1982.

Geraci, V.J. and Prewo, W. 1977. Bilateral trade and transport costs. *Review of Economics and Statistics* 59(1), February, 67–74.

Geweke, J.F. 1977. The dynamic factor analysis of economic time-series models. In *Latent Variables in Socioeconomic Models*, ed. D.J. Aigner and A.S. Goldberger, Amsterdam: North-Holland, ch. 19.

Geweke, J.F. and Singleton, K.J. 1981. Latent variable models for time series: a frequency domain approach with an application to the permanent income hypothesis. *Journal of Econometrics* 17(3), December, 287–304.

Goldberger, A.S. 1971. Econometrics and psychometrics. *Psychometrika* 36, June, 83–107.

Goldberger, A.S. 1972a. Maximum-likelihood estimation of regressions containing unobservable independent variables. *International Economic Review* 13(1), February, 1–15.

Goldberger, A.S. 1972b. Structural equation methods in the social sciences. *Econometrica* 40(6), November, 979–1001.

Griliches, Z. 1974. Errors in variables and other unobservables. *Econometrica* 42(6), November, 971–98.

Griliches, Z. and Mason, W.M. 1972. Education, income and ability. *Journal of Political Economy* 80(3), Pt II, May–June, 74–103.

Hausman, J. 1977. Errors in variables in simultaneous equation models. *Journal of Econometrics* 5(3), May, 389–401.

Hsiao, C. 1976. Identification and estimation of simultaneous equation models with measurement error. *International Economic Review* 17(2), June, 319–39.

Hsiao, C. 1977. Identification of a linear dynamic simultaneous error-shock model. *International Economic Review* 18(1), February, 181–94.

Hsiao, C. and Robinson, P.M. 1978. Efficient estimation of a dynamic error-shock model. *International Economic Review* 19(2), June, 467–79.

Hurwicz, L. and Anderson, T.W. 1946. Statistical models with disturbances in equations and/or disturbances in variables. Unpublished memoranda. Chicago: Cowles Commission.

Jöreskog, K.G. 1970. A general method for the analysis of covariance structures. *Biometrika* 57(2), August, 239–51.

Jöreskog, K.G. and Goldberger, A.S. 1975. Estimation of a model with multiple indicators and multiple causes of a single latent variable. *Journal of the American Statistical Association* 70, Pt I, September, 631–9.

Kadane, J.B., McGuire, T.W., Sanday, P.R. and Stuelin, P. 1977. Estimation of environmental effects on the pattern of I.Q. scores over time. In *Latent Variables in Socioeconomic Models*, ed. D.J. Aigner and A.S. Goldberger, Amsterdam: North-Holland, ch. 17.

Koopmans, T.C. 1937. *Linear Regression Analysis of Economic Time Series*. Haarlem: De Erven F. Bohn N.V.

Koopmans, T.C. 1979. Economics among the sciences. *American Economic Review* 69(1), March, 1–13.

Lahiri, K. 1977. A joint study of expectations formation and the shifting Phillips curve. *Journal of Monetary Economics* 3(3), July, 347–57.

Leontief, W. 1971. Theoretical assumptions and nonobserved facts. *American Economic Review* 61(1), March, 1–7.

Liviatan, N. 1961. Errors in variables and Engel curve analysis. *Econometrica* 29, July, 336–62.

Madansky, A. 1959. The fitting of straight lines when both variables are subject to error. *Journal of the American Statistical Association* 54, March, 173–205.

Maravall, A. and Aigner, D.J. 1977. Identification of the dynamic shock-error model. In *Latent Variable Models in Socioeconomic Models*, ed. D.J. Aigner and A.S. Goldberger, Amsterdam: North-Holland, ch. 18.

Morgenstern, O. 1950. *On the Accuracy of Economic Observations*. 2nd edn, Princeton:

Princeton University Press, 1963.

Pareto, V. 1927. *Manual of Political Economy.* New York: Augustus M. Kelley, 1971.

Reiersl, O. 1950. Identifiability of a linear relation between variables which are subject to error. *Econometrica* 18, October, 375–89.

Robins, P.K. and West, R.W. 1977. Measurement errors in the estimation of home value. *Journal of the American Statistical Association* 73, June, 290–94.

Robinson, P.M. and Ferrara, M.C. 1977. The estimation of a model for an unobservable variable with endogenous causes. In *Latent Variable Models in Socioeconomic Models,* ed. D.J. Aigner and A.S. Goldberger, Amsterdam: North-Holland, ch. 9.

Sargan, J.D. 1958. The estimation of economic relationships using instrumental variables. *Econometrica* 26, July, 393–415.

Singleton, K.J. 1977. The cyclical behavior of the term structure of interest rates. Unpublished PhD dissertation, Madison: University of Wisconsin.

Stapleton, D. 1984. Errors-in-variables in demand systems. *Journal of Econometrics* 26(3), December, 255–70.

Zellner, A. 1970. Estimation of regression relationships containing unobservable independent variables. *International Economic Review* 11, October, 441–54.

Full and Limited Information Methods

THOMAS J. ROTHENBERG

Econometricians have developed a number of alternative methods for estimating parameters and testing hypotheses in simultaneous equations models. Some of these are limited information methods that can be applied one equation at a time and require only minimal specification of the other equations in the system. In contrast, the full information methods treat the system as a whole and require a complete specification of all the equations.

The distinction between limited and full information methods is, in part, simply one of statistical efficiency. As is generally true in inference problems, the more that is known about the phenomenon being studied, the more precisely the unknown parameters can be estimated with the available data. In an interdependent system of equations, information about the variables appearing in one equation can be used to get better estimates of the coefficients in other equations. Of course, there is a trade-off: full information methods are more efficient, but they are also more sensitive to specification error and more difficult to compute.

Statistical considerations are not, however, the only reason for distinguishing between limited and full information approaches. Models of the world do not come off the shelf. In any application, the choice of which variables to view as endogenous (i.e. explained by the model) and which to view as exogenous (explained outside the model) is up to the analyst. The interpretations given to the equations of the model and the specification of the functional forms are subject to considerable discretion. The limited information and full information distinction can be viewed not simply as one of statistical efficiency but one of modelling strategy.

The simultaneous equations model can be applied to a variety of economic situations. In each case, structural equations are interpreted in light of some hypothetical experiment that is postulated. In considering the logic of econometric model building and inference, it is useful to distinguish between two general classes of applications. On the one hand, there are applications where the basic economic question involves a single hypothetical experiment and the problem is to draw inferences about the parameters of a single autonomous structural equation. Other relationships are considered only as a means for learning about the given equation. On the other hand, there are applications where the basic economic question being asked involves in an essential way an interdependent system of experiments. The goal of the analysis is to understand the interaction of a set of autonomous equations.

An example may clarify the distinction. Consider the standard competitive supply-demand model where price and quantity traded are determined by the interaction of consumer and producer behaviour. One can easily imagine situations where consumers are perfectly-competitive price takers and it would be useful to know the price elasticity of market demand. One might be tempted to use time-series data and regress quantity purchased on price (including perhaps other demand determinants like income and prices of substitutes as additional explanatory variables) and to interpret the estimated equation as a demand function. If it could plausibly be assumed that the omitted demand determinants constituting the error term were uncorrelated over the sample period with each of the included regressors, this interpretation might be justified. If, however, periods where the omitted factors lead to high demand are also the periods where price is high, then there will be simultaneous equations bias. In order to decide whether or not the regression of quantity on price will produce satisfactory estimates of the demand function, the mechanism determining movements in price must be examined. Even though our interest is in the behaviour of consumers, we must consider other agents who influence price. In this case a model of producer behaviour is needed.

This example captures the essence of many econometric problems: we want to learn about a relationship defined in terms of a hypothetical isolated experiment but the data we have available were in fact generated from a more complex experiment. We are not particularly interested in studying the process that actually generated the data, except in so far it helps us to learn about the process we *wish* had generated the data. A simultaneous equations model is postulated simply to help us estimate a single equation of interest.

Some economic problems, however, are of a different sort. Again in the supply-demand set-up, suppose we are interested in learning how a sales tax will affect market price. If tax rates had varied over our sample period, a regression of market price on tax rate might be informative. If, however, there had been little or no tax rate variation, such a regression would be useless. But, in a correctly specified model, the effects of taxes can be deduced from knowledge of the structure of consumer and producer decision making in the absence of taxes. Under competition, for example, one needs only to know the slopes of the demand and supply curves. Thus, in order to predict the effect of a sales tax, one might wish to estimate the system of structural equations describing market equilibrium.

The distinction between these two situations can be summarized as follows: in the one case we are interested in a structural equation for its own sake; in the other case our interest is in the reduced-form of an interdependent system. If our concern is with a single equation, we might prefer to make few assumptions about the rest of the system and to estimate the needed parameters using limited information methods. If our concern is with improved reduced-form estimates, full-information approaches are natural since specification of the entire system is necessary in any case. A further discussion of these methodological issues can be found in Hood and Koopmans (1953, chs 1 and 6).

LIMITED INFORMATION METHODS. Consider a single structural equation represented by

$$y = Z\alpha + u, \tag{1}$$

where y is a T-dimensional (column) vector of observations on an endogenous variable, Z is a $T \times n$ matrix of observations on n explanatory variables, α is an n-dimensional parameter vector, and u is a T-dimensional vector of random errors. The components of α are given a causal interpretation in terms of some hypothetical experiment suggested by economic theory. For example, the first component might represent the effect on the outcome of the experiment of a unit change in one of the conditions, other things held constant. In our sample, however, other conditions varied across the T observation. The errors represent those conditions which are not accounted for by the explanatory variables and are assumed to have zero mean.

The key assumption underlying limited-information methods of inference is that we have data on K predetermined variables that are unrelated to the errors. That is, the error term for observation t is uncorrelated with each of the predetermined variables for that observation. The $T \times K$ matrix of observations on the predetermined variables is assumed to have rank K and is denoted by X. By assumption, then, $E(X'u)$ is the zero vector. Some of the explanatory variables may be predetermined and hence some columns of Z are also columns of X. The remaining explanatory variables are thought to be correlated with the error term and are considered as endogenous. Implicitly, equation (1) is viewed as part of a large system explaining all the endogenous variables. The predetermined variables appearing in X but not in Z are assumed to be explanatory variables in some other structural equation. Exact specification of these other equations is not needed for limited information analysis.

In most approaches to estimating α it is assumed that nothing is known about the degree of correlation between u and the endogenous components of Z. Instead, the analysis exploits the zero correlation between u and X. The simplest approach is the method of moments. Since $X'u$ has mean zero, a natural estimate of α is that vector a satisfying the vector equation $X'(y - Za) = 0$. This is a system of K linear equations in n unknowns. If K is less than n, the estimation method fails. If K equals n, the estimate is given by $(X'Z)^{-1} X'y$, as long as the inverse exists. The approach is often referred to as the method of instrumental variables and the columns of X are called instruments.

If K is greater than n, any n independent linear combinations of the columns of X can be used as instruments. For example, for any $n \times K$ matrix D, α can be estimated by

$$(D'X'Z)^{-1}D'X'y, \tag{2}$$

as long as the inverse exists. Often D is chosen to be a selection matrix with each row containing zeros except for one unit element; that is, n out of the K predetermined variables are selected as instruments and the others are discarded. If Z contains no endogenous variables, it is a submatrix of X; least squares can then be interpreted as instrumental variables using the regressors as instruments.

The estimator (2) will have good sampling properties if the instruments are not only uncorrelated with the errors but also highly correlated with the explanatory variables. To maximize that correlation, a natural choice for D is the coefficient matrix from a linear regression of Z on X. The instruments are then the predicted values from that regression. These predicted values (or projections) can be written as NZ where N is the indempotent projection matrix $X(X'X)^{-1}X'$; the estimator becomes

$$(Z'NZ)^{-1}Z'Ny. \tag{2'}$$

Because $N = NN$, the estimator (2) can be obtained by simply regressing y on the predicted values NZ. Hence, this particular instrumental variables estimator is commonly called *two-stage least squares*.

The two-stage least-squares estimator is readily seen to be the solution of the minimization problem

$$\min(y - Za)'N(y - Za). \tag{3}$$

As an alternative, it has been proposed to minimize the ratio

$$\frac{(y - Za)'N(y - Za)}{(y - Za)'M(y - Za)} \tag{4}$$

where $M = I - N$ is also an indempotent projection matrix. This yields the *limited-information maximum-likelihood* estimator. That is, if the endogenous variables are assumed to be multivariate normal and independent from observation to observation, and if no variables are excluded a priori from the other equations in the system, maximization of the likelihood function is equivalent to minimizing the ratio (4). This maximum likelihood estimate is also an instrumental variable estimate of the form (2). Indeed, the matrix D turns out to be the maximum likelihood estimate of the population regression coefficients relating Z and X. Thus the solutions of (3) and (4) are both instrumental variable estimates. They differ only in how the reduced-form regression coefficients used for D are estimated.

The sampling distribution of the instrumental variable estimator depends, of course, on the choice of D. The endogenous variables in Z are necessarily random. Hence, the estimator behaves like the ratio of random variables; its moments and exact sampling distribution are difficult to derive even under the assumption of normality. However, large-sample approximations have been developed. The

91

two-stage least-squares estimate and the limited information maximum-likelihood estimate have, to a first order of approximation, the same large-sample probability distribution. To that order of approximation, they are optimal in the sense that any other instrumental variable estimators based on X have asymptotic variances at least as large. The asymptotic approximations tend to be reasonably good when T is large compared with K. When $K - n$ is large, instrumental variable estimates using a subset of the columns of X often outperform two-stage least squares. Further small-sample results are discussed by Fuller (1977).

FULL INFORMATION METHODS. Although limited-information methods like two-stage least squares can be applied to each equation of a simultaneous system, better results can usually be obtained by taking into account the other equations. Suppose the system consists of G linear structural equations in G endogenous variables. These equations contain K distinct predetermined variables which may be exogenous or values of endogenous variables at a previous time period. The crucial assumption is that each predetermined variable is uncorrelated with each structural error for the same observation.

Let $y_1, \ldots, y_G$ be T-dimensional column vectors of observations on the G endogenous variables. As before, the $T \times K$ matrix of observations on the predetermined variables is denoted by X and assumed to have rank K. The system is written as

$$y_i = Z_i \alpha_i + u_i, \qquad (i = 1, \ldots, G) \tag{5}$$

where Z_i is the $T \times n_i$ matrix of observations on the explanatory variables, u_i is the error vector, and α_i is the parameter vector for equation i. Some of the columns of Z_i are columns of X; the others are endogenous variables.

Again, estimates can be based on the method of moments. Consider the set of GK equations

$$X'(y_i - Z_i a_i) = 0. \qquad (i = 1, \ldots, G) \tag{6}$$

If, for any i, K is less than n_i, the corresponding parameter α_i cannot be estimated; we shall suppose that any equation for which this is true has already been deleted from the system so that G is the number of equations whose parameters are estimable. If $n_i = K$ for all i, the solution to (6) is obtained by using limited information instrumental variables on each equation separately. If, for some i, $n_i < K$, the system (6) has more equations than unknowns. Again, linear combinations of the predetermined variables can be used as instruments. The optimal selection of weights, however, is more complicated than in the limited-information case and depends on the pattern of correlation among the structural errors.

If the structural errors are independent from observation to observation but are correlated across equations, we have the specification

$$E(u_i u_j') = \sigma_{ij} I, \qquad (i, j = 1, \ldots, G)$$

where the σ's are error covariances and I is a T-dimensional identity matrix. As a generalization of (3), consider the minimization problem

$$\min \sum_i \sum_j (y_i - Z_i a_i)' N (y_j - Z_j a_j) \sigma^{ij}, \tag{7}$$

where the σ^{ij} are elements of the inverse of the matrix $[\sigma_{ij}]$. For given σ's, the first-order conditions are

$$\sum_j Z_i' N (y_j - Z_j a_j) \sigma^{ij} = 0, \qquad (i = 1, \ldots, G) \tag{8}$$

which are linear combinations of the equations in (6). It can be demonstrated that the solution to (8) is an instrumental variables estimator with asymptotically optimal weights. In practice, the σ's are unknown but can be estimated from the residuals of some preliminary fit. This approach to estimating the α's is called *three-stage least squares* since it involves least-squares calculations at three stages, first to obtain the projections NZ_j, again to obtain two-stage least-squares estimates of the σ's, and finally to solve the minimization problem (7). For details, see Zellner and Theil (1962).

If the structural errors are assumed to be normal, the likelihood function for the complete simultaneous equations system has a relatively simple expression in terms of the reduced-form parameters. However, since the reduced form is nonlinear in the structural parameters, analytic methods for maximizing the likelihood function are not available and iterative techniques are used instead. Just as in the limited-information case, the maximum-likelihood estimator can be interpreted as an instrumental variables estimator. If in (8) the least-squares predicted values NZ_i are replaced by maximum-likelihood predictions and if the σ's are replaced by their maximum-likelihood estimates, the resulting solution is the (full-information) maximum-likelihood estimate of the α's. See Malinvaud (1970, ch. 19) for details.

At one time full-information methods (particularly those using maximum likelihood) were computationally very burdensome. Computer software was almost non-existent, rounding error was hard to control, and computer time was very expensive. Many econometric procedures became popular simply because they avoided these difficulties. Current computer technology is such that computational burden is no longer a practical constraint, at least for moderate-sized models. The more important constraints at the moment are the limited sample sizes compared with the number of parameters to be estimated and limited confidence we have in the orthogonality conditions that must be imposed to get any estimates at all.

BIBLIOGRAPHY

Fuller, W. 1977. Some properties of a modification of the limited information estimator. *Econometrica* 45, May, 939–53.

Hood, W. and Koopmans, T. (eds) 1953. *Studies in Econometric Method.* Cowles Foundation Monograph No. 14, New York: Wiley.

Malinvaud, E. 1970. *Statistical Methods of Econometrics.* 2nd edn, Amsterdam: North-Holland.

Zellner, A. and Theil, H. 1962. Three-stage least squares: simultaneous estimation of simultaneous equations. *Econometrica* 30, January, 54–78.

Identification

CHENG HSIAO

In economic analysis we often assume that there exists an underlying structure which generated the observations of real-world data. However, statistical inference can relate only to characteristics of the distribution of the observed variables. A meaningful statistical interpretation of the real world through this structure can be achieved only if there is no other structure which is also capable of generating the observed data.

To illustrate, consider X as being normally distributed with mean $E(X) = \mu_1 - \mu_2$. Then $\mu_1 - \mu_2$ can be estimated using observed X. But the parameters μ_1 and μ_2 are not uniquely estimable. In fact, one can think of an infinite number of pairs $(\mu_i, \mu_j), i, j = 1, 2, \ldots, (i \neq j)$ such that $\mu_i - \mu_j = \mu_1 - \mu_2$. In order to determine $\mu_1 - \mu_2$ uniquely, we need additional prior information, such as $\mu_2 = 3\mu_1$ or some other assumption.

The problem of whether it is possible to draw inferences from the probability distribution of the observed variables to an underlying theoretical structure is the concern of econometric literature on identification. The first economist to raise this issue was Working (1925; 1927). The general formulations of the identification problems were made by Frisch (1934), Marschak (1942), Haavelmo (1944), Hurwicz (1950), Koopmans and Reiersøl (1950), Koopmans, Rubin and Leipnik (1950), Wald (1950) and many others. An extensive treatment of the theory of identification in simultaneous equation systems was provided by Fisher (1966). A survey of recent advances in the subject can be found in Hsiao (1983).

1 DEFINITIONS

It is generally assumed in econometrics that economic variables whose formation an economic theory is designed to explain have the characteristics of random variables. Let $\mathbf{y}$ be a set of such observations. A structure S is a complete specification of the probability distribution function of $\mathbf{y}$. The set of all a priori possible structures, T, is called a model. In most applications, $\mathbf{y}$ is assumed to

95

be generated by a parametric probability distribution function $F(\mathbf{y}, \boldsymbol{\theta})$, where the probability distribution function F is assumed known, but the $m \times 1$ parameter vector $\boldsymbol{\theta}$ is unknown. Hence, a structure is described by a parametric point $\boldsymbol{\theta}$, and a model is a set of points $A \subset R^m$.

Definition 1: Two structures, $S^0 = F(y, \boldsymbol{\theta}^0)$ and $S^* = F(\mathbf{y}, \boldsymbol{\theta}^*)$ are said to be *observationally equivalent* if $F(y, \boldsymbol{\theta}^0) = F(\mathbf{y}, \boldsymbol{\theta}^*)$ for ('almost') all possible y. A model is identifiable if A contains no two distinct structures which are observationally equivalent. A function of $\boldsymbol{\theta}, g(\boldsymbol{\theta})$, is identifiable if all observationally equivalent structures have the same value for $g(\boldsymbol{\theta})$.

Sometimes a weaker concept of identifiability is useful.

Definition 2: A structure with parameter value $\boldsymbol{\theta}^0$ is said to be *locally identified* if there exists an open neighbourhood of $\boldsymbol{\theta}^0, \Omega$, such that no other $\boldsymbol{\theta}$ in Ω is observationally equivalent.

2 GENERAL RESULTS

Lack of identification is a reflection that a random variable has the same distribution for different values of the parameter. R.A. Fisher's information matrix provides a measure of sensitivity of the distribution of a random variable due to small changes in the value of the parameter point (Rao, 1962). It can, therefore, be shown that subject to the regularity conditions, $\boldsymbol{\theta}^0$ is locally identified if and only if the information matrix evaluated in the neighbourhood of $\boldsymbol{\theta}^0$ is nonsingular (Rothenberg, 1971).

It is clear that unidentified parameters cannot be consistently estimated. There are also pathological cases where identified models fail to possess consistent estimators (e.g. Gabrielson, 1978). However, for most practical cases we may treat identifiability and the existence of a consistent estimator as equivalent (for precise conditions, see Le Cam, 1956; Deistler and Seifert, 1978).

3 SPECIFIC MODELS

The choice of model structure is one of the basic ingredients in the formulation of the identification problem. In this section we briefly discuss some identification conditions for different types of models in order to demonstrate the kind of prior restrictions required.

3.1 Linear models. Consider a theory which predicts a relationship among the variables as

$$B\mathbf{y}_t + \Gamma\mathbf{x}_t = \mathbf{u}_t, \tag{1}$$

where $\mathbf{y}_t$ and $\mathbf{u}_t$ are $G \times 1$ vectors of observed and unobserved random variables, respectively, $\mathbf{x}_t$ is a $K \times 1$ vector of observed non-stochastic variables, B and Γ are $G \times G$ and $G \times K$ matrices of coefficients, with B being nonsingular. We assume that $\mathbf{u}_t$ is independently normally distributed with mean $\mathbf{O}$ and variance-covariance matrix Σ. Equations (1) are called *structural equations*. Solving the endogenous variables, $\mathbf{y}$, as a function of the exogenous variables, $\mathbf{x}$, and the disturbance $\mathbf{u}$, we obtain

$$\mathbf{y}_t = -B^{-1}\Gamma\mathbf{x}_t + B^{-1}\mathbf{u}_t = \Pi\mathbf{x}_t + v_t, \tag{2}$$

with $E v_t = 0$, $E v_t v_t' = \mathbf{V} = B^{-1}\Sigma B^{-1'}$. Equations (2) are called the *reduced form* equations derived from (1) and give the conditional likelihood of $\mathbf{y}_t$ for given $\mathbf{x}_t$.

Premultiplying (1) by a $G \times G$ nonsingular matrix D, we get a second structural equation

$$B^*\mathbf{y}_t + \Gamma^*\mathbf{x}_t = \mathbf{u}_t^*, \tag{3}$$

where $B^* = DB$, $\Gamma^* = D\Gamma$, and $\mathbf{u}_t^* = D\mathbf{u}_t$. It can be readily seen that (3) has the same reduced form (2) as (1). Therefore, the two structures are observationally equivalent and the model is non-identifiable.

To make the model identifiable, additional prior restrictions have to be imposed on the matrices B, Γ and/or Σ. Consider the problem of estimating the parameters of the first equation in (1), out of a system of G equations. If the parameters cannot be estimated, the first equation is called *unidentified* or *underidentified*. If given the prior information, there is a unique way of estimating the unknown parameters, the equation is called *just identified*. If the prior information allows the parameters to be estimated in two or more linearly independent ways, it is called *overidentified*. A necessary condition for the first equation to be identified is the number of restrictions on this equation be no less than $G - 1$ (order condition). A necessary and sufficient condition is that a specified submatrix of B, Γ and Σ be of rank $G - 1$ (rank condition) (Fisher, 1966; Hausman and Taylor, 1983). For instance, suppose the restrictions on the first equation are in the form that certain variables do not appear. Then this rank condition says that the first equation is identified if and only if the submatrix obtained by taking the columns of B and Γ with prescribed zeros in the first row is of rank $G - 1$ (Koopmans and Reiersøl, 1950).

3.2 Dynamic models. When both lagged endogenous variables and serial correlation in the disturbance term appear, we need to impose additional conditions to identify a model. For instance, consider the following two-equation system (Koopmans, Rubin and Leipnik, 1950)

$$y_{1t} + \beta_{11}y_{1,t-1} + \beta_{12}y_{2,t-1} = u_{1t}, \qquad \beta_{21}y_{1t} + y_{2t} = u_{2t}. \tag{4}$$

If (u_{1t}, u_{2t}) are serially uncorrelated, (4) is identified. If serial correlation in (u_{1t}, u_{2t}) is allowed, then

$$y_{1t} + \beta_{11}^*y_{1,t-1} + \beta_{12}^*y_{2,t-1} = u_{1t}^*, \qquad \beta_{21}y_{1t} + y_{2t} = u_{2t}, \tag{5}$$

is observationally equivalent to (4), where $\beta_{11}^* = \beta_{11} + d\beta_{21}$, $\beta_{12}^* = \beta_{12} + d$, and $u_{1t}^* = u_{1t} + du_{2t}$.

Hannan (1971) derives generalized rank conditions for the identification of this type of model by first assuming that the maximum orders of lagged endogenous and exogenous variables are known, then imposing restrictions to eliminate redundancy in the specification and to exclude transformations of the equations that involve shifts in time. Hatanaka (1975), on the other hand, assumes that the prior information takes only the form of excluding certain variables from an equation, and derives a rank condition which allows common roots to appear in each equation.

3.3 Non-linear models. For linear models we have either global identification or else an infinite number of observationally equivalent structures. For models linear in the variables but nonlinear in the parameters the state of the mathematical art is such that we can only talk about local properties. That is, we cannot tell the true structure from any other substitute; however, we may be able to distinguish it from other structures which are close to it. A sufficient condition for local identification is that the Jacobian matrix formed by taking the first partial derivatives of

$$\omega_i = \boldsymbol{\Psi}_i(\boldsymbol{\theta}), \qquad i = 1,\ldots,n$$
$$0 = \phi_j(\boldsymbol{\theta}), \qquad j = 1,\ldots,R \qquad (6)$$

with respect to $\boldsymbol{\theta}$ be of full column rank (in the neighbourhood of true $\boldsymbol{\theta}$), where ω_i are the n population moments of $\mathbf{y}$ and ϕ_j are the R *a priori* restrictions on $\boldsymbol{\theta}$ (Fisher, 1966).

When the Jacobian matrix of (6) has less than full column rank and the rank of this matrix does not stay constant around θ, the model may still be locally identifiable via conditions implied by the higher order derivatives. However, the estimator of a model suffering from first order lack of identification will in finite samples behave in a way that is difficult to distinguish from the behaviour of an unidentified model (Sargan, 1983).

3.4 Bayesian analysis. In Bayesian analysis all quantities, including the parameters, are random variables. Thus, a model is said to be identified in probability if the posterior distribution for θ is proper. When the prior distribution for θ is proper, so is the posterior, regardless of the likelihood function of $\mathbf{y}$. In this sense unidentifiability causes no real difficulty in the Bayesian approach. However, basic to the Bayesian argument is that all probability statements are conditional. That is, it consists essentially in revising the probability of a fixed event in the light of various conditioning events, the revision being accomplished by Bayes' theorem. Therefore, in order for an experiment to be informative with regard to unknown parameters (i.e. the prior to be different from the posterior) the parameter must be identified or estimable in the classical sense and identification remains as a property of the likelihood function (Kadane, 1975).

Drèze (1975) has commented that exact restrictions are unlikely to hold with probability one and has suggested using probabilistic prior information. In order to incorporate a stochastic prior, he has derived necessary rank conditions for the identification of a linear simultaneous equation model.

4 CONCLUDING REMARKS

The study of identifiability is undertaken in order to explore the limitations of statistical inference (when working with economic data) or to specify what sort of a priori information is needed to make model parameters estimable. It is a fundamental problem concomitant with the existence of a structure. Logically it precedes all problems of estimation or of testing hypotheses.

An important point that arises in the study of identification is that without a priori restrictions imposed by economic theory it would be almost impossible to estimate economic relationships. In fact, Liu (1960) and Sims (1980) have argued that economic relations are not identifiable because the world is so interdependent as to have almost all variables appearing in every equation, thus violating the necessary condition for identification. However, almost all the models we discuss in econometrics are only approximate. We use convenient formulations which behave in a general way that corresponds to our economic theories and intuitions, and which cannot be rejected by the available data. In this sense, identification is a property of the model but not necessarily of the real world.

The problem of identification arises in a number of different fields such as automatic control, biomedical engineering, psychology, systems science, etc., where the underlying physical structure may be deterministic (e.g. see Aström and Eykhoff, 1971). It is also aptly linked to the design of experiments (e.g. Kempthorne, 1947; Bailey, Gilchrist and Patterson, 1977). Here, we restrict our discussion to economic applications of statistical identifiability involving random variables.

BIBLIOGRAPHY

Aström, K.J. and Eykhoff, P. 1971. System identification – a survey. *Automatica* 7, 123–62.

Bailey, R.A., Gilchrist, F.H.L. and Patterson, H.D. 1977. Identification of effects and confounding patterns in factorial designs. *Biometrika* 64, 347–54.

Deistler, M. and Seifert, H. 1978. Identifiability and consistent estimability in econometric models. *Econometrica* 46, 969–80.

Drèze, J. 1975. Bayesian theory of identification in simultaneous equations models. In *Studies in Bayesian Econometrics and Statistics*, ed. S.E. Fienberg and A. Zellner, Amsterdam: North-Holland.

Fisher, F.M. 1966. *The Identification Problem in Econometrics*. New York: McGraw-Hill.

Frisch, R. 1934. *Statistical Confluence Analysis by Means of Complete Regression Systems*. Publication No. 5, Oslo: Universitets Økonomiske Institutt.

Gabrielson, A. 1978. Consistency and identifiability. *Journal of Econometrics* 8, 261–83.

Haavelmo, T. 1944. The probability approach in econometrics. *Econometrica* 12, Supplement, 1–115.

Hannan, E.J. 1971. The identification problem for multiple equation systems with moving average errors. *Econometrica* 39, 751–65.

Hatanaka, M. 1975. On the global identification of the dynamic simultaneous equations model with stationary disturbances. *International Economic Review* 16, 545–54.

Hausman, J.A. and Taylor, W.E. 1983. Identification, estimation and testing in simultaneous equations models with disturbance covariance restrictions. *Econometrica* 51, 1527–49.

Hsiao, C. 1983. Identification. In *Handbook of Econometrics*, Vol. I, ed. Z. Griliches and M. Intriligator, Amsterdam: North-Holland.

Hurwicz, L. 1950. Generalization of the concept of identification. In *Statistical Inference in Dynamic Economic Models*, Cowles Commission Monograph no. 10, New York: John Wiley.

Kadane, J.B. 1975. The role of identification in Bayesian theory. In *Studies in Bayesian Econometrics and Statistics*, ed. S.E. Fienberg and A. Zellner, Amsterdam: North-Holland.

Kempthorne, O. 1947. A simple approach to confounding and factorial replication in factorial experiments. *Biometrika* 34, 255–72.

Koopmans, T.C. and Reiersøl, O. 1950. The identification of structural characteristics. *Annals of Mathematical Statistics* 21, 165–81.

Koopmans, T.C., Rubin, H. and Leipnik, R.B. 1950. Measuring the equation systems of dynamic economics. In *Statistical Inference in Dynamic Economic Models*, Cowles Commission Monograph No. 10, New York: John Wiley.

Le Cam, L. 1956. On the asymptotic theory of estimation and testing hypotheses. In *Proceedings of the Third Berkeley Symposium on Mathematical Statistics and Probability*, Vol. 1, Berkeley: University of California Press.

Liu, T.C. 1960. Underidentification, structural estimation, and forecasting. *Econometrica* 28, 855–65.

Marschak, J. 1942. Economic interdependence and statistical analysis. In *Studies in Mathematical Economics and Econometrics*, Chicago: University of Chicago Press, 135–50.

Rao, C.R. 1962. Problems of selection with restriction. *Journal of the Royal Statistical Society*, Series B 24, 401–5.

Rothenberg, T.J. 1971. Identification in parametric models. *Econometrica* 39, 577–92.

Sargan, J.D. 1983. Identification and lack of identification. *Econometrica* 51, 1605–33.

Sims, C.A. 1980. Macroeconomics and reality. *Econometrica* 48, 1–48.

Wald, A. 1950. Note on the identification of economic relations. In *Statistical Inference in Dynamic Economic Models*, Cowles Commission Monograph No. 10, New York: John Wiley.

Working, E.J. 1925. The statistical determination of demand curves. *Quarterly Journal of Economics* 39, 503–43.

Working, E.J. 1927. What do statistical 'demand curves' show? *Quarterly Journal of Economics* 41, 212–35.

Information Theory

ESFANDIAR MAASOUMI

Information theory is a branch of mathematical statistics and probability theory. Thus, it can and has been applied in many fields, including economics, that rely on statistical analysis. As we are concerned with it, the technical concept of 'information' must be distinguished from the semantic concept in common parlance. The simplest and still the most widely used technical definitions of information were first introduced (independently) by Shannon and Wiener in 1948 in connection with communication theory. Though decisively and directly related, these definitions must also be distinguished from the definition of 'information' introduced by R.A. Fisher in 1925 for estimation theory.

Whenever observations are made or experiments conducted, we seek information about the underlying populations. Information theory provides concepts and definitions by means of which we may measure formally what can be inferred from the sampled data. More narrowly interpreted, we may view these concepts and definitions as summary statistics representing the associated (empirical) distributions, much like the moments of distributions. These concepts, however, also admit the intuitive meanings not unlike the notions of 'information' and 'uncertainty' in common parlance. One such concept, the *entropy* of a distribution is central to information theory and is a measure of disorder or uncertainty. It was the definition of entropy that first caught the attention of Henri Theil and led to the use of information theory in *economics* in the 1960s. Following this discovery two measures of income inequality, measures of divergence and/or concentration in trade and industry, and many other economic applications were introduced in Theil (1967). Further applications in economic theory and other social sciences are discussed in Theil (1972, 1980).

A somewhat different but equally important set of developments of information theory have taken place in *econometrics*. Information criteria exist which measure the 'divergence' between populations. The use of such criteria helps to discriminate statistically between hypotheses, select models and evaluate their forecasting performance. These are essential steps in model evaluation and inference in econometrics.

Given a sample and (possibly) some prior information, a so-called 'maximum entropy (ME)' distribution of the underlying continuous process may be derived. This distribution and its quantiles and moments can be used in order to resolve a number of important problems including that of undersized samples. Theil and Laitinen (1980) formulated the ME distribution, and Theil and Fiebig (1984), give a complete coverage of this topic.

More general concepts of entropy and the associated measures of divergence can be used to develop a family of Generalized Entropy (GE) measures of inequality and in the area of 'multidimensional' welfare analysis. A by-product of this is the development of a 'summary welfare attribute' which serves as an index of several miscellaneous attributes such as income, wealth, and physical quality of life indices. Another by-product is the development of 'information efficient' functional forms when the regression function is unkown *a priori*.

Applications to the classical theory of consumer and producer demand equations is noteworthy. The feature of this theory that provides the connection with information theory is the concept of 'value shares', the expenditure on a given commodity (input factor) divided by total expenditure. Thus the value shares have the same mathematical properties as probabilities ($0 \leqslant p_i \leqslant 1$). Theil (1967) noted some of the first attempts by Lisman (1949) and Pikler (1951) to draw analogies between econometric and information theory concepts. Emphasizing a point elaborated upon by De Jongh (1952), Theil wrote: 'the reason information theory is nevertheless important in economics is that it is more than a theory dealing with information concepts. It is actually a general partitioning theory in the sense that it presents measures for the way in which some set is divided into subsets....' And then, 'it may amount to dividing certainty (probability 1) into various possibilities none of which is certain, but it may also be an allocation problem in economics.'

Our account begins with the introduction of some basic concepts.

1 CENTRAL DEFINITIONS AND CONCEPTS

An extensive literature exists which treats information theory in an axiomatic manner, much of it stimulated by the work of Shannon (1948) and Wiener's suggestive remarks in Wiener (1948). Kullback (1959) provides a comprehensive bibliography. From Stumpers (1953) it is clear, however, that some important contributions had appeared prior to 1948. For our purposes it will suffice to note that the occurrence of an event contains (or conveys) information. Thus one needs 'information functions' that measure the amount of information conveyed. If, as is usual, we are concerned with random events, there usually exist prior probabilities of occurrence of events and posterior probabilities. Hence, given an information function, we may measure the 'information gain' as between the prior and the posterior probabilities. Further, given an experiment and a *set* of observations, we may measure the 'expected information gain'.

The most widely used information function is $-\log p_i$, where p_i denotes the probability of a random variable X taking a value x_i. This function is non-negative and satisfies the 'additivity axiom' for *independent events*. That is, the information that both of two independent events have occurred is equal to the sum of the information in the occurrence of each of the events. More general information functions will be discussed later. The base of the logarithm (usually e or 2) determines the desired 'information unit', 'bits' when 2 is the base, and 'nits' when the natural base is employed. It may be useful to list some of the axioms that are employed to restrict the form of information functions:

Let such functions be denoted by $h(\cdot)$.

Axiom $1 - h(\cdot)$ is a function only of the probability of events (p, say).

Axiom $2 - h(p)$ is continuous in $p, 0 < p \leqslant 1$.

Axiom $3 - h(p)$ is a monotonically decreasing function of p.

This last axiom is quite intuitive. For instance, when we receive a definite message (observation) that a most unlikely event (p close to zero) has occurred, we are more highly surprised (informed) than if the event had a high probability (p close to 1) of occurrence. Thus, we may impose the following restrictions:

$$h(0) = \infty, \quad h(1) = 0 \quad \text{and} \quad h(p_1) > h(p_2), \quad \text{if } 0 \leqslant p_1 < p_2 \leqslant 1.$$

There are many functions that satisfy these axioms. $\log 1/p = -\log p$ is uniquely identified (apart from its base) on the basis of a further axiom, the *additivity of* $h(\cdot)$ in the case of independent events.

A generalization of the above definition is needed for general situations in which the messages received are not completely reliable. An important example is the case of forecasts of weather or economic conditions. Suppose p_1 is the probability of occurrence of an event (perhaps calculated on the basis of frequency of occurrence in the past), and p_2 the probability of the same event *given that it had been predicted to occur* (calculated in the same manner). We may then enquire as to the merit or the 'information gain' of such predictions. Given the observation that the predicted event has occurred, this information gain is defined as follows:

$$h(p_1) - h(p_2) = \log p_2/p_1.$$

More generally, the information content of data which may be used to 'update' prior probabilities is defined by:

Information gain (IG) = log (posterior probability/prior probability). Since typically, data are subject to sampling variability, the 'expected information gain' is the appropriate measure of information gain. Thus, the expected value of IG defined above may be obtained with respect to either the prior or the posterior distributions over the range of the possible values for the random event. This gain is the difference between the 'expected information' in the two distributions. Consider a set of n mutually exclusive and exhaustive events $E_1, \ldots, E_n$ with corresponding probabilities $p_1, \ldots, p_n$ ($\Sigma p_n = 1, p_i \geqslant 0$). Then occurrence of an event contains $h(p_i)$ information with probability p_i. *Before* any observation is made, the 'expected information' in the distribution $p = (p_1, \ldots, p_n)$ is given by:

$$0 \leqslant \sum_{i=1}^{n} p_i h(p_i) = H(p) \leqslant \log n. \tag{1}$$

When $h(p_i) = -\log p_i$, the convention: $p_i \log p_i = 0$ if $p_i = 0$, is used. The maximum, $\log n$, occurs when $p_i = 1/n$ for all $i = 1, \ldots, n$. This is a situation of maximum prior 'uncertainty' or 'disorder' in the distribution p. Contrast this with $p_1 = 1, p_i = 0 \forall i \neq 1$, in which case $H(p) = 0$.

A dual concept to 'expected information' may be defined. This is the 'Entropy' which measures the 'uncertainty' or 'disorder' in a distribution p as defined by $H(p)$ in equation (1). Entropy is a central concept in information theory and its applications. It is also considered as an index of how close a distribution is to the uniform distribution. Note that an otherwise unknown distribution (p) may be determined by maximizing its entropy subject to any available restrictions. For instance the first few moments of the distribution may be specified *a priori*. The distribution so obtained is called the 'Maximum Entropy' (ME) distribution. In Theil and Laitinen (1980), *continuity* as well as the first moment of the observed data are utilized in order to obtain the ME distribution of the data and its higher moments.

The concept of 'divergence' or 'distance' between distributions naturally follows those of expected information gain and entropy. Instead of the prior and posterior distributions referred to earlier, it may be more suggestive to consider competing distributions (perhaps resulting from competing hypotheses), $f(x)$ and $g(x)$, which may generate a random variable x with the range denoted by R. There are two *directional* measures of divergence between $f(\cdot)$ and $g(\cdot)$. These are:

$$I(2, 1) = \int_R g(x) \log \frac{g(x)}{f(x)} \, dx$$

and

$$I(1, 2) = \int_R f(x) \log \frac{f(x)}{g(x)} \, dx.$$

A *non-directional* measure in the same context may be an average of the two directional criteria given above. For instance:

$$J(1, 2) = \int_R [\log f(x) - \log g(x)][f(x) - g(x)] \, dx = I(1, 2) + I(2, 1).$$

This is the well known Kullback–Leibler information criterion used extensively in many applications.

Various generalizations of these criteria are obtained either by generalizations of the form of the information function (which typically include the logarithmic form as a special case), or by generalizations of the *metrics* that include $J(1, 2)$ above.

Some properties of these central concepts and their generalizations will be discussed in the following sections. It will be illuminating, however, to close this section by demonstrating an interesting connection between the information concepts defined so far and an important definition given by R.A. Fisher (1925):

Let x be a random variable taking values in the space S with the p.d.f. $f(\cdot, \theta)$ with respect to a σ-finite measure v. Assume $f(\cdot, \theta)$ differentiable w.r.t. θ and:

$$\frac{d}{d\Theta} \int_c f(x, \Theta) dv = \int_c \frac{df(x, \Theta)}{d\Theta} dv$$

for any measurable set $c \in S$. Fisher defined the following measure of information on Θ contained in x:

$$\phi(\Theta) = E\left(\frac{d \log f}{d\Theta}\right)^2 = V\left(\frac{d \log f}{d\Theta}\right)$$

where V denotes the variance when $E(d \log f / d\Theta) = 0$.

If there is a unique observation (of x) with probability 1 corresponding to *each value of* Θ, then the random variable (i.e. its distribution) has the maximum information. The least information exists if the random variable has the *same distribution* for all Θ. Thus, one might measure the sensitiveness of x with respect to Θ by the extent to which its distribution changes in response to (infinitesimal) changes in Θ. If Θ and $\Theta' = \Theta + \delta\Theta$ are two values of Θ, a suitable measure of 'distance' or 'divergence', $D[f(\Theta), f(\Theta')]$, is required. An example of $D[\cdot]$ was given earlier, and many more criteria have been proposed. It may be shown that many such criteria are *increasing* functions of Fisher's information $[\phi(\Theta) \geqslant 0]$. To give an example, consider the Hellinger distance:

$$\cos^{-1} \int [f(x, \Theta) \cdot f(x, \Theta')]^{1/2} dv.$$

Using a Taylor expansion of $f(x, \Theta')$ and neglecting terms of power 3 or more in $\delta\Theta$, we find:

$$\cos^{-1} \int f(\Theta) \left\{ 1 - \frac{1}{8} \left[\frac{f'(\Theta)}{f(\Theta)} \right]^2 (\delta\Theta)^2 \right\} dv = \cos^{-1} [1 - \tfrac{1}{8}\phi(\Theta)(\delta\Theta)^2],$$

where $\phi(\Theta)$ is indeed Fisher's information. Thus, such divergence criteria and $\phi(\Theta)$ are equivalent measures of the sensitivity of the random variables (p.d.f., s) with respect to small changes in the parameter values. These observations provide a basis for measuring the distance between competing hypotheses (on Θ) and model selection techniques in econometrics.

2 APPLICATIONS IN ECONOMICS AND ECONOMETRICS

2.1 Measurement of economic inequality. Theil (1967) observed that the entropy, $H(y)$, was a remarkably useful measure of 'equality'. If $y = (y_1, \ldots, y_N)$ denotes the non-negative income *shares* of N individuals, the entropy of y, by definition, measures its distance from the rectangular distribution, $y_i = 1/N$, which is the case of complete equality. Thus, the difference between $H(y)$ and its maximum value, $\log N$, may be used as a measure of *inequality*. This measure satisfies the 'three fundamental welfare requirements', namely symmetry (S), Homogeneity (H), and the Pigou–Dalton principle of transfers (PT). In addition, Theil (1967) demonstrated extremely useful *additive decomposability* properties of this measure. In recent axiomatic treatments by Bourguignon (1979), Shorrocks (1980), Cowell and Kuga (1981) and Foster (1983), the following question is posed: what is a suitable measure of inequality among general classes of functional forms which are restricted to satisfy the above three requirements in addition to Theil's decomposability? The last condition identifies Theil's first measure, $T1 = \log N - H(y)$, and a second information measure proposed in Theil (1967). The latter is defined as follows:

$$T2 = -\log N - \frac{1}{N} \sum \log y_i.$$

The choice between these two measures implies preferences that may be formulated by Social Welfare Functions (SWF). From a practical viewpoint, however, the choice between T1 and T2 may also be made on the basis of their decomposability properties. These may be briefly described as follows:

Let there be G exclusive sets (groups) of individuals, $S_1, \ldots, S_G$, with N_g denoting the number of individuals in S_g, $g = 1, \ldots, G$ ($\Sigma N_g = N$). Let y_g be the *share* of S_g in total income. Then we have:

$$T1(y) = \sum_{g=1}^{g} y_g \log \frac{y_g}{N_g/N} + \sum_g y_g [\log N_g - H_g(y)].$$

Here, $H_g(y)$ denotes the entropy of group g calculated from (y_i/y_g) for all $i \in S_g$. The first term above is the 'between-group' inequality, and the second term is a weighted average of the 'within-group' inequalities (the term in the square brackets). This decomposition is essential in analysing the incidence of inequality amongst the population subgroups (e.g. defined by age, race, region, etc.)

A similar decomposition formula holds for the second measure T2. The major difference is that the 'within-group' inequalities in T2 are weighted by the groups' *population shares* (N_g/N) rather than their income shares (y_g). The decomposition for T2 is somewhat preferable to that for T1 (see Shorrocks, 1980) as it permits a less ambiguous discussion of such questions as: what is the contribution of the inequality in the gth group to total inequality? This is partly because y_g are sensitive to redistributions (distributional changes) whereas population shares (N_g/N) are not so by design.

A generalization of the concept of information functions and the entropy has been employed by Toyoda, Cowell and Kuga to define the family of Generalized Entropy (GE) inequality indices. The GE is defined as follows:

$$\mu_\gamma(y) = \frac{1}{N} \sum_i [(Ny_i)^{1+\gamma} - 1]/\gamma(\gamma + 1),$$

where $\mu_0(\cdot)$ and $\mu_{-1}(\ )$ are, respectively, the T1 and T2 defined earlier. $\gamma \leqslant 0$ ensures the convexity of GE members, and for values of $\gamma \ll 0$ the GE is ordinally equivalent to the class of measures proposed earlier by Atkinson (1970) by direct reference to the SWFs. $-\gamma = v \geqslant 0$ is referred to as the 'degree of inequality aversion' exhibited by the underlying SWF. The information function underlying the GE indices is $-1/\gamma(y_i^\gamma - 1)$ which includes $-\log y_i$ as a special case. The generalized entropy corresponding to this function is given by:

$$H_\gamma(y) = \sum_i \frac{1}{\gamma(\gamma+1)}[(Ny_i)^\gamma - 1] \cdot y_i.$$

The GE measures are also decomposable in the manner described above.

2.2 Multi-dimensional welfare analysis. The recognition that welfare depends on more than any single attribute (e.g. income) has led to analyses of welfare functions and inequality in the multi-dimensioned space of several attributes, such as incomes (and its factor components), wealth, quality of life and basic needs indices. Pioneering work that deals directly with individual utilities (as functions of these attributes) and Social Welfare Functions is primarily due to Kolm (1977) and Atkinson and Bourguignon (1982). The measurement approach due to Maasoumi (1986a) poses the same question statistically and, surprisingly provides a pure measurement (index number) interpretation of the SWF approach with equivalent solutions. The measurement approach seeks a 'summary share' or an index which may be employed to represent the miscellaneous attributes of interest. Information theory is utilized to obtain 'summary share' distributions without explicitly imposing any restrictive structure on preferences and behaviour. Noting that a measure of inequality is a summary statistic for a distribution (much as the moments of a p.d.f.). Maasoumi (1986a) poses the following question: Which summary distribution (index) is the 'closest' to the distribution of the welfare attributes of interest? Given suitable information criteria for measuring the 'distance' between distributions, one can find a summary (or representative) *share vector* (distribution) that minimizes this distance. Briefly: let y_{if} be the share of the ith individual, $i \in [1, N]$, from the fth attribute, $f \in [1, M]$. There are M distributions, $y_f = (y_{1f}, \ldots, y_{Nf})$, and we seek a distribution, $S = (S_1, \ldots, S_N)$, which is closest to these M distributions as measured by the following generalized information measure of divergence:

$$D(\gamma) = \frac{1}{\gamma(\gamma+1)} \sum_{f=1}^M \alpha_f \sum_{i=1}^N S_i[(S_i/y_{if})^\gamma - 1],$$

where α_f is the weight given to the fth attribute. Minimizing $D(\gamma)$ with respect to S_i subject to $\Sigma S_i = 1$, we find:

$$S_i \propto \left(\sum_f \delta_f y_{if}^{-1} \right)^{-1/\gamma}, \qquad \sum_f \delta_f = 1.$$

This is a functional of the CES variety which includes the Cobb–Douglas ($\gamma = 0$)

and the linear ($\gamma = -1$) forms as special cases. The S_i may be regarded as individual utility functions with the optimal distributional characteristics implied from $D(\gamma)$.

Once $S = (S_1, \ldots, S_N)$ is so determined, any of the existing measures of inequality may be used to measure multivariate inequality represented in S. Members of GE have been used for this purpose in Maasoumi (1986a). It may be shown that only two members of GE, Theil's T1 and T2, and some values of γ, provide fully decomposable measures of multi-dimensional inequality. Full decomposition refers to decomposition by population subgroups as well as by the inequality in individual welfare attributes. An interesting alternative method, Principal Components, is seen to be a special case of the above approach. It corresponds to the case $\gamma = -1$, with α_f being the elements of the first characteristic vector of $y'y$, $y = (y_{if})$ being the distribution matrix. This feature of information theory is not surprising. As S. Kullback and others have noted, one of its great advantages is the generality that it affords in the analysis of statistical issues, with the suggestion of new solutions and useful interpretations of the old.

2.3 'Information efficient' functional forms. Economic theory is generally silent on the specific form of functional relationships between variables of interest. Certain restrictions on the general characteristics of such relations are typically available, but ideally one must use the available data to determine the appropriate functional form as well as its parameters. The common practice in econometrics is either to specify flexible functional families, or to test specific functional forms for statistical adequacy (e.g. see Judge et al., 1980, ch. 11). The criteria of section 2.2 may be used, however, to obtain functions of the data with distributions which most closely resemble the empirical distribution of the observations. For instance, using $D(\gamma)$ from the previous section, let $S_i = f(x_i)$ be the indeterminate functional relationship between the variables $x_i = (x_{1i}, \ldots, x_{ki})$ at each observation point $i = 1, \ldots, T$. The variable set x_i may or may not include the endogenous (dependent) variable in an explicit regression context. Maasoumi (1986b) shows that, in the latter case, the CES functional form is 'ideal' according to $D(\gamma)$, and in the former the usual Box–Cox transformation is obtained. According to $D(\gamma)$, any other functional forms will distort the distributional information in the sample. The value of $D(\gamma)$ for any approximate regression functions, less its minimum, is an interesting measure of the informational inefficiency of that regression function.

2.4 Tests of hypotheses and model selection. Sample estimates of the measures of divergence $I(1, 2)$, $I(2, 1)$ and $J(1, 2)$ defined above may be used to test hypotheses or to choose the 'best' models. For instance, the minimum value of $I(1, 2)$, denoted by $I(*:2)$ and called 'the minimum discrimination information', is obtained for a given distribution $f_2(x)$ with respect to all $f_1(x)$, such that

$$\int T(x) f_1(x) \mathrm{d}x = \boldsymbol{\Theta},$$

where Θ are constants and $T(x)$ are measurable statistics. For example, $T(x) = x$ and $\Theta = \mu$, restricts the mean of possible distributions $f_1(x)$. General solutions for $f_1(x)$ [denoted $f^*(x)$] and $I(*:2)$ are given in Kullback (1959, ch. 3) and elsewhere.

$I(*:2)$, and the corresponding values for $I(1:*)$ and $J(*)$, may be estimated by replacing Θ (and the other unknown parameters) by their sample estimates ($\hat{\Theta}$) when $f_2(x)$ is the generalized density of n independent observations. Given a sample 0_n, we denote this estimate by $\hat{I}(*:2;0_n)$. This statistic measures the minimum discrimination information between a population with density $f^*(x)$ (with $\Theta = \hat{\Theta}$ etc.), and the population with the density $f_2(x)$. The justification for its use in tests of hypotheses and model selection is that the non-negative statistic $\hat{I}(\cdot)$ is zero when $\hat{\Theta}$ is equal to Θ of the population with density $f_2(x)$, becoming larger the worse is the resemblance between the sample and the hypothesized population $f_2(x)$.

To illustrate, consider the linear regression model

$$y = X\beta + u,$$

where $U \sim N(0, \Sigma)$ and $X \sim T \times K$ and of rank K.

Consider two competing hypotheses:

$$H_1: \beta = \beta \text{ (no restriction)}, \qquad H_2: \beta = \beta^2.$$

Then, it may be verified that:

$$J(1, 2) = 2I(1, 2) = (X\beta - X\beta^2)' \Sigma^{-1} (X\beta - X\beta^2)$$

$$= \frac{1}{\sigma^2}(X\beta - X\beta^2)'(X\beta - X\beta^2), \qquad \text{if } \Sigma = \sigma^2 I$$

$$= (\beta - \beta^2)'(X'X)(\beta - \beta^2)/\sigma^2.$$

Replacing the unknown parameters, $\Theta = (\beta, \sigma^2)$, with their respective unbiased OLS estimates, we find:

$$\hat{J}(H_1; H_2) = (\hat{\beta} - \beta^2)'(X'X)(\hat{\beta} - \beta^2)/\hat{\sigma}^2.$$

And if $\beta^2 = 0$:

$$\hat{J}(H_1, H_2) = \hat{\beta}'(X'X)\hat{\beta}/\hat{\sigma}^2$$

which may be recognized as proportional to Hotelling's T^2 statistic with an F distribution with K and $T - K$ degrees of freedom.

The above example produced a statistic with a known finite sample distribution. In this situation, we are in effect rejecting H_2 if:

$$\text{Prob}\{\hat{I}(*:H_2) - \hat{I}(*H_1) \geqslant C | H_2\} \leqslant \alpha,$$

where C is chosen to control the size (α) and the power of the test.

More generally, when the exact distributions are not known, asymptotic procedures may be employed. Suppose, for instance, that the competing populations (hypotheses), H, are members of the exponential family (which includes $f^*(x)$). Let the admissible range of parameter values be denoted by Ω, and the range (value) specified by $H_i \in H$ denoted by ω_i. It may be shown that (see Kullback, 1959):

$$\hat{I}(*:H) = \log\left[\max_\Omega f^*(x) \bigg/ \max_{\omega_i} f^*(x) \right] = -\log \lambda_i,$$

where λ_i is the Neyman–Pearson (likelihood-ratio) statistic. Under certain regularity conditions, the statistic $-2 \log \lambda_i$ is asymptotically distributed as X^2. Also, in the same situation, for two competing hypotheses $H_1 : \Theta \in \omega_1, H_2 : \Theta \in \omega_2$ it may be shown that:

$$\hat{I}(*:H_2) - \hat{I}(*:H_1) = -\log \lambda*,$$

where $\lambda* = \max_{\Theta \in \omega_2} f^*(x)/\max_{\Theta \in \omega_1} f^*(x)$. Variants of such statistics are also useful for tests of 'non-tested' hypotheses. For the distribution of $\lambda*$ and its extensions see (e.g.) Chernoff (1954) and Cox (1961). Finally, we note that the above test reduces to $\hat{I}(*:H_2)$ when $H_2 : \Theta \in \omega$ and $H_1 : \Theta \in \Omega - \omega$. In such cases $\hat{I}(*:H_1) = 0$.

Variations to the information criteria described above have been proposed for 'model selection' in econometrics. Akaike (1973) proposed a measure based on the Kullback–Leibler criterion. We give this criterion (AIC) for the problem of choosing an optimal set of regressors in the standard regression model. As before, let $y = X\beta + U, U \sim N(0, \sigma_u^2 I)$, be the 'comprehensive' model, with $X = [X_1, X_2]$ and $\beta = (\beta_1', \beta_2')'$ representing a full rank partition $K_1 + K_2 = K$. Under the null hypothesis $R\beta = [0, I_{K_2}]\beta = 0(\beta_2 = 0)$, the AIC is as follows:

$$\text{AIC} = -\frac{2}{T}\log l(y, \beta_1) + 2K_1/T = \log(y'M_1 y/T) + 2K_1/T,$$

where $l(\ )$ is the likelihood function and $M_1 = I - X_1(X_1'X_1)^{-1}X_1'$. One proceeds to choose K_1 (and hence M_1) so as to minimize AIC. The first term decreases with K_1, thus the above criterion incorporates the trade-off between parsimony and 'fit' of a model. If one proceeds as though σ^2 were known in the likelihood function. Amemiya (1976) shows that:

$$\text{AIC} \ (\sigma^2 \text{ known}) = y'M_1 y/T + \sigma^2(2K_1)/T.$$

An estimate of this last criterion may be based on the unbiased OLS estimates of σ^2 with or without the restrictions ($\beta_2 = 0$). The latter estimate is equivalent to the so-called 'Cp criterion', and the former is equivalent to the 'Prediction Criterion' for model selection. For other variations to AIC (e.g. Sawa's BIC criterion) see Judge et al. (1980, Section 11.5).

CONCLUSIONS

The above examples do not do justice to a remarkable range of currently available applications in the information criteria in economics and econometric inferences. We hope, however, that they suffice to show: (1) the usefulness of the general approach in encompassing many different and often ad hoc procedures in econometric inference; and (2) how new methods with plausible and intuitive appeal may be derived in order to resolve many hitherto unresolved problems. The full potential for further applications of information theory and its formal discipline in economic and econometric theory is great. The current level of interest in this potential is extremely promising.

BIBLIOGRAPHY

Akaike, H. 1973. Information theory and the extension of the maximum likelihood principle. In *International Symposium on Information Theory*, ed. B.N. Petrov and F. Csaki, Budapest: Akadémiaikiado.

Amemiya, T. 1976. Selection of regressors. Technical Report No. 225, Stanford: Stanford University.

Atkinson, A.B. 1970. On the measurement of inequality. *Journal of Economic Theory* 2, 244–63.

Atkinson, A.B. and Bourguignon, F. 1982. The comparison of multi-dimensional distributions of economic status. *Review of Economic Studies* 49, 183–201.

Bourguignon, F. 1979. Decomposable income inequality measures. *Econometrica* 47, 901–20.

Chernoff, H. 1954. On the distribution of the likelihood ratio. *Annals of Mathematical Statistics* 25, 573–8.

Cowell, F.A. and Kuga, K. 1981. Inequality measurement: an axiomatic approach. *European Economic Review* 13, 147–59.

Cox, D.R. 1961. Test of separate families of hypotheses. In *Proceedings of the Fourth Berkeley Symposium on Mathematical Statistics and Probability*, Vol. 1, Berkeley: University of California Press.

De Jongh, B.H. 1952. *Egalisation, Disparity and Entropy.* Utrecht: A.W. Bruna en Zoons-Uitgevers Maatschapij.

Fisher, R.A. 1925. *Statistical Methods for Research Workers.* London: Oliver & Boyd.

Foster, J.E. 1983. An axiomatic characterization of the Theil measure of income inequality. *Journal of Economic Theory* 31(1), October, 105–21.

Judge, G.G., Griffiths, W.W., Hill, R.C. and Lee, T.C. 1980. *The Theory and Practice of Econometrics.* New York: Wiley.

Kolm, S.-Ch. 1977. Multi-dimensional egalitarianism. *Quarterly Journal of Economics* 91, 1–13.

Kullback, S. 1959. *Information Theory and Statistics.* New York: Wiley.

Lisman, J.H.C. 1949. Econometrics and thermodynamics: a remark on Davis' theory of budgets. *Econometrica* 17, 59–62.

Maasoumi, E. 1986a. The measurement and decomposition of multi-dimensional inequality. *Econometrica* 54(5), September.

Maasoumi, E. 1986b. Unknown regression functions and information efficient functional forms: an interpretation. In *Innovations in Quantitative Economics*, ed. D. Slottje, Greenwich, Conn.: JAI Press.

Pikler, A. 1951. Optimum allocation in econometrics and physics. *Weltwirtschaftliches Archiv* 66, 97–132.

Shannon, C.E. 1948. A mathematical theory of communication. *Bell System Technical Journal* 27, 379–423, 623–56.

111

Shorrocks, A.F. 1980. The class of additively decomposable inequality measures. *Econometrica* 48, 613–25.

Stumpers, F.L.H.M. 1953. A bibliography of information theory; communication theory–cybernetics. *IRE Transactions*, PGIT-2.

Theil, H. 1967. *Economics and Information Theory*. Amsterdam: North-Holland.

Theil, H. 1972. *Statistical Decomposition Analysis With Applications in the Social and Administrative Sciences*. Amsterdam: North-Holland.

Theil, H. 1980. The increased use of statistical concepts in economic analysis. In *Developments in Statistics*, Vol. 3, ed. P.R. Krishnaiah, New York: Academic Press.

Theil, H. and Fiebig, D. 1984. *Exploiting Continuity: Maximum Entropy Estimation of Continuous Distributions*. Cambridge, Mass: Ballinger.

Theil, H. and Laitinen, K. 1980. Singular moment matrices in applied econometrics. In *Multivariate Analysis V*, ed. P.R. Krishnaiah, Amsterdam: North-Holland.

Wiener, N. 1948. *Cybernetics*. New York: John Wiley.

Instrumental Variables

CHARLES E. BATES

In one of its simplest formulations the problem of estimating the parameters of a system of simultaneous equations with unknown random errors reduces to finding a way of estimating the parameters of a single linear equation of the form $Y = X\beta_0 + \varepsilon$, where β_0 is unknown, Y and X are vectors of data on relevant economic variables and ε is the vector of unknown random errors. The most common method of estimating β_0 is the method of least squares: $\hat{\beta}_{OLS} \equiv$ argmin $\varepsilon(\beta)' \varepsilon(\beta)$, where $\varepsilon(\beta) \equiv Y - X\beta$. Under fairly general assumptions $\hat{\beta}_{OLS}$ is an unbiased estimator of β_0 provided $E(\varepsilon_t | X) = 0$ for all t, where ε_t is the tth-coordinate of ε.

Unfortunately for the empirical economist, it is often the case that the basic orthogonality condition between the errors and the explanatory variables is not satisfied by economic models, due to correlation between the errors and the explanatory variables. Particularly relevant examples of this situation include (1) any case where the data contain errors introduced by the process of collection (errors in variables problem); (2) the inclusion of a dependent variable of one equation in a system of simultaneous equations as an explanatory variable in another equation in the system (simultaneous equations bias); and (3) the inclusion of a lagged dependent variable as an explanatory variable in the presence of serial correlation. For all of these cases,

$$E(\hat{\beta}_{OLS}) = E[(X'X)^{-1}X'Y] = \beta_0 + E\left[(X'X)^{-1} \sum_{t=1}^{n} X_t' E(\varepsilon_t | X) \right] \neq \beta_0$$

in general, and the bias introduced cannot be determined because the errors ε are unknown. Furthermore, in every case the bias fails to go to zero as the sample size increases. Clearly the method of least squares is unsatisfactory for many situations of relevance to economists.

In 1925 the US Department of Agriculture published a study by the zoologist Sewall Wright where the parameters of a system of six equations in thirteen

113

unknown variables were estimated using a method he referred to as 'path analysis'. In essence his approach exploited zero correlations between variables within his system of equations to construct a sufficient number of equations to estimate the unknown parameters. The idea which underlies this approach is that if two variables are uncorrelated, then the average of the product of repeated observations of these variables will approach zero as the number of observations is increased without bound except for a negligible number of times. Thus if we know that a variable of the system Z_i is uncorrelated with the errors of ε, we can exploit the fact that $n^{-1}\Sigma_{t=1}^n Z_{ti}\varepsilon_t \equiv n^{-1}\Sigma_{t=1}^n Z_{ti}(Y_t - X_t\beta_0)$ approaches zero to construct a useful relationship between parameters of the system by setting such averages equal to zero. Provided a sufficient number of such relationships can be constructed which are independent, this provides a method for estimating the parameters of a system of simultaneous equations which should become more accurate as the number of observations increases.

Since the 1940s, when Reiersøl (1941, 1945) and Geary (1949) presented the formal development of this procedure, the variables Z which are instrumental in the estimation of the parameters β_0 have been called 'instrumental variables'. Associated with each instrumental variable Z_i is an equation formed as described in the previous paragraph, called a normal equation, which can be used to form the estimates of the unknown parameters. Frequently there are more instrumental variables than parameters to be estimated. As the equations are formed from relationships between random variables, generally no solution will exist to a system of estimating equations formed in this manner using all possible instrumental variables. As each estimating equation contains relevant information about the parameters to be estimated, it is undesirable just to ignore some of them. Thus we can define a fundamental problem in the application of this method: how can we make effective use of all the information available from the instrumental variables? This problem will occupy the rest of this essay.

Let $\varepsilon_t(\theta) \equiv F_t(X_t, Y_t, \theta)$ be a $p \times 1$ vector-valued function defined on a domain of possible parameter values $\Theta \subseteq \mathbb{R}^k$ which represents a system of p simultaneous equations with dependent variables Y_t, a $p \times 1$ random vector, and an $m \times s$ random matrix of explanatory variables X_t for all $t = 1, 2, \ldots, n$. Standard formulations of $F_t(X_t, Y_t, \theta)$ are the linear model $\varepsilon_t(\theta) \equiv Y_t - X_t\theta$ and the nonlinear model $\varepsilon_t(\theta) \equiv Y_t - f_t(X_t, \theta)$. Let $W_t(\theta)$ be a $p \times r$ random valued matrix defined on Θ for all $t = 1, 2, \ldots, n$. Assume that there exists a unique value θ_0 in Θ such that $E(\varepsilon_1^0 | W_1^0) = 0$ for all $t = 1, 2, \ldots, n$, where $\varepsilon_t^0 \equiv F_t(X_t, Y_t, \theta_0)$ and $W_t^0 \equiv W_t(\theta_0)$. Finally, let $Z_t(\theta)$ be a $p \times 1$ random matrix such that $E(Z_t(\theta) | W_t(\theta)) = Z_t(\theta)$ for all θ in Θ. Any such variables $Z_t(\theta_0)$ may serve as instrumental variables for the estimation of the unknown parameters θ_0 since

$$E(Z_t^{0\prime}\varepsilon_t^0) = E(E(Z_t^{0\prime}\varepsilon_t | W_t^0)) = E(Z_t^0 E(\varepsilon_t^0 | W_t^0)) = 0$$

for all $t = 1, 2, \ldots, n$, as long as the functions F_t and W_t and the data generating process satisfy sufficiently strong regularity assumptions to ensure that the uniform law of large numbers is satisfied, i.e.

$$n^{-1} \sum_{t=1}^{n} Z_t(\theta)' \varepsilon_t(\theta) \xrightarrow{P} n^{-1} \sum_{t=1}^{n} E[Z_t(\theta)' \varepsilon_t(\theta)]$$

uniformly in θ on Θ.

Identification of the unknown parameters θ_0 requires that there be at least as many instrumental variables as there are parameters to be estimated, i.e. $l \geqslant k$. On the other hand, if there are more instrumental variables than parameters to be estimated, there will be no solution to $n^{-1} \sum_{t=1}^{n} Z_t(\theta)' \varepsilon_t(\theta) = 0$ in general for finite n as indicated above. One possible solution to this problem is simply to use k of the instrumental variables in the estimation of θ_0. The omitted instrumental variables may then be used to construct statistical tests of the $l - k$ over-identifying restrictions of the unknown parameter vector. A drawback of this approach is that not all of the information available to us is used in the estimation of the unknown parameters and hence, the estimates will not be as precise as they should be. An alternative approach which effectively uses all of the available instrumental variables is to be preferred.

Even though in general the moment function $n^{-1} \sum_{t=1}^{n} Z_t'(\theta) \varepsilon_t(\theta) \neq 0$ for any value of θ, its limiting function $n^{-1} \sum_{t=1}^{n} E[Z_t'(\theta) \varepsilon_t(\theta)]$ does vanish when $\theta = \theta_0$. This suggests estimating θ_0 with that value of Θ which makes $n^{-1} \sum_{t=1}^{n} Z_t'(\theta) \varepsilon_t(\theta)$ as close to zero as possible. The criterion of closeness is of some interest to the econometrician. It affects the size of the confidence ellipsoids of the estimator about θ_0 and hence the precision of the estimate. The Nonlinear Instrumental Variables Estimator (NLIV), $\hat{\theta}_{n,\text{NLIV}} = \text{argmin}_{\theta \in \Theta}$

$$\left[\sum_{t=1}^{n} Z_t'(\theta) \varepsilon_t(\theta) \right]' \cdot \left[\text{Var} \sum_{t=1}^{n} Z_t'(\theta_0) \varepsilon_t(\theta_0) \right]^{-1} \cdot \left[\sum_{t=1}^{n} Z_t'(\theta) \varepsilon_t(\theta) \right]$$

is the optimal instrumental variables estimator in this respect (Bates and White, 1986a).

The NLIV estimator simplifies to well-known econometric estimators in a variety of alternative specifications of the underlying probability model which generated the variables. When the data generating process is independent and identically distributed, $\hat{\theta}_{n,\text{NLIV}}$ is the Nonlinear Three-stage Least Squares estimator of Jorgenson and Laffont (1974). The additional restriction of consideration to a single equation ($p = 1$) results in the Nonlinear Two-stage Least Squares estimator of Amemiya (1974). Furthermore, if the model $\varepsilon(\theta)$ is linear in θ, $\hat{\theta}_{n,\text{NLIV}}$ then simplifies to the Three-stage Least Squares estimator of Zellner and Theil (1962) for a system of simultaneous equations and to the Two-stage Least Squares Estimator of Theil (1953). Basmann (1957) and Sargan (1958) for the estimation of the parameters of a single equation. On the other hand, if we allow for heterogeneity by restricting the data generating process only to be independent, $\hat{\theta}_{n,\text{NLIV}}$ simplifies to White's (1982) Two-stage Instrumental Variables estimator of the parameters of a single linear equation.

As indicated above, it is desirable from consideration of asymptotic precision to include as many instrumental variables as are available for the estimation of the unknown parameters θ_0. This raises the question of the existence of a set of

115

instrumental variables $\{Z^*\} \in \Gamma$ that renders the inclusion of any further instrumental variables redundant, where Γ is the set of all sequences of instrumental variables such that $\hat{\theta}_{n,\text{NLIV}}$ is a consistent estimator of θ_0 with an asymptotic covariance matrix. Bates and White (1986b) provide conditions which imply that such instrumental variables exist, though it may not be possible to obtain them in practice. Suppose there exists a sequence of k instrumental variables $\{\mathcal{Z}\}$ such that for all $\{Z\}$ in Γ

$$E[\mathcal{Z}(\theta_0)'\nabla_\theta\varepsilon(\theta_0)] = E[\mathcal{Z}(\theta_0)'\varepsilon(\theta_0)\varepsilon(\theta_0)'Z(\theta_0)].$$

Then $\{\mathcal{Z}(\theta_0)\}$ is optimal in Γ in the sense of asymptotic precision. Suppose it is also the case that Σ an $np \times np$ matrix with representative element $\sigma_{th\tau g} \equiv E(\varepsilon_{th}(\theta_0)\cdot\varepsilon_{\tau g}(\theta_0)| W_{th}(\theta_0), W_{\tau g}(\theta_0))$, is nonsingular a.s. and that

$$E[E(\nabla_\theta\varepsilon_{th}(\theta_0)| W_{th}(\theta_0))| W_{\tau g}] = E(\nabla_\theta\varepsilon_{th}(\theta_0)| W_{th}(\theta_0))$$

for all t, $\tau = 1, 2, \ldots, n$ and $h, g = 1, 2, \ldots, p$ such that $\sigma^{th\tau g} \neq 0$, where $\sigma^{th\tau g}$ is a representative element of Σ^{-1}. Let Z^* be an $np \times k$ matrix with rows

$$Z^*_{th} \equiv \sum_{\tau=1}^{n} \sum_{g=1}^{p} \sigma^{th\tau g} E[\nabla_\theta\varepsilon_{\tau g}(\theta_0)| W_{\tau g}(\theta_0)].$$

If $\{Z^*\}$ is in Γ then $\{Z^*\}$ is optimal in Γ.

In many situations it will not be possible to make use of such instrumental variables in practice. However, for some important situations optimal instrumental variables are available. Suppose that $\varepsilon(\theta) \equiv Y - X\theta$ and the explanatory variables X are independent of the errors $\varepsilon(\theta_0)$. If the errors are independent and identically distributed for all $t = 1, 2, \ldots, n$ and $h = 1, 2, \ldots, p$, then $Z^* = X$. Thus the optimal instrumental variables estimator is given by

$$\hat{\theta}_{n,\text{NLIV}} \equiv \underset{\theta\in\Theta}{\text{argmin}}\, \varepsilon(\theta)'X[\sigma^2 E(X'X)]^{-1}X'\varepsilon(\theta),$$

where $\sigma^2 \equiv \text{var}[\varepsilon_{th}(\theta_0)]$ is a real, nonstochastic scalar for all t and h. If it is also the case that $n^{-1}E(X'X) - n^{-1}X'X^P \to 0$ as $n \to \infty$, $\hat{\theta}_{n,\text{NLIV}}$ is asymptotically equivalent to $\text{argmin}_{\theta\in\Theta}\varepsilon(\theta)'X(X'X)^{-1}X'\varepsilon(\theta)$, that is Ordinary Least Squares is the optimal instrumental variables estimator. If there is contemporaneous correlation only, i.e. $\text{var}(\varepsilon_t(\theta_0)) = \Omega$, a $p \times p$ nonstochastic matrix, then Zellner's (1962) Seemingly Unrelated Regression Estimator (SURE), is the optimal instrumental variables estimator. If we further relax these assumptions so that $\text{var}(\varepsilon(\theta_0))$ is an arbitrary positive definite $np \times np$ matrix, the Generalized Least Squares (Aitken, 1935) is the optimal instrumental variables estimator.

Since the development of the Two-stage Least Squares estimator in the mid-1950s, the method of instrumental variables has come to play a prominent role in the estimation of economic relationships. Without this method much of economic theory cannot be tested in any concrete way. But it is inherently a large sample estimation method based as it is on the law of large numbers and the central limit theorem. Since in general it is not possible to know how much data are required to arrive at acceptable estimates, all conclusions derived from instrumental variables estimates should be tempered with a healthy dose of scepticism.

BIBLIOGRAPHY

Aitken, A.C. 1935. On least squares and linear combinations of observations. *Proceedings of the Royal Society of Edinburgh* 55, 42–8.

Amemiya, T. 1974. The nonlinear two-stage least-squares estimator. *Journal of Econometrics* 2, 105–10.

Basmann, R.L. 1957. A generalized classical method of linear estimation of coefficients in a structural equation. *Econometrica* 25, 77–83.

Bates, C.E. and White, H. 1986a. Efficient estimation of parametric models. Johns Hopkins University, Department of Political Economy, Working Paper No. 166.

Bates, C.E. and White, H. 1986b. An asymptotic theory of estimation and inference for dynamic models. Johns Hopkins University, Department of Political Economy.

Geary, R.C. 1949. Determination of linear relations between systematic parts of variables with errors in observation, the variances of which are unknown. *Econometrica* 17, 30–58.

Goldberger, A.S. 1972. Structural equation methods in the social sciences. *Econometrica* 40, 979–1001.

Hausman, J.A. 1983. Specification and estimation of simultaneous equation models. In *Handbook of Econometrics*, Amsterdam: North-Holland, ch. 7.

Jorgenson, D.W. and Laffont, J. 1974. Efficient estimation of nonlinear simultaneous equations with additive disturbances. *Annals of Economic and Social Measurement* 3(4), 615–40.

Reiersøl, O. 1941. Confluence analysis by means of lag moments and other methods of confluence analysis. *Econometrica* 9, 1–24.

Reiersøl, O. 1945. Confluence analysis by means of instrumental sets of variables, *Arkiv for Mathematik, Astronomi och Fysik*, 32A.

Sargan, J.D. 1958. The estimation of economic relationships using instrumental variables. *Econometrica* 26, 393–415.

Theil, H. 1953. Estimation and simultaneous correlation in complete equation systems. The Hague: Centraal Planbureau.

White, H. 1982. Instrumental variables regression with independent observations. *Econometrica* 50, 483–500.

White, H. 1984. *Asymptotic Theory for Econometricians*. Orlando: Academic Press.

White, H. 1985. Instrumental variables analogs of generalized least squares estimators. *Journal of Advances in Statistical Computing and Statistical Analysis* 1.

Wright, S. 1925. Corn and Hog Correlations. Washington, DC: US Department of Agriculture, Bulletin 1300.

Zellner, A. 1962. An efficient method of estimating seemingly unrelated regressions and tests for aggregation bias. *Journal of the American Statistical Association* 57, 348–68.

Zellner, A. and Theil, H. 1962. Three-stage least squares: simultaneous estimation of simultaneous equations. *Econometrica* 30, 54–78.

Latent Variables

DENNIS J. AIGNER

A cursory reading of recent textbooks on econometrics shows that historically the emphasis in our discipline has been placed on models that are without measurement error in the variables but instead have stochastic 'shocks' in the equations. To the extent that the topic of errors of measurement in variables (or latent variables) is treated, one will usually find that for a classical single-equation regression model, measurement error in the dependent variable, y, causes no particular problem because it can be subsumed within the equation's disturbance term. But when it comes to the matter of measurement errors in the independent variables, the argument will usually be made that consistent parameter estimation is unobtainable unless repeated observations on y are available at each data point, or strong a priori information can be employed. The presentation usually ends there, leaving us with the impression that the errors-in-variables 'problem' is bad enough in the classical regression model and surely must be worse in more complicated models.

But in fact this is not so. For example, in a simultaneous equations setting one may employ over-identifying restrictions that appear in the system in order to identify error variances associated with exogenous variables, and hence to obtain consistent parameter estimates (not always, to be sure, but at least *sometimes*). Moreover, *ceteris paribus*, the dynamics in an equation can also be helpful in parameter identification. Finally, restrictions on a model's covariance structure, which are commonplace in sociometric and psychometric modelling, may also serve to aid identification. These are the three main themes of research with which we will be concerned.

To begin, let each observation (y_i, x_i) in a random sample be generated by the stochastic relationships:

$$y_i = \eta_i + u_i, \tag{1}$$

$$x_i = \xi_i + v_i, \tag{2}$$

$$\eta_i = \alpha + \beta \xi_i + \varepsilon_i, \qquad i = 1, \ldots, n. \tag{3}$$

Equation (3) is the heart of the model, and we shall assume $E(\eta_i|\xi_i) = \alpha + \beta\xi_i$, so that $E(\varepsilon_i) = 0$ and $E(\xi_i\varepsilon_i) = 0$. Also, we denote $E(\xi_i^2) = \sigma_{\varepsilon\varepsilon}$. Equations (1) and (2) involve the measurement errors and their properties are taken to be $E(u_i) = E(v_i) = 0$, $E(u_i^2) = \sigma_{uu}$, $E(v_i^2) = \sigma_{vv}$ and $E(u_iv_i) = 0$. Furthermore, we will assume that the measurement errors are each uncorrelated with ε_i and with the latent variables η_i and ξ_i. Inserting the expressions $\xi_i = x_i - v_i$ and $\eta_i = y_i - u_i$ into (3), we get:

$$y_i = \alpha + \beta x_i + w_i, \tag{4}$$

where $w_i = \varepsilon_i + u_i - \beta v_i$. Now since $E(v_i|x_i) \neq 0$, we readily conclude that least squares methods will yield biased estimates of α and β.

By assuming that all random variables are normally distributed we eliminate any concern over estimation of the ξ_i's as 'nuisance' parameters. This is the so-called *structural* latent variables model, as contrasted to the *functional* model, wherein the ξ_i's are assumed to be fixed variates. Even so, under the normality assumption no consistent estimators of the primary parameters of interest exist. This can be seen easily by writing out the so-called 'covariance' equations that relate consistently estimable variances and covariances of the observables (y_i and x_i) to the underlying parameters of the model. Under the assumption of joint normality, these equations exhaust the available information and so provide necessary and sufficient conditions for identification. They are obtained by 'covarying' (4) with y_i and x_i, respectively. Doing so, we obtain:

$$\sigma_{yy} = \beta\sigma_{yx} + \sigma_{\varepsilon\varepsilon} + \sigma_{uu},$$
$$\sigma_{yx} = \beta\sigma_{xx} - \beta\sigma_{vv},$$
$$\sigma_{xx} = \sigma_{\xi\xi} + \sigma_{vv}. \tag{5}$$

Obviously there are but three equations (involving three consistently estimable quantities, σ_{yy}, σ_{xx} and σ_{yx}) and five parameters to be estimated. Even if we agree to give up any hope of disentangling the separate influences of ε_i and u_i (by defining, say, $\sigma^2 = \sigma_{\varepsilon\varepsilon} + \sigma_{uu}$) and recognize that the equation $\sigma_{xx} + \sigma_{\xi\xi} + \sigma_{vv}$ will always be used to identify $\sigma_{\xi\xi}$ alone, we are still left with two equations in three unknowns (β, σ^2, and σ_{vv}).

The initial theme in the literature develops from this point. One suggestion to achieve identification in (5) is to assume that we know something about σ_{vv} relative to σ^2, or to σ_{xx}. Suppose this *a priori* information is in the form $\lambda = \sigma_{vv}/\sigma^2$. Then we have $\sigma_{vv} = \lambda\sigma^2$ and

$$\sigma_{yy} = \beta\sigma_{yx} + \sigma^2,$$
$$\sigma_{yx} = \beta\sigma_{xx} - \beta\lambda\sigma^2,$$
$$\sigma_{xx} = \sigma_{\xi\xi} + \sigma_{vv}. \tag{5a}$$

From this it follows that β is a solution to:

$$\beta^2\lambda\sigma_{yx} - \beta(\lambda\sigma_{yy} - \sigma_{xx}) - \sigma_{yx} = 0, \tag{6}$$

and that

$$\sigma^2 = \sigma_{yy} - \beta\sigma_{yx}. \tag{7}$$

Clearly this is but one of several possible forms that prior information on the underlying covariance structure may take (Jöreskog, 1970): a Bayesian treatment also suggests itself (Zellner, 1971).

Suppose that instead of having such information to help to identify the parameters of the simple model (1)–(3), there exists a variate z_i, observable, with the properties that z_i is correlated with x_i but uncorrelated with w_i. That is, z_i is an *instrumental variable* (for x_i). This is tantamount to saying that there exists another equation relating z_i to x_i, for example,

$$x_i = \gamma z_i + \delta_i, \tag{8}$$

with $E(z_i\delta_i) = 0$, $E(\delta_i) = 0$ and $E(\delta_i^2) = \sigma_{\delta\delta}$. Treating (4) and (8) as our structure (multinormality is again assumed), and forming the covariance equations we get, in addition to (5):

$$\sigma_{yz} = \beta\sigma_{xz},$$

$$\sigma_{xx} = \gamma\sigma_{zx} + \sigma_{\delta\delta},$$

$$\sigma_{zx} = \gamma\sigma_{zz}. \tag{9}$$

It is apparent that the parameters of (8) are identified through the last two of these equations. If, as before, we treat $\sigma_{\varepsilon\varepsilon} + \sigma_{uu}$ as a single parameter, σ^2, then, (5) and the first equation of (9) will suffice to identify β, σ^2, σ_{vv} and $\sigma_{\xi\xi}$.

This simple example illustrates how additional equations containing the same latent variable may serve to achieve identification. This 'multiple equations' approach spawned the revival of latent variable models in the 1970s (Zellner, 1970; Jöreskog and Goldberger, 1975).

From consideration of (4) and (8) together we saw how the existence of an instrumental variable (equation) for an independent variable subject to measurement error could resolve the identification problem posed. This is equivalent to suggesting that an over-identifying restriction exists somewhere in the system of equations from which (4) is extracted to provide an instrument for a variable like x_i. But over-identifying restrictions cannot be traded-off against measurement error variances without qualification. Indeed, the *locations* of the exogenous variable measured with error, relative to those of the over-identifying restrictions appearing elsewhere in the equation system, are crucial (Geraci, 1976). To elaborate, consider the following equation system,

$$y_1 + \beta_{12}y_2 = \gamma_{11}\xi_1 + \varepsilon_1,$$

$$\beta_{21}y_1 + y_2 = \gamma_{22}\xi_2 + \gamma_{23}\xi_3 + \varepsilon_2, \tag{10}$$

where ξ_j ($j = 1, 2, 3$) denote the latent exogenous variables in the system. Were they regarded as *observable*, the first equation – conditioned on this supposition – is over-identified (one over-identifying restriction), while the second equation is conditionally just-identified. Therefore, at most one measurement error variance can be identified.

Consider first the specifications $x_1 = \xi_1 + v_1$, $x_2 = \xi_2$, $x_3 = \xi_3$, and let σ_{11} denote the variance of v_1. The corresponding system of covariance equations, under our standard assumption of multinormality, suffices to examine the state of identification of all the parameters. There are six equations available to determine the six unknowns, β_{12}, β_{21}, γ_{11}, γ_{22}, γ_{23}, and σ_{11}, and in this case all parameters are exactly identified. Were the observation error instead associated with ξ_2, the conclusion would be different. Under that specification β_{12} and γ_{11} are overdetermined, while there are only three covariance equations available to solve for β_{21}, γ_{22}, γ_{23}, and σ_{22}. Hence these latter four parameters, all of them associated with the second equation in (10), are not identified.

The results presented and discussed thus far apply only to models depicting *contemporaneous* behaviour. When dynamics are introduced into either the dependent or the independent variables in a linear model with measurement error, the results are usually beneficial. To illustrate, we revert to a single-equation setting, one that parallels the development of (4). In particular, suppose that the sample at hand is a set of time-series observations and that (4) is instead:

$$\eta_t = \beta \eta_{t-1} + \varepsilon_t,$$
$$y_t = \eta_t + u_t, \qquad t = 1, \ldots, T, \tag{11}$$

with all the appropriate previous assumptions imposed, except that now we will also use $|\beta| < 1$, $E(u_t) = E(u_{t-1}) = 0$, $E(u_t^2) = E(u_{t-1}^2) = \sigma_{uu}$, and $E(u_t u_{t-1}) = 0$. Then, analogously to (5), we have:

$$\sigma_{yy} = \beta \sigma_{yy-1} + \sigma_{\varepsilon\varepsilon} + \sigma_{uu},$$
$$\sigma_{yy-1} = \beta(\sigma_{yy} - \sigma_{uu}), \tag{12}$$

where σ_{yy-1} is our notation for the covariance between y_t and y_{t-1} and by assumption we equate the variances of y_t and y_{t-1}. This eliminates one parameter from consideration (σ_{vv}), and there is now a system of two equations in only three unknowns. Unfortunately, we are not now helped any further by our earlier agreement to combine the effects of the equation disturbance term (ε_t) and the measurement error in the dependent variable (u_t).

Fortunately, however, there is some additional information that can be utilized to resolve things: it lies in the covariance between current y_t and lags beyond one period (y_{t-s} for $s \geqslant 2$). These covariances are of the form:

$$\sigma_{yy-s} = \beta \sigma_{yy-s+1}, \qquad s \geqslant 2, \tag{13}$$

so that any one of them taken in conjunction with (12) will suffice to solve for β, $\sigma_{\varepsilon\varepsilon}$, and σ_{uu}. See Maravall and Aigner (1977) and Hsiao (1977) for more details and extension to the simultaneous equations setting.

Structural modelling with latent variables is not only appropriate from a conceptual viewpoint, in many instances it also provides a means to enhance model specifications by taking advantage of information that otherwise might be misused or totally ignored. Several interesting applications of latent variables models in econometrics have appeared since the early 1970s. Numerous others have been published in the psychometrics and sociometrics literature over the years. An in-depth presentation of the theoretical developments outlined here with references to the applied literature is contained in Aigner et al. (1984).

BIBLIOGRAPHY

Aigner, D.J., Hsiao, C., Kapteyn, A. and Wansbeek, T. 1984. Latent variable models in econometrics. Chapter 23 in *Handbook of Econometrics*, Vol. 2, ed. Z. Griliches and M. Intriligator, Amsterdam: North-Holland.

Geraci, V. 1976. Identification of simultaneous equations models with measurement error. *Journal of Econometrics* 4, 263–83.

Hsiao, C. 1977. Identification of a linear dynamic simultaneous error-shock model. *International Economic Review* 18, 181–94.

Jöreskog, K. 1970. A general method for the analysis of covariance structures. *Biometrika* 57, 239–51.

Jöreskog, K.G. and Goldberger, A.S. 1975. Estimation of a model with multiple indicators and multiple causes of a single latent variable. *Journal of the American Statistical Association* 70, 631–9.

Maravall, A. and Aigner, D.J. 1977. Identification of the dynamic shock-error model: the case of dynamic regression. Chapter 18 in *Latent Variables in Socioeconomic Models*, ed. D.J. Aigner and A.S. Goldberger, Amsterdam: North-Holland.

Zellner, A. 1970. Estimation of regression relationships containing unobservable independent variables. *International Economic Review* 11, 441–54.

Zellner, A. 1971. *An Introduction to Bayesian Inference in Econometrics*. New York: Wiley.

Leads and Lags

OLIVIER JEAN BLANCHARD

The notion that an economic variable leads or lags another variable is an intuitive and simple notion. Nevertheless, it has proven difficult to go from this intuitive notion to a precise, empirically testable, definition.

The first attempt was made by Burns and Mitchell in their work on business cycles (1946). Their interest was in characterizing whether individual variables led or lagged the cycle. Their approach was roughly as follows. It was first to divide time into separate business cycles, then to look at the deviation of each variable from its mean value during each cycle and finally to average across cycles. If the variable reached its maximum – or minimum – value on average before the peak of the cycle, the variable was said to lead the cycle; if it reached its maximum or minimum after the peak, it was said to lag the cycle. Following the same line, Burns and Mitchell constructed an index of leading indicators, composed of a dozen series. The series were chosen by taking into account several criteria, the most relevant – for our purposes – being timing at troughs and peaks. This index is still in use today and is regularly published by the US Department of Commerce.

The implicit definition offered by Burns and Mitchell of a leading variable is quite sophisticated, being a relation between timings of turning points between series. It is also partly judgemental, as the procedure used by Burns and Mitchell implies finding business cycles in the data, deciding on what average behaviour of a series in a typical cycle is and so on. The development of time series methods has led to a quest for a less judgemental and more easily testable definition; this has led to tighter, testable but less sophisticated definitions.

The focus has shifted from looking at the relation between two time series at specific points, such as turning points in the Burns–Mitchell work, to looking at characteristics of the joint behaviour of the two time series in general, throughout the business cycle for example. A simple definition is the following: a variable may be said to lead another series if it tends to move – increase,

123

decrease,...– before this other series. This still vague statement can be given precise statistical meaning. For example, a series can be said to lead another in the business cycle if the phase difference cross spectral density of the two series is positive at business cycle frequencies. This definition does not capture exactly the same thing as the Burns–Mitchell definition which focuses on particular points, namely turning points, rather than on specific frequencies. But it is close and is easily testable.

This definition, as well as the Burns–Mitchell definition, partly fails however to capture what the intuitive notion of a leading variable is about. In this intuitive notion is the idea that a variable which leads another contains information about future values of the other that one could not obtain by just looking at current and past values of this other variable. For example, the formal definition given above implies that, if one looked at two sinusoids with close peaks, one would define the one which peaks first as leading the other; it is clear however that the leading sinusoid would contain no information about the other. Thus, one is led to look for a definition which takes into account this notion of additional information.

Such a definition is the following. A variable x leads a variable y if in the following regression,

$$y = a_1 y(-1) + \cdots + a_n y(-n) + b_1 x(-1) + \cdots + b_n x(-n) + e$$

the set of coefficients $(b_1, \ldots, b_n)$ is significant.

This definition captures the notion that x helps predict y, even when one looks at the history of y. If the set of b's is significant, x is also said to cause or 'Granger-cause' y. This definition is easily testable and has become widely accepted. Interestingly, most of the components of the index of leading indicators turn out to lead industrial production in that sense. They help forecast industrial production.

It should be clear, and this is partly obscured by the use of the word causality in this context, that a variable may lead another one, not because it affects it with a lag, but just because it reflects information about its future values. The stock market for example is a leading indicator; this may be because stock prices incorporate information about the future of the economy which one cannot obtain by looking only at current and past values of output, not because stock prices affect economic activity. It may also be a combination of both effects.

BIBLIOGRAPHY

Burns, A.F. and Mitchell, W.G. 1946. *Measuring Business Cycles*. New York: Columbia University Press.

Limited Dependent Variables

TAKESHI AMEMIYA

1. INTRODUCTION

The term *limited dependent variable* was first used by Tobin (1958) to denote the dependent variable in a regression equation that is constrained to be non-negative. In Tobin's study the dependent variable is the household's monetary expenditure on a durable good, which of course must be non-negative. Many other economic variables are non-negative. However, non-negativity alone does not invalidate standard linear regression analysis. It is the presence of many observations at zero which causes bias to the least squares estimator and requires special analysis. For example, Tobin's data contain many households for which the expenditure on a durable good in a given year is zero.

Figure 1 shows a scatter diagram of a hypothetical expenditure–income relationship. It is clear from the diagram that the linear least squares fit of all the points will not accurately describe the relationship between expenditure and income. Later I shall indicate what statistical model will generate the data such as depicted in Figure 1 and what estimators are more appropriate than least squares.

Tobin's model may be called a *censored regression model*. The word *censored* in this context refers to a situation where a researcher knows both the number of observations for which the dependent variable takes zero value and the value of the independent variables for those observations. In contrast, in the *truncated* regression model, those zero observations are totally lost for a researcher. An example of the data for a truncated regression model is obtained by removing the four dots lying on the horizontal axis in Figure 1.

The study of censored or truncated data in the independent and identically distributed (i.i.d.) case predates Tobin's study in the statistical literature. However, Tobin was the first to generalize the analysis to a regression model. Censored or truncated regression models are now extensively used in many disciplines, including economics.

125

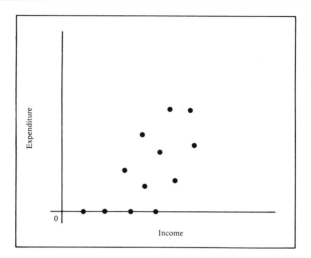

Figure 1   An example of a non-negative dependent variable

Many generalizations of Tobin's model have been proposed, a very simple example being to constrain the dependent variable to lie in an interval not necessarily $[0 \ \infty]$. A more interesting generalization is to consider a model which involves more than one limited dependent variable. In this essay I shall discuss the three most frequently used multivariate limited dependent models: Gronau's wage-rate model, Heckman's labour supply model, and the endogenous switching regression model.

For greater detail than is possible here, the reader is referred to Maddala (1983) and Amemiya (1985). *Discrete choice models*, which are closely related to censored regression models, are discussed in a separate essay.

2. TOBIN'S MODEL

2.1 Definition. Tobin's model for explaining a household's expenditure on a durable good can be derived from a simple theory of utility maximization subject to the budget constraint and a boundary constraint. Define the following symbols:

y a household's expenditure on a durable good.
y_0 the price of the cheapest available durable good.
z all the other expenditures.
x income.

A household is assumed to maximize utility $U(y, z)$ subject to the budget constraint $y + z \leqslant x$ and the boundary constraint $y \geqslant y_0$ or $y = 0$. Suppose y^* is the solution of the maximization subject to $y + z \leqslant x$ but not subject to the other constraint, and assume $y^* = \beta_1 + \beta_2 x + u$, where u may be interpreted as the sum of all the unobservable variables which affect the utility function. Then the solution to the original problem, denoted by y, is defined by

$$y = y^* \quad \text{if} \quad y^* > y_0 = 0 \quad \text{or} \quad y_0 \quad \text{if} \quad y^* \leqslant y_0. \tag{2.1}$$

Now, if we assume further that u is i.i.d. over individual households with a normal distribution and that y_0 is the same for all the individual households, we obtain the following statistical model:

$$y_i^* = x_i'\beta + u_i, \quad y_i = y_i^* \quad \text{if} \quad y_i^* > 0 = 0 \quad \text{if} \quad y_i^* \leqslant 0, \quad i = 1, 2, \ldots, n, \tag{2.2}$$

where u_i are independent and identically distributed as $N(0, \sigma^2)$. This is the model proposed and estimated by Tobin (1958). It is sometimes called the *Tobit* model in analogy to the probit model. If we call its various generalizations also by the name of Tobit models, (2.2) may be called the *standard Tobit* model.

The statistical model (2.2) will produce data like those shown in Figure 1. I shall consider various estimators of the parameters β and σ^2 in this model in the next two subsections.

2.2 Estimation. Earlier I noted that the least squares method applied to all the observations of Figure 1 will yield biased estimates. This can be mathematically demonstrated for model (2.2) as follows. From (2.2) we obtain

$$Ey_i = P(x_i'\beta + u_i > 0) E(x_i'\beta + u_i | x_i'\beta + u_i > 0) = \Phi(x_i'\alpha)[x_i'\beta + \sigma\lambda(x_i'\alpha)], \tag{2.3}$$

where $\alpha = \beta/\sigma$, $\lambda(x_i'\alpha) = \phi(x_i'\alpha)/\Phi(x_i'\alpha)$, and Φ and ϕ are the standard normal distribution and density function, respectively. Thus, the least squares estimator is biased to the extent that the last expression of (2.3) is not equal to $x_i'\beta$.

The least squares applied to only the positive observations also produces bias, although this is not apparent from Figure 1. This can be mathematically demonstrated by considering

$$E(y_i | y_i > 0) = E(x_i'\beta + u_i | x_i'\beta + u_i > 0) = x_i'\beta + \sigma\lambda(x_i'\alpha), \tag{2.4}$$

which is clearly not equal to $x_i'\beta$.

The term $\lambda(x_i'\alpha)$ which appears in both (2.3) and (2.4) is called *Mill's ratio* and plays an important role in a simple consistent estimator to be discussed later.

The least squares estimator, whether it is applied to all the observations or to only the positive observations, is not only biased but also inconsistent. A consistent and asymptotically efficient estimator is provided, as usual, by the maximum likelihood (ML) estimator. Tobin (1958) used it in the empirical work reported in his article. The likelihood function of Tobin's model (2.2) is given by

$$L = \prod_0 [1 - \Phi(x_i'\alpha)] \prod_1 \sigma^{-1}\phi[(y_i - x_i'\beta)/\sigma], \tag{2.5}$$

where Π_0 refers to the product over those i for which $y_i = 0$, and Π_1, for $y_i > 0$. The first term is equal to the probability of the observed event $x_i'\beta + u_i < 0$, and the second term is equal to the density of the observed y_i. Thus, the likelihood function is the product of probabilities and densities. Despite this unusual

127

characteristic of the likelihood function, it can be shown that the ML estimator is consistent and asymptotically normal with its asymptotic variance–covariance matrix given by the usual formula $-[E\partial^2 \log L/\partial\theta\partial\theta']^{-1}$. See Amemiya (1973).

Note that in Tobin's model (2.2), we observe $x_i'\beta + u_i$ when it is positive. If, instead, we do not observe it and merely learn that $x_i'\beta + u_i$ is positive, we have the so-called probit model. The likelihood function of the probit model is given by

$$L = \prod_0 [1 - \Phi(x_i'\alpha)] \prod_1 \Phi(x_i'\alpha). \tag{1.6}$$

The probit ML estimator of α, which maximizes the above, is consistent but not as asymptotically efficient as the ML estimator which maximizes (2.5). Moreover, as one can see from the form of the likelihood function (2.6), one cannot estimate β and σ^2 separately by the probit ML estimator.

Heckman (1976) noted that by inserting the probit ML estimator of α into the right-hand side of (2.4), one can obtain consistent estimates of β and σ by least squares, that is, by regressing positive y_i's on x_i and $\lambda(x_i'\hat{\alpha})$, where $\hat{\alpha}$ is the probit ML estimate. This estimator is called *Heckman's two-step estimator* and can also be used for generalized Tobit models, which I shall discuss later. In fact, it is more useful for those models than for the standard Tobit model because the ML estimator is computationally burdensome for some of the generalized Tobit models. Heckman used his estimator in the two-equation Tobit model, to be discussed in section 4 below.

Heckman's principle can be similiarly applied to equation (2.3). In that case, one would regress all the y_i's, both positive and zero on $\Phi(x_i'\hat{\alpha})x_i$ and $\Phi(x_i\hat{\alpha})$. Not much is known as to which method is more preferred.

Several Monte Carlo studies have shown that Heckman's estimator can be considerably less efficient than the ML estimator in certain cases.

2.3 Nonstandard conditions. It is well known that the least squares estimator (or equivalently, the ML estimator) in the standard normal regression model retains its consistency (although not its efficiency) when some of the basic assumptions of the model – namely, normality, homoscedasticity, and serial independence – are removed. In contrast, it has been shown that the ML estimator derived under the assumptions of model (2.2) is no longer consistent when u_i is not normal or when u_i is not homoscedastic, although it is consistent if the u_i are serially correlated. The same is true of the probit ML estimator and Heckman's estimator.

This is a serious problem because non-normality and heteroscedasticity are common occurrences in econometrics. It is recommended, therefore, that a researcher should perform a statistical test against non-normality or heteroscedasticity, and if their intensity is suspected to be high, one should incorporate non-normality or heteroscedasticity directly into one's model.

I conjecture that the normal ML estimator will do reasonably well if the degree of non-normality or heteroscedasticity is 'small'. A Monte Carlo study has shown that the normal Tobit ML estimator performs reasonably well even when u_i is distributed according to the Laplace distribution, that is, with the density

$f(u) = 2^{-1} \exp(-|u|)$. Powell (1981) proposed the least absolute deviations (LAD) estimator in Tobin's model. It is defined as the value of β that minimizes $\Sigma_{i=1}^{n} |y_i - \max(x_i'\beta, 0)|$. He has shown the estimator to be consistent under general distributions of u_i as well as under heteroscedasticity, and derived its asymptotic distribution. The intuitive appeal for the LAD estimator in a censored regression model arises from the fact that in the case of an i.i.d. sample, the median (of which the LAD estimator is a generalization) is not affected by left censoring below the mean. A main drawback of the LAD estimator is the computational difficulty it entails. It is hoped that a reasonably efficient algorithm for computing the LAD estimator will be developed in the near future.

3. GRONAU'S WAGE-RATE MODEL

Gronau (1973) studied the effect of children on the housewife's value of time and consequently on her wage rate, using US census data. A censored regression model is appropriate because there are many housewives who do not work and therefore for whom the wage rate is not observed.

Gronau assumed that, given the exogenously determined offered wage W^0, a housewife maximizes her utility function $U(C, X)$ subject to $X = W^0 H + V$ and $C + H = T$, where C is time spent at home for child care, X represents all other goods, T is total available time, and V is other income. In Figure 2, the budget constraint is represented by a solid line, and two possible indifference curves are drawn in broken lines.

Depending on the shape of the indifference curves, there are two possible types of solutions to this maximization problem: the interior solution A or the corner solution B. In B the housewife does not work, and in A she works for H hours.

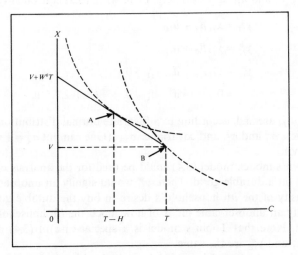

Figure 2 A housewife's determination of hours worked

To put it algebraically, the housewife does not work if

$$\left[\frac{\partial U}{\partial C} \bigg/ \frac{\partial U}{\partial X} \right]_{H=0} > W^0 \tag{3.1}$$

and works if the inequality above is reversed. If she works, the hours worked H are obtained by solving

$$\frac{\partial U}{\partial C} \bigg/ \frac{\partial U}{\partial X} = W^0, \tag{3.2}$$

and the actual wage rate W is equal to the offered wage W^0. Gronau calls the left-hand side of (3.1) the housewife's value of time or, more commonly, the reservation wage, denoted W^r. In the statistical model he estimates, Gronau is concerned only with the determination of the wage rate and not with the hours worked. (A statistical model which explains both the wage rate and the hours worked will be discussed in the next section.) Assuming that both W^0 and W^r can be written as linear combinations of independent variables plus error terms, Gronau specifies his statistical model as follows:

$$W_i^0 = x_{i2}' \beta_2 + u_{i2}$$
$$W_i^r = z_i' \alpha + v_i$$
$$W_i^0 = W_i, \quad \text{if} \quad W_i^0 > W_i^r$$
$$ = 0, \quad \text{if} \quad W_i^0 \leqslant W_i^r, \quad i = 1, 2, \ldots, n, \tag{3.3}$$

where (u_{i2}, v_i) are i.i.d. according to a bivariate normal distribution.

I shall write the model (3.3) in such a way that its similarity to Tobin's model (2.2) becomes more apparent. By defining $y_{i1}^* = W_i^0 - W_i^r$ and $y_{i2}^* = W_i^0$ and defining x_{i1}, β_i, and u_{i1} appropriately, I can write (3.3) equivalently as

$$y_{i1}^* = x_{i1}' \beta_1 + u_{i1}$$
$$y_{i2}^* = x_{i2}' \beta_2 + u_{i2}$$
$$y_{i2} = y_{i2}^*, \quad \text{if} \quad y_{i1}^* > 0$$
$$\phantom{y_{i2}} = 0, \quad \text{if} \quad y_{i1}^* \leqslant 0, \quad i = 1, 2, \ldots, n, \tag{3.4}$$

where (u_{i1}, u_{i2}) are i.i.d. according to a bivariate normal distribution with mean zero, variances σ_1^2 and σ_2^2, and covariance σ_{12}. (One can put $\sigma_1^2 = 1$ without loss of generality.)

Like Tobin's model, model (3.4) could be used for the analysis of household expenditure on a durable good. Then, y_{i1}^* would signify an unobservable index of the intensity of the ith household's desire to buy the durable good, and y_{i2}^* would signify an unobservable index of how much the ith household wishes to spend on it. Note that Tobin's model is a special case of (3.4) obtained by assuming y_{i1}^* and y_{i2}^* are the same.

The other extreme special case of (3.4) is obtained by assuming independence between y_{i1}^* and y_{i2}^*. In this special case, the computation of the ML estimators is simple: the ML estimator of β_1/σ_1 is obtained by applying the probit ML estimator of the equation for y_{i1}^*, and the ML estimator of β_2 is obtained by the least squares regression of positive y_{i2} on x_{i2}. Because of its computational ease, this model was often used before the advance of computer technology. However, in economic applications it is generally unrealistic to assume the independence of y_{i1}^* and y_{i2}^*.

The likelihood function of model (3.4) can be written as

$$L = \prod_0 P(y_{i1}^* \leqslant 0) \prod_1 \int_0^\infty f(y_{i1}^*, y_{i2}) dy_{i1}^*, \tag{3.5}$$

where Π_0 denotes the product over those i for which $y_{i2} = 0$ and Π_1 over those i for which $y_{i2} > 0$. The maximization of (3.5) is relatively simple. Using (3.5), the hypothesis of the equality of y_{i2}^* and y_{i2}^* (Tobin's hypothesis) or the hypothesis of independence between y_{i1}^* and y_{i2}^* can be tested by the likelihood ratio test or by any other asymptotically equivalent test.

Heckman's two-step estimator can be used for this model. From (3.4) we can obtain an equation analogous to (2.4) as follows:

$$E(y_{i2}|y_{i2} > 0) = x_{i2}'\beta_2 + \sigma_{12}\sigma_1^{-1}\lambda(x_{i1}'\sigma_1), \tag{3.6}$$

where $\alpha_1 = \beta_1/\alpha_1$. In the first step one estimates α_1 by applying the probit ML estimator applied to the equation for y_{i1}^*, denoted $\hat{\alpha}_1$, and in the second step one regresses positive y_{i2} on x_{i2} and $\lambda(x_{i1}'\hat{\alpha}_1)$.

Heckman's estimator is consistent as long as (3.6) is valid. In particular, the consistency of Heckman's estimator does not require the joint normality of y_{i1}^* and y_{i2}^*, for (3.6) is valid as long as y_{i1}^* is normal and y_{i2}^* can be written as a sum of a linear function of y_{i1}^* and a random variable (not necessarily normal) distributed independent of y_{i1}^*.

4. HECKMAN'S LABOUR SUPPLY MODEL

The theoretical model of labour supply discussed in section 3 determines both the wage rate and the hours worked, but, as we noted earlier, Gronau's statistical model defines the distribution of only the wage rate. Heckman's (1974) statistical model which defines the joint distribution of the wage rate and the hours worked is developed as follows:

Heckman's equation for the offered wage rate (actually, its logarithm) is, like Gronau's given by

$$W_i^0 = x_{i2}'\beta_2 + u_{i2}. \tag{4.1}$$

Heckman specifies $W^r \equiv (\partial U/\partial C)/(\partial U/\partial X)$ explicitly as a function of the hours worked H and a linear function of exogenous variables plus an error term as

$$W_i^r = \gamma H_i + z_i\alpha + v_i. \tag{4.2}$$

It is assumed that the ith individual works if

$$W_i^r(H_i = 0) \equiv z'\alpha + x_i < W_i^0 \tag{4.3}$$

131

and then the wage rate W_i and the hours worked H_i are determined by simultaneously solving (4.1) and (4.2) after putting $W_i^0 = W_i^r = W_i$. Therefore, we can define Heckman's statistical model as

$$W_i = x'_{i2}\beta_2 + u_{i2}$$

and

$$W_i = \gamma H_i + z'_i\alpha + v_i, \qquad \text{if} \quad H_i^* \equiv x'_{i1}\beta_1 + u_{i1} > 0$$

$$W_i = 0 \quad \text{and} \quad H_i = 0, \qquad \text{if} \quad H_i^* \leqslant 0, \tag{4.4}$$

where $x'_{i1}\beta_1 = \gamma^{-1}(x'_{i2}\beta_2 + z'_i\alpha)$ and $u_{i1} = \gamma^{-1}(u_{i2} - v_i)$. Note that H_i^* may be interpreted as the desired hours of work.

The first two equations of (4.4) constitute the structural equations of a simultaneous equations model since an endogenous variable H appears in the right-hand side of the second equation. In order to make Heckman's model (4.4) comparable to Tobin's model (2.2) or Gronau's model (3.4), I shall write the reduced-form version of Heckman's model. By defining $y_i^* = H^*, y_i = H, y_2^* = W^0$, and $y_2 = W$, the reduced-form version of Heckman's model (assuming normality) can be defined by

$$y_{i1}^* = x_{i1}\beta_1 + u_{i1}$$

$$y_{i2}^* = x'_{i2}\beta_2 + u_{i2}$$

$$y_{i1} = y_{i1}^*, \qquad \text{if} \quad y_{i1}^* > 0 \quad = 0, \qquad \text{if} \quad y_{i1}^* \leqslant 0$$

$$y_{i2} = y_{i2}^*, \qquad \text{if} \quad y_{i1}^* > 0 \quad = 0, \qquad \text{if} \quad y_{i1}^* \leqslant 0, \qquad i = 1, 2, \ldots, n, \tag{4.5}$$

where (u_{i1}, u_{i2}) are i.i.d. according to a bivariate normal distribution with mean zero, variances σ_1^2 and σ_2^2, and covariance σ_{12}.

The likelihood function of model (4.5) is given by

$$L = \prod_0 P(y_{i1}^* \leqslant 0) \prod_1 f(y_{i1}, y_{i2}), \tag{4.6}$$

where the definitions of the symbols are the same as in (3.5). The maximization of (4.6) is also a fairly routine problem. Heckman's two-step method can also be applied to this model in a way very similar to that discussed in section 3.

The estimation of the structural parameters of model (4.4) requires an additional procedure because of its simultaneity problem. However, as noted by Amemiya (1979), the problem of deriving the estimates of the structural parameters from the estimates of the reduced form parameters in the simultaneous equations censored regression model can be solved by means of the same principle as in the standard simultaneous equations model.

5. ENDOGENOUS SWITCHING REGRESSION MODEL

The endogenous switching regression model is defined as follows:

$$y_{i1}^* = x_{i1}'\beta_1 + u_{i1}$$
$$y_{i2}^* = x_{i2}'\beta_2 + u_{i2}$$
$$y_{i3}^* = x_{i3}'\beta_3 + u_{i3}$$
$$y_i = y_{i2}^*, \quad \text{if} \quad y_{i1}^* > 0 = y_{i3}^*, \quad \text{if} \quad y_{i1}^* \leqslant 0$$
$$w_i = 1, \quad \text{if} \quad y_{i1}^* > 0 = 0, \quad \text{if} \quad y_{i1}^* \leqslant 0, \tag{5.1}$$

where (u_{i1}, u_{i2}, u_{i3}) are i.i.d. according to a trivariate normal distribution. Note that the variables with the asterisks are unobserved, and y_i, w_i, and x_is are observed.

It is called a switching regression model because the regression equation which the observed dependent variable follows switches back and forth between two equations. It is called endogenous switching because the switching is controlled by the outcome of a random variable y_{i1}^*, which may be correlated with y_{i2}^* and y_{i3}^*. The fact that w_i is observed may be characterized by the statement that the sample separation is known in this model. A variety of switching regression models arise depending on whether the switching is endogenous or exogenous and whether the sample separation is known or unknown.

The likelihood function of model (5.1) is given by

$$L = \prod_0 \int_{-\infty}^0 f_3(y_{i1}^*, y_i) \, dy_{i1}^* \prod_1 \int_0^\infty f_2(y_{i1}^*, y_i) \, dy_{i1}^*, \tag{5.2}$$

where Π_0 denotes the product over those i for which $w_i = 0$, Π_1 over those i for which $w_i = 1$, f_2 denotes the joint density of y_{i1}^* and y_{i2}^*, and f_3 the joint density of y_{i1}^* and y_{i3}^*. As in the prceding models, the ML estimation is computationally feasible, and Heckman's two-step estimation yields consistent estimates.

An interesting example of model (5.1) is given by Lee (1978), who studied the effect of union membership on the wage rate. In Lee's model, y_{i2}^* represents the logarithm of the wage rate of the ith worker in case he or she joins the union, and y_{i3}^* represents the same in case he or she does not join the union, and y_i represents the observed wage rate. Whether or not the worker joins the union is determined by the sign of the variable

$$y_{i1}^* = y_{i2}^* - y_{i3}^* + z_i'\alpha + v_i. \tag{5.3}$$

Another interesting example of model (5.1) is the so-called *disequilibrium model*, first proposed by Fair and Jaffee (1972). In their model, y_{i2}^* represents the quantity supplied, y_i is the observed quantity traded, and $y_{i1}^* = y_{i3}^* - y_{i2}^*$. Many extensions of the disequilibrium model have been proposed and the ensuing statistical problems have been discussed in the economic literature: for a recent survey, see Quandt (1982).

Model (5.1) can be generalized to the multinomial case where the regression equation which the observed dependent variable follows switches from one to another among more than two regression equations. To get a concrete idea, I shall describe Duncan's model (1980).

He analyses the joint determination of the location of a firm and its output (for simplicity I consider a scalar dependent variable-output, but the analysis can be generalized to the case of a vector of dependent variables, as Duncan does). A firm chooses the location at which profits are maximized, and only the output at the chosen location is observed. Let s_k^i be the profit of the ith firm when it chooses the kth location, $i = 1, 2, \ldots, n$ and $k = 1, 2, \ldots, K$, and let y_k^i be the output of the ith firm at the kth location. Then Duncan postulates

$$s_k^i = x_{k1}^i{}' \beta + u_k^i \qquad (5.4)$$

and

$$y_k^i = x_{k2}^i{}' \beta + v_k^i, \qquad (5.5)$$

where x_{k1}^i and x_{k2}^i are vector functions of the input–output prices and $(u_1^i, u_2^i, \ldots, u_k^i, v_1^i, v_2^i, \ldots, v_k^i)$ are i.i.d. according to a $2K$-variate normal distribution. (Economic theory dictates that the same β appear in both equations.) Suppose $s_k^i > s_j^i$ for any $j \neq k$. Then a researcher observes y_k^i but does not observe y_j^i for $j \neq k$.

I shall indicate how to derive the likelihood function of Duncan's model. Let us assume $K = 3$ for simplicity. We consider a typical firm and assume that we observe the firm to choose location 1, which implies that we observe y_1 and the event characterized by the inequalities $s_1 > s_2$ and $s_1 > s_3$. (I have suppressed the superscript which would indicate this particular firm.) Therefore, the contribution of this firm to the likelihood function is

$$P(s_1 > s_2, s_1 > s_3) f(y_1 | s_1 > s_2, s_1 > s_3). \qquad (5.6)$$

The total likelihood function is the product of these over all the firms.

Thus the likelihood function of Duncan's model consists of the probability part and the density part, like the likelihood function of the other models we have considered so far. If K is large, the maximization of the likelihood function of this model may involve a costly computation. Duncan maximizes the probability part and the density part separately and obtains two different estimates of β. Then he estimates β by using the optimal weighted average of the two estimates.

A model similar to Duncan's can be also used, for example, to analyse the joint determination of the consumer's choice of a particular brand of a durable good and the amount of expenditure on that brand; see for example Dubin and McFadden (1984).

BIBLIOGRAPHY

Amemiya, T. 1973. Regression analysis when the dependent variable is truncated normal. *Econometrica* 41, 997–1016.

Amemiya, T. 1979. The estimation of a simultaneous-equation Tobit model. *International Economic Review* 20, 169–81.

Amemiya, T. 1985. *Advanced Enconometrics*. Cambridge, Mass: Harvard University Press.

Dubin, J.A. and McFadden, D.L. 1984. An econometric analysis of residential electric appliance holdings and consumption. *Econometrica* 52, 345–62.

Duncan, G.M. 1980. Formulation and statistical analysis of the mixed, continuous discrete dependent variable model in classical production theory. *Econometrica* 48, 839–52.

Fair, R.C. and Jaffee, D.M. 1972. Methods of estimation for markets in disequilibrium. *Econometrica* 40, 497–514.

Gronau, R. 1973. The effects of children on the housewife's value of time. *Journal of Political Economy* 81, S168–S199.

Heckman, J.J. 1974. Shadow prices, market wages, and labor supply. *Econometrica* 42, 679–93.

Heckman, J.J. 1976. The common structure of statistical models of truncation, sample selection and limited dependent variables and a simple estimator for such model. *Annals of Economic and Social Measurement* 5, 475–92.

Lee, L.F. 1978. Unionism and wage rates: a simultaneous equations model with quantitative and limited dependent variables. *International Economic Review* 19, 415–33.

Maddala, G.S. 1983. *Limited-Dependent and Qualitative Variables in Econometrics.* Cambridge: Cambridge University Press.

Powell, J.L. 1981. Least absolute deviations estimation for censored and truncated regression models. Technical Report No. 356, Institute for Mathematical Studies in the Social Sciences, Stanford University.

Quandt, R.E. 1982. Econometric disequilibrium models. *Econometric Reviews* 1, 1–63.

Tobin, J. 1958. Estimation of relationships for limited dependent variables. *Econometrica* 26, 24–36.

Logit, Probit and Tobit

FORREST D. NELSON

Two convenient classifications for variables which are not amenable to treatment by the principal tool of econometrics, regression analysis, are *quantal responses* and *limited responses*. In the quantal response (all or nothing) category are dichotomous, qualitative and categorical outcomes, and the methods of analysis identified as *probit* and *logit* are appropriate for these variables. Illustrative applications include decisions to own or rent, choice of travel mode, and choice of professions. The limited response category covers variables which take on mixtures of discrete and continuous outcomes, and the prototypical model and analysis technique is identified as *tobit*. Examples are samples with both zero and positive expenditures on durable goods, and models of markets with price ceilings including data with both limit and non-limit prices. While the tobit model evolved out of the probit model and the limited and quantal response methods share many properties and characteristics, they are sufficiently different to make separate treatment more convenient.

DICHOTOMOUS LOGIT AND PROBIT MODELS. The simplest of the logit and probit models apply to dependent variables with dichotomous outcomes. If Y can take on only two possible outcomes, say 0 and 1, then the stochastic behaviour of Y is described by the probability of a positive response, $P(Y = 1 | X)$, which is here taken to depend on a vector valued variable X. The specification of the functional form for P in the probit model is the normal CDF, while the logit model uses the logistic equation. Specifically, for the probit model

$$P(Y = 1 | X) = \int_{-\infty}^{\theta' X} \frac{1}{\sqrt{2\pi}\sigma} \exp\left[\frac{-1}{2}u^2\right] du \equiv \Phi(\theta' X) \tag{1}$$

while for the logit model

$$P(Y = 1 | X) = \frac{\exp(\theta' X)}{1 + \exp(\theta' X)} \equiv \Lambda(\theta' X). \tag{2}$$

136

In both forms, θ is a parameter vector, and the choice of a linear, additive form for the way X enters Φ and Λ is common but not necessary.

A rudimentary derivation of these otherwise ad hoc specifications from an explicit description of behaviour is as follows. Suppose the underlying theory of behaviour posits a continuous but latent (or observable) variable, say W, embodying that behaviour, with the dichotomous realization on Y determined by comparing W with some 'threshold'. For convenience, take the threshold to be zero. Then Y is determined by

$$Y = \begin{cases} 1 & \text{if } W > 0 \\ 0 & \text{if } W \leqslant 0 \end{cases}.$$

If W is related to X linearly with an additive random component,

$$W = \beta' X - u,$$

then outcome probabilities are determined by

$$P(Y = 1 | X) = P(\beta' X - u > 0) = F\left(\frac{\beta' X}{\delta}\right), \tag{3}$$

where δ is a scale parameter used to standardize the random variable u, and F is the CDF for this standardized random variable u/δ. The choice of F is dictated by the distribution of u. If u/δ is $N(0, 1)$, then (3) is the probit model of equation (1); and if u/δ is logistic with mean 0 and variance $\pi^2/3$, then (3) is the logit model of equation (2). In both cases, $\theta = \beta/\delta$, and β and δ are not separately identifiable.

The similarities in the shapes of the logistic and normal distributions suggest that results of probit and logit analysis will differ by very little. Indeed, the inferences drawn from the two methods applied to the same data are invariably similar, and even parameter estimates from the two models will agree, approximately, up to a factor of proportionality. (Logit coefficients tend to exceed probit coefficients by a scale factor in the range 1.6 to 1.8.) A choice between the two models, therefore, is not an important one and may often be ruled by convenience factors, such as availability of appropriate computer programs.

One superficially attractive alternative to probit or logit is the linear probability model (LPM). The LPM specification is

$$P(Y = 1 | X) = \theta' X. \tag{4}$$

Since in the dichotomous case $E(Y|X) = P(Y = 1|X)$, this model lends itself to a simple linear regression formulation,

$$Y = \theta' X + u. \tag{5}$$

If (4) is correct, then the disturbance term u defined implicitly in (5) has mean zero and is uncorrelated with X. Least squares would thus appear to be a viable estimator for θ. But least squares does not recognize the implicit constraint in (4) that $\theta' X$ must lie in the interval from zero to one. Indeed this constraint

137

makes the linear form unattractive except as a local approximation, and, if (4) is merely an approximation, the independence of u and X will not hold, so least squares will produce biased estimates of even the linear approximation. Such problems generally outweigh the advantages of the linear specification, and sigmoid shapes for P, particularly the logit and probit models, are more commonly selected.

The most frequently used estimation technique for the dichotomous logit and probit models of equations (1) and (2) is maximum likelihood (ML). For a random sample of observations on the $0-1$ dependent variable Y_i and independent variables X_i, $i = 1,\ldots,N$, the maximum likelihood estimator, θ, is found as the solution to

$$\max_{\theta} \left\{ \ln L(\mathbf{Y}|\mathbf{X}, \theta) = \sum_{i=1}^{N} [Y_i \ln P_i + (1 - Y_i)\ln(1 - P_i)] \right\} \qquad (6)$$

where $\mathbf{Y} = (Y_1,\ldots,Y_N)'$, $\mathbf{X} = (X_1,\ldots,X_N)'$ and $P_i = \Phi(\theta' X_i)$ for the probit model or $P_i = \Lambda(\theta' X_i)$ for the logit model. The first order conditions ($\partial(\ln L)/\partial\theta = 0$) are nonlinear in θ, so explicit solutions do not exist, and iterative maximization methods must be employed. Fortunately, the log likelihood is globally concave for probit and logit models, so any of a number of common algorithms will suffice. The Newton–Raphson algorithm, for example, is quite satisfactory and yields a consistent estimate of the covariance matrix of θ, the negative inverse of the matrix of second derivatives of the log likelihood, as a by-product.

An alternative estimation method is applicable when the data consist of replicated observations on Y. Suppose that corresponding to each of the N observations on X_i, there are n_i observations on Y, say $Y_{ij}, j = 1,\ldots,n$. A sufficient statistic for the n_i observations Y_{ij} is given by the fraction of positive responses, $p_i = (\Sigma_j Y_{ij})/n_i$. Using the logit model as an example, define the 'observed logit' as $w_i = \Lambda^{-1}(p_i)$, note that the 'true logit' is $\Lambda^{-1}(P_i) = \theta' X$, and let the difference between them be $u_i = w_i - \theta' X_i$. A Taylor series expansion of $\Lambda^{-1}(p_i)$ about P_i reveals that, for large enough n_i, u_i is approximately $N\{0, 1/[n_i p_i(1 - p_i)]\}$. Thus, weighted least squares estimation of θ from the regression equation,

$$w_i = \theta' X_i + u_i \qquad (7)$$

yields an estimator $\hat{\theta}$ with the same asymptotic properties as the MLE. In the logit model the transformation Λ^{-1} is the log-odds ratio, so $w_i = \ln[p_i/(1 - p_i)]$. The analysis is similar for the probit model. The estimator was first derived by Berkson (1944) using the estimation principle of minimum chi-square, and Theil (1969) obtained it for the more general multinomial case using the weighted least squares principle as described here. Thus the estimator is interchangeably referred to as the Berkson–Theil WLS estimator and the MIN chi-square estimator.

The ML and WLS estimators are both consistent, asymptotically efficient and asymptotically normal with the same covariance matrix, so there is little basis for choice between the two except for the computational advantages of WLS. Of course, WLS applies only to replicated data, and the two estimators differ in terms of sample size requirements – the properties of the MLE rely on the total number of observations, $\Sigma_i n_i$, while the asymptotic approximations of the WLS estimator are valid only if the number of replications, n_i, is large for each i. Both estimators have been criticized for lack of robustness against misspecification of the functional form of $P(Y=1|X)$. Estimators which are robust against this misspecification have been proposed by Manski (1975) and Cosslett (1983). The basic idea is to restrict $P(Y=1|X) = F(\theta'X)$ only so far as to require F to be monotonic and estimate the parameters θ and the function F simultaneously.

These simple models have been extended in a number of ways, and they are closely related to a number of other analysis techniques. (Amemiya (1981) provides a comprehensive survey.) The most obvious extension is to allow Y to take on more than two values – the resulting extension for the logit model is referred to as multinomial logit, while the corresponding extension for probit turns out to be computationally onerous for more than four alternatives. McFadden obtained a multinomial logistic form for probabilistic discrete choice behaviour from a random utility model which incorporates such additional features as alternative specific attributes (McFadden, 1973). Models with multiple, ordered outcomes for the dependent variable have also been proposed (McKelvey and Zavoina, 1975).

While probit and logit models specify the conditional distribution of Y given X, discriminant analysis begins with a specification of the conditional distribution of X given Y. Interestingly, the implied form for $P(Y|X)$ in the normal discriminant analysis model with two populations is the same as equation (2), but the differences in assumptions made under the two approaches lead to different estimators with different properties. In a similar comparison, the log-linear models for contingency tables (see, for example, Bishop, Fienberg and Holland, 1975) specify a functional form for the joint distribution of a set of qualitative variables. It is easy to show that the implied conditional probability of one of these variables, conditional on the rest, has the multinomial logistic form.

TOBIT MODEL. In the standard regression model, the dependent variable is generally assumed to take on any of an infinite continuum of values, and the probability of any particular value is zero. In the dichotomous probit model, the dependent variable assumes only two values, each of which is assigned probability mass. Tobin (1958) proposed a limited variable model, later called the Tobit model, to handle dependent variables which are mixtures of these two cases, specifically mass points at the low end and continuous values above. An example is the analysis of durable goods expenditures when negative values cannot occur but there are frequent observations of zero. The specification of the model is

$$Y = \begin{cases} \beta'X + u & \text{if RHS} > 0, \\ 0 & \text{if RHS} \leqslant 0. \end{cases} \tag{8}$$

In the statistics literature, the term 'truncated' is applied to a univariate model in which there is no record of observations beyond the limit point, and the term 'censored' is used for situations in which the number of limit observations is recorded even though their values are not. Though the Tobit model is a multivariate one, it is closest to the censored variable case with the additional requirement that all exogenous variables be recorded for both limit and non-limit observations.

Even under the standard assumptions of the regression model, namely that the error terms u are independent of X and of each other, have zero mean, and are homoscedastic, it is easily seen that ordinary least squares regression of Y on X will lead to biased estimates of β. Observations with large negative disturbances u are more likely to be censored than are observations with large positive value of u, so the regression disturbance, defined as $v = Y - \beta'X$ for both limit and non-limit observations, will have a mean which is greater than zero and in fact depends on X. Thus, the least squares estimator of β will be biased, usually toward zero, and that is true whether or not limit observations are included in the sample.

An estimator with desirable asymptotic properties is maximum likelihood. Under the assumption that the error terms u are iid normal, the likelihood function is given by

$$L(\mathbf{Y}|\mathbf{X}, \beta, \sigma) = \prod^{\Psi_0} \Phi\left(\frac{-\beta'X_i}{\sigma}\right) \cdot \prod^{\Psi_1} \frac{1}{\sigma}\phi\left(\frac{Y_i - \beta'X_i}{\sigma}\right), \tag{9}$$

where Ψ_0 and Ψ_1 are the sets of observation subscripts i corresponding to limit and non-limit observations, respectively, and Φ and ϕ are the standard normal distribution and density functions. The first order conditions for maximization of the logarithm of (9) are non-linear, so iterative techniques are required. Olsen (1978) pointed out that, under the reparameterization $(\alpha', \alpha_0) = (\beta'/\sigma, -1/\sigma)$, the log-likelihood is globally concave, so an algorithm such as Newton-Raphson will yield the MLE starting from any initial estimate of the parameters. Amemiya (1973) demonstrated the conditions under which the MLE will be consistent, asymptotically efficient and asymptotically normal.

It is widely recognized that the MLE for this Tobit model is not robust against misspecifications which would be innocuous in the corresponding regression model. (See Hurd (1979), Arabmazar and Schmidt (1981) and Goldberger (1983) for examples, Robinson (1982) for an exception involving serial correlation, and Nelson (1981) for a specification test.) This lack of robustness has stimulated the development of alternative estimators such as Powell's (1984) least absolute deviation estimator. These alternatives, unfortunately, are computationally difficult, do not carry over easily to related models, and are not in widespread use.

The Tobit model has been extended in various ways. Trivial adaptations include non-zero thresholds which are constant or at least exogenous and censoring from above rather than below. The truncated variable case with no limit observations is easily handled with modification of the likelihood function (Hausman and Wise, 1977). Similar modifications allow for interior censoring and for both upper and lower truncation (Rosett, 1959; Rosett and Nelson, 1975).

Richer generalizations of the Tobit model involve multiple equations. Three examples are simultaneous equations models, models of markets in disequilibrium and models with self-selection. The first of these is a generalization of the simultaneous equation techniques for linear models. (Lee (1981) surveys and extends this literature.) In the second example, quantities supplied and demanded serve as the upper truncation points for each other, and the two equations are estimated simultaneously (see Quandt (1982) for a survey). In models with self-selection, one behavioural relation determines whether the dependent variable of a second equation will be observed. Heckman (1974) develops such a model in which the decision to participate in the labour force and the level of participation are the two equations of interest.

An extensive treatment of limited dependent variable models can be found in Maddala (1983), and Amemiya (1984) provides a comprehensive yet compact survey.

ORIGIN AND EVOLUTION OF PROBIT, LOGIT AND TOBIT ANALYSIS. Credit for invention of the method of analysis later to be called probit is generally given to the psychophysicist Fechner (1860). In assessing the ability of subjects to perceive differences in the weight of inanimate objects, Fechner converted the proportion of correct responses to normal deviates and plotted those deviates against the true weight difference. Urban (1909) collected extensive data on problems of this nature and introduced such extensions as the use of the Cauchy cdf in place of the normal curve.

Introduction of these quantal response techniques to bioassay came as early as the 1920s, the most influential early contributors being Gaddum and Bliss. (Biological assay is the measurement of the potency of some stimulus by means of the reactions which it produces in living matter.) Gaddum (1933) transformed the proportion of positive quantal responses into its 'normal equivalent deviation' (n.e.d.) by the inverse normal cdf. Then he fitted straight lines to the plot of this n.e.d. against the stimulus level. In parallel but independent research, Bliss (1934) applied the term 'probit', a contraction of 'probability unit', to the n.e.d. increased by 5 and thus christened the method of analysis. (That increment of 5 served to avoid working with negative numbers.)

Despite these firm and wide foundations, Berkson and Finney are the names most commonly associated with the logit and probit analysis, respectively. Berkson (1944, 1949) advocated the use of the logistic transformation in place of the normal (thus, 'logit' refers to 'logistic probability unit') and introduced the computationally efficient minimum chi-square estimation procedure. In 1947, Finney published the first edition of the treatise *Probit Analysis*, which became the standard reference and computational handbook for applications of the probit technique.

An application of probit to the problem of automobile demand by Farrell (1954) appears to have been its first use in economics and was inspired by the literature in bioassay. Farrell's 'stimulus' variable was income and conceptually he sought an estimate of the mean of the random income threshold above which a household would make a purchase. Soon after, Tobin (1955) examined the demand for durable goods with a probit model. He included two exogenous variables, conceived of a latent index made up of a linear combination of them as the stimulus, and framed the problem in a multiple regression analysis setting rather than the anova structure more common in bioassay. While Tobin's paper apparently did not impress contemporary editors, its wide citation in the econometrics literature over the next two decades suggests that it was indeed a landmark contribution.

Sporadic contributions to the probit–logit literature appeared throughout the 1960s. Zellner and Lee (1965) adapted Berkson's MIN chi-square estimator to multiple dichotomous relationships, Goldberger (1964) was the first to mention probit in an econometrics text, and, in work which appears to have been independent of the bioassay literature, Theil (1969) suggested a multinomial logit model and derived the weighted least squares estimator for it.

Parallel to but independent of the development of probit and logit for empirical work in bioassay, the probit and logit functions were being used in theoretical models of behaviour in psychology, and this literature led to independent introduction of the techniques to economics. Following the early work of Fechner, Urban and others, Thurstone (1927) obtained the probit model as a solution to the derivation of choice probabilities in a theoretical model of random utility, and Luce (1959) derived the multinomial logit model from an axiomatic approach to this same problem. This literature was introduced to economics by Marschak (1960) and inspired empirical research using the multinomial logit model in the area of travel demand. The new results and careful elucidation of the theoretical and statistical foundations of the multinomial logit model by McFadden (1973, 1981) serves as a major stimulus to the application and further development of these techniques in economics.

Limited dependent variable models have a much shorter history, and, aside from univariate censored and truncated variable models, a history which is more closely confined to economics. The seminal contribution was by Tobin (1958) who considered the zero mass point and continuous positive observations on durable goods expenditures to reflect a hybridization of probit models and regression models. The truncated variable model he proposed was christened 'Tobit' by Goldberger (1964). Aside from sporadic applications and extensions through the 1960s, the next major contributions were proofs of the asymptotic properties of the MLE by Amemiya (1973) and Heckman's (1974) careful derivation of a limited variable model from an underlying theory of economic behaviour. Subsequent developments have flourished, particularly in new models and applications involving self-selection and in properties and performance of various estimators.

BIBLIOGRAPHY

Amemiya, T. 1973. Regression analysis when the dependent variable is truncated normal. *Econometrica* 41, 997–1016.
Amemiya, T. 1981. Qualitative response models: a survey. *Journal of Economic Literature* 19, 1483–536.

Amemiya, T. 1984. Tobit models: a survey. *Journal of Econometrics* 24, 3–61.

Arabmazar, A. and Schmidt, P. 1981. Further evidence on the robustness of the Tobit estimator to heteroscedasticity. *Journal of Econometrics* 17, 253–8.

Berkson, J. 1944. Application of the logistic function to bio-assay. *Journal of the American Statistical Association* 39, 357–65.

Berkson, J. 1949. Maximum likelihood and minimum chi-square estimates of the logistic function. *Journal of the American Statistical Association* 44, 273–8.

Bishop, Y., Fienberg, S. and Holland, P. 1975. *Discrete Multivariate Analysis*. Cambridge, Mass.: MIT Press.

Bliss, C. 1934. The method of probits. *Science* 79, 38–9.

Cosslett, S. 1983. Distribution-free maximum likelihood estimator of the binary choice model. *Econometrica* 51, 765–82.

Farrell, M. 1954. The demand for motor cars in the United States. *Journal of the Royal Statistical Society*, Series A 117, 171–93.

Fechner, G. 1860. *Elemente der Psychophysik*. Leipzig: Breitkopf & Härtel.

Finney, D. 1947. *Probit Analysis*. Cambridge: Cambridge University Press.

Gaddum, J. 1933. Reports on biological standards III. Methods of biological assay depending on a quantal response. *Special Report Series Medical Research Council* No. 183, London.

Goldberger, A. 1964. *Economic Theory*. New York: Wiley.

Goldberger, A. 1983. Abnormal selection bias. In *Studies in Econometrics: Time Series and Multivariate Statistics*, ed. S. Karlin, T. Amemiya and L.A. Goodman, New York: Academic Press.

Hausman, J. and Wise, D. 1977. Social experimentation, truncated distributions and efficient estimation. *Econometrica* 45, 319–39.

Heckman, J. 1974. Shadow prices, market wages, and labor supply. *Econometrica* 42, 679–93.

Hurd, M. 1979. Estimation in truncated samples when there is heteroscedasticity. *Journal of Econometrics* 11, 247–58.

Lee, L.F. 1981. Simultaneous equations models with discrete and censored variables. In *Structural Analysis of Discrete Data with Econometric Applications*, ed. C. Manski and D. McFadden, Cambridge, Mass.: Harvard University Press.

Luce, R. 1959. *Individiaul Choice Behavior: a Theoretical Analysis*. New York: Wiley.

McFadden, D. 1974. Conditional logit analysis of qualitative choice behavior. In *Frontiers in Econometrics*, ed. P. Zarembka, New York: Academic Press.

McFadden, D. 1981. Econometric models of probabilistic choice. In *Structural Analysis of Discrete Data with Econometric Applications*, ed. C. Manski and D. McFadden, Cambridge, Mass.: Harvard University Press.

McKelvey, R. and Zavoina, W. 1975. A statistical model for the analysis of ordinal level dependent variables. *Journal of Mathematical Sociology* 4, 103–120.

Maddala, G.S. 1983. *Limited Dependent and Qualitative Variables in Econometrics*. Cambridge: Cambridge University Press.

Manski, C. 1975. Maximum score estimation of the stochastic utility model of choice. *Journal of Econometrics* 3, 205–28.

Marschak, J. 1960. Binary-choice constraints and random utility indicators. In *Mathematical Methods in the Social Sciences*, ed. K. Arrow, S. Karlin and P. Suppes, Stanford: University Press.

Nelson, F. 1981. A test for misspecification in the censored-normal model. *Econometrica* 49, 1317–29.

Olsen, R. 1978. A note on the uniqueness of the maximum likelihood estimator for the Tobit model. *Econometrica* 46, 1211–15.

Powell, J. 1984. Least absolute deviations estimation for the censored regression model. *Journal of Econometrics* 25, 303–25.

Quandt, R. 1982. Econometric disequilibrium models. *Econometric Review* 1, 1–63.

Robinson, P. 1982. On the asymptotic properties of estimators of models containing limited dependent variables. *Econometrica* 50, 27–41.

Rosett, R. 1959. A statistical model of friction in economics. *Econometrica* 27, 263–7.

Rosett, R. and Nelson, F.D. 1975. Estimation of a two-limit probit regression model. *Econometrica* 43, 141–6.

Theil, H. 1969. A multinomial extension of the linear logit model. *International Economic Review* 10, 251–9.

Thurstone, L. 1927. A law of comparative judgement. *Psychological Review* 34, 273–86.

Tobin, J. 1955. The application of the multivariate probit analysis to economic survey data. Cowles Foundation Discussion Paper No. 1, New Haven.

Tobin, J. 1958. Estimation of relationships for limited dependent variables. *Econometrica* 26, 24–36.

Urban, F. 1909. Die Psychophysichen Massmethoden als Grundlagen Empirischer Messungen. *Archiv für die Gesammte Psychologie* 15, 261–355.

Zellner, A. and Lee, T. 1965. Joint estimation of relationships involving discrete random variables. *Econometrica* 33, 383–94.

Lognormal Distribution

P.E. HART

If there is a number, θ, such that $Y = \log_e(X - \theta)$ is normally distributed, the distribution of X is *lognormal*. The important special case of $\theta = 0$ gives the two-parameter lognormal distribution, $X \sim \Lambda(\mu, \sigma^2)$ with $Y \sim N(\mu, \sigma^2)$, where μ and σ^2 denote the mean and variance of $\log_e X$. The classic work on the subject is by Aitchison and Brown (1957). A useful survey is provided by Johnson and Kotz (1970). They also summarize the history of this distribution: the pioneer contributions by Galton (1879) on its genesis, and by McAlister (1879) on its measures of location and dispersion, were followed by Kapteyn (1903), who studied its genesis in more detail and also devised an analogue machine to generate it. Gibrat's (1931) study of economic size distributions was a most important development and his law of proportionate effect is given in equation (1) below.

Since then there has been an immense number of applications of the lognormal distribution in the natural, behavioural and social sciences. The many hundreds of applications in the social sciences vary from the duration of strikes to securities markets.

Why does the lognormal distribution occur so frequently? One plausible answer is based on the Central Limit Theorems used to explain the genesis of a normal curve. If a large number of random shocks, some positive, some negative, change the size of a particular variable, X, in an additive fashion, the distribution of that variable will tend to become normal as the number of shocks increases. But if these shocks act multiplicatively, changing the value of X by randomly distributed proportions instead of absolute amounts, the Central Limit Theorems apply to $Y = \log_e X$ which tends to be normally distributed. Hence X has a lognormal distribution.

The substitution of multiplicative for additive random shocks generates a positively skew, leptokurtic, lognormal distribution instead of the symmetric, mesokurtic normal curve. But the degree of skewness and kurtosis of the two-parameter lognormal curve depends solely on σ^2, so if this is low enough,

145

the lognormal approximates the normal curve. The important difference is that X cannot take zero or negative values which may make the lognormal distribution a more appropriate representation of variables, such as height and weight, which must take positive values. Clearly, the widespread occurrence of positive variables in practice, coupled with the great flexibility of the shape of the lognormal, provide further reasons for its frequent application.

A convenient illustration of the application of the lognormal distribution in economics is provided by Hart and Prais (1956). After noting the approximation of the size distribution of UK firms to a lognormal curve, they used σ^2 to measure changes in business concentration 1885–1950. Prais (1976) updated this analysis to 1969. The justification for using σ^2 to measure the extent to which business is concentrated in large firms is that in the lognormal case there is a one-to-one relationship between σ^2 and all the other measures of concentration such as the Gini coefficient of concentration, the coefficient of variation, the first order or Shannon entropy, the second order entropy or Hirschman–Herfindahl statistic, and other orders of entropy such as the Atkinson index of inequality. The principle of transfers criticism of the use of σ^2, namely that a transfer of business from a smaller to a larger firm need not increase σ^2, does not apply in the lognormal case. Indeed, Creedy (1977) has shown that the principle of transfers criticism is not important even if the lognormal distribution does not hold.

More important is the criticism that a lognormal model cannot readily include births, deaths or marriages (mergers) of firms which are known to be important in practice. The same limitation arises in other fields since X, denoting the size of the ith observation, cannot take zero value in a lognormal model.

Another limitation is that in the simple Gibrat (1931) model

$$y_i(t) = y_i(t-1) + \varepsilon_i(t), \tag{1}$$

where $y_i = Y_i - \bar{Y}$, and $\varepsilon_i(t)$ is independent of $y_i(t-1)$ with $E(\varepsilon_i) = 0$ and $E(\varepsilon_i^2) = \sigma_\varepsilon^2$ for all t, concentration must increase over time since

$$\sigma_t^2 = V(y)_t = V(y)_{t-1} + \sigma_\varepsilon^2. \tag{2}$$

Yet $\hat{\sigma}^2$ did not increase between 1939 and 1950. Again, in the context of income distributions, $\hat{\sigma}^2$ does not increase continuously over time which has led some authors to reject a lognormal model of incomes. This problem may be overcome by (3)

$$y_i(t) = \beta y_i(t-1) + \varepsilon_i(t) \tag{3}$$

which is the regression model implicit in Galton (1889, 1892) and repeated by Kalecki (1945). Equation (2) is replaced by (4)

$$V(y)_t = \beta^2 V(y)_{t-1} + \sigma_\varepsilon^2 \tag{4}$$

and $\sigma^2 = V(y)$ can fall over time if $\beta^2 < \rho^2$ where the correlation coefficient is given by $\rho^2 = 1 - \{\sigma_\varepsilon^2 / V(y_t)\}$. Thus there is no need to introduce births and deaths to prevent an ever increasing variance.

Unfortunately, the Central Limit Theorems of Lindeberg–Levy, or of Lyapunov, which generate a lognormal distribution from (1) cannot be used for (3) when $\beta < 1$. By repeated substitution,

$$y_i(t) = \beta^t y_i(0) + \sum_{\tau=1}^{t} \beta^{t-\tau} \varepsilon_i(\tau), \qquad t \geqslant \tau, \tag{5}$$

and we could assume that ε_i is normally distributed to obtain a normal distribution for $Y = \log_e X$, but this is tantamount to assuming that X is lognormally distributed.

Alternatively it may be shown that the departure of $y_i(t)$ from normality will not be very large if β is near but below unity. Since the rth cumulant of a sum of independent variables is the sum of the rth cumulants of the separate variables, we have

$$K_r\{y(t)\} = \frac{K_r\{\varepsilon\}}{(1 - \beta^r)} \tag{6}$$

for large t, assuming the $\varepsilon(\tau)$ are identically distributed. The skewness of $y(t)$ is $\mu_3/\mu_2^{1.5}$ and its kurtosis is $(\mu_4/\mu_2^2) - 3$. Both may be obtained from (6) and expressed as ratios of the skewness and kurtosis of the ε. For example, suppose the lowest value of β is 0.7, then the skewness of $y(t)$ is about half, and its kurtosis about a third, of those of $\varepsilon(\tau)$. Clearly, the skewness and kurtosis of $\varepsilon(\tau)$ would have to be very large to make $y(t)$ depart very much from normality. Hence the widespread use of the lognormal distribution in practice is justified even if the $\varepsilon(\tau)$ are not normal.

BIBLIOGRAPHY

Aitchison, J. and Brown, J.A.C. 1957. *The Lognormal Distribution.* Cambridge: Cambridge University Press.

Creedy, J. 1977. The principle of transfers and the variance of logarithms. *Oxford Bulletin of Economics and Statistics* 39, 152–8.

Galton, F. 1879. The geometric mean in vital and social statistics. *Proceedings of the Royal Society of London* 29, 365–7.

Galton, F. 1889. *Natural Inheritance.* London: Macmillan.

Galton, F. 1892. *Hereditary Genius.* London: Macmillan; New York: Horizon Press, 1952.

Gibrat, R. 1931. *Les inégalites économiques.* Paris; Libraire du Recueil Sirey.

Hart, P.E. and Prais, S.J. 1957. The analysis of business concentration: a statistical approach. *Journal of the Royal Statistical Society* Series A 119, 150–91.

Johnson, N.L. and Kotz, S. 1970. *Continuous Univariate Distributions* 1. Boston: Houghton Mifflin.

Kalecki, M. 1945. On the Gibrat distribution. *Econometrica* 13, 161–70.

Kapteyn, J.C. 1903. *Skew Frequency Curves in Biology and Statistics.* Astronomical Laboratory, Groningen: Noordhoff.

McAlister, D. 1879. The law of the geometric mean. *Proceedings of the Royal Society of London* 29, 367–75.

Prais, S.J. 1976. *The Evolution of Giant Firms in Britain.* Cambridge and New York: Cambridge University Press.

Macroeconometric Models

RAY C. FAIR

The topic 'macroeconometric models' is very broad. Conceivably it could include any study in which at least one equation was estimated using macroeconomic data. I will limit my discussion to structural models that try to explain the overall economy, although I will also have a few things to say about vector autoregressive models.

One might have thought at the beginning of large-scale model construction in the early 1950s that there would be a gradual and fairly systematic improvement in the accuracy of the specification of the equations, so that by the late 1980s there would exist a generally agreed upon model. This is not the case. Macroeconomics has now been in a state of flux for more than a decade. There is currently much disagreement among macroeconomists about the structure of the economy, and there is certainly no generally agreed upon model. This lack of agreement manifests itself in quite different monetary and fiscal policy recommendations that are made at any one time by different economists.

The unsettled nature of macroeconomics makes it an exciting research area, but also a difficult one to review in a short essay. Any current review of macroeconometric models must be selective and somewhat idiosyncratic, and this is certainly true of the present review. I have chosen some topics that I think are important in the area, but the list is by no means exhaustive.

I. A BRIEF HISTORY. A comprehensive discussion of the history of macroeconometric model-building is in Bodkin, Klein and Marwah (1986). The following discussion is very brief. The beginning of the construction of macroeconometric models is usually traced back to Tinbergen's (1939) work on business cycles in the late 1930s, although there were earlier efforts by Tinbergen and others that could be classified as macroeconometric models. Tinbergen's model was an annual model and consisted of 31 behavioural equations and 17 identities. It was estimated by ordinary least squares for the period 1919–32. There are few exogenous variables in the model; Bodkin, Klein and Marwah (1986) have identified only five. Tinbergen never 'solved' his model in the modern sense. He did, however, spend considerable time analysing the dynamic properties of the model analytically after reducing the model to a linear difference equation in corporate profits.

Work on macroeconometric models began in earnest after World War II. The leading figure in the postwar period has been Lawrence Klein, who built his first models while at the Cowles Commission in the mid-1940s. The results of this work were published in Klein (1950). This monograph contained three models. Model I contains three behavioural equations and three identities, and it was estimated by full-information maximum likelihood, limited-information maximum likelihood and ordinary least squares. This model has been an important pedagogical tool for many decades. Model II contains a consumption function and two identities. Model III contains 12 behavioural equations and 4 identities. It is best known today as the precursor of the Klein–Goldberger model.

The Klein–Goldberger model (1955) began as a project of the Research Seminar in Quantitative Economics at the University of Michigan. It was an annual model, estimated for the split-sample period 1929–41, 1946–52. It consisted of 15 behavioural equations and 5 identities and was estimated by limited-information maximum likelihood. It was the first model to be used for regular *ex ante* forecasting purposes. The first forecast was for the year 1953.

The 1960s was an active time for model-builders. One of the major efforts of the decade was the Brookings model, a quarterly model which at its peak contained nearly 400 equations. This model was a joint effort of many individuals, and although it never achieved the success that was initially expected, much was learned during the effort. The model was laid to rest around 1972.

The 1970s was a time in which many models became commercially successful, the most successful being DRI (Data Resources, Inc.), Wharton, and Chase. The commercialization of the models changed the focus of research somewhat. Less time was spent on what one might call basic research on the models, such as experimenting with alternative estimation techniques and statistical testing. More time was spent on the month-to-month needs of keeping the models up to date. The 1970s was also a time in which macroeconomic models came under attack on academic grounds. The key attack was the Lucas (1976) critique, which argued that the models are not likely to be useful for policy purposes. More will be said about this later. These attacks had the effect of moving academics away from research on large-scale models to other things, and very little academic research was done on models in the 1970s. This has continued to be true to some extent in the first half of the 1980s.

II. METHODOLOGY. Economic theory is used to guide the specification of macro-econometric models. The 'traditional' procedure is to use theory to guide the choice of explanatory variables in the equations to be estimated. Consider, for example, the multi-period utility-maximization theory of household behaviour. This theory tells us that a household's consumption and labour-supply decisions are a function of the prices of the goods, the wage rate, non-labour income,

149

interest rates and the initial value of wealth. The traditional procedure is thus to use these as explanatory variables in the equations explaining consumption and labour supply. In many cases theory indicates the signs of the coefficients of the explanatory variables. Theory is generally not used to decide the functional forms of the estimated equations and the lengths of the lag distributions. Functional forms and lag lengths are generally chosen empirically, by trying alternative forms and lengths to see which produces the best results.

The transition from theoretical models to empirical models is a difficult problem in macroeconomics. One is usually severely constrained by the quantity and quality of the available data, and many restrictive assumptions are generally needed in the transition from the theory to the data. In other words, extra 'theorizing' occurs during the transition, and it is usually theory that is less appealing than that of the purely theoretical model.

The place where extra theorizing occurs most is the treatment of expectations. Expected future values play an important role in most theoretical models. In the multi-period utility-maximization model, for example, expected future values of prices, the wage rate, non-labour income and interest rates affect current consumption and labour-supply decisions. Since expected values are generally not observed, one needs to make some assumption about how expectations are formed when specifying the empirical equations to estimate. A common approach is to assume that expectations of a particular variable are a function of current and lagged values of the variable. Under this assumption one simply replaces the expected future values with current and lagged values. This assumption is fairly ad hoc, and much of the research in macroeconomics in the last decade is on the question of how expectations are formed. More will be said about expectations later.

Once enough assumptions have been made so that only observed variables appear in the equations, the equations are ready to be estimated. The estimation techniques range from ordinary least squares and two-stage least squares to three-stage least squares and full information maximum likelihood. Many equations in macroeconometric models have serially correlated error terms, and a common procedure is to estimate the equations under the assumption that the error terms are first-order autoregressive. If the model is simultaneous, which almost all models are, ordinary least squares produces inconsistent estimates.

Much experimentation takes place at the estimation stage. Different functional forms and lag lengths are tried, and explanatory variables are dropped if they have coefficient estimates of the wrong expected sign. Variables with coefficient estimates of the right sign may also be dropped if the estimates have t-statistics that are less than about two in absolute value, although practice varies on this. If things are not working out very well in the sense that very few significant estimates of the correct sign are being obtained, one may go back and rethink the theory or the transition from the theory to the estimated equations. This process may lead to new equations to try and perhaps to better results. This back-and-forth movement between theory and results can be an important part of the construction of the model.

The estimation technique that is used in experimenting with alternative specifications is usually a limited-information technique, such as two-stage least squares. These techniques have the advantage that one can experiment with a particular equation without worrying very much about the other equations in the model. Knowledge of the general features of the other equations is used in the choice of the first-stage regressors for the two-stage least squares technique, for example, but one does not need to know the exact features of each equation when making this choice. If a full-information technique is used, it is usually used at the end of the search process to estimate the final version of the model. If the full-information estimates are quite different from the limited-information ones, it may again be necessary to go back and rethink the theory and transition. In particular, this may indicate that the version of the model that has been chosen by the limited-information searching is seriously misspecified. Sometimes ordinary least squares is used in the searching process even though the model is simultaneous. This, however, has little to recommend it since the ordinary least squares estimates are inconsistent, and consistent alternatives like two-stage least squares are not expensive to use.

The next step after the model has been estimated is to test and analyse it. One way in which models are tested is to compute predicted values from solving the overall model and compare the predicted values to the actual values. The accuracy of the predictions is usually examined by calculating room mean-squared errors. The properties of models are analysed by performing 'multiplier' experiments. These experiments involve changing one or more exogenous variables and observing how the predicted values of the endogenous variables change. Models can also be analysed by performing optimal-control experiments. Given a particular objective function and given a set of policy variables, one can find the values of the policy variables that maximize the objective function subject to the constraints imposed by the model.

It may also be the case that things are not working out well at the testing and analysis stage. Poor fits may be obtained; multipliers that seem (according to one's *a priori* views) too large or too small may be obtained; and optimal control experiments may yield optimal values that do not seem sensible. This may also lead one to rethink the theory, the transition to the estimated equations, or both, and perhaps to try alternative specifications. The back-and-forth movement between theory and results may thus occur at both the estimation and analysis steps.

It is important to note that the back-and-forth movement between theory and results may yield a model that fits the data well and seems on other grounds to be quite good, when it is in fact a poor approximation of the structure of the economy. If one searches hard enough, it is usually possible with macro time-series data to come up with what seems to be a good model. The searching for models in this way is sometimes called 'data mining' and sometimes called 'specification searches', depending on one's mood. Fortunately, there is a way of testing whether one has mined the data in an inappropriate way, which is to do outside sample tests. If a model is poorly specified, it should not fit well outside the sample period for which it was estimated, even though it looks good within sample. It is thus possible to test for misspecification by examining outside sample results. A method for doing this is discussed in the next section.

Because of the dropping of variables with wrong signs and (possibly) the back-and-forth movement from multiplier results to theory, an econometric model is likely to have multiplier properties that are similar to what one expects from the theory. Therefore, the fact that an econometric model has properties that are consistent with the theory is in no way a confirmation of the model, at least in my view. Models must be tested by using methods like the one discussed in the next section, not by examining the 'reasonableness' of their multiplier properties.

There are two main alternatives to the traditional procedure just outlined. One, which is discussed in section IV, is to take more seriously the theoretical restrictions that are implied by the assumption that decisions are made by maximizing objective functions. The other alternative is to estimate vector autoregressive models, where very few theoretical restrictions are imposed. This alternative has been stressed by Sims (1980). A vector autoregressive (VAR) model is one in which each variable is regressed on lagged values of itself and lagged values of all the other variables in the model. This approach imposes some restrictions on the data – in particular, the number of variables to use, the lengths of the lags and (sometimes) cross-equation restrictions on the coefficients – but the restrictions are in general less restrictive than the exclusionary ones used by the traditional approach. As discussed in the next section, VAR models are useful for comparison purposes even if one otherwise does not agree with the VAR methodology.

Macroeconometric models are also used to make forecasts. Given a set of coefficient estimates, a set of values of the future-error terms, and a set of guesses of the future values of the exogenous variables, one can use a model to make predictions of the future values of the endogenous variables. A forecast beyond the data, where guessed values of the exogenous variables must be used, is called an *ex ante* forecast. A forecast within the data, where actual values of the exogenous variables are used, is called an *ex post* forecast. The values chosen for the error terms are usually the expected values, which are almost always zero. If an equation has been estimated under the assumption of a first-order autoregressive error, the estimate of the autoregressive coefficient and last period's estimated-error term are used in estimating the current period's error term.

In practice, *ex ante* forecasts are often 'subjectively adjusted'. If, when unadjusted, the model is not forecasting what the model-builder thinks is going to happen, the equations are changed by adding or subtracting values from the constant terms. In many cases a constant term in an equation is changed more than once over the forecast horizon. Adjusting the values of constant terms is equivalent to adjusting the values of the error terms, given that a different value of the constant term can be used each period. This procedure can thus be looked on as the model-builder guessing the future values of the error terms. Instead of setting the future-error terms equal to their expected values, the model-builder overrides this aspect of the model and sets values based on his or her own feelings about what is going to happen. With enough adjustments it is possible to have the forecasts be whatever the user wants, subject to the restriction that the identities must be satisfied. This means, of course, that in practice one can never be sure how much of the forecast is due to the model and how much is due to the model-builder. It also means that *ex ante* forecasts are of little use for testing and comparing models *qua* models.

III. TESTING. The testing of macroeconometric models is extremely difficult, and this is undoubtedly one of the reasons that there is so little agreement in the area. There are two main problems in comparing different models. First, models may differ in the number and types of variables that are taken to be exogenous. If, for example, one model takes prices as exogenous whereas a second model does not, the first model has an obvious advantage over the second in predictive tests. Second, data mining may make a model look good within sample when it is in fact a poor approximation of the structure.

I have developed a method for comparing models that helps account for these problems (Fair, 1980). The method is briefly as follows. There are four main sources of uncertainty of a forecast from a model: uncertainty due to (1) the error terms, (2) the coefficient estimates, (3) the exogenous variables and (4) the possible misspecification of the model. Uncertainty from the error terms and coefficient estimates can be estimated using stochastic simulation. From the estimation of the model one has estimates of the covariance matrix of the error terms and the covariance matrix of the coefficient estimates. Given these estimates and given an assumption about the functional form of the distributions, such as normality, one can draw error terms and coefficients. For a given set of draws the model can be solved and the predicted values of the endogenous variables recorded. This is one trial. Many trials can be performed, and after, say, J trials, one has J predicted values of each endogenous variable for each period of the forecast. From the J values one can compute the mean of the forecast and the variance of the forecast error.

In order to account for exogenous-variable uncertainty, one needs some assumption about the uncertainty itself. One polar assumption is that the exogenous variables are in some sense as uncertain as the endogenous variables. One might, for example, estimate autoregressive equations for each exogenous variable and add these equations to the model. This would produce a model with no exogenous variables, which could then be tested. The other polar assumption is that there is no uncertainty attached to the exogenous variables. This might be true of some policy variables. I have generally worked with an in-between case, where I estimate an autoregressive equation for each exogenous variable and use the estimated variance from this equation as an estimate of the variance of the exogenous-variable forecast error. I then use these estimated variances and the normality assumption to draw values for the exogenous variables. Each trial of the stochastic simulation thus consists of draws of the error terms, coefficients and exogenous variables.

Estimating the degree of misspecification of the model is based on a comparison of two estimated forecast-error variances. One is the stochastic simulation estimate; the other is the square of the outside-sample forecast error. If the model is correctly specified, the expected value of the difference between the two estimates is zero (ignoring simulation error). If one has data mined in an inappropriate way and the model is misspecified, one would expect the stochastic simulation estimate to be smaller than the estimate from the outside-sample error. The expected value of the difference is thus likely to be positive for a misspecified model. By repeated re-estimation and stochastic simulation of the model, where one observation is added at the end of the sample period for each estimation, the expected value of the difference between the estimated variances can be estimated. The differences are then estimates of the degree of misspecification of the model.

The final estimated forecast-error variance for each variable for each period is obtained by adding the estimated difference to the stochastic-simulation estimate that is based on draws of the error terms, coefficients and exogenous variables. This estimated variance has accounted for the four main sources of uncertainty of a forecast, and it can be compared across models. Speaking loosely, each model is on an equal footing for comparison purposes. If one model has smaller estimated variances than another, this is evidence in favour of the model. Autoregressive and vector autoregressive models are useful for comparison purposes. Estimated variances of a structural model can be compared to those of an autoregressive or vector autoregressive model. If the estimated variances of the structural model are in general larger after taking all the sources of uncertainty into account, this is a cause of some concern.

IV. THE LUCAS CRITIQUE AND THE ESTIMATION OF DEEP STRUCTURAL PARAMETERS. The theory that is used to guide the specification of econometric equations in what I am calling the traditional approach is generally based on some implicit objective function that is being maximized. The parameters of the objective function are not, however, directly estimated. The parameters of the derived-decision equations are estimated instead, where the estimated parameters are combinations of the parameters of the objective function, the parameters of expectation-formation mechanisms, and other things. A problem with estimating combinations is that if, say, one wants to examine the effects of changing an exogenous variable or a policy rule on the decision variables, there is always the possibility that this change will change something in the combinations. If so, then it is inappropriate to use the estimated-decision equations, which are based on fixed estimates of the combinations, to examine the effects of the change. This is the point emphasized by Lucas (1976) in his critique of macroeconometric models.

Lucas's critique has led to a line of research concerned with estimating parameters of objective functions, which are sometimes called 'deep' structural parameters. These parameters, which are primarily taste and technology parameters, are assumed not to change when policy rules and exogenous variables change, and so one can use them and the associated model to examine the effects of policy changes. The approach is appealing in this sense, although many restrictive assumptions are involved in setting up the estimation problem, such as the specification of a particular form for the objective function. It is too early to know how useful this approach will be in practice.

If the approach of estimating deep structural parameters turns out not to lead to econometric models that are good approximations, this does not invalidate Lucas's critique. The critique is a logical one. If parameters that are taken to be constant change when policy changes, the estimated effects of the change are clearly in error. The key question for any experiment with a model is the likely size of the error. There are many potential sources of error, and even the best econometric model is only an approximation. One of the most important sources of error in my view is the use of aggregate data. As the age and income distributions of the population change, the coefficients in aggregate equations are likely to change, and this is a source of error in the estimated equations. This problem may be quantitatively much more important than the problem raised by Lucas.

One encouraging feature regarding the Lucas critique is the following. Assume that for an equation or set of equations the parameters change considerably when a given policy variable changes. Assume also that the policy variable changes frequently. In this case the method discussed in section III is likely to reject a model that includes this equation or set of equations. The model is obviously misspecified, and the method should be able to pick up this misspecification if there have been frequent changes in the policy variable. One may, of course, still be misled regarding the Lucas critique if the policy variable has changed not at all or very little in the past. In this case the model will still be misspecified, but the misspecification has not been given a change to be picked up in the data. One should thus be wary of drawing conclusions about the effects of seldom-changed policy variables unless one has strong reasons for believing that the Lucas critique is not quantitatively important for the particular policy variable in question.

V. MODELS WITH RATIONAL EXPECTATIONS. In the past few years research has begun on macroeconometric models with rational expectations. Consider a model in which some of the explanatory variables are expected future values. In particular, assume that y_{t+1}^e appears as an explanatory variable in the first equation, where y_{t+1}^e is the expected value of y for period $t+1$ based on information through period $t-1$. In the utility-maximization model in section I, the equation being estimated might be a consumption equation and y might be the wage rate. If expectations are assumed to be rational in the sense of Muth (1961), then the value of y_{t+1}^e is equal to the model's prediction of y for period $t+1$. In other words, the expectation of a variable is equal to the model's prediction of it. Under the assumption of rational expectations, agents know the model and use it to generate their expectations. Agents are obviously assumed to be much more sophisticated in this case than they are in the case in which expectations of a variable are simply a function of current and lagged values of the variable.

Models with rational expectations are more difficult to estimate and solve than are standard models. Two types of estimation methods have been proposed for these models. One is full-information maximum likelihood, FIML (Fair and Taylor, 1983). This method accounts for all the restrictions that are implied by the rational-expectations hypothesis, including all cross-equation restrictions. Unfortunately, the method is expensive to use, and it is not currently computationally feasible for large non-linear models.

There are limited information alternatives to FIML. The main alternative is Hansen's (1982) method of moments estimator. Limited information methods like Hansen's estimator are based on the assumption that agents form expectations rationally and that there is an observed vector of variables (observed by the econometrician), denoted Z_i, that is used in part by agents in forming their (rational) expectations. The methods do not require for consistent estimates that Z_t include all the variables used by agents in forming their expectations, Limited-information techniques are not very expensive to compute, and they have been widely used in practice.

The solution of rational expectations models is more difficult than the solution of standard models because future predicted values affect present predicted values. In other words, one cannot solve for the present without knowing the future. The solution method that has come to be used (Fair and Taylor, 1983) iterates on solution *paths*. One guesses paths for the future values of the expectations and then solves the model period by period, treating the paths as predetermined. This solution yields new paths for the future values of the expectations, and so the model can be solved again period by period, treating the new paths as predetermined. This then yields new solution paths, which can be used for a new period-by-period solution, and so on. Convergence is achieved when the solution paths on one iteration are within some prescribed tolerance level of the solution paths on the next iteration. This method turns out to work quite well in practice and is not that expensive.

Work is essentially just beginning on macroeconometric models with rational expectations, and no strong conclusions can as yet be drawn. Results are presented in Fair (1985) that provide only mild support for the use of more sophisticated expectational hypotheses than are traditionally used in model-building. More work, however, is clearly needed. It should be noted finally that macroeconometric models with rational expectations in the sense described here do not necessarily satisfy the Lucas critique. Depending on the set up, the coefficients that are estimated in the stochastic equations are not necessarily deep structural parameters even if there are expected future variables among the explanatory variables.

CONCLUSION. Work in macroeconometrics has the advantage that new observations are continually being generated. The current range of disagreement in macro-economics may be narrowed in the future as more data are generated and more tests performed. Whether this will happen and whether there will be a return to more academic research on macroeconometric models is hard to say. Academic research on models clearly peaked in the 1960s, and it may have reached a trough in the late 1970s or early 1980s. But trying to predict research cycles is probably more hazardous than trying to predict business cycles.

BIBLIOGRAPHY

Bodkin, R.G., Klein, L.R. and Marwah, K. 1986. *A History of Macro-Econometric Model-Building.*

Fair, R.C. 1980. Estimating the expected predictive accuracy of econometric models. *International Economic Review* 21, June, 355–78.

Fair, R.C. 1985. The use of expected future variables in macroeconometric models. Mimeo, May.

Fair, R.C. and Taylor, J. 1983. Solution and maximum likelihood estimation of dynamic rational expectations models. *Econometrica* 51, July, 1169–85.

Hansen, L. 1982. Large sample properties of generalized method of moments estimators. *Econometrica* 50, July, 1029–54.

Klein, L.R. 1950. *Economic Fluctuations in the United States, 1921–1941.* Cowles Monograph No. 11, New York: Wiley.

Klein, L.R. and Goldberger, A.S. 1955. *An Econometric Model of the United States 1929–1952.* Amsterdam: North-Holland.

Lucas, R.E., Jr. 1976. Econometric policy evaluation: a critique. In *The Phillips Curve and Labor Markets*, ed. K. Brunner and A.H. Meltzer, Amsterdam: North-Holland.

Muth, J.F. 1961. Rational expectations and the theory of price movements. *Econometrica* 29, 315–35.

Sims, C.A. 1980. Macroeconomics and reality. *Econometrica* 48, January, 1–48.

Tinbergen, J. 1939. *Statistical Testing of Business Cycle Theories.* Geneva: League of Nations.

Multicollinearity

WILFRED CORLETT

Exact multicollinearity means that there is at least one exact linear relation between the column vectors of the $n \times k$ data matrix of n observations on k variables. More commonly, multicollinearity means that the variables are so intercorrelated in the data that the relations are 'almost exact'. The term was used by Frisch (1934) mainly in the context of attempts to estimate an exact relation between the systematic components of variables whose observed values contained disturbances or errors of measurement but where there might also be other relations between the systematic components which made estimates dangerous or even meaningless. In more recent work the data matrix has usually been the matrix X of regressor values in the linear regression model $Y = X\beta + \varepsilon$ with no measurement errors. Confusion between the two cases led at one time to some misunderstanding in the literature. Other terms used for the same phenomenon are collinearity and ill-conditioned data – although the latter may contain aspects of the scaling of variables which are irrelevant to multicollinearity.

For the linear regression model, exact multicollinearity means that it is impossible to separate out the effects of the individual variables is an exact relation. Some (or all) of the parameters of the model can not be estimated although some linear functions of them can. However, exact multicollinearity is rare except in badly specified models. Multicollinearity that is not exact is liable to lead to high variances and standard errors for least squares estimators of the parameters, although now some linear functions of the parameters can be estimated with much smaller variances. As a result, tests of hypotheses about the parameters may have little power, so that very inaccurate hypotheses may not be rejected, and confidence intervals for the parameters may be very wide. If a test rejects an hypothesis, multicollinearity has not done any serious harm; if it does not reject it, multicollinearity *may* be the cause but there are other reasons for not rejecting. The sample may be too small; the variance of the error ε may be too high; there may be too little variation in the relevant variable – although

158

this is sometimes considered as collinearity with a constant in the model; or the hypothesis may be correct or almost correct.

Various methods have been suggested for assessing the importance of multi-collinearity. One was the use of bunch maps (Frisch, 1934) which involved calculating regressions in all possible subsets of the variables, which minimization in the direction of each variable in the subset in turn, followed by a diagrammatic presentation. Interpretation was difficult. Several methods use the matrix R of correlations between the X variables. High off-diagonal elements indicate possible harmful effects from relations between two variables but relations involving more variables are difficult to spot in this way. Following Farrar and Glauber (1967) attention was paid to the determinant of R, with value near zero indicating serious multicollinearity. The diagonal elements of the inverse of R, the variance inflation factors, show how much multicollinearity multiplies the variance which would be achieved for the least squares estimator of a parameter if the variable associated with it were orthogonal to all the other variables. Possibly the most fruitful method is the use of the eigenvalues of R or of $X'X$, where each column of X has been scaled to have unit length but has not been centred. Belsley, Kuh and Welsch (1980) use this scaled X and the singular values of X (which are the square roots of the eigenvalues of $X'X$) to detect the number of apparently harmful relations between the variables, the effects of each on the estimation of each parameter and, hence, in combination with auxiliary regressions, an indication of which variables they contain.

If multicollinearity causes serious problems in some application, there are various possible ways of improving the situation. It may be possible to obtain more data. If the data really satisfy the model, this will improve matters – particularly if the new data do not have the same collinearities as the old. It may be possible to impose exact restrictions on the parameters. These restrictions, usually derived from economic theory, can give considerable improvements to the properties of estimators, but only if they are really justified. Finally, it may be possible to use stochastic information on the parameters or linear functions of them. This may be done by pure Bayesian techniques, or, following Theil and Goldberger (1961), by a form of mixed estimation using stochastic information on the values of the parameters, or linear functions of them, obtained from previous samples or from introspection (cf. Theil, 1971).

BIBLIOGRAPHY

Belsley, D.A., Kuh, E. and Welsch, R.E. 1980. *Regression Diagnostics*. New York: John Wiley.

Farrar, D.E. and Glauber, R.R. 1967. Multicollinearity in regression analysis: the problem revisited. *Review of Economics and Statistics* 49, 92–107.

Frisch, R. 1934. *Statistical Confluence Analysis by Means of Complete Regression Systems*. Oslo: University Institute of Economics.

Theil, H. 1971. *Principles of Econometrics*. New York: John Wiley.

Theil, H. and Goldberger, A.S. 1961. On pure and mixed statistical estimation in economics. *International Economic Review* 2, 65–78.

Non-linear Methods in Econometrics

A. RONALD GALLANT

Economic theory guides empirical research primarily by suggesting which variables ought to enter a relationship. But as to the functional form that this relationship ought to take, it only gives general information such as stating that certain first and second partial derivatives of a relationship must be positive or such as ruling out certain functional forms. In some applications, notably consumer demand systems, the theory rules out models that are linear in the parameters such as $y = \Sigma x_i \beta_i + e$ and thus provides a natural impetus to the development of statistical methods for models that are non-linear in the parameters such as

$$y = \left(\sum x_i \beta_i \right) \Big/ \left(\sum x_i \gamma_i - 1 \right) + e.$$

A more subtle but more profound influence in the same direction is exerted by the converse aspect of suggesting what variables ought to enter a relationship, that is variables not suggested ought not be present. Thus, when searching for a model that explains data better than an existing model, one will prefer a more complicated model involving only the suggested variables to a model of equal complexity in additional variables. One will inevitably fit models to data that are nonlinear in the parameters during the search.

It is not surprising, therefore, that the subject of nonlinear statistical models developed primarily within econometrics, once advances in computing technology and probability theory occurred that would permit it. What is surprising is the rapidity of the development and the speed at which the frontier of econometric research has passed beyond the study of nonlinear statistical models to the natural focus of study, a focus that takes the view that it is best to think of a model as being a point in a function space. Since, as indicated above, the most that economic theory can really say is that a model is a point in a function space, it would seem that the model ought to be studied as such. The process of moving from linear statistical models, through nonlinear models, to the new frontier has taken about fifteen years. Here we shall give an accounting of the statistical aspects of the process. A more detailed development of the subject that follows approximately the same lines as this survey and includes discussion of computations and applications in Gallant (1987).

Prior to 1969, there were scattered papers on nonlinear models with Hartley (1961, 1964) being the most notable contributor. A paper by Jennrich (1969) sparked research in nonlinear statistical models by econometricians. It considered the univariate, nonlinear explicit model

$$y_t = f(x_t, \theta^0) + e_t, \qquad t = 1, 2, \ldots, n$$

where y_t is a univariate response, x_t is a k-vector of explanatory variables, θ^0 is a p-vector of unknown parameters to be estimated, and e_t is an additive error assumed to be independently and identically distributed with mean zero and unknown variance σ^2. In the paper, sufficient conditions were obtained such that the least squares estimator, that is, the estimator $\hat{\theta}$ that minimizes

$$s_n(\theta) = (1/n) \sum_{t=1}^{n} [y_t - f(x_t, \theta)]^2,$$

over a parameter space Θ, is consistent and asymptotically normally distributed. What had blocked development of an asymptotic theory along conventional lines was the fact that the random variables y_t are not independently and identically distributed. Jennrich showed that the key to overcoming this technical difficulty was a uniform strong law of large numbers that holds if Θ is compact and a central limit theorem that holds for independently but not identically distributed random variables. The compactness assumption is somewhat restrictive but a paper by Malinvaud (1970) showed how the compactness assumption can be circumvented if need be.

These papers set the stage. Over the next ten years there followed a stream of papers extending econometric methods for linear models with a regression structure – ancillary explanatory variables and independent errors – to the analogous nonlinear model. Practical applications proceeded apace. Examples include papers on the asymptotic theory of estimation and inference for multivariate nonlinear models and for nonlinear simultaneous equations models.

From the long-run perspective, the most important outcome of this activity for econometric theory was a reasonable set of conditions such that a triangular array of data generated according to an implicit, nonlinear, simultaneous equations model (the most general model that need be considered) given by

$$q(y_t, x_t, \gamma_n^0) = e_t, \qquad t = 1, 2, \ldots, n, \qquad n = 1, 2, \ldots$$

will obey a uniform strong law of large numbers

$$\lim_{n \to \infty} \sup_{\theta \in \Theta} \left| (1/n) \sum_{t=1}^{n} [g(y_t, x_t, \theta) - \mathscr{E}g(y_t, x_t, \theta)] \right| = 0 \qquad \text{a.s.}$$

161

and will follow a continuously convergent central limit theorem

$$\mathscr{I}_n^{-1/2}(1/\sqrt{n}) \sum_{t=1}^{n} [g(y_t, x_t, \theta_n^0) - \mathscr{E}g(y_t, x_t, \theta_n^0)] \xrightarrow{\mathscr{L}} N(0, I).$$

Above, y_t is an M-variate response, x_t is a k-vector of explanatory variables, γ_n^0 is a sequence of (possibly infinite dimensional) parameters that converges with respect to some metric, $\{e_t\}$ is a sequence of independent, M-variate errors, θ_n^0 is a convergent sequence of p-vectors from a compact set Θ, and $\mathscr{I}_n^{-1/2}$ is the Cholesky factorization of the inverse of

$$\mathscr{I}_n = \operatorname{Var}\left[(1/\sqrt{n}) \sum_{t=1}^{n} g(y_t, x_t, \theta_n^0) \right].$$

The dependence of the parameter γ_n^0 on the sample size n is a technical expedient that allows one to deduce to a non-null, asymptotic distribution of test statistics. Other than that application, one usually presumes that there is no drift, which is to say that γ_n^0 is equal to some value γ^0 for all n.

With these results in hand, a unified treatment of nonlinear statistical models became possible. It was accomplished in a paper by Burguete, Gallant, and Souza (1982). The unifying concept was that estimators $\hat{\theta}_n$ are solutions to an optimization problem: minimize $s_n(\theta)$ subject to θ in Θ. From this concept, an asymptotic theory of estimation and inference follows by mimicking the standard methods of proof used in maximum likelihood theory but replacing the classical strong law and central limit theorem with those above.

The types of sample objective functions $s_n(\theta)$ that arise in econometrics can be divided into two groups. The first group is least mean distance estimators which have the form

$$s_n(\theta) = (1/n) \sum_{t=1}^{n} s(y_t, x_t, \hat{\tau}_n, \theta),$$

where $\hat{\tau}_n$ is a (possibly matrix valued) estimator of nuisance parameters and $s(y, x, \tau, \theta)$ is real valued. The leading example of this type of estimator is multivariate least squares (seemingly unrelated regressions) where data are presumed to be generated according to the explicit, multivariate model

$$y_t = f(x_t, \theta^0) + e_t,$$

with

$$s_n(\theta) = (1/n) \sum_{t=1}^{n} [y_t - f(x_t, \theta)]' \hat{\tau}_n^{-1} [y_t - f(x_t, \theta)];$$

$\hat{\tau}_n$ is some estimate of $\operatorname{var}(e_t)$, the errors are assumed to be independently and identically distributed. Other examples are maximum likelihood estimators, M-estimators and iteratively rescaled M-estimators for nonlinear (univariate or multivariate) explicit models, and maximum likelihood estimators for non-linear, simultaneous systems.

162

The second group is method of moments estimators which have the form

$$s_n(\theta) = (1/2)m_n'(\theta)\hat{D}_n m_n(\theta), \qquad m_n(\theta) = (1/n)\sum_{t=1}^{n} m(y_t, x_t, \hat{\tau}_n, \theta),$$

where $\hat{\tau}_n$ is an estimator of nuisance parameters and $\hat{D}_n$ is some matrix valued function of $\hat{\tau}_n$. The leading example of this type of estimator is the three-stage least-squares estimator where data are presumed to be generated according to the implicit, simultaneous equations model

$$q(y_t, x_t, \theta^0) = e_t,$$

and

$$m_n(\theta) = (1/n)\sum_{t=1}^{n} q(y_t, x_t, \theta) \otimes Z(x_t).$$

In the expression above, q, y_t, e_t are M-vectors, x_t is a k-vector, $Z(x)$ is some (possibly nonlinear) vector-valued function of the explanatory variables x_t, usually low order monomials in the components of x, and $\hat{D}_n$ is some estimator of $\text{Var}[\sqrt{n}m(\theta^0)]$. Other examples are the two-stage least-squares estimator, scale invariant M-estimators, and the Hartley–Booker (1965) estimator.

As regards estimation, the result which follows from the unifying concept are that $\hat{\theta}_n$ is estimating that value θ_n^0 which minimizes a function of the form $\bar{s}_n(\theta, \gamma_n^0)$ in the sense that $\sqrt{n}(\hat{\theta}_n - \theta_n^0)$ is asymptotically normally distributed. In the case of least mean distance estimators, this function is computed as

$$\bar{s}_n(\theta, \gamma_n^0) = \mathcal{E}(1/n)\sum_{t=1}^{n} s(y_t, x_t, \tau_n^0, \theta),$$

where $\{\tau_n^0\}$ is some sequence for which $\sqrt{n}(\hat{\tau}_n - \hat{\tau}_n^0)$ is bounded in probability and in the case of method of moments estimators this function is computed as

$$\bar{s}_n(\theta, \gamma_n^0) = (1/2)\bar{m}_n'(\theta, \gamma_n^0)D(\tau_n^0)\bar{m}_n(\theta, \gamma_n^0),$$

$$\bar{m}_n(\theta, \gamma_n^0) = \mathcal{E}(1/n)\sum_{t=1}^{n} m(y_t, x_t, \tau_n^0, \theta).$$

The expectation $\mathcal{E}(.)$ in the expression above is computed according to the model

$$q(y_t, x_t, \gamma_n^0) = e_t, \qquad t = 1, 2, \ldots, n, \qquad n = 1, 2, \ldots$$

that actually generates the data, which may be different from the model that was presumed to hold for the purpose of defining the estimation procedure. As a consequence, θ_n^0 will depend on the (possibly infinite dimensional) parameter vector γ_n^0 and, hence, will depend on n. In general, there will be a dependence on n even if γ_n^0 does not drift because the function $\bar{s}_n(\theta, \gamma)$ that defines θ_n^0 depends on n none the less. We will have $\theta_n^0 = \theta^0$ for all n when the presumed model and the actual model coincided and there is no drift.

Nearly every scientist regards a model as an approximation to nature not a description of nature. Thus, the importance of the result above derives not from the fact that it gives an asymptotic approximation to the sampling distribution of an estimator when the presumed model generates the data but from the fact that it gives an approximation when it does not. This provides a scientist with the tools with which to assess the adequacy of the approximation under alternative states of nature.

Above is the statement that $\sqrt{n}(\hat{\theta}_n - \theta_n^0)$ is asymptotically normally distributed. More precisely,

$$\mathscr{I}_n^{-1/2} \mathscr{J}_n \sqrt{n}(\hat{\theta}_n - \theta_n^0) \xrightarrow{\mathscr{L}} N(0, I).$$

In the case of least mean distance estimators, $\mathscr{I}_n$ is computed as

$$\mathscr{I}_n = \mathrm{Var}\left[(1/\sqrt{n}) \sum_{t=1}^{n} (\partial/\partial\theta)s(y_t, x_t, \tau_n^0, \theta_n^0) \right]$$

and in the case of method of moments estimators as

$$\mathscr{I}_n = [(\partial/\partial\theta')\bar{m}_n(\theta_n^0, \gamma_n^0)]' D(\tau_n^0) S_n D(\tau_n^0)[(\partial/\partial\theta')\bar{m}_n(\theta_n^0, \gamma_n^0)],$$

$$S_n = \mathrm{Var}\left[(1/\sqrt{n}) \sum_{t=1}^{n} m(y_t, x_t, \tau_n^0, \theta_n^0) \right].$$

In either case

$$\mathscr{J}_n = (\partial^2/\partial\theta\,\partial\theta')\bar{s}_n(\theta_n^0, \gamma_n^0).$$

All computations above are carried out using the actual model to define the expectation and variance operator, not the presumed model. An estimator $\hat{\mathscr{I}}_n$ is obtained using the obvious sample analogs of $\mathscr{I}_n$ in each instance; for example,

$$\hat{\mathscr{I}}_n = [(\partial/\partial\theta')m_n(\hat{\theta}_n)]' D(\hat{t}_n)\hat{S}_n D(\hat{t}_n)[(\partial/\partial\theta')m_n(\hat{\theta}_n)],$$

$$\hat{S}_n = (1/n) \sum_{t=1}^{n} [m(y_t, x_t, \hat{t}_n, \hat{\theta}_n)][m(y_t, x_t, \hat{t}_n, \hat{\theta}_n)]'.$$

In either case $\hat{\mathscr{J}}_n = (\partial^2/\partial\theta\,\partial\theta')s_n(\hat{\theta}_n)$.

For testing the hypothesis

$$H: h(\theta^0) = 0 \quad \text{against} \quad A: h(\theta^0) \neq 0,$$

where h is a q-vector one has a Wald test statistic

$$W = n\hat{h}'(\hat{H}\hat{V}\hat{H}')^{-1}\hat{h},$$

a 'likelihood ratio' test statistic

$$L = 2n[s_n(\tilde{\theta}_n) - s_n(\hat{\theta}_n)],$$

and a Lagrange multiplier test statistic

$$R = n[(\partial/\partial\theta)s_n(\tilde{\theta}_n)]'\tilde{\mathscr{J}}^{-1}\tilde{H}'(\tilde{H}\tilde{V}\tilde{H}')^{-1}\tilde{H}\tilde{\mathscr{J}}^{-1}[(\partial/\partial\theta)s_n(\tilde{\theta}_n)],$$

where $\tilde{\theta}_n$ minimizes $s_n(\theta)$ subject to $h(\theta) = 0$, $\tilde{h} = h(\tilde{\theta}_n)$, $\tilde{H} = (\partial/\partial\theta')h(\tilde{\theta}_n)$, $\tilde{V} = \tilde{\mathcal{J}}^{-1}\tilde{\mathcal{I}}\tilde{\mathcal{J}}^{-1}$, and the $\sim$ denotes the same quantities evaluated at $\tilde{\theta}_n$ instead of at $\hat{\theta}_n$.

The Wald test can be computed from knowledge of the unconstrained estimate alone; the Lagrange multiplier test from knowledge of the constrained estimate alone. Often one of these will be much easier to compute than the other, thus dictating a choice of test statistics. The 'likelihood ratio' test requires knowledge of both and requires, in addition, that $\mathcal{I}_n = \mathcal{J}_n$ when the presumed model generates the data. It is the preferred statistic when available.

In each instance, one rejects the null hypothesis when the statistic exceeds the upper $\alpha \cdot 100$ percentage point of the chi-square distribution with q degrees of freedom. If the presumed model generates the data then each statistic is asymptotically distributed as a non-central chi-square random variable with q degrees of freedom; if some other model generates the data then each statistic is asymptotically distributed as the ratio of quadratic forms in normal random variables.

As seen from the results summarized above, twelve years after the seminal papers by Jennrich and Malinvaud the literature on nonlinear models with a regression structure was fairly mature. The literature on dynamic models was not. Dynamic models are those where time indexes the observations, where lagged dependent variables, y_{t-1}, y_{t-2} are permitted as explanatory variables amongst the components of x_i, and where errors may be serially correlated. However, some progress in accommodating models with serially correlated errors was made during this period.

The literature failed to accommodate fully dynamic models in the sense that no general, theoretical developments specifically demonstrated that linear models with lagged dependent variables as explanatory variables were included within their scope. This was due to the use of stationary stochastic processes and martingales (which are essentially linear concepts) as the underpinnings of the theory; for instance, a nonlinear transformation of a martingale is in general itself not a martingale. The exceptions to this failure were a monograph by Bierens (1981) and a paper by White and Domowitz (1984). White and Domowitz relied on mixing conditions and a notion of asymptotic martingales due to McLeish (1975, 1977) – notions that will withstand nonlinear transformation – and pointed the way to a general asymptotic theory similar to that outlined above, which was accomplished in a monograph by Gallant and White (1987). The results are the same as those outlined above, with two exceptions.

The first is that the theory cannot accommodate a drift in the traditional fashion where the parameter γ_n^0 tends to a point γ^0 fast enough that $\sqrt{n}h(\theta_n^0)$ is bounded. Rather, γ_n^0 must be held fixed for all n with drift accomplished by formulating the null hypothesis as $H: h(\theta_n^0) = h_n^0$ and bounding $\sqrt{n}[h(\theta_n^0) - h_n^0]$. This is irrelevant as a practical matter because the formulas that one uses to approximate power do not change.

The second exception is that estimating the variance of a sum becomes much more troublesome. For instance, to estimate

$$S_n = \text{Var}\left[(1/\sqrt{n}) \sum_{t=1}^{n} m(y_t, x_t, \tau_n^0, \theta_n^0) \right]$$

one uses

$$\hat{S}_n = \sum_{\tau = -l(n)}^{l(n)} w[\tau/l(n)]\hat{S}_{n\tau},$$

when $l(n)$ is the integer nearest $n^{1/5}$ and

$$w(x) = \begin{cases} 1 - 6|x|^2 + 6|x|^3 & 0 \leqslant |x| \leqslant 1/2 \\ 2(1 - |x|)^3 & 1/2 \leqslant |x| \leqslant 1. \end{cases}$$

$$\hat{S}_{n\tau} = \begin{cases} (1/n) \sum_{t=1+\tau}^{n} m(y_t, x_t, \hat{\tau}_n, \hat{\theta}_n) \times m'(y_{t-\tau}, x_{t-\tau}, \hat{\tau}_n, \hat{\theta}_n) & \tau \geqslant 0, \\ (\hat{S}_{n,-\tau})' & \tau < 0. \end{cases}$$

The progress in nonlinear models has indeed been rapid. The developments just described provide an essentially complete asymptotic theory for nonlinear models in as much generality as is likely ever to be useful. There will be refinements over the years but, in the broad sense, the frontier has moved on.

BIBLIOGRAPHY

Bierens, H.J. 1981. Robust methods and asymptotic theory. In *Lecture Notes in Economics and Mathematical Systems*, 192, Berlin: Springer-Verlag.

Burguete, J.F., Gallant, A.R. and Souza, G. 1982. On unification of the asymptotic theory of nonlinear econometric models. *Econometric Reviews* 1, 151–90.

Gallant, A.R. 1987. *Nonlinear Statistical Models*. New York: John Wiley & Sons.

Gallant, A.R. and White, H.L. 1987. *Consistency and Asymptotic Normality for Parametric Estimation with Dependent Observations*. Oxford: Basil Blackwell.

Hartley, H.O. 1961. The modified Gauss–Newton method for the fitting of nonlinear regression functions by least squares. *Technometrics* 3, 269–80.

Hartley, H.O. 1964. Exact confidence regions for the parameters in nonlinear regression laws. *Biometrika* 51, 347–53.

Hartley, H.O. and Booker, A. 1965. Nonlinear least squares estimation. *Annals of Mathematical Statistics* 36, 638–50.

Jennrich, R.I. 1969. Asymptotic properties of nonlinear least squares estimators. *Annals of Mathematical Statistics* 40, 633–43.

Malinvaud, E. 1970. The consistency of nonlinear regressions. *Annals of Mathematical Statistics* 41, 956–69.

McLeish, D.L. 1975. A maximal inequality and dependent strong laws. *Annals of Probability* 3, 829–39.

McLeish, D.L. 1977. On the invariance principle for nonstationary mixingales. *Annals of Probability* 5, 616–21.

White, H.L. and Domowitz, I. 1984. Nonlinear regression with dependent observations. *Econometrica* 52, 143–62.

Non-nested Hypotheses

M. HASHEM PESARAN

In recent years considerable attention has been paid to the role of hypothesis testing in econometrics and its links with the problem of model selection in econometrics. One important topic considered in this recent work is the testing of 'non-nested' or separate models. Broadly speaking, two models (or hypotheses) are said to be 'non-nested' if neither can be obtained from the other by the imposition of appropriate parametric restrictions or as a limit of a suitable approximation; otherwise they are said to be 'nested'. (A more formal definition can be found in Pesaran, 1987.) Non-nested models can arise from differences in the underlying theoretical paradigms and/or from differences in the way a particular relationship suggested by economic theory is modelled. Examples of non-nested econometric models abound in the literature: demand systems (Deaton, 1978; Murray, 1984), Keynesian and new classical models of unemployment (Pesaran, 1982a; Dadkhah and Valbuena, 1985), effects of dividend taxes on corporate investment decisions (Poterba and Summers, 1983), money demand functions (McAleer, Fisher and Volker, 1982) and empirical models of exchange rate determination (Backus, 1984), to mention just a few. Other examples of non-nested hypotheses arise when the probability distributions under consideration belong to separate parametric families, such as log-normal versus exponential, or Poisson versus geometric distributions.

In assessing the empirical adequacy of non-nested models, two general approaches can be employed, namely, model selection and hypothesis testing. In the case of model selection, the rival models are treated symmetrically and the model which is expected to perform best with respect to a particular loss function is chosen. In econometrics the popular criterion for model selection is Theil's adjusted multiple correlation coefficient ($\bar{R}$). This criterion is based on a simple trade-off between 'fit' and 'parsimony' and is applicable primarily to single equation classical linear regression models. Other more generally applicable model selection rules include Akaike's information criterion, and Schwarz's

167

Bayesian information criterion, both of which can be derived formally within a decision theoretic framework.

Almost all of the non-nested hypothesis testing procedures in econometrics build on the pioneering work of Cox (1961, 1962). The basic idea behind what is now known as the Cox test is rather simple and involves centring the log-likelihood ratio statistic so that under the null hypothesis it has mean zero, at least in large samples. This modification is needed because the unadjusted log-likelihood ratio statistic does not have the usual central chi-squared distribution under the null hypothesis when the alternative happens to be non-nested. An alternative approach to non-nested hypothesis testing, also suggested by Cox (1961) and then taken up by Atkinson (1970), is the comprehensive model approach, whereby the models are tested by means of an artificially constructed general model which includes the non-nested models as special cases. A third approach to the problem, also based on a suggestion by Cox (1961), has been considered by Dastoor (1983), Deaton (1982), and Gourieroux et al. (1983) and recently popularized in econometrics as 'encompassing tests' by Mizon and Richard (1986).

Let two non-nested models, available for the analysis of the process generating the n observations $\mathbf{y} = (y_1, y_2, \ldots, y_n)'$ on the variable of interest Y, be represented by H_f and H_g. Suppose also that under H_f, the joint probability density function of $\mathbf{y}$ is given by $L_f(\mathbf{y}; \theta)$, and under H_g by $L_g(\mathbf{y}; \gamma)$, where θ and γ are unknown parameter vectors under H_f and H_g, respectively. The Cox statistic for the test of H_f (say) against H_g can be written as

$$T_{fg} = \{l_f(\hat{\theta}_n) - l_g(\hat{\gamma}_n)\} - E_{\theta_n}\{l_f(\hat{\theta}_n) - l_g(\hat{\gamma}_n)\}, \tag{1}$$

where $l_f(\hat{\theta}_n) = \log\{L_f(\mathbf{y}; \hat{\theta}_n)\}$ and $l_g(\hat{\gamma}_n) = \log\{L_g(\mathbf{y}; \hat{\gamma}_n)\}$ are the maximized log-likelihood values under H_f and H_g, respectively, and $\hat{\theta}_n$ and $\hat{\gamma}_n$ are the maximum likelihood estimators of θ and γ under H_f and H_g respectively. The second term in (1) represents the estimate of the expectation under H_f of the maximized log-likelihood difference $\hat{l}_{fg} = l_f(\hat{\theta}_n) - l_g(\hat{\gamma}_n)$. In practice, it is often necessary to replace $E_{\theta_n}(\hat{l}_{fg})$ by a suitable approximation. In the case where H_f is nested within H_g, the term $E_{\theta_n}(\hat{l}_{fg})$ will be identically equal to zero and no correction to the log-likelihood ratio statistic $\hat{l}_{fg}$ is needed. In general, however, the correction suggested by Cox is required if T_{fg} is to have mean zero, at least in large samples. Under certain regularity conditions, it can be shown that the statistic $N_f = T_{fg}/\{V_{\theta_n}(T_{fg})\}^{1/2}$ is asymptotically distributed under H_f as $N(0, 1)$. The estimate of the variance of T_{fg}, $V_{\theta_n}(T_{fg})$, can be computed using results in Cox (1961, 1962), or Pesaran (1974, p. 156). Taking H_g as the null hypothesis, the statistic N_g can also be obtained for the test of H_g against H_f by interchanging the roles of H_f and H_g. Four outcomes are then possible:

(i) Accept H_f and reject H_g, if $|N_f| < C_\alpha$ and $|N_g| \geqslant C_\alpha$.
(ii) Reject H_f and accept H_g, if $|N_f| \geqslant C_\alpha$ and $|N_g| < C_\alpha$.
(iii) Reject both H_f and H_g, if $|N_f| \geqslant C_\alpha$ and $|N_g| \geqslant C_\alpha$.
(iv) Accept both H_f and H_g, if $|N_f| < C_\alpha$ and $|N_g| < C_\alpha$,

where C_α is the α-per cent critical value of the standard normal distribution. In the case of non-nested hypotheses, there is no way of ranking the models by the level of their generality. Therefore, unlike the nested case, it is not unusual, given the data, for both non-nested models to be rejected when tested against one another.

Atkinson's comprehensive model approach is based on an artificially constructed general model such as

$$L(\mathbf{y}; \theta, \gamma, \lambda) = L\{L_f(\mathbf{y}, \theta), L_g(\mathbf{y}, \gamma), \lambda\},$$

where $L(.)$ represents the probability density function of the combined or the comprehensive model (say H_λ) and λ is a scalar nesting or mixing parameter. A relatively simple form of $L(.)$ used extensively in the literature is the exponential combination.

$$H_\lambda: L(\mathbf{y}; \theta, \gamma, \lambda) = \frac{\{L_f(\mathbf{y}; \theta)\}^{1-\lambda}\{L_g(\mathbf{y}, \gamma)\}^\lambda}{\displaystyle\int \{L_f(\mathbf{y}; \theta)\}^{1-\lambda}\{L_g(\mathbf{y}, \gamma)\}^\lambda \mathrm{d}\mathbf{y}}. \tag{2}$$

The Atkinson approach to testing H_f against H_g is now reduced to testing $\lambda = 0$ against $\lambda = 1$ in the context of the combined hypothesis H_λ. This approach is, however, subject to a number of drawbacks, arising primarily from the fact that under $\gamma = 0$ (or $\lambda = 1$) the unknown parameter vector γ (or θ) disappears from the combined model (Pesaran, 1981). The problem can be circumvented in a number of different ways, as discussed for example in Pesaran (1982b); thus leading to a proliferation of Atkinson-type test statistics.

An 'encompassing test' of H_f against H_g can be carried out either by considering all the unknown parameters or by focusing on certain combinations of the parameters of interest. The former is referred to as the 'complete parameteric encompassing test', and is based on the statistic $\hat{\gamma}_n - \hat{\gamma}_{*n}$, where $\hat{\gamma}_{*n}$ is an estimate of $\gamma_* = \mathrm{plim}_{n \to \infty}(\hat{\gamma}_n | H_f)$, the pseudo-true value of γ under H_f. Therefore, like the Cox statistic above, by construction the encompassing statistic $E_f = \hat{\gamma}_n - \hat{\gamma}_{*n}$ has mean zero when H_f is true, at least in large samples. The encompassing test can be regarded as the application of Cox's basic idea to the whole (or to a subset) of the parameters of the alternative hypothesis. By interchanging the roles of H_f and H_g, the complete parametric encompassing statistic for the test of H_g against H_f is given by $E_g = \hat{\theta}_n - \hat{\theta}_{*n}$, where $\hat{\theta}_{*n}$ is an estimate of $\theta_* = \mathrm{plim}_{n \to \infty}(\hat{\theta}_n | H_g)$ evaluated under H_g.

All of the above three approaches originate from or are directly based on the seminal work of Cox. There is, however, a fourth approach proposed by Epps et al. (1982) which is based on the deviation of the sample moment generating function from its theoretical counterpart under the null hypothesis. This approach is, however, difficult to apply in practice and in general requires very large sample sizes, and so far has had little impact on econometric analysis of non-nested models.

As an important example of a non-nested hypothesis testing problem in econometrics, consider the following two classical linear regression models:

$$H_f: \mathbf{y} = X\mathbf{a} + \mathbf{u}_f, \quad \mathbf{u}_f \sim N(0, \sigma^2 I_n), \quad 0 < \sigma^2 < \infty \tag{3}$$

$$H_g: \mathbf{y} = Z\mathbf{b} + \mathbf{u}_g, \quad \mathbf{u}_g \sim N(0, \omega^2 I_n), \quad 0 < \omega^2 < \infty \tag{4}$$

where X and Z are $n \times k_f$ and $n \times k_g$ matrices of observations on the explanatory variables of models H_f and H_g, respectively. These variables are assumed to be distributed independently of $n \times 1$ disturbance vectors $\mathbf{u}_f$ and $\mathbf{u}_g$. The parameters $\mathbf{a}$ and $\mathbf{b}$ are the $k_f \times 1$ and $k_g \times 1$ vectors of unknown regression coefficients, and I_n is the identity matrix of order n. It is also assumed that the probability limits of $n^{-1}(X'X)$, $n^{-1}(Z'Z)$ and $n^{-1}(X'Z)$ exist with the first two (denoted by Σ_{xx} and Σ_{zz}, respectively) positive definite and the third (denoted by Σ_{xz}) non-zero. Sufficient (but not necessary) conditions for H_f and H_g to be non-nested are

$$\Sigma_f = \Sigma_{xx} - \Sigma_{xz}\Sigma_{zz}^{-1}\Sigma_{zx} \neq 0,$$

$$\Sigma_g = \Sigma_{zz} - \Sigma_{zx}\Sigma_{xx}^{-1}\Sigma_{xz} \neq 0.$$

These conditions ensure that, even in the limit, all the columns of X (or Z) cannot be expressed as linear combinations of the columns of Z (or X).

For this example, a large sample approximation for T_{fg}, using (1), is given by

$$T_{fg} = \frac{n}{2}\log(\hat{\omega}_n^2 / \hat{\omega}_{*n}^2),$$

where

$$\hat{\omega}_n^2 = n^{-1}(\mathbf{y} - Z\hat{\mathbf{b}}_n)'(\mathbf{y} - Z\hat{\mathbf{b}}_n), \quad \hat{\omega}_{*n}^2 = \hat{\sigma}_n^2 + \hat{\mathbf{a}}_n'\hat{\Sigma}_f\hat{\mathbf{a}}_n,$$

in which

$$\hat{\sigma}_n^2 = n^{-1}(\mathbf{y} - X\hat{\mathbf{a}}_n)'(\mathbf{y} - X\hat{\mathbf{a}}_n), \quad \hat{\mathbf{a}}_n = (X'X)^{-1}X'\mathbf{y}, \quad \hat{\mathbf{b}}_n = (Z'Z)^{-1}Z'\mathbf{y},$$

and

$$\sum_f = n^{-1}(X'X) - n^{-1}X'Z(Z'Z)^{-1}Z'X.$$

Finally, for the estimate of the variance of T_{fg}, we have

$$V_{\theta_n}(T_{fg}) = (\hat{\sigma}_n^2 / \hat{\omega}_{*n}^4)\hat{\mathbf{a}}_n'X'M_zM_xX\hat{\mathbf{a}}_n,$$

where $M_x = I - X(X'X)^{-1}X'$ and $M_z = I - Z(Z'Z)^{-1}Z'$. The Cox statistic, $N_f = T_{fg}/\{V_{\theta_n}(T_{fg})\}^{1/2}$, can now be computed straightforwardly by means of four ordinary least squares regressions as described in Pesaran (1974).

Application of Atkinson's comprehensive approach to the linear regression models, using the exponential combination (2), yields the following result (Pesaran, 1982b)

$$H_\lambda: \mathbf{y} = (1 - \xi)X\mathbf{a} + \xi Z\mathbf{b} + \mathbf{u}, \tag{5}$$

where $\xi = \lambda\sigma_\lambda^2/\omega^2$ and $\sigma_\lambda^{-2} = \{(1 - \lambda)\sigma^{-2} + \lambda\omega^2\}$. For a given value of $\mathbf{b}$, a test of H_f against H_g can now be carried out by testing the hypothesis $\xi = 0$ against $\xi = 1$ in (5). As pointed out above, notice that under $\xi = 0$ (or $\lambda = 0$), the unknown parameter vector **b** disappears from the combined hypothesis. Different choices for **b** results in different test statistics. Substituting $\hat{\mathbf{b}}_n$ for **b** in (5) yields the J-test proposed by Davidson and MacKinnon (1981). Whilst replacing **b** by a consistent estimate of the probability limit of $\hat{\mathbf{b}}_n$ under H_f (i.e. $\hat{\mathbf{b}}_{*n}$), gives the JA-test of Fisher and McAleer (1981). Godfrey (1983) shows that the JA-test has the exact $t(n - k_f - 1)$ distribution under H_f if X and Z are non-stochastic and the errors are normally distributed. It is also interesting to note that the application of Roy's union-intersection principle of the test of $\xi = 0$ in (5) yields the standard F statistic for the test $\delta_2 = 0$ in the combined model $y = X\delta_1 + Z\delta_2 + u$. A proof of the result can be found in McAleer and Pesaran (1986).

The result of the 'encompassing test' applied to non-nested linear regression models crucially depends on the choice of the 'parameters of interest'. When all the regression coefficients are considered to be of interest, the encompassing test of H_f against H_g turns out to be the same as Roy's union intersection test discussed above. But when the parameter of interest is the error variance ω^2, the encompassing test of H_f against H_g will be asymptotically equivalent to the Cox test.

Extensions of the above procedures for dealing with serial correlation of residuals, stochastic regressors, non-normality of the disturbances, presence of correlation between regressors and disturbances, limited dependent variables and non-linearities have also been considered in the literature. See, for example, Pesaran (1974, Supplement), Pesaran and Deaton (1978), Davidson and MacKinnon (1981, 1982), Godfrey (1983), Ericsson (1983), MacKinnon et al. (1983) and Smith and Maddala (1983). Work has also been done on the small sample properties of some of the non-nested tests and their power characteristics. The simulation results carried out in the literature suggest that Cox-type tests for non-nested regression models tend to over-reject the 'true' model in small samples. Adjustments designed to overcome this problem are proposed in Godfrey and Pesaran (1983), where it is also shown that the small-sample adjusted Cox-test performs favourably when compared with the J-test or the F-test applied to the combined model $y = X\delta_1 + Z\delta_2 + u$. For further details and relevant references, the interested reader is advised to consult McAleer and Pesaran (1986).

BIBLIOGRAPHY

Atkinson, A. 1970. A method for discriminating between models. *Journal of the Royal Statistical Society*, Series B 32, 323–53.

Backus, D. 1984. Empirical models of the exchange rate: separating the wheat from the chaff. *Canadian Journal of Economics* 17, 824–46.

Cox, D.R. 1961. Test of separate families of hypotheses. In *Proceedings of the Fourth Berkeley Symposium on Mathematical Statistics and Probability*, Vol. 1, Berkeley: University of California Press, 105–123.

Cox, D.R. 1962. Further results on tests of separate families of hypotheses. *Journal of the Royal Statistical Society*, Series B 24, 406–424.

Dadkhah, K. and Valbuena, S. 1985. Non-nested test of New Classical vs Keynesian models: evidence from European countries. *Applied Economics* 17, 1083–98.

Dastoor, N.K. 1983. Some aspects of testing non-nested hypotheses. *Journal of Econometrics* 21, 213–28.

Davidson, R. and MacKinnon, J.G. 1981. Several tests for model specification in the presence of alternative hypotheses. *Econometrica* 49, 781–93.

Davidson, R. and MacKinnon, J.G. 1982. Some non-nested hypothesis tests and the relations among them. *Review of Economic Studies* 49, 551–65.

Deaton, A.S. 1978. Specification and testing in applied demand analysis. *Economic Journal* 88, 524–36.

Deaton, A.S. 1982. Model selection procedures, or, does the consumption function exist? In *Evaluating the Reliability of Macroeconomic Models*, ed. G.C. Chow and P. Corsi, New York: Wiley, 43–65.

Epps, T.W., Singleton, K.J. and Pulley, L.B. 1982. A test of separate families of distributions based on the empirical moment generating function. *Biometrika* 69, 391–9.

Ericsson, N.R. 1983. Asymptotic properties of instrumental variables statistics for testing non-nested hypotheses. *Review of Economic Studies* 50, 287–304.

Fisher, G.R. and McAleer, M. 1981. Alternative procedures and associated tests of significance for non-nested hypotheses. *Journal of Econometrics* 16, 103–19.

Godfrey, L.G. 1983. Testing non-nested models after estimation by instrumental variables or least squares. *Econometrica* 51, 355–65.

Godfrey, L.G. and Pesaran, M.H. 1983. Tests of non-nested regression models: small sample adjustments and Monte Carlo evidence. *Journal of Econometrics* 21, 133–54.

Gourieroux, C., Montfort, A. and Trognon, A. 1983. Testing nested or non-nested hypotheses. *Journal of Econometrics* 21, 83–115.

MacKinnon, J.G., White, H. and Davidson, R. 1983. Tests for model specification in the presence of alternative hypotheses: some further results. *Journal of Econometrics* 21, 53–70.

McAleer, M., Fisher, G. and Volker, P. 1982. Separate misspecified regressions and the US long run demand for money function. *Review of Economics and Statistics* 64, 572–83.

McAleer, M. and Pesaran, M.H. 1986. Statistical inference in non-nested econometric models. *Applied Mathematics and Computation*.

Mizon, G.E. and Richard, J.-F. 1986. The encompassing principle and its application to non-nested hypotheses. *Econometrica* 54(3), 657–78.

Murray, J. 1984. Retail demand for meat in Australia: a utility theory approach. *Economic Record* 60, 45–56.

Pesaran, M.H. 1974. On the general problem of model selection. *Review of Economic Studies* 41, 153–71.

Pesaran, M.H. 1981. Pitfalls of testing non-nested hypotheses by the Lagrange multiplier method. *Journal of Econometrics* 17, 323–31.

Pesaran, M.H. 1982a. A critique of the proposed tests of the natural rate-rational expectations hypothesis. *Economic Journal* 92, 529–54.

Pesaran, M.H. 1982b. On the comprehensive method of testing non-nested regression models. *Journal of Econometrics* 18, 263–74.

Pesaran, M.H. 1987. Global and partial non-nested hypotheses and asymptotic local power. *Econometric Theory* 3, 69–97.

Pesaran, M.H. and Deaton, A.S. 1978. Testing non-nested nonlinear regression models. *Econometrica* 46, 677–94.

Poterba, J.M. and Summers, L.H. 1983. Dividend taxes, corporate investment, and 'Q'. *Journal of Public Economics* 22, 135–67.

Smith, M.A. and Maddala, G.S. 1983. Multiple model testing for non-nested heteroskedastic censored regression models. *Journal of Econometrics* 21, 71–81.

Path Analysis

INSAN TUNALI

Path analysis is a method for estimating and testing the internal consistency of models with a postulated causal structure. The postulated structure is displayed in the form of path diagrams, where one-way arrows link causal variables to their outcomes, and curved two-headed arrows connect related variables whose causal links are not under study. Estimation proceeds along the lines of method of moments and instrumental variables theory: the causal ordering of variables along distinct paths are exploited to express the unknown structural parameters in terms of the population moments of the observed and the unobserved variables. Estimating equations are obtained by replacing the population moments of the observed variables by their sample counterparts, which are then solved for the unknown parameters and the estimates of the moments of the unobservables (which themselves can be thought of as structural parameters).

Consider the following simple example discussed in Wright (1960) and Duncan (1975). The structural model consists of

$$y_1 = \beta_1 x + u$$

Model (1)

$$y_2 = \beta_2 x + v,$$

where y's denote the observed (endogenous) variables, x the observed (exogenous) variable, u and v the unobserved (exogenous) variables or disturbances, and β's the unknown parameters. To keep the algebra simple, all exogenous variables are assumed to have zero means here and below. The disturbances are assumed to have non-zero variances and covariance, and are uncorrelated with x. The path diagram depicting the postulated causal structure is given in Figure 1. The relationships between the population moments and the structural parameters are easily derived to be

174

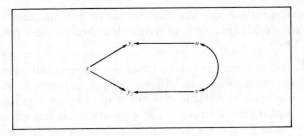

Figure 1. Path diagram for Model (1)

$$\sigma_{11} = \beta_1^2 \sigma_{xx} + \sigma_{uu}, \qquad \sigma_{12} = \beta_1 \beta_2 \sigma_{xx} + \sigma_{uv}, \qquad \sigma_{1x} = \beta_1 \sigma_{xx},$$

$$\sigma_{22} = \beta_2^2 \sigma_{xx} + \sigma_{vv}, \qquad \sigma_{2x} = \beta_2 \sigma_{xx}, \qquad (1')$$

where the variance–covariance structures of the observables y_1, y_2, x and the unobservables u, v are respectively given by

$$\begin{bmatrix} \sigma_{11} & \sigma_{12} & \sigma_{1x} \\ & \sigma_{22} & \sigma_{2x} \\ & & \sigma_{xx} \end{bmatrix}, \qquad \begin{bmatrix} \sigma_{uu} & \sigma_{uv} \\ & \sigma_{vv} \end{bmatrix}.$$

Inspection reveals that the five equations in $(1')$ will uniquely determine the five unknowns, $\beta_1, \beta_2, \sigma_{uu}, \sigma_{vv}, \sigma_{uv}$, using estimates obtained from a random sample on the observables to replace $\sigma_{11}, \sigma_{22}, \sigma_{12}, \sigma_{xx}, \sigma_{1x}$ and σ_{2x}.

To see how path analysis can be utilized to test the internal consistency of a postulated structure, consider the same set of equations as in model (1), but omit the curved arrow from Figure 1. This is equivalent to setting $\sigma_{uv} = 0$ in the equation system $(1')$. The five equations now over-determine the four unknowns, $\beta_1, \beta_2, \sigma_{uu}$ and σ_{vv}. Simple algebraic manipulation of the covariance terms reveals that the solution to the system will be unique if and only if $\sigma_{12} = \sigma_{1x}\sigma_{2x}/\sigma_{xx}$. This condition (referred to as an 'over-identifying restriction' in the econometrics literature) can be tested using the sample counterparts of the population moments involved. Note that no such check on the internal consistency of the original model is available: Model (1) is 'just-identified'.

The preceding example illustrates the basic ideas behind path analysis, cast within the conventional linear regression framework. The method's origins, however, lie elsewhere. Path analysis was invented by the geneticist Sewall Wright, whose work in the 1920s foreshadowed the econometric literature on structural estimation. Wright formulated complex models with unobservables and wrestled with simultaneity and identification long before econometricians began their systematic study of these topics. Wright's main subject of study, heritability, offered him the necessary insights for modelling the links between cause and effect. His objective was to infer correlations between the traits of interest – bone sizes of rabbits, skin colour and birth weight of guinea-pigs, etc. – across different generations in a population. Towards this end, Wright devised an algorithm for reading off the estimating equations directly from the path diagram. For a model which does not depict simultaneity, Wright described his algorithm as follows (cf. Wright, 1960):

> The correlation between any two variables in a properly constructed diagram of relations is equal to the sum of contributions pertaining to the paths by which one may trace from one to the other in the diagram without going back after going forward along an arrow and without passing through any variable twice in the same path. A coefficient pertaining to the whole path connecting two variables, and thus measuring the contribution of that path to the correlation, is known as a *compound path coefficient*. Its value is the product of the coefficients pertaining to the elementary paths along its course. One, but not more than one of these, may pertain to a two-headed arrow without violating the rule against going back after going forward.

Since the analysis of correlations constituted his primary interest, Wright worked with standardized variables, having zero means and unit variances. His algorithm applied to the model above without standardization of the variances would yield the system in (1'). If standardized variables were utilized instead, the resulting equations would be in terms of simple correlations and beta coefficients, referred to as 'path coefficients' by Wright. It is a matter of simple algebra to convert the above equations to Wright's equations, and vice versa. For example, taking the first expression in (1') above and dividing by σ_{11}, we get the equivalent representation.

$$1 = [(\beta_1)(\sigma_{xx}/\sigma_{11})^{1/2}]^2 + [(1)(\sigma_{uu}/\sigma_{11})^{1/2}]^2 = p_{1x}^2 + p_{1u}^2,$$

where p's denote the path coefficients. (Note that the structural coefficient of u has been entered as '1' in this expression.) Wright's representation has the advantage of providing a readily interpretable goodness of fit measure: p_{1x}^2 and p_{1u}^2 are respectively the proportion of the variation in y_1 that can be explained by x, and that which is left unexplained.

Path analysis is capable of handling a much more general class of problems than the one discussed above. To illustrate the nature of the extensions, we look at some other simple models. These and other examples may be found in Goldberger (1973) and Duncan (1975). We first consider the simultaneous equations model

$$y_1 = \gamma_1 y_2 + \beta_1 x + u$$

Model (2)

$$y_2 = \gamma_2 y_1 + \beta_2 x + v,$$

where u and v are unobserved, and are assumed to be uncorrelated with x. The associated path diagram is given in Figure 2. It is straightforward to show that this model is not identified without further assumptions. Clearly, setting $\gamma_1 = \gamma_2 = 0$ gives model (1). Setting $\gamma_1 = \sigma_{uv} = 0$ (which is equivalent to removing the arrow going from y_2 to y_1 and the double-headed arrow connecting u and v in

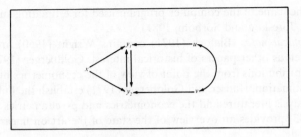

Figure 2. Path diagram for Model (2)

Figure 2) gives a recursive model, which can be shown to be just-identified. Recursive models have been studied extensively in the sociology literature, where Wright's work has had its significant impact (cf. Boudon, 1965; Duncan, 1966).

Next, we consider the latent variable model

$$x^* = \alpha x + w$$

Model (3)
$$y_1 = \beta_1 x^* + u$$

$$y_2 = \beta_2 x^* + v,$$

where y's are observed, x^* is unobserved, w is unobserved and uncorrelated with the other disturbances u and v, and x is observed and uncorrelated with w, u, v. The path diagram corresponding to this specification is given in Figure 3.

It can be shown that Model (3) is not identified without further assumptions. Clearly, setting $\alpha = 1$ and $w = 0$ yields Model (1), which is just-identified. The versatility of path analysis can be underscored by noting other versions of (3) that appear under various names in the literature on linear structural equation models. (We ignore the issue of identification for these models.) Setting $\alpha = 1$ we obtain an errors in variables (or measurement error) model. Dropping the x^* equation from (3), we get a factor analytic model, with x^* as the common factor, and u, v as the specific factors. If we replace the scalars α and x by conformable vectors α' and x, we obtain a multiple indicator-multiple cause (MIMIC) model. Finally, note that the simultaneous equation model (2) and the latent variable model (3) can be combined to arrive at a more general structural model, widely

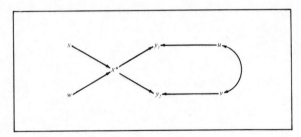

Figure 3. Path diagram for Model (3)

known by the name of the computer program used for estimating such models, LISREL (cf. Jöreskog and Sörbom, 1981).

Bibliographical notes. Blalock (1971) contains Wright (1960) and Duncan (1966), as well as other papers of historical interest. Goldberger (1972) reviews Wright's contributions from the point of view of the econometrics literature on structural estimation. Hauser and Goldberger (1971) establish the links between the path analysis literature and the econometrics and psychometrics literatures. Bentler (1983) provides an overview of the state of the art on linear structural equation models.

BIBLIOGRAPHY

Bentler, P.M. 1983. Simultaneous equation systems as moment structure models – with an introduction to latent variable models. *Journal of Econometrics* 22, 13–42.

Blalock, H.M. (ed.) 1971. *Causal Models in the Social Sciences.* Chicago: Aldine.

Boudon, R. 1965. A method of linear causal analysis: dependence analysis. *American Sociological Review* 30, 365–73.

Duncan, O.D. 1966. Path analysis: sociological examples. *American Journal of Sociology* 72, 1–16.

Duncan, O.D. 1975. *Introduction to Structural Equation Models.* New York: Academic Press.

Goldberger, A.S. 1972. Structural equation methods in the social sciences. *Econometrica* 40, 979–1001.

Goldberger, A.S. 1973. Structural equation models: an overview. In *Structural Equation Models in the Social Sciences*, ed. A.S. Goldberger and O.D. Duncan, New York: Seminar Press.

Hauser, R.M. and Goldberger, A.S. 1971. The treatment of unobservable variables in path analysis. In *Sociological Methodology 1971*, ed. H.L. Costner, San Francisco: Jossey-Bass.

Jöreskog, K.G. and Sörbom, D. 1981. *LISREL: Analysis of Linear Structural Relationships by the Method of Maximum Likelihood – User's Guide.* Chicago: National Educational Resources.

Wright, S. 1960. Path coefficients and path regressions: alternative or complementary concepts? *Biometrics* 16, 189–202.

Random Coefficients

P.A.V.B. SWAMY AND J.R. BARTH

Random coefficients models generalize conventional fixed coefficients models to avoid inconsistent and inaccurate assessments of relationships among variables.

FIXED COEFFICIENTS MODELS. As Goldberger (1964, pp. 380–88) indicates, there are three alternative ways to formulate fixed coefficients models: (1) structural-form, (2) reduced-form and (3) recursive-form. The view of the economic mechanism underlying these formulations is that there is a joint probability distribution of the current endogenous (random) variables $y_i^* = (y_{1t}^*, \ldots, y_{Lt}^*)'$ conditional on the values of the predetermined variables $x_t = (x_{1t}, \ldots, x_{Kt})'$. This conditional distribution may be written as

$$p(y_t | x_t, \theta), \tag{1}$$

where θ is a fixed parameter vector taking values in a parameter space Ω and Y is a sample space in which y_t takes on its values.

One way to specify this distribution is to postulate a reduced-form model. The vector θ then includes the fixed coefficients as well as the disturbance variances and covariances of the reduced-form. Alternatively, one could postulate a structural-form model and then deduce the conditional distribution by transforming the structural-form into the reduced-form. Finally, one could postulate a model in recursive-form, thereby imposing upon the structural-form the triangularity restriction on the coefficients matrix of the endogenous variables and the diagonality restriction of the covariance matrix of the disturbances.

INACCURACIES AND INCONSISTENCIES. Regardless of the formulation postulated, the usefulness of fixed coefficients models is limited because of inherent inconsistencies and inaccuracies. For example, even when the fixed coefficients model is formulated in structural-form, the equations frequently are subjected to episodic breakdowns that are usually handled by judgemental 'add factors' and

179

dummy variables. Even in those situations when microeconomic relationships remain invariant under changed circumstances, the corresponding macroeconomic relationships obtained by aggregating across individual units may not remain invariant, as shown by Swamy et al. (1982).

Besides these inaccuracies, the reduced-form is invariant under nonsingular transformations of the structural-form, see Goldberger (1964, p. 312). Different values of the structural parameters therefore imply the same conditional distribution so that the structural equations may not be identified. Yet identification is a necessary condition for statistical consistency, see Gabrielsen (1978). Of course, one can achieve identification by imposing restrictions on the parameters of structural equations. But if these restrictions are over-identifying, they can be inconsistent, as shown by Conway et al. (1984, p. 7). Furthermore, there are cases in which the reduced-form parameters are also not identified without appropriate restrictions. Imposing identifying restrictions on the reduced-form parameters, however, may contradict the structural identifying restrictions, see Swamy (1980) and Swamy and Mehta (1983), leading to a logically inconsistent model. Surely no one would wish to construct this type of model, since as Boland convincingly argues, even if one cannot prove a model is true, to be true it must be at least logically consistent, see Swamy et al. (1985). Furthermore, if a model is logically inconsistent, the notion of the true value of a parameter and the related concept of statistical consistency do not apply.

Finally, according to Lane (1984), there are three possible interpretations of the elements of Ω:

(a) θ is compatible with the conditional distribution;
(b) Ω is an abstract set and θ merely indexes the conditional distribution;
(c) θ is a possible value for some 'real' physical parameter and function (1) is to be regarded as the distribution of the random quantity y^* (conditional on x) should θ be the true value of that parameter.

Interpretation (c) raises the difficult philosophical question: When and in what sense do 'real' physical parameters exist? Furthermore, must one believe that each structural parameter has a propensity to take a single value? It is difficult to believe that there are model-free physical quantities underlying each model parameter, without guidance as to what constitutes reality and how reality is linked to the mathematics embodied in specific models. Such guidance is impossible, however, because the truth status of a logically consistent model cannot be established, see Swamy et al. (1985). Thus, one never knows when interpretation (c) is appropriate. An appeal to statistical consistency based on the notion of the true values of parameters therefore cannot be made with any conviction.

Since interpretations (a) and (b) are defined solely in terms of the assumed (mathematical) model and do not necessarily refer to the physical reality that model is intended to represent, they are mathematically precise. However, interpretation (a) provides no scope for the mixture principle (that is, permitting an assumed underlying distribution for the parameters to affect the ultimate values of the endogenous variables), since only models whose sampling distributions are identical share 'the same Ω'. Fixed coefficients models thus apply only to situations when the model structure can be represented solely in terms of probability distributions on the sample space indexed by the fixed and unknown θ.

Interpretation (b), on the other hand, does provide wide scope for mixing. Indeed, any two fixed coefficients models with the same index set can be mixed. Consequently, if there exists a pair of observations, one from each model, yielding the same likelihood function on the index set Ω, the likelihood principle holds that the 'evidence' or 'inference' derived from the two models with these two observations must be identical. Yet, this conclusion may not only be incorrect, but is inconsistent with the Bayesian approach, as Lane (1984) points out.

In sum, the foundational status of a fixed coefficients model cannot be determined until Ω is interpreted. Depending upon whether one adopts interpretation (a), (b), or (c), fixed coefficients models are either devoid of interesting consequences (since θ is fixed and unknown), wrong (since inferences may be incorrect and unacceptable to Bayesians), or severely and ambiguously restricted in its domain of applicability (since the truth status of models cannot be known).

RANDOM COEFFICIENTS MODELS. A way to avoid the difficulties mentioned in the preceding section is to use the following random coefficients model (for earlier models, see Swamy (1971) and the references therein) developed by Swamy and Tinsley (1980):

$$\text{(i)} \quad y_t^* = x_t' \beta_t^*;$$

$$\text{(ii)} \quad \beta_t^* = Bz_t + J\xi_t^*; \tag{2}$$

$$\text{(iii)} \quad \xi_t^* = \Phi\xi_{t-1}^* + v_t^*;$$

with $E(v_t^* | z_t, x_t, \xi_{t-1}) = E(v_t^*) = 0$ for all z_t, x_t, and ξ_{t-1}, $E(v_t^* v_s^{*'} | z_t, x_t, \xi_{t-1}) = \Delta_v$ if $t = s$ and 0 if $t \neq s$. One element of each of x_t and z_t may be identically equal to 1 for all t, with the coefficients corresponding to these unit elements representing a random intercept and a constant vector, respectively. Although Swamy and Tinsley set $J = [I, 0, \ldots, 0]$, alternative choices for J are possible.

Since the disturbance term is indistinguishable from a time-dependent random element of β_t^* corresponding to the unit element of x_t, both specifications are combined into a single element of β_t^*. When an equation is part of a larger model, regressors may be jointly determined with the regressand and hence correlated with the contemporaneous disturbance term, see Goldberger (1964, p. 292). If so, elements of x_t in equation (2) (i) are correlated with β_t^*, which means they also appear in z_t. Equation (2)(ii) admits such correlations. The term $J\xi_t^*$ is that part of β_t^* that is mean-independent of x_t and z_t.

Clearly, fixed coefficients models are special cases of random coefficients models. This is the case, for instance, when all the elements of β_t^* corresponding to the non-constant elements of x_t have zero variances and when the columns of B corresponding to the non-constant elements of z_t are null. Thus, in fixed coefficients models, the intercept but not the slopes may be interpreted as random, see Swamy (1970; 1971, p. 8).

When time series of cross-sections data are available, equation (2) has been generalized by Swamy and Mehta (1975) to

$$\text{(i)} \quad y_{it}^* = x_{it}' \beta_{it}^* = \sum_{j=1}^{K} x_{jit} \beta_{jit}^*$$

$$\text{(ii)} \quad \beta_{it}^* = \beta + \alpha_i^* + \xi_{it}^*, \tag{3}$$

where i indexes cross-section observations, t indexes time series observations, the α_i^* are independently distributed with mean vector zero and constant covariance matrix Δ_α, the ξ_{it}^* are distributed with mean vector zero and a general covariance matrix Δ, the α_i^* are independent of the ξ_{it}^* and the β_{it}^* are mean-independent of the x_{it}.

Since these random coefficients models are designed to provide only a convenient approach to modelling relationships, they do not carry a metaphysical burden of 'reality' for the parameters they contain. Furthermore, equations (2)(ii) and (3)(ii) provide rich classes of coherent mixing functions. Swamy and Mehta (1975) and Swamy and Tinsley (1980) use data based methods to select the mixing functions, though purely subjective beliefs can form the basis for these functions. Based on these observations, the correct interpretation for the coefficients β_t^* and β_{it}^* is Lane's interpretation (b). Unlike fixed coefficients, random coefficients are not subject to inconsistent restrictions. Since the ultimate aim of inference is typically to generate an accurate prediction about the value of some future observations, Swamy and Lad (1985) employed a random coefficients model to generate predictions about the future values of stock prices based upon the current and past values of dividends. The resulting forecasts are substantially better than those obtained from the corresponding fixed coefficients model, demonstrating the potential gain in accuracy provided by this consistent approach to modelling relationships among variables.

In conclusion, rather than indicting fixed coefficients models, the comments presented here emphasize the shortcomings of that approach as compared with random coefficients models, thereby providing the researcher with more complete information when deciding upon an empirical model.

BIBLIOGRAPHY

Conway, R.K., Swamy, P.A.V.B., Yanagida, J.F. and von zur Muehlen, P. 1984. The impossibility of causality testing. *Agricultural Economic Research* 36(3), Summer, 1–19.

Gabrielsen, A. 1978. Consistency and identifiability. *Journal of Econometrics* 8(2), October, 261–63.

Goldberger, A.S. 1964. *Econometric Theory*. New York: Wiley.

Lane, D.A. 1984. Discussion of the likelihood principle by J.O. Berger and R.L. Wolpert. Lecture Notes – Monograph Series, Vol. 6, Hayward, California, Institute of Mathematical Statistics.

Swamy, P.A.V.B. 1970. Efficient inference in a random coefficient regression model. *Econometrica* 38(2), March, 311–23.

Swamy, P.A.V.B. 1971. *Statistical Inference in Random Coefficient Regression Models*. New York: Springer-Verlag.

Swamy, P.A.V.B. 1980. A comparison of estimators for undersized samples. *Journal of Econometrics* 14(2), October, 161–81.

Swamy, P.A.V.B. and Lad, F. 1985. Forecasting stock prices with the stochastic coefficients models. Special Studies, Federal Reserve Board, Washington, DC.

Swamy, P.A.V.B. and Mehta, J.S. 1975. Bayesian and non-Bayesian analysis of switching regressions and of random coefficient regression models. *Journal of the American Statistical Association* 70, Pt I, September, 593–602.

Swamy, P.A.V.B. and Mehta, J.S. 1983. Further results on Zellner's minimum expected loss and full information maximum likelihood estimators for undersized samples. *Journal of Business and Economic Statistics* 1(2), April, 154–62.

Swamy, P.A.V.B. and Tinsley, P.A. 1980. Linear prediction and estimation methods for regression models with stationary stochastic coefficients. *Journal of Econometrics* 12(2), February, 103–42.

Swamy, P.A.V.B., Barth, J.R. and Tinsley, P.A. 1982. The rational expectations approach to economic modelling. *Journal of Economic Dynamics and Control* 4(2), May, 125–47.

Swamy, P.A.V.B., Conway, R.K. and von zur Muehlen, P. 1985. The foundations of econometrics – are there any? (With discussion.) *Econometric Reviews* 4(1), November, 1–61.

Rational Expectations:
Econometric Implications

N.E. SAVIN

It has long been recognized that forecasts affect outcomes. Similarly, outcomes affect expectations. Thus, there is a mapping from expectations to outcomes and back to expectations and so from expectations to expectations. A rational expectations equilibrium is a fixed point of this mapping in which expectations generate outcomes which confirm the original expectations. A rational expectations equilibrium is a natural solution concept in a model with expectations. The heuristic reasoning is that outside rational expectations equilibria agents make systematic mistakes; expectations are not confirmed by outcomes in that the expectations are not correct on the average. Consequently, it is very plausible that outside rational expectations equilibria, agents will eventually notice that they are making systematic mistakes and attempt to revise the way they forecast in order to eliminate the sources of the systematic errors. This suggests that agents are not in equilibrium until they have learned to form rational expectations.

Econometric analysis typically assumes that the econometrician is an outside observer: nothing which the econometrician does affects the generation process. In particular, it is assumed that the forecasts based on the econometrician's estimated model do not influence the forecasts of the agents in the economy. By contrast, the agents in the economy are inside econometricians. If the agents' forecasts are derived from an estimated econometric model, then the data generation process changes when the agents update the parameter estimates or change the model specification. A single atomistic agent can act like the outside econometrician, but this is not so for agents as a whole. The collective impact of the forecasting activity of the agents is to change the data generation process; this is the essence of forecast feedback.

This essay concentrates on three topics which involve the econometric implications of rational expectations: solutions, estimation and learning. The issues surrounding the solutions are discussed in section 1 in the context of a second order linear expectational difference equation. Section 2 considers maximum likelihood and general method of moment estimators which can be used by an outside econometrician to estimate the parameters of a rational expectations model. The question of whether agents – inside econometricians – can learn to form rational expectations is addressed in section 3. The concluding comments are in section 4.

1. SOLUTIONS

A prototype for many rational expectations models is the second order expectational difference equation

$$E_t y_{t+1} - (\rho_1 + \rho_2)y_t + \rho_1\rho_2 y_{t-1} = x_t, \tag{1}$$

where t indexes the integers, $\{x_t\}$ and $\{y_t\}$ are scalar stochastic processes and where for expositional purposes ρ_1 and ρ_2 are assumed to be real numbers. The variable x is called the 'driving process' and '$E_t y_{t+1}$' is the forecast of y based on the information available at time t. The reduced form of the model is the solution of the equation which expresses y as a function of current and past values of x_t, which is the information available at time t. Second order expectational difference equations arise as necessary conditions for optima in linear-quadratic versions of costly adjustment models and in this context are called Euler equations. Examples can be found in Kennan (1979), Sargent (1979), Hansen and Sargent (1980), Eichenbaum (1983) and Hansen and Singleton (1982).

There is a long list of methods for finding solutions to linear expectational difference equations. These include 'state-space' techniques in Lucas (1972), 'methods of undetermined coefficients' in Muth (1961) and Aoki and Canzoneri (1979), 'forward and backward' solutions in Blanchard (1979) and Blanchard and Kahn (1980) and a 'method of undetermined coefficients in the frequency domain' in Saracoglu and Sargent (1978), Futia (1981) and Whiteman (1983).

The solutions presented below are those obtained by the approach of Whiteman (1983). This method is analytically straightforward and has the virtue that it finds all the solutions within a certain set. Whiteman assumes that the driving process is covariance stationary and looks for solutions with the same general structure as the driving process, that is, for solutions in the same 'space' as the driving process. The motivation for this approach is twofold. The first is that without any restrictions on the $\{x_t\}$ and without any side conditions there is a plethora of solutions. The second is that stationarity is assumed in the estimation theory for expectational difference equations.

The Whiteman solution technique employs four assumptions. First, x_t has a known Wold decomposition

$$x_t = \sum_{j=0}^{\infty} A_j \varepsilon_{t-j}, \tag{2}$$

with $\varepsilon_t = x_t - E(x_t|x_{t-1}, x_{t-2}, \ldots)$, $\sum_{j=0}^{\infty} A_j^2 < \infty$ and the function $A(z) = \sum_{j=0}^{\infty} A_j z^j$

must be analytic on the open unit disk. Thus (2) can be written as

$$x_t = \sum_{j=0}^{\infty} A_j L^j \varepsilon_t = A(L)\varepsilon_t, \tag{2'}$$

where L is the lag operator: $L^n = x_{t-n}$. Second, the solutions are in the space of the driving process (2) and are of the form

$$y_t = \sum_{j=0}^{\infty} C_j \varepsilon_{t-j} = C(L)\varepsilon_t. \tag{3}$$

Third, the forecasting procedure is rational and the forecasts are computed using the Wiener–Kolmogorov formula

$$
\begin{aligned}
E_t y_{t+1} &= E_t[C_0 \varepsilon_{t+1} + C_1 \varepsilon_t + C_2 \varepsilon_{t-1} + \cdots] \\
&= C_1 \varepsilon_t + C_2 \varepsilon_{t-1} + \cdots = [C(L) - C_0]L^{-1}\varepsilon_t
\end{aligned}
\tag{4}
$$

since $E_t \varepsilon_{t+1} = 0$. Note that the forecast is computed using a solution to the model and hence is model consistent. Fourth, the rational expectations restrictions hold for all realizations of the driving process. Using (2), (3) and (4) equation (1) can be written as

$$[C(L) - C_0]L^{-1}\varepsilon_t - (\rho_1 + \rho_2)C(L)\varepsilon_t + \rho_1 \rho_2 C(L)L\varepsilon_t = A(L)\varepsilon_t, \tag{5}$$

where it is assumed that (5) holds for all realizations of $\{\varepsilon_t\}$. The solutions are obtained by exploiting the property that the z transforms of the sequences represented in (5) must be identical as analytic functions on the open unit disk.

The solutions are now presented for the three cases corresponding to three different sets of values for the parameters ρ_1 and ρ_2. First suppose $|\rho_1| < 1$, $|\rho_2| < 1$. The Wold representation for the solutions $\{y_t\}$ is

$$y_t = \{(1 - \rho_1 L)(1 - \rho_2 L)\}^{-1}\{A(L)L + C_0\}\varepsilon_t, \tag{6}$$

which can be written as

$$y_t = \{(1 - \rho_1 L)(1 - \rho_2 L)\}^{-1}\{L - C_0 A(L)^{-1}\}x_t, \tag{6'}$$

provided that $\{x_t\}$ has an autoregressive representation. In this case the expectational difference equation (1) does not uniquely determine the solution $\{y_t\}$. For any finite value of C_0 (6) gives a process lying in the space of the driving process which satisfies equation (1). Since C_0 is a parameter in the forecasting formula the model does not completely determine the forecasting procedure of the agents.

The second case is $|\rho_1| < 1 < |\rho_2|$. In this case (1) and (2) determine a unique solution for y_t:

$$y_t = \{(1 - \rho_1 L)(1 - \rho_2 L)\}^{-1}\{(L - \rho_2^{-1}A(\rho_2^{-1}A)L)^{-1}\}x_t. \tag{7}$$

This case applies when (1) is interpreted as the Euler equation in a linear-quadratic costly adjustment model; see Kennan (1979).

The third case is where $1 < |\rho_1|$, $1 < |\rho_2|$. In this case there is no solution lying in the space of the driving process.

There are several econometric implications of the solutions. First, the parameters of (6) and (7) depend on the parameters of both the driving process and the expectational difference equation. Thus, there are cross-equation restrictions between the parameters of the reduced form and the driving process. Sargent (1981) has called the cross-equation restrictions the 'hallmark of rational expectations'. If x is a policy variable and if a change in policy is described by a change in the parameters of the x process, then a policy change induces a change in the values of the reduced form parameters. The consequence is that if the reduced form parameters are estimated from data generated by the existing policy regime, the resulting estimates may produce a misleading forecast of what will happen under a different policy regime. This point is spelled out in Lucas's (1976) critique of econometric policy evaluation. The connection between the notion of exogeneity and the Lucas critique is discussed by Engle, Hendry and Richard (1983). See also Sims (1982).

The second point is that when $|\rho_1| < 1$ and $|\rho_2| < 1$ there may be many stationary solutions in the space of the driving process. The nature and implication of the multiple solutions has been discussed by Gourieroux, Laffont and Monfort (1982), Broze, Gourieroux and Szafarz (1985) and Evans and Honkapohja (1986). A number of criteria have been proposed for eliminating some of the solutions. Examples include Taylor's (1977) 'minimum variance' criterion, which chooses the solution with the smallest variance, McCallum's (1983) 'minimum state variable' criterion, which chooses the solution which depends on the fewest other variables and Evans's (1985) 'expectational stability' criterion, which chooses solutions that are stable given a small deviation of the expectations functions from rational expectations equilibrium.

The search for selection criteria in linear rational expectations models has a resemblance to a parallel activity in game theory. Games of complete as well as incomplete information can have multiple equilibria. Several selection criteria – 'refinements' to the concept of Nash equilibrium – have been developed for the purpose of eliminating some of these equilibria. These criteria, or refinements, include Selten's (1965) 'subgame perfection', Selten's (1975) 'trembling hand perfection' and the Kohlberg and Mertens (1986) 'stability' criterion. It is difficult to find appealing arguments for eliminating solutions for linear rational expectations models when the expectational difference equation is not the first order condition to a well posed optimization problem.

Third, in the case of the unique solution (7) it is the relation between the C_j's and not the absolute size of these coefficients that is determined. This can be seen from the renormalization $C^* = C_0^{-1} C_j$ and $v_t^* = C_0^{-1} \varepsilon_t$. The same rescaling procedure can be applied to the representation for x_t.

Fourth, the second order case is the simplest case where all three possibilities exist: many, one and no solutions in the space of a stationary driving process. The case of no solutions is of special interest since in empirical studies the estimation procedures assume that a stationary solution exists.

187

Fifth, there are solutions lying outside the space of the driving process, some of which are nonstationary. Nonstationary solutions exist whether or not the driving process is stationary.

2. ESTIMATION

The problem considered here is the estimation of a rational expectations model by an outside econometrician. Hansen (1982) has shown that under certain assumptions there are strongly consistent estimators for the parameters of linear and nonlinear rational expectations models. A key assumption is that the driving process and the solution are stationary and ergodic. This assumption again highlights the importance of the driving process.

A stationary and ergodic driving process $\{x_t\}$ is illustrated by the first order autoregressive process:

$$x_t = ax_{t-1} + \varepsilon_t, \qquad |a| < 1, \tag{8}$$

where $\{\varepsilon_t\}$ is independently identically normally distributed. The moving average representation of the $\{x_t\}$ process (8) is

$$x_t = (1 - aL)^{-1}\varepsilon_t = A(L)\varepsilon_t. \tag{8'}$$

If $\{y_t\}$ is in the space of the driving process, then it is also stationary and ergodic.

For empirical work the assumption of stationarity and ergodicity is a demanding one, especially for times series as opposed to cross-sectional series. Nelson and Plosser (1982) have provided evidence that a number of macroeconomic variables such as GNP and the money supply behave very similarly to random walks or integrated processes rather than stationary processes about a trend. In practice the driving variables are often detrended. The detrending of a random walk produces a number of spurious effects. For example, Nelson and Kang (1981, 1983) have shown that regressing a trend-free random walk against a time trend will result in the misleading inference that the trend is significant and that the detrended series is serially correlated. Some examples of the empirical implications of trends versus random walks for rational expectations models are discussed in Deaton (1986). The general asymptotic theory for testing the random walk versus the time trend model has been recently developed by Durlauf and Phillips (1986). They examine analytically the effects of spuriously detrending random walks.

The fact that the driving process is stationary does not imply that the solution is stationary since the solution may not be in the space of the driving process. Hence there is the additional problem of testing whether the solution is stationary.

Turning to estimation, the objective is to estimate the parameters of the structural equation rather than the parameters of the driving process. The parameters of the expectational difference equation (1) are often interpreted as the coefficients of the utility function or production function of a representative agent or firm and hence it is these parameters which are of economic interest.

There are two approaches to the estimation of the structural parameters. One is to estimate the structural parameters via the reduced form. The estimates produced by the reduced form approach depend on the specification of the driving process and on which solution is selected. Suppose the driving process is the first order autoregression (8) and the parameters of equation (1) are estimated from the non-unique solution (6). Substituting $(1 - aL)^{-1}$ for $A(L)$ in (6) gives

$$y_t = \{(1 - \rho_1 L)(1 - \rho_2 L)\}^{-1}\{L + C_0(1 - aL)\}x_t, \tag{9}$$

which can be rearranged as

$$y_t = (\rho_1 + \rho_2)y_{t-1} - \rho_1\rho_2 y_{t-2} + C_0 x_t + (1 - C_0 a)x_{t-1}. \tag{9'}$$

Since (9') is an exact relation the coefficients of (9') can be calculated exactly from four sample points of the form $(y_{t'}, y_{t'-1}, y_{t'-2}, x_{t'}, x_{t'-1})$. Given the prior information $|\rho_1| < 1$ and $|\rho_2| < 1$ only the sum and the product of ρ_1 and ρ_2 can be identified from the data.

Assume next that $|\rho_1| < 1 < |\rho_2|$. Then substituting $(1 - aL)^{-1}$ for $A(L)$ in the unique solution (7) yields

$$y_t - \{(a - \rho_2)(1 - \rho_1 L)\}^{-1}x_t, \tag{10}$$

which can be rewritten as

$$y_t - \rho_1 y_{t-1} = (a - \rho_2)^{-1}x_t. \tag{10'}$$

The parameter a can be consistently estimated by applying least squares to (8). In this case (10) and (10') are also exact relations so that the coefficients of y_{t-1} and x_t can be determined exactly from the two sample points (y_t, y_{t-1}, x_t) and (y_{t+1}, y_t, x_{t+1}). Given an estimate of a an estimate of ρ_2 is obtained from the coefficient of x_t in (10') and the ρ_1 is determined exactly since it is the coefficient of y_{t-1} in (10'). In this case the prior information $|\rho_1| < 1 < |\rho_2|$ allows the parameters ρ_1 and ρ_2 to be identified.

In empirical studies the sample data does not satisfy exact relations such as (9') and (10'). This has led to the construction of models based on stories where the agents have more information than the outside econometrician. For example, in a model in which agents face several driving variables, the econometrician may have observations on only some of the driving variables. This is illustrated by

$$E_t y_{t+1} - (\rho_1 + \rho_2)y_t + \rho_1\rho_2 y_{t-1} = x_t = x_t' + \eta_t. \tag{11}$$

where the outside econometrician observes only x_t'. Whiteman calls (11) a 'perturbed equation'.

Observe that in the perturbed version of (9') the parameters C_0 and a are over-identified since given an estimate of a from the driving process two estimates of C_0 can be calculated from the perturbed version of (9') and also two estimates of a; one obtained from the driving process and one from (9').

The coefficients of the perturbed equation (11) can be consistently estimated from the reduced form provided certain conditions are satisfied. As an illustration suppose the autoregression (8) is the driving process where the ε_t's and n_t's are serially and mutually independent. Applying least squares to the driving process and to the perturbed version of (10') produces consistent estimates of the coefficients in these equations. A consistent estimate of the structural parameter ρ_2 is derived from the coefficient of x_t in the perturbed version of (10') using the least squares estimate of the parameter a in the autoregression (8).

Asymptotically efficient estimators of the parameters of the driving process and the structure can be obtained by using the method of maximum likelihood. Hansen and Sargent (1980) show that the maximum likelihood estimator is asymptotically efficient only if it maximizes the joint likelihood function of the driving process and the reduced form.

Two problems are encountered using maximum likelihood. First, it is difficult to solve explicitly for the reduced form if structural equation is nonlinear and the driving process is complicated. For the case of nonlinear expectational difference equations Fair and Taylor (1983) have proposed an approximate maximum likelihood procedure which circumvents some of the computational difficulties of obtaining a complete characterization of the reduced form. In particular, they develop a method for solving numerically for the reduced form. The second is that the maximum likelihood estimator may not be consistent, or, if consistent, not efficient, when the model is misspecified. Hansen and Singleton (1982) present an example in which the maximum likelihood estimator fails to be consistent due to a misspecification of the stochastic properties of the driving process.

The other approach is to estimate the structural parameters directly. This approach applied to equation (1) can be motivated as follows. The difference between y_{t+1} and the conditional expectation $E_t y_{t+1}$ is

$$u_{t+1} = y_{t+1} - E_t y_{t+1} = [C(L) - (C(L) - C_0)]L^{-1}\varepsilon_t = C_0\varepsilon_{t+1}, \qquad (12)$$

which implies that

$$E_t u_{t+1} = 0 \qquad (12')$$

and hence that y_{t+1} is a conditionally unbiased estimate of the conditional expectation. This condition can be interpreted as the first order condition to a linear-quadratic optimization problem. By assumption the forecast error is orthogonal to the observed forecast and to any other variables in the information set of agents when the forecast is made. Substituting y_{t+1} for $E_t y_{t+1}$ in (1) and rearranging gives

$$y_{t+1} = (\rho_1 + \rho_2)y_t - \rho_1\rho_2 y_{t-1} + x_t + u_{t+1}. \qquad (13)$$

From (13) it is seen that the 'error' (12) introduced by the substitution is contemporaneously uncorrelated with the 'regressors' y_t, y_{t-1} and x_t provided that the ε_t's are serially uncorrelated. Thus, consistent estimates of the parameters ρ_1 and ρ_2 can be obtained by applying least squares to (13). If instead of (1) the starting point is the perturbed equation (11), least squares is consistent if the error η_t in (11) is independent of the error u_{t+1}. The direct structural approach was used by Kennan (1979) to estimate a perturbed version of an Euler equation.

Note that the value of C_0 and the variance of ε_{t+1} combine to determine the variance of the error (12) and that the direct structural approach gives a consistent estimate of the error variance. As a consequence, the value of C_0 in the multiple solutions case (6) is (implicitly) consistently estimated.

An alternative motivation for the direct structural approach exploits certain orthogonality conditions. Define

$$h(z_{t+1}, b_0) = y_{t+1} - (\rho_1 + \rho_2)y_t + \rho_1\rho_2 y_{t-1} - x_t = 0, \tag{14}$$

where $z_{t+1} = (y_{t+1}, y_t, y_{t-1}, x_t)$ is the vector of variables and $b_0 = [(\rho_1 + \rho_2), (\rho_1\rho_2)]$ is the vector of parameters in (1). Using these definitions (1) can be written as

$$E_t h(z_{t+1}, b_0) = 0, \tag{14'}$$

so that given a set of variables $\{w_q\}$ in the agents' information set which are observed by the econometrician

$$E_t[h(z_{t+1}, b_0)w_{q,t}] = 0, \tag{15}$$

where the variables w_q can be thought of as instrumental variables. Taking the expectation of (15) over the variables in information set gives the unconditional expectation

$$EE_t[h(z_{t+1}, b_0)w_{q,t}] = E[h(z_{t+1}, b_0)w_{q,t}] = 0. \tag{15'}$$

Hansen (1982) defines the general method of moments estimator of the true parameter b_0 as the estimator which makes the sample versions of the population orthogonality conditions (15') as close to zero as possible according to some measure of distance. Examples of this method include the least squares procedure of Kennan (1979) and a variety of instrumental variable techniques. For identification there must be at least as many orthogonality conditions as parameters to be estimated.

The general method of moments estimators are in general less asymptotically efficient than maximum likelihood if the model is correctly specified. Heuristically, this is because the method of moments does not use all the stochastic properties of the driving process and all the orthogonality conditions. The chief advantages of the method of moments estimators are robustness to misspecification and computational convenience. The method is robust in the sense that the model does not have to be completely specified; in particular, it is not necessary to make precise assumptions about the stochastic properties of the driving process. The computational advantage is that least squares type procedures can be used and that the model does not have to be solved for the reduced form. Hence, the method is especially suited to the estimation of nonlinear rational expectations models. In many applications of interest the u_{t+1}'s are serially correlated and conditionally heteroskedastic. Hansen (1982) has also stated conditions under which the method is consistent in the presence of serial correlation and conditional heteroskedasticity.

3. LEARNING

One possible and appealing justification for the use of rational expectations is that agents learn to form rational expectations. There is a large literature on learning to form rational expectations, much of which is surveyed in Blume, Bray and Easley (1982). The literature falls into two parts: one is concerned with 'rational learning' in which the model is correctly specified and agents form rational expectations given knowledge of the model and estimates of its parameters. Examples include Townsend (1978, 1983), Brandenburger (1984) and Bray and Kreps (1986). Rational learning is the natural extension of the standard methodology, based on optimization, to learning. Bray and Kreps (1986) show that it also guarantees convergence to rational expectations equilibrium under quite mild assumptions. The case which has been studied suppose a substantial degree of insight and prior knowledge of the part of agents.

The other part of this literature assumes some degree of bounded rationality. Examples of this type include Bray (1982, 1983), Radner (1982), Frydman (1982), Bray and Savin (1986), Fourgeaud, Gourieroux and Pradel (1986) and Marcet and Sargent (1986). In the bounded rationality framework agents are assumed to learn using reasonable model specifications which are often correct in rational expectations equilibrium, but misspecified when there is learning.

Following the classic paper by Muth (1961), the cobweb model has been used in the discussion of expectations formation of Townsend (1978), Brandenburger (1984), Frydman (1982), Bray and Savin (1986), Fourgeaud, Gourieroux and Pradel (1986) and others. Townsend (1978) and Bray and Savin (1986) consider a continuum of firms producing a homogeneous good where the set of firms is the unit interval $[0, 1]$ indexed by i. The firms make their production decisions at each date t before the realization of an exogenous stochastic demand which depends linearly on p_t, the market clearing price of the good, and on an unobserved exogenous demand shock. Each firm has a quadratic cost function so that the optimal output of firm i at date t is proportional to p_{it}^e, the mean of firm i's prior on p_t at date t. Setting the average supply to the market equal to the demand gives

$$p_t = x_t'm + a\bar{p}_t^e + u_t, \tag{16}$$

where x_t is a vector of exogenous supply shocks observable by firms when the production decision is made, u_t is the difference between the unobservable exogenous shocks in the demand and supply equations and

$$\bar{p}_t^e = \int_0^1 p_{it}^e \, di \tag{17}$$

is the average of the price expectations (prior means) of the firms. In Bray and Savin (1986) the description of the model is completed by assuming that the stochastic processes x_t and u_t are independently identically distributed random variables with bounded forth moments. The equation (16) is a special type of expectational difference equation called a 'withholding equation'. The simplest example of such an equation is

$$E_{t-1}y_t - \rho y_t = x_t. \tag{18}$$

The equation (16) is a perturbed version of (18) due to the addition of the error

u_t. Withholding equations are very prevalent in the rational expectations literature. One reason is that a class of models stemming from the absolute versus relative-price confusion paradigm of Lucas (1972, 1975) employs (18). Another reason is that Muth's (1961) cobweb model produces such an equation. The unique solution y_t to (18) lying in the space of a driving process when the ε_t's are independently identically distributed is

$$y_t = (1 - \rho)^{-1} x_t \tag{19}$$

provided ρ is not equal to unity. It is important to note that this unique solution exists regardless of the value of ρ. For further details see Whiteman (1983).

From (16) the rational expectations equilibrium price forecast is

$$p_{it}^e = x_t' m (1 - a)^{-1} \tag{20}$$

for all i, provided a is not equal to unity. This solution is essentially the same as (19). Substituting this forecast in (16) the price in rational expectations equilibrium is the random variable

$$p_t = x_t' m (1 - a)^{-1} + u_t. \tag{21}$$

Hence if agents know the numerical value of $m(1 - a)^{-1}$ they can form rational expectations.

The learning procedure followed by agents should depend on how much they know about the model and the way other agents learn. Suppose all agents know the numerical value of a and can observe or infer $\bar{p}_t^e$. Then (16) can be written as $y_t = x_t' m + u_t$ where $y_t = p_t - a \bar{p}_t^e$ is an observable variable. This equation satisfies the assumptions of the standard linear model so that m can be consistently estimated using classical or Bayesian methods.

Townsend (1978) assumes that the agents are Bayesians who know a and have enough common knowledge to infer $\bar{p}_t^e$ and hence can use Bayesian methods to infer m. A similar result under weaker common knowledge assumption has been obtained by Brandenburger (1984). In Townsend and Brandenburger the agents know that they are in a market game where the actual price depends on the collective output decisions of all the firms. Each agent calculates the Bayesian Nash equilibrium price of the game at each date and uses this as the price forecast. These examples assume Bayesian learning based on correctly specified likelihood functions, that is, likelihood functions which take into account the forecast feedback.

By contrast, in Bray and Savin (1986) and Fourgeaud, Gourieroux and Pradel (1986) the agents do not know the value of a and use a misspecified model for forecasting price. The agents assume that

$$p_t = x_t b + u_t \tag{22}$$

and that (22) satisfies the assumptions of the standard linear model and estimate b using classical or Bayesian techniques. For simplicity, suppose that the agents are classical statisticians and that b is estimated after observing

$(x_1, p_1, \ldots, (x_{t-1}, p_{t-1})$ by

$$b_{t-1} = \left[\sum_{j=1}^{t-1} x_j x_j' \right]^{-1} \left[\sum_{j=1}^{t-1} x_j p_j \right]. \tag{22}$$

The agent's forecast of p_t is $x_t' b_{t-1}$. Substituting this forecast into (16) gives

$$p_t = x_t'(m + a b_{t-1}) + u_t. \tag{23}$$

Equations (22) and (23) describe the true data generation process. Comparing (23) with (21) it is clear that agents are using a misspecified model since they are assuming that b in (21) is a constant when in fact the learning process induces a time-varying parameter $m + a b_{t-1}$. The specification (21) is not arbitrary since it would be correct in rational expectations equilibrium, that is, if the value $m(1 - a)^{-1}$ were known and used in forecasting. On the other hand, the agents are not fully rational because they fail to employ the relevant model to deduce (16) and hence to deduce that the forecasting procedure based on (21) implies the time-varying parameter model (23), which in turn implies that the forecasting procedure based on (21) is inconsistent with the model.

It can be shown that b_t cannot converge to any other value than the rational expectations equilibrium value $m(1 - a)^{-1}$ and that if $a < 1$, b_t strongly converges to $m(1 - a)^{-1}$. In this case agents eventually learn how to form rational expectations. When $a < 1$ the demand curve crosses the supply curve from above, which is the standard economically plausible case. Fourgeaud, Gourieroux and Pradel (1986) and Marcet and Sargent (1986) present proofs for the case where b is estimated by least squares and Bray and Savin (1986) for the case where agents are Bayesian statisticians.

When $a > 1$ it appears that b_t does not converge. In this case b_t follows one of a variety of divergent processes including a random walk. The nonconvergence is due to the unstable cobweb since the driving process is stable.

The question of the rate of convergence of b_t to the rational expectations equilibrium value is of considerable interest and has been investigated by Bray and Savin (1986). If the rate of convergence is fast, then the learning procedure works in the sense of generating expectations which are very nearly rational in a short time. Rapid convergence justifies the use of the rational expectations equilibrium as a good asymptotic approximation to a learning process and encourages the application of rational expectations models to actual data.

If convergence is slow or does not appear to occur, then the agents will eventually detect that the model (21) is misspecified. As a consequence, the specification of the model may be revised. Whether the sequence of model revisions adopted by agents will eventually lead to rational expectations equilibrium is an open question.

Time-varying models are widely used in empirical studies. Since learning processes can generate data which closely mimics that generated by standard time-varying parameter models, learning is a potentially attractive explanation for the observed phenomenon of time-varying coefficients.

4. CONCLUDING COMMENTS

The implicit assumption made in the case of an outside econometrician estimating a rational expectations model is that the actions of the outside econometrician do not influence the agents in the economy. This is true if the model estimated by the econometrician is ignored by the agents. If the empirical work of the outside econometrician is in fact ignored, then this raises the question of the motivation for such work. On the other hand, if the outside econometrician's model specification and estimates do have influence, then it is no longer true that the outside econometrician is indeed outside the economy. In this situation the econometrician's model may be misspecified due to forecast feedback.

The stationarity of the driving process and the solution plays an important role in the analysis of the solutions and in the theory of estimation. Nonstationarity appears to be a characteristic of many macroeconomic time series. It is this which accounts for the popularity of time-varying parameter methods in econometrics. This nonstationarity may be in part a product of agents learning how to form rational expectations. Even if the agents are fully rational in the sense that they can calculate the Bayesian Nash equilibrium, this does not rule out nonstationarity. The assumption of stationarity may not be consistent with the notion of agents learning to form rational expectations.

In the typical rational expectations model forecasting is assumed to be a costless activity. In practice forecasting is costly, if for no other reason, because it is a time consuming activity; agents may be playing many market games simultaneously or agents may be playing one game which involves substantial amounts of data collection and processing. This suggests that the choice of a forecasting procedure is the outcome of a constrained optimization problem. Thus the assumption of bounded rationality is not necessary to explain why agents do not forecast with all available information. Alternatively, bounded rationality can be interpreted as the result of a budget constraint. Rule of thumb forecasting procedures may closely approximate the procedures selected by constrained optimization. The time constraint also naturally suggests why there is a market for forecasting services. Given the opportunity cost of time it may be optimal for agents to buy forecasts rather than make their own. The econometricians who supply these forecasts are inside the economy which means that econometric modelling is complicated by the presence of forecast feedback. This in turn may explain why econometric models require frequent revision.

BIBLIOGRAPHY

Aoki, A. and Canzoneri, M. 1979. Reduced forms of rational expectation models. *Quarterly Journal of Economics* 93, 59–71.

Blanchard, O.J. 1979. Backward and forward solutions for economies with rational expectations. *American Economic Review* 69, 114–118.

Blanchard, O.J. and Kahn, C.M. 1980. The solution of linear difference models under rational expectations. *Econometrica* 48, 1305–11.

Blume, L., Bray, M.M. and Easley, D. 1982. Introduction to the stability of rational expectations equilibrium. *Journal of Economic Theory* 26, 313–17.

Brandenburger, A. 1984. Information and learning in market games. Churchill College, Cambridge Mimeo, August 1984.

Bray, M.M. 1982. Learning estimation, and the stability of rational expectations. *Journal of Economic Theory* 26, 318–39.

Bray, M.M. 1983. Convergence to rational expectations equilibrium. In *Individual Forecasting and Aggregate Outcomes*, ed. R. Frydman and E.S. Phelps, Cambridge: Cambridge University Press.

Bray, M.M. and Kreps, D. 1986. Rational learning and rational expectations. In *Essays in Honour of K.J. Arrow*, ed. W. Heller, R. Starr and D. Starrett, Cambridge: Cambridge University Press.

Bray, M.M. and Savin, N.E. 1986. Rational expectations equilibria, learning and model specification. *Econometrica* 57, 1129–60.

Broze, L., Gourieroux, C. and Szafarz, A. 1985. Solutions of linear rational expectations models. *Econometric Theory* 1, 341–68.

Deaton, A. 1986. Life-cycle models of consumption: is the evidence consistent with the theory? Woodrow Wilson School, Princeton University, Mimeo.

Durlauf, S.N. and Phillips, P.C.B. 1986. Trends versus random walks in time series analysis. Cowles Foundation Discussion Paper No. 788.

Eichenbaum, M.S. 1983. A rational expectations equilibrium model of finished goods and employment. *Journal of Monetary Economics* 12, 259–77.

Engle, R.F., Hendry, D.F. and Richard, J.-F. 1983. Exogeneity. *Econometrica* 50, 227–304.

Evans, G. 1985. Expectational stability and multiple solutions in linear rational expectations models. *Quarterly Journal of Economics* 99, 1217–33.

Evans, G. and Honkapohja, S. 1986. A complete characterization of ARMA solutions to linear rational expectations models. *Review of Economic Studies* 53, 227–39.

Fair, R.C. and Taylor, J.B. 1983. Solution and maximum likelihood estimation of dynamic nonlinear rational expectations models. *Econometrica* 51, July, 1169–85.

Fourgeaud, C., Gourieroux, C. and Pradel, J. 1986. Learning procedure and convergence to rationality. *Econometrica*, 54, 845–68.

Frydman, R. 1982. Towards an understanding of market processes: individual expectations, learning and convergence to rational expectations equilibrium. *American Economic Review* 72, 652–68.

Futia, C.A. 1981. Rational expectations in stationary linear models. *Econometrica* 49, 171–92.

Gourieroux, C., Laffont, J.J. and Monfort, A. 1982. Rational expectations in linear models: analysis of solutions. *Econometrica* 50, 409–25.

Hansen, L.P. 1982. Large sample properties of generalized method of moments estimators. *Econometrica* 50, 1029–54.

Hansen, L.P. and Sargent, T.J. 1980. Formulating and estimating dynamic linear rational expectations. *Journal of Economic Dynamics and Control* 2, 7–46.

Hansen, L.P. and Singleton, K.J. 1982. Generalized instrumental variable estimation of nonlinear rational expectations models. *Econometrica* 50, 1269–86.

Kennan, J. 1979. The estimation of partial adjustment models with rational expectations. *Econometrica* 47, 1441–6.

Kohlberg, E. and Mertens, J.-F. 1986. On the strategic stability of equilibria. *Econometrica* 57, 1003–38.

Lucas, R.E. Jr. 1972. Econometric testing of the natural rate hypothesis. In *Econometrics of Price Determination Conference*, ed. O. Eckstein, Washington, DC: Board of Governors of the Federal Reserve System.

Lucas, R.E. Jr. 1975. An equilibrium model of the business cycle. *Journal of Political Economy* 83, 1113–144.

Lucas, R.E. Jr. 1976. Econometric policy evaluation: a critique. In *The Phillips Curve and Labor Markets*, Carnegie-Rochester Conference on Public Policy, Vol. 1, ed. K. Brunner and A.H. Meltzer, Amsterdam: North-Holland.

Marcet, A. and Sargent, T.J. 1986. Convergence of least squares learning mechanisms in self referential linear stochastic models. University of Minnesota, Mimeo.

McCallum, B.T. 1983. On non-uniqueness in rational expectations models: an attempt at perspective. *Journal of Monetary Economics* 11, 139–68.

Muth, J.F. 1961. Rational expectations and the theory of price movements. *Econometrica* 29, 315–35.

Nelson, C.R. and Plosser, C. 1982. Trends and random walk in macroeconomic time series: some evidence and implications. *Journal of Monetary Economics* 10, 139–62.

Nelson, C.R. and Kang, H. 1981. Spurious periodicity in inappropriately detrended time series. *Econometrica* 49, 741–51.

Nelson, C.R. and Kang, H. 1983. Pitfalls in the use of time as an explanatory variable in regression. NBER Technical Working Paper No. 30.

Radner, R. 1982. Equilibrium under uncertainty. In *Handbook of Mathematical Economics*, Vol. II, ed. K.J. Arrow and M.D. Intriligator, Amsterdam: North-Holland.

Saracoglu, R. and Sargent, T.J. 1978. Seasonality and portfolio balance under rational expectations. *Journal of Monetary Economics* 4, 511–21.

Sargent, T.J. 1979. *Macroeconomic Theory*. New York: Academic Press.

Sargent, T.J. 1981. Interpreting economic time series. *Journal of Political Economy* 89, 403–10.

Selten, R. 1965. Spieltheoretische Behandlung eines Oligopomodells mit Nachfragetragheit. *Zeitschrift fur die Gesamte Staatswissenschaft* 122, 301–24.

Selten, R. 1975. A re-examination of the perfectness concept for equilibrium points in extensive games. *International Journal of Game Theory* 4, 25–55.

Sims, C.A. 1982. Policy analysis with econometric models. *Brookings Papers on Economic Activity* No. 1, 107–52.

Taylor, J.B. 1977. Conditions for unique solutions in stochastic macroeconomic models with rational expectations. *Econometrica* 45, 1337–85.

Townsend, R.M. 1978. Market anticipations, rational expectations and Bayesian analysis. *International Economic Review* 19, 481–94.

Townsend, R.M. 1983. Forecasting the forecasts of others. *Journal of Political Economy* 91, 545–88.

Whiteman, C.H. 1983. *Linear Rational Expectations Models*. Minneapolis: University of Minnesota Press.

Seasonal Variation

PIETRO BALESTRA

When observations are taken at regular intervals within a year (by month or by quarter), most economic time series are likely to exhibit some degree of seasonal variation. An obvious example, known to everyone, is the existence of a 'high' and 'low' season for air transportation and other recreational activities. Perhaps less obvious, but equally important, is the presence of a seasonal pattern in most economic aggregates such as the index of production, price indices, the unemployment rate and so on.

In order to appraise the economic situation and take appropriate action, it is extremely important to be able to 'isolate' or 'extract' the seasonal component from an economic time series. Take, for instance, the case of an increase of one-half of a percentage point in the unemployment rate between two successive quarters. Does that not mean that the conditions in the labour market are deteriorating? Not necessarily, if typically between those two quarters of the year the economy experiences a rise in seasonal unemployment. Conversely, the situation may be more alarming than that indicated by the mere increase of one-half of a percentage point if the past record shows a declining rate between the two quarters.

The main difficulty in assessing the seasonal pattern is that an economic time series is the aggregate outcome of many different forces and not simply the result of a pure seasonal movement. Traditionally, in time series analysis, one thinks of an economic time series (E) as being composed of three elements: a seasonal component (S), a trend-cycle component (T) and a residual component (R). The two widely adopted specifications are the linearly additive one ($E = S + T + R$) and the multiplicative one ($E + S \cdot T \cdot R$). In both cases, the seasonal component is intimately tangled with the others and the task of eliminating it from the series (known as the problem of seasonal adjustment) is a delicate one.

Related to the seasonal adjustment problem is the question of how one should estimate an economic relationship in the presence of seasonal data. These two aspects of seasonality are briefly addressed below.

198

SEASONAL ADJUSTMENT. A seasonally adjusted series is one from which the seasonal component has been removed ($E - S$ and E/S for the additive and multiplicative cases respectively). Two characteristics common to practically all seasonal adjustment procedures may be stressed. Firstly, they all belong to the class of univariate methods, in the sense that each series is adjusted individually. Secondly, they do not offer any real explanation of seasonality, as it is implicitly assumed that the seasonal movement is an intrinsic phenomenon governed by the rhythms of nature.

The two most commonly used procedures are the moving average method and the regression method.

THE MOVING AVERAGE METHOD. It is the official method used by most government agencies. The best known variant is the programme X-11 of the US Bureau of Census. In brief (neglecting the complications arising from the treatment of extreme points) it consists of three main steps: (1) a preliminary estimation of the seasonal component; (2) the estimation of the trend-cycle component from the preliminary deseasonalized series; and (3) the final estimation of the seasonal component from the original series from which the trend-cycle has been removed.

In spite of its technical complexity, the moving average method is easy to use (as computer programs are readily available) and has the great advantage of being able to handle, in an effective way, a changing seasonal pattern. Its major drawback is that, as in the case of all moving average procedures, the results tend to be less reliable at each end of the time series and consequently the most recent data are subject to frequent revisions. To eliminate (or at least attenuate) this adverse effect, it has been proposed to extend the original series at each end by one year by means of an autoregressive moving average process prior to deseasonalizing the series (as in the programme X-11 ARMMI developed by Dagum; see Dagum, 1978).

THE REGRESSION METHOD. Contrary to the moving average method, in which all the three components are implicitly assumed to be stochastic, the regression method is based on the assumption that the seasonal component and the trend component can be represented by deterministic functions of time, the stochastic element being confined to the residual term.

By far the simplest way to model the seasonal component is to use dummy variables. In the case of quarterly data, and neglecting the trend-cycle for the moment, the proper specification reads

$$E_t = a_1 S_{1t} + a_2 S_{2t} + a_3 S_{3t} + a_4 S_{4t} + u_i,$$

where s_{it}, $i = 1, \ldots, 4$, are the four dummies, one for each season and u_i represents the residual. The seasonal coefficients a_i are estimated by the least squares method. The above specification implies a constant seasonal pattern, but more complex items of seasonal variation can be contemplated. Furthermore, to account for the trend-cycle, we can easily add to the above equation the term bt (where t represents time) or a higher polynomial expression in t.

199

The regression method does have some appeal to economists because it satisfies some simple consistency requirements that might reasonably be expected from a seasonal adjustment procedure (sum preserving, orthogonality and indempotency, see Lovell, 1963). In addition, it is extremely easy to implement.

ESTIMATION OF ECONOMIC RELATIONSHIPS WITH SEASONAL DATA. Two options are available to the econometrician interested in the estimation of economic relations in the presence of seasonal data: the use of seasonally adjusted series for all the relevant variables or, alternatively, the use of the original series accompanied by the explicit inclusion in the relation of a time function representing the seasonal pattern (such as seasonal dummy variables).

Although there is still lack of consensus concerning the most suitable technique for handling seasonal movements, many economists prefer the second alternative on the grounds that the seasonal adjustment procedure applied individually to each variable eliminates too much variability from the underlying economic phenomena. However, when seasonal adjustment is performed by regression methods, the above two alternatives produce exactly the same results (Lovell, 1963).

BIBLIOGRAPHY

Dagum, E.B. 1978. Modelling, forecasting and seasonally adjusting economic time series with the X-11-ARIMA method. *The Statistician* 27 (3, 4) 203–16.

Lovell, M.C. 1963. Seasonal adjustment of economic time series and multiple regression analysis. *Journal of the American Statistical Association* 58(304), 993–1010.

Selection Bias and Self-selection

JAMES J. HECKMAN

The problem of selection bias in economic and social statistics arises when a rule other than simple random sampling is used to sample the underlying population that is the object of interest. The distorted representation of a true population as a consequence of a sampling rule is the essence of the selection problem. Distorting selection rules may be the outcome of decisions of sample survey statisticians, self-selection decisions by the agents being studied or both.

A random sample of a population produces a description of the population distribution of characteristics that has many desirable properties. One attractive feature of a random sample generated by the *known rule* that all individuals are equally likely to be sampled is that it produces a description of the population distribution of characteristics that becomes increasingly accurate as sample size expands.

A sample selected by any rule not equivalent to random sampling produces a description of the population distribution of characteristics that does not accurately describe the true population distribution of characteristics no matter how big the sample size. Unless the rule by which the sample is selected is known or can be recovered from the data, the selected sample cannot be used to produce an accurate description of the underlying population. For certain sampling rules, even knowledge of the rule generating the sample does not suffice to recover the population distribution from the sampled distribution.

This essay defines the problem of selection bias and presents conditions required to solve the problem. Examples of various types of commonly encountered sampling frames are given and specific economic selection mechanisms are presented. Assumptions required to use selected samples to determine features of the population distribution are discussed.

The analytical framework developed to understand the inferential problems raised by selection bias is also fruitful in understanding the economics of self-selection. The prototypical choice theoretic model of self-selection is that of

Roy (1951). In his model, agents choose among a variety of discrete 'occupational' opportunities. Agents can pursue only one 'occupation' at a time. While every person can, in principle, do the work in each 'occupation', at least at some level of competence, self-interest drives individuals to choose that 'occupation' which produces the highest income (utility) for them. As in the statistical selection bias problem, there is a latent population (of skills). Observed (utilized) skill distributions are the outcome of a selection rule by agents. The relationship between observed and latent skill distributions is of considerable interest and underlies recent work on worker hierarchies (see Willis and Rosen, 1979). The 'occupations' can be: (a) market work or non-market work (b) unemployed and searching or working at the offered wage (c) working in one province or working in another, or (d) any choice among a set of mutually exclusive opportunities.

Because the insights in the Roy model underly much recent research, we present a brief exposition of it and demonstrate how it can be or has been fruitfully extended to a variety of settings. An important issue, closely linked to the problem of identifying population parameters from selected sample distributions, is the empirical content of economic models of self-selection and worker hierarchies. Are they artefacts of distributional assumptions for unobservable skills or are they genuine behavioural hypotheses?

1. A DEFINITION AND SOME EXAMPLES OF SELECTION BIAS

Any selection bias model can be described by the following set-up. Let $\mathbf{Y}$ be a vector of outcomes of interest and let $\mathbf{X}$ be a vector of 'control' or 'explanatory' variables. The population distribution of $(\mathbf{Y}, \mathbf{X})$ is $F(\mathbf{y}, \mathbf{x})$. To simplify the exposition we assume that the density is well defined and write it as $f(\mathbf{y}, \mathbf{x})$.

Any sampling rule can be interpreted as producing a non-negative weighting function $\omega(\mathbf{y}, \mathbf{x})$ that alters the population density. Let $(\mathbf{Y}^*, \mathbf{X}^*)$ denote the sampled random variables. The density of the sampled data $g(\mathbf{y}^*, \mathbf{x}^*)$ may be written as

$$g(\mathbf{y}^*, \mathbf{x}^*) = \omega(\mathbf{y}^*, \mathbf{x}^*)\mathbf{f}(\mathbf{y}^*, \mathbf{x}^*)/ \int \omega(\mathbf{y}^*, \mathbf{x}^*)f(\mathbf{y}^*, \mathbf{x}^*)dy^*\, dx^*, \qquad (1.1)$$

where the denominator of the expression is introduced to make the density $g(\mathbf{y}^*, \mathbf{x}^*)$ integrate to one as is required for proper densities.

Alternatively, the weight may be defined as

$$\omega^*(\mathbf{y}^*, \mathbf{x}^*) = \frac{\omega(\mathbf{y}^*, \mathbf{x}^*)}{\int \omega(\mathbf{y}^*, \mathbf{x}^*)\mathbf{f}(\mathbf{y}^*, \mathbf{x}^*)dy^*\, dx^*}$$

so that

$$g(\mathbf{y}^*, \mathbf{x}^*) = \omega^*(\mathbf{y}^*, \mathbf{x}^*)f(\mathbf{y}^*, \mathbf{x}^*). \qquad (1.2)$$

Sampling schemes for which $\omega(\mathbf{y}, \mathbf{x}) = 0$ for some values of $(\mathbf{Y}, \mathbf{X})$ create special problems. For such schemes, not all values of $(\mathbf{Y}, \mathbf{X})$ are sampled. Let indicator variable $i(\mathbf{x}, \mathbf{y}) = 0$ if a potential observation at values $\mathbf{y}, \mathbf{x}$ cannot be sampled and let $i(\mathbf{y}, \mathbf{x}) = 1$ otherwise. Let $\Delta = 1$ record the occurrence of the event 'a potential observation is sampled, i.e. the value of $\mathbf{y}, \mathbf{x}$ is observed' and let $\Delta = 0$ if it is not. In the population, the proportion that is sampled is

$$\Pr(\Delta = 1) = \int i(\mathbf{y}, \mathbf{x}) f(\mathbf{y}, \mathbf{x}) dy \, dx. \tag{1.3}$$

while

$$\Pr(\Delta = 0) = 1 - \Pr(\Delta = 1).$$

For samples in which $\omega(\mathbf{y}, \mathbf{x}) = 0$ for a non-negligible proportion of the population ($\Pr(\Delta = 0) > 0$), it is clarifying to consider two cases. A *truncated sample* is one for which $\Pr(\Delta = 1)$ is not known and cannot be consistently estimated. For such a sample, (1.1) is the density of all of the sampled $\mathbf{Y}$ and $\mathbf{X}$ values. A *censored sample* is one for which $\Pr(\Delta = 1)$ is known or can be consistently estimated. The sampling rule in this case is such that values of $\mathbf{y}, \mathbf{x}$ for which $\omega(\mathbf{y}, \mathbf{x}) = 0$ are not known but it is known whether or not $i(\mathbf{y}, \mathbf{x}) = 0$ for all values of $\mathbf{Y}, \mathbf{X}$. In this case it is notationally convenient to define $(\mathbf{Y}^*, \mathbf{X}^*) = (\mathbf{0}, \mathbf{0})$ for values of $\mathbf{y}, \mathbf{x}$ such that $\omega(\mathbf{y}, \mathbf{x}) = i(\mathbf{y}, \mathbf{x}) = 0$. Such a definition is innocuous provided that in the population there is no point mass (concentration of probability mass) at $(\mathbf{0}, \mathbf{0})$. (Any value other than $(\mathbf{0}, \mathbf{0})$ can be selected provided that there is no point mass at that value.) Given $\Delta = 0$, the distribution of $\mathbf{Y}^*, \mathbf{X}^*$ is

$$G(\mathbf{y}^*, \mathbf{x}^*) = 1 \quad \text{for} \quad \Delta = 0$$

at

$$\mathbf{Y}^* = \mathbf{0} \quad \text{and} \quad \mathbf{X}^* = \mathbf{0}.$$

The joint density of $\mathbf{Y}^*, \mathbf{X}^*, \Delta$ for the case of a censored sample is obtained by combining (1.1) and (1.3). Thus

$$g(\mathbf{y}^*, \mathbf{x}^*, \delta) = \left[\frac{\omega(\mathbf{y}^*, \mathbf{x}^*) f(\mathbf{y}^*, \mathbf{x}^*)}{\int \omega(\mathbf{y}^*, \mathbf{x}^*) f(\mathbf{y}^*, \mathbf{x}^*) \, dy^* \, dx^*} \right]^{\delta}$$

$$\times \left[\int i(\mathbf{y}, \mathbf{x}) f(\mathbf{y}, \mathbf{x}) \, dy \, dx \right]^{\delta}$$

$$\times [1]^{1-\delta} \left[\int (1 - i(\mathbf{y}, \mathbf{x})) f(\mathbf{y}, \mathbf{x}) dy \, dx \right]^{1-\delta} \tag{1.4}$$

The first term on the right-hand side of (1.4) is the conditional density of $\mathbf{Y}^*, \mathbf{X}^*$ given $\Delta = 1$. The second term is the probability that $\Delta = 1$. The third term is the conditional density of $\mathbf{Y}^*, \mathbf{X}^*$ given $\Delta = 0$. This density assigns unit mass to $\mathbf{y}^* = \mathbf{0}, \mathbf{x}^* = \mathbf{0}$ when $\Delta = 0$. The fourth term is the probability that $\Delta = 0$. Notice that in the case in which $\omega(\mathbf{y}, \mathbf{x}) > 0$ for all $\mathbf{y}, \mathbf{x}, \Delta = 1$ and (1.4) is identical to (1.1).

In a random sample $\omega(\mathbf{y}^*, \mathbf{x}^*) = 1$ (and so $\omega^*(\mathbf{y}^*, \mathbf{x}^*) = 1$). In a selected sample, the sampling rule weights the data differently. Values of $(\mathbf{Y}, \mathbf{X})$ are over-sampled

203

or under-sampled relative to their occurrence in the population. In the case of truncated samples, the weight is zero for certain values of the outcome.

In many problems in economics, attention focuses on $f(\mathbf{y}|\mathbf{x})$, the conditional density of $\mathbf{Y}$ given $\mathbf{X} = \mathbf{x}$. In such problems knowledge of the population distribution of $\mathbf{X}$ is of no direct interest. If samples are selected solely on the $\mathbf{x}$ variables ('selection on the exogenous variables'), $\omega(\mathbf{y}, \mathbf{x}) = \omega(\mathbf{x})$ and there is no problem about using selected samples to make valid inference about the population conditional density. This is so because in the case of selection on the exogenous variables

$$g(\mathbf{y}^*, \mathbf{x}^*) = f(\mathbf{y}^*|\mathbf{x}^*)\frac{\omega(\mathbf{x}^*)f(\mathbf{x}^*)}{\displaystyle\int \omega(\mathbf{x}^*)f(\mathbf{x}^*d\mathbf{x}}$$

and

$$g(\mathbf{x}^*) = \frac{\omega(\mathbf{x}^*)f(\mathbf{x}^*)}{\displaystyle\int \omega(\mathbf{x}^*)f(\mathbf{x}^*)d\mathbf{x}^*}.$$

Thus

$$g(\mathbf{y}^*|\mathbf{x}^*) = \frac{g(\mathbf{y}^*, \mathbf{x}^*)}{g(\mathbf{x}^*)} = f(\mathbf{y}^*|\mathbf{x}^*).$$

For such problems, sample selection distorts inference only if selection occurs on $\mathbf{y}$ (or $\mathbf{y}$ and $\mathbf{x}$). Sampling on both $\mathbf{y}$ and $\mathbf{x}$ is termed *general stratified sampling*.

From a sample of data, it is not possible to recover the true density $f(\mathbf{y}, \mathbf{x})$ without knowledge of the weighting rule. On the other hand, if the weighting rule is known ($\omega(\mathbf{y}^*, \mathbf{x}^*)$), the density of the sampled data is known ($g(\mathbf{y}^*, \mathbf{x}^*)$), the support of $(\mathbf{y}, \mathbf{x})$ is known and $\omega(\mathbf{y}, \mathbf{x})$ is nonzero, then $f(\mathbf{y}, \mathbf{x})$ can always be recovered because

$$\frac{g(\mathbf{y}^*, \mathbf{x}^*)}{\omega(\mathbf{y}^*, \mathbf{x}^*)} = \frac{f(\mathbf{y}^*, \mathbf{x}^*)}{\displaystyle\int \omega(\mathbf{y}^*, \mathbf{x}^*)f(\mathbf{y}^*, \mathbf{x}^*)d\mathbf{y}^* \, d\mathbf{x}^*} \qquad (1.5)$$

and by hypothesis both the numerator and denominator of the left-hand side are known. From the requirement that $(\mathbf{y}^*, \mathbf{x}^*)$ has a well defined density

$$\int f(\mathbf{y}^*, \mathbf{x}^*)d\mathbf{y}^* \, d\mathbf{x}^* = 1.$$

Integrating the left-hand side of (1.5) it is possible to determine $\int \omega(\mathbf{y}^*, \mathbf{x}^*) f(\mathbf{y}^*, \mathbf{x}^*)d\mathbf{y}^* \, d\mathbf{x}^*$ and hence to use (1.5) to recover the population density of the data.

The requirements that (a) the support of $(\mathbf{y}, \mathbf{x})$ is known and (b) $\omega(\mathbf{y}, \mathbf{x})$ is nonzero are not innocuous. In many important problems in economics requirement (b) is not satisfied: the sampling rule excludes observations for certain values of $\mathbf{y}, \mathbf{x}$ and hence it is impossible without invoking further assumptions to determine the population distribution of $(\mathbf{Y}, \mathbf{X})$ at those values. If neither the support nor the weight is known, it is impossible, without invoking strong assumptions, to determine whether the fact that data are missing at certain $\mathbf{y}, \mathbf{x}$ values is due to the sampling plan or that the population density has no support at those values. We now turn to some specific sampling plans of interest in economics.

Example 1. Data are collected on incomes of individuals whose income Y exceeds a certain value c (for cutoff value). The rule is to observe Y if $Y > c$. Thus $\omega(y) = 1$ if $y > c$ and $\omega(y) = 0$ if $y \leqslant c$. Because the weight is zero for some values of y, we know that knowledge of the sampling rule does *not* suffice to recover the population distribution. From a random sample of the entire population, the social scientist knows or can consistently estimate (a) the sample distribution of Y above c and (b) the proportion of the original random sample with income below c ($F(c)$ where F is the distribution function of Y). The social scientist does not observe values of Y below c.

In this example, observed income is a *truncated random variable*. The point of truncation is c. The *sample* of observed income is said to be *censored*. If the proportion of the original random sample with income below c is not known and cannot be consistently estimated, the *sample* is *truncated*. In a truncated sample, nothing is known about the proportion of the underlying population that can appear in the sample. A sample is truncated only if $\omega(\mathbf{y}) = 0$ for some intervals of $\mathbf{y}$ (for $\mathbf{y}$ continuous) or if $\omega(\mathbf{y}) = 0$ at values of $\mathbf{y}$ at which there is finite probability mass. In a censored sample, the proportion of the underlying population that can appear in the sample is known, at least to an arbitrarily high degree of approximation, as sample size increases.

Let $Y^* = Y$ if $Y > c$. Define $Y^* = 0$ otherwise (the choice of the value for Y^* when Y is not observed is inessential and any value can be used in place of 0 provided that the true distribution places no mass at the selected value). Define an indicator variable $\Delta = 1$ if $Y > c$. $\Delta = 0$ otherwise. Then the distribution of Y^* is

$$G(y^* | Y > 0) = F(y^* | Y > c) = F(y^* | \delta = 1) = \frac{F(y^*)}{1 - F(c)}, y^* > c. \quad (1.6a)$$

$$G(y^* | Y^* > 0) = 1 \quad \text{for} \quad Y^* = 0 (\Delta = 0). \quad (1.6b)$$

Observe that (1.6a) is obtained from (1.1) by setting $\omega(y^*) = 1$ if $y > c$, and $\omega(y^*) = 0$ otherwise, and integrating up with respect to y^*. The distribution of Δ is

$$\mathrm{pr}(\Delta) = [1 - F(c)]^\delta [F(c)]^{1-\delta}.$$

The joint distribution of (Y^*, Δ) is

$$F(y^*, \delta) = F(y^* | \delta) \mathrm{Pr}(\delta) = \left\{ \frac{F(y^*)}{(1 - F(c))} \right\}^\delta [1 - F(c)]^\delta (1)^{1-\delta} [F(c)]^{1-\delta}$$

$$= [F(y^*)]^\delta [F(c)]^{1-\delta}. \quad (1.7)$$

Note that (1.7) is obtained from (1.4) by setting $\omega(y) = 0, y < c, \omega(y) = 1$ otherwise, by setting $i(y) = \omega(y)$, and by integrating up with respect to y^*. For normally distributed Y, (1.7) is the 'Tobit' distribution.

The difference between the information in a truncated sample and the information in a censored sample is encapsulated in the contrast between (1.6a) and (1.7). Clearly there is more information in a censored sample than in a truncated sample because one can obtain (1.6a) from (1.7) (by conditioning on $\Delta = 1$) but not vice versa.

Inferences about the population distribution based on assuming that $F(y^*|Y > c)$ closely approximates $F(y)$ are potentially very misleading. A description of population income inequality based on a subsample of high income people may convey no information about the true population distribution.

Without further information about F and its support, it is not possible to recover F from $G(y^*)$ from either a censored or a truncated sample. Access to a censored sample enables the analyst to recover $F(y)$ for $y > c$ but obviously does not provide any information on the shape of the true distribution for values of $y \leqslant c$.

This problem is routinely 'solved' by assuming that F is of a known functional form. This solution strategy does not always work. If F is normal, then it can be recovered from a censored or truncated sample (Pearson, 1901). If F is Pareto, F cannot be recovered from either a truncated or a censored sample (see Flinn and Heckman, 1982). If F is real analytic (i.e. possesses derivatives of all order) and the support of Y is known, then F can be recovered (Heckman and Singer, 1985).

Example 2. Expand the discussion in the previous example to a linear regression setting. Let

$$Y = \mathbf{X}\boldsymbol{\beta} + U \tag{1.8}$$

be the population earnings function where Y is earnings, $\mathbf{X}$ is a regressor vector assumed to be distributed independently of mean zero disturbance U. '$\boldsymbol{\beta}$' is a suitably dimensioned parameter vector. Conventional assumptions are invoked to ensure that ordinary least squares applied to a random sample of earnings data consistently estimates $\boldsymbol{\beta}$.

Data are collected on incomes of persons for whom Y exceeds c. Again the weight depends solely on y, i.e. $\omega(y, \mathbf{x}) = 0, y \leqslant c, \omega(y, \mathbf{x}) = 1, y > c$. The social scientist knows or can consistently estimate (a) the sample distribution of Y above c (b) the sample distribution of the $\mathbf{X}$ for Y above c and (c) the proportion of the original random sample with income below c. The social scientist does not observe values of Y below c.

As before, let $Y^* = Y$ if $T > c$. Define $Y^* = 0$ otherwise. $\Delta = 1$ if $Y > c$, $\Delta = 0$ otherwise. The probability of the event $\Delta = 1$ given $\mathbf{X} = \mathbf{x}$ is

$$\Pr(\Delta = 1 | \mathbf{X} = \mathbf{x}) = \Pr(Y > c | \mathbf{X} = \mathbf{x}) = \Pr(Y > c - \mathbf{x}\boldsymbol{\beta} | \mathbf{X} = \mathbf{x}).$$

Invoking independence between U and $\mathbf{X}$ and letting F_u denote the distribution of U,

$$\Pr(\Delta = 1 | \mathbf{X} = \mathbf{x}) = 1 - F_u(c - \mathbf{x}\boldsymbol{\beta}) \tag{1.9a}$$

and

$$\Pr(\Delta = 0 | \mathbf{X} = \mathbf{x}) = F_u(c - \mathbf{x}\boldsymbol{\beta}). \tag{1.9b}$$

The distribution of Y^* conditional on $\mathbf{X}$ is

$$G(y^* | Y > 0, \mathbf{X} = \mathbf{x}) = F(y^* | X = x, Y > c) = F(y^* | \mathbf{X} = \mathbf{x}, \Delta = 1)$$

$$= \frac{F_u(y^* - \mathbf{x}\boldsymbol{\beta})}{1 - F_u(c - \mathbf{x}\boldsymbol{\beta})}, \qquad y^* > c. \tag{1.10a}$$

$$G(y^* | Y \leqslant 0) = 1 \quad \text{for} \quad Y^* = 0 (\Delta = 0). \tag{1.10b}$$

The joint distribution of (Y^*, Δ) given $\mathbf{X} = \mathbf{x}$ is

$$F(y^*, \delta | \mathbf{X} = \mathbf{x}) = F(y^* | \delta, \mathbf{x}) \Pr(\delta | \mathbf{x}) = \{F_u(y^* - \mathbf{x}\boldsymbol{\beta})\}^\delta \{F_u(c - \mathbf{x}\boldsymbol{\beta})\}^{1-\delta}. \tag{1.11}$$

In particular,

$$E(Y^* | \mathbf{X} = \mathbf{x}, \Delta = 1) = \mathbf{x}\boldsymbol{\beta} + E(U | \mathbf{X} = \mathbf{x}, \delta = 1) = \mathbf{x}\boldsymbol{\beta} + \int_{c - \mathbf{x}\boldsymbol{\beta}}^{\infty} \frac{z \, dF_u(z)}{(1. - F_u(c - \mathbf{x}\boldsymbol{\beta}))}, \tag{1.12}$$

where z is a dummy variable of integration. In contrast, the population mean regression function is

$$E(Y | \mathbf{X} = \mathbf{x}) = \mathbf{x}\boldsymbol{\beta}. \tag{1.13}$$

The contrast between (1.12) and (1.13) is illuminating. Many behavioural theories in social science produce empirical counterparts of (1.8) with population conditional expectations like (1.13). Such theories sometimes restrict the signs, permissible values and other relationships among the coefficients in $\boldsymbol{\beta}$. When the theoretical model is estimated on a selected sample ($\Delta = 1$), the true conditional expectations is (1.12) not (1.13). The conditional mean of U depends on $\mathbf{x}$. In terms of conventional omitted variable analysis, $E(U | \mathbf{X} = \mathbf{x}, \Delta = 1)$ is omitted from the regression. Since this term is a function of $\mathbf{x}$ it is likely to be correlated with $\mathbf{x}$. Least squares estimates of $\boldsymbol{\beta}$ obtained on selected samples which do not account for selection are biased and inconsistent.

To illustrate the nature of the bias, it is useful to draw on the work of Cain and Watts (1973). Suppose that X is a scalar random variable (e.g. education) and that its associated coefficient is positive ($\beta > 0$). Under conventional assumptions about U (e.g. mean zero, independently and identically distributed and distributed independently of X), the population regression of Y on X is a straight line. The scatter about the regression line and the regression line are given in Figure 1. When $Y > c$ is imposed as a sample inclusion requirement, lower population values of U are excluded from the sample in a way that systematically depends on x. ($Y > c$ or $U > c - x\beta$). As x increases, the conditional mean of

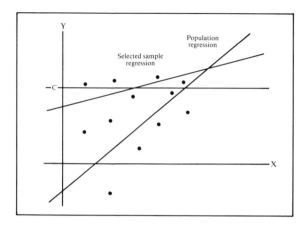

Figure 1

$U[E(U|X = x, \Delta = 1)]$ decreases. Regression estimates of β that do not correct for sample selection (i.e. include $E(U|X = x, \Delta = 1)$ as a regressor) are downward biased because of the negative correlation between x and $E(U|X = x, \Delta = 1)$. See the flattened regression line for the selected sample in Figure 1.

In models with more than one regressor, no sharp result on the sign of the bias in the regression estimate that results from ignoring the selected nature of the sample is available except when the **X** variables are from certain distributions (e.g. normal, see Goldberger, 1983). None the less, the key result – that conventional least squares estimates of $\boldsymbol{\beta}$ obtained from selected samples are biased and inconsistent remains true.

As in example 1, it is fruitful to distinguish between the case of a truncated sample and the case of a censored sample. In the truncated sample case, no information is available about the fraction of the population that would be allocated to the truncated sample $[Pr(\Delta = 1)]$. In the censored sample case, this fraction is known or can be consistently estimated. In the censored sample case it is fruitful to distinguish two further cases: (a) the case in which **X** is not observed when $\Delta = 0$ and (b) the case in which it is. Case (b) is the one most fully developed in the literature (Heckman and MaCurdy, 1981).

Note that the conditional mean $E(U|X = x, \Delta = 1)$ is a function of $c - x\beta$ solely through $Pr(\Delta = 1|x)$. Since $Pr(\Delta = 1|x)$ is monotonic in $c - x\beta$, the conditional mean depends solely on $Pr(\Delta = 1|x)$ and the parameters F_u i.e. since

$$F_u^{-1}(1 - Pr(\Delta = 1|x)) = c - x\beta,$$

$$E(U|X = x, \Delta = 1) = \int_{F_u^{-1}[1 - Pr(\Delta = 1|x)]}^{\infty} \frac{z \, dF_u(z)}{Pr(\Delta = 1|x)}.$$

This relationship demonstrates that the conditional mean is a function of the probability of selection. As the probability of selection goes to 1, the conditional mean goes to zero. For samples chosen so that the values of **x** are such that the observations are certain to be included in the sample, there is no problem in using ordinary least squares on selected samples to estimate β. Thus in Figure 1, ordinary least squares regressions fit on samples selected to have large $\mathbf{x}$ values closely approximate the true regression function and become arbitrarily close as $\mathbf{x}$ becomes large. The condition mean in (1.12) is a surrogate for $\Pr(\Delta = 1|\mathbf{x})$. As this probability goes to one, the problem of sample selection in regression analysis becomes negligibly small.

Heckman (1976) demonstrates that β and F_u are identified if U is normally distributed and standard conditions invoked in regression analysis are satisfied. Gallant and Nychka (1984) and Cosslett (1984) establish conditions for identification for non-normal U. In their analyses, F_u is consistently non-parametrically estimated.

Example 3. The next example considers *censored random variables*. This concept extends the notion of a truncated random variable by letting a more general rule than truncation on the outcome of interest generate the selected sample. Because the sample generating rule may be different from a simple truncation of the outcome being studied, the concept of a censored random variable in general requires at least two distinct random variables.

Let Y_1 be the outcome of interest. Let Y_2 be another random variable. Denote observed Y_1 by Y_1^*. If $Y_2 < c$, Y_1 is observed. Otherwise Y_1 is not observed and we can set $Y_1^* = 0$ or any other convenient value (assuming that Y_1 has no point mass at $Y_1 = 0$ or at the alternative convenient value). In terms of the weighting function ω, $\omega(y_1, y_2) = 0$ if $y_2 > c$, $\omega(y_1, y_2) = 1$ if $y_2 \leq c$.

Selection rule $Y_2 < c$ does not necessarily restrict the range of Y_1. Thus Y_1^* is not in general a truncated random variable. Define $\Delta = 1$ if $Y_2 < c$; $\Delta = 0$ otherwise. If $F(y_1, y_2)$ is the population distribution of (Y_1, Y_2), the distribution of Δ is

$$\Pr(\Delta = \delta) = [1 - F_2(c)]^{1-\delta}[F_2(c)]^{\delta}, \qquad \delta = 0, 1,$$

where F_2 is the marginal distribution of Y_2. The distribution of Y_1^* is

$$G(y_1^*) = F(y_1^*|\delta = 1) = \frac{F(y_1^*, c)}{F_2(c)}, \qquad \Delta = 1, \qquad (1.14a)$$

$$G(y_1^* = 0) = 1, \qquad \Delta = 0. \qquad (1.14b)$$

Note that (1.14a) is the distribution function corresponding to the density in (1.1) when $\omega(y_1, y_2) = 1$ if $y_2 \leq c$ and $\omega(y_1, y_2) = 0$ otherwise.

The joint distribution of (Y_1^*, Δ) is

$$G(y_1^*, \delta) = [F(y_1^*, c)]^{\delta}[1 - F_2(c)]^{1-\delta}. \qquad (1.15)$$

This is the distribution function corresponding to density (1.4) for the special weighting rule of this example. In a censored sample, under general conditions it is possible to consistently estimate $\Pr(\Delta = \delta)$ and $G(y_1^*)$. In a truncated sample, only conditional distribution (1.14a) can be estimated. A degenerate version of this model has $Y_1 \equiv Y_2$. In that case, censored random variable Y_1 is also a truncated random variable. Note that a censored random variable may be defined for a truncated or censored sample.

Example 3 and variants of it have wide applicability in economics. Let Y_1 be the wage of a woman. Wages of women are observed only if women work. Let Y_2 be an index of a woman's propensity to work. In Gronau (1974) and Heckman (1974), Y_2 is postulated as the difference between reservation wages (the value of time at home determined from household preference functions) and potential market wages Y_1. Then if $Y_2 < 0$, the woman works. Otherwise, she does not. $Y_1^* = Y_1$ if $Y_2 < 0$ is the observed wage.

If Y_1 is the offered wage of an unemployed worker, and Y_2 is the difference between reservation wages (the return to searching) and offered market wages, $Y_1^* = Y_1$ if $Y_2 < 0$ is the accepted wage for an unemployed worker (see Flinn and Heckman, 1982). If Y_1 is the potential output of a firm and Y_2 is its profitability, $Y_1^* = Y_1$ if $Y_2 > 0$. If Y_1 is the potential income in occupation one and Y_2 is the potential income in occupation two, $Y_1^* = Y_1$ if $Y_1 - Y_2 < 0$ while $Y_2^* = Y_2$ if $Y_1 - Y_2 \geqslant 0$. We develop this example at length in section 2 where we consider explicit economic models of self-selection. There we discuss the identifiability of this model.

Example 4. This example builds on example 3 by introducing regressors. This produces the *censored regression model* (Heckman, 1976; 1979). In example 3 set

$$Y_1 = \mathbf{X}_1 \boldsymbol{\beta}_1 + U_1, \tag{1.16a}$$

$$Y_2 = \mathbf{X}_2 \boldsymbol{\beta}_2 + U_2, \tag{1.16b}$$

where $(\mathbf{X}_1, \mathbf{X}_2)$ are distributed independently of (U_1, U_2), a mean zero, finite variance random vector. Conventional assumptions are invoked to ensure that if Y_1 and Y_2 can be observed, least squares applied to a random sample of data on $(Y_1, Y_2, \mathbf{X}_1, \mathbf{X}_2)$ would consistently estimate $\boldsymbol{\beta}_1$ and $\boldsymbol{\beta}_2$. $Y_1^* = Y_1$ if $Y_2 < 0$. If $Y_2 < 0$, $\Delta = 1$. Then the regression function for the selected sample is

$$E(Y_1^*|\mathbf{X}_1 = \mathbf{x}_1, Y_2 < 0) = E(Y_1^*|\mathbf{X}_1 = \mathbf{x}_1, \Delta = 1)$$

$$= \mathbf{X}_1 \boldsymbol{\beta}_1 + E(U_1|\mathbf{X}_1 = \mathbf{x}_1, \Delta = 1) \tag{1.17}$$

and the regression function for the population is

$$E(Y_1|\mathbf{X}_1 = \mathbf{x}_1) = \mathbf{X}_1 \boldsymbol{\beta}_1. \tag{1.18}$$

As in the regression analysis of truncated random variables, there is an illuminating contrast between the conditional expectation for the selected sample (1.17) and the population regression function (1.18). The two functions differ by the conditional mean of $U_1 [E(U_1|\mathbf{X}_1 = \mathbf{x}_1, \Delta = 1)]$. In the regression analysis of truncated random variables, ordinary least squares estimates of $\boldsymbol{\beta}$ (in equation (1.14)) are biased and inconsistent because the conditional mean is improperly omitted from the selected sample regression. The same analysis applies to the regression analysis of censored random variables. The conditional mean is a surrogate for the probability of selection $[\Pr(\Delta = 1 | \mathbf{x}_2)]$. As $\Pr(\Delta = 1 | \mathbf{x}_2)$ goes to one, the problem of sample selection bias becomes negligible. However, in the censored regression case, a new phenomenon appears. If there are variables in $\mathbf{X}_2$ not in $\mathbf{X}_1$, such variables may appear to be statistically important determinants of Y_1 when ordinary least squares is applied to data generated from censored samples.

As an example, suppose that survey statisticians use some extraneous (to $\mathbf{X}_1$) variables to determine sample enrolment. Such variables may appear to be important determinants of Y_1 when in fact they are not. They are important determinants of Y_1^*. In an analysis of self-selection, let Y_1 be the wage that a potential worker could earn were he to accept a market offer. Let Y_2 be the difference between the best non-market opportunity available to the potential worker and Y_1. If $Y_2 < 0$, the agent works. The conditional expectation of observed wages ($Y_1^* = Y$, if $Y_2 < 0$) given $\mathbf{x}_1$ and $\mathbf{x}_2$ will be a non-trivial function of $\mathbf{x}_2$. Thus variables determining non-market opportunities will determine Y_1^*, even though they do not determine Y_1. For example, the number of children less than six may appear to be significant determinants of Y_1 when inadequate account is taken of sample selection, even though the market does not place any value or penalty on small children in generating wage offers for potential workers.

Heckman (1976) develops the analysis of this model when (U_1, U_2) is normally distributed. Gallant and Nychka (1984) and Cosslett (1984) demonstrate that under mild restrictions on $F(u_1, u_2)$, if there is one continuous valued variable in $\mathbf{X}_2$ not in $\mathbf{X}_1$ (so that there is no exact linear dependence between $\mathbf{X}_2$ and $\mathbf{X}_1$), $\boldsymbol{\beta}_1$, $\boldsymbol{\beta}_2$ and $F(u_1, u_2)$ can be consistently non-parametrically estimated. Heckman and MaCurdy (1986) develop this class of models at length.

Example 5. This example demonstrates how self-selection bias affects the interpretation placed on estimated consumer demand functions when there is self-selection. We postulate a population of consumers with a quasi-concave utility function $U(\mathbf{Z}, E)$ which depends on the consumption of goods and preference shock E which represents heterogeneity in preferences among consumers. The support of E is $\mathbf{E}$. For price vector $\mathbf{P}$ and endowment income M, the consumer's problem is to

$$\text{Max } U(\mathbf{Z}, E) \quad \text{subject to} \quad \mathbf{P}'\mathbf{Z} \leqslant M.$$

In the population $\mathbf{P}$ and M are distributed independently of E. First order conditions for this problem are

$$\frac{\partial U(\mathbf{Z}, E)}{\partial \mathbf{Z}} \leqslant \lambda \mathbf{P}, \tag{1.19}$$

where λ is the Lagrange multiplier associated with the budget constraint. Focusing on the demand for the first good, Z_1, none of it is purchased if at zero consumption of Z_1

$$\left. \frac{\partial U(\mathbf{Z}, E)}{\partial Z_1} \right|_{Z_1 = 0} \leqslant \lambda P_1 \tag{1.20}$$

211

i.e. marginal valuation is less than marginal cost in utility terms. Conventional interior solution demand functions for Z_1 are defined for a given $\mathbf{P}$, M only for values of E such that

$$\left.\frac{\partial U(\mathbf{Z}, \mathbf{E})}{\partial Z_1}\right|_{Z_{1=0}} \geq \lambda P_1. \tag{1.21}$$

Let the set of E for which conventional interior solution consumer demand functions for Z_1 are defined be denoted by $\underline{\underline{E}}$. Then

$$\underline{\underline{E}} = \left\{ E \left\| \left.\frac{\partial U(\mathbf{Z}, \mathbf{E})}{\partial Z_1}\right|_{Z_{1=0}} \geq \lambda P_1 \quad \text{for given} \quad \mathbf{P}, M \right. \right\}.$$

Let $\Delta_1 = 0$ if the consumer does not purchase Z_1. Let $\Delta_1 = 1$ otherwise. If $F(\varepsilon)$ is the population distribution of E, the proportion purchasing none of good Z_1 given $\mathbf{P}$, M is

$$\Pr(\Delta_1 = 0 | \mathbf{P}, M) = 1 - \int_{\underline{\underline{E}}} dF(\varepsilon).$$

Provided inequality (1.21) is satisfied, $\Delta_1 = 1$ and interior solution demand function

$$Z_1 = Z_1(\mathbf{P}, M, E) \tag{1.22}$$

is well defined and $Z_1 = Z_1^*$. When $\Delta_1 = 0$, observed $Z_1 = Z_1^* = 0$.

Equation (1.22) is the conventional object of interest in consumer theory. Partial derivatives of that function *holding E and the other arguments constant* have well defined economic interpretations. Suppose that some non-negligible proportion of the population buys none of good Z_1. Regression estimates of the parameters of (1.22) using Z_1^* approximate the conditional expectation

$$E(Z_1 | \Delta_1 = 1, \mathbf{P}, M) = \int_{\underline{\underline{E}}} Z_1(\mathbf{P}, M, \varepsilon) dF(\varepsilon). \tag{1.23}$$

The derivatives of (1.23) are different from the derivatives of (1.22). In order to define these derivatives, it is helpful to define $I_{\underline{\underline{E}}}(E)$ as an indicator function for set $\underline{\underline{E}}$ which equals one if $E \in \underline{\underline{E}}$ and equals zero otherwise. When prices or income change, the set of values of E that satisfy inequality (1.21) changes. Let $\underline{\underline{E}} + \Delta \underline{\underline{E}}_{\mathbf{P}}$ be the set of E values that satisfy (1.21) when there is a finite price change $\Delta \mathbf{P}$. $I_{\underline{\underline{E}} + \Delta \underline{\underline{E}}_{\mathbf{P}}}(E)$ is an indicator function which equals one when $E \in \underline{\underline{E}} + \Delta \underline{\underline{E}}_{\mathbf{P}}$. Then the derivatives of (1.23) are, for the jth price

$$\frac{\partial E(Z_1 | \Delta = 1, \mathbf{P}, M)}{\partial P_j} = \int_{\underline{\underline{E}}} \frac{\partial Z_1(\mathbf{P}, M, \varepsilon)}{\partial P_j} dF(\varepsilon)$$

$$+ \lim_{\Delta P_j \to 0} \int_{\underline{\underline{E}}} \frac{[(I_{\underline{\underline{E}} + \Delta \underline{\underline{E}}_{\mathbf{P}}}(\varepsilon) - I_{\underline{\underline{E}}}(\varepsilon)] Z(\mathbf{P}, M, \varepsilon)}{\Delta P_j} dF(\varepsilon) \tag{1.24}$$

When the limit in the second term does not exist, the derivative does not exist. We assume for expositional convenience that the limit is well defined.

The first expression on the right-hand side of (1.24) is the *average effect* of price change on commodity demand. The second term on the right-hand side of (1.24) arises from the change in sample composition of E as the proportion of non-purchasers changes in response to price change. This term generates the selection bias.

Neither term is the same as the price derivative of (1.22) for an arbitrary value of $E = \varepsilon$ although the first term on the right-hand side of (1.24) approximates the price derivative of (1.22) for some value of $E = \varepsilon$.

A similar decomposition of the derivatives of the conditional demand function can be performed if it is defined solely for a sample of non-zero purchasers (see Heckman and MaCurdy, 1981, 1986).

Just as in the statistical sample selection bias problem, there is a population of interest. In this case, the population parameters of interest are the distribution of E and the parameters of $U(\mathbf{Z}, E)$. Those who buy Z_1 are a self-selected sample of the population. Estimates of population parameters estimated on self-selected samples are biased and inconsistent. There is a population distribution of $Z_1(\mathbf{P}, M, E)$ generated by the distribution of E. Observations of Z_1 are obtained only if $E \in \underline{\underline{E}}(\omega(E) = 1$ if $E \in \underline{\underline{E}}$, $\omega(E) = 0$ otherwise). Alternatively one can express the inclusion criteria in terms of the latent population distribution of Z_1 induced by E (given $\mathbf{P}$ and M) and write $\omega(z_1) = 1$ if $z_1 > 0$, $\omega(z_1) = 0$ if $z_1 \leq 0$.

Heckman (1974) and Heckman and MaCurdy (1981) provide further discussion of this type of model which is widely used in applied economics and consider issues of identifiability for such models.

Example 6. Length biased sampling. Let T be the duration of an event such as a completed unemployment spell or a completed duration of a job with an employer. The population distribution of T is $F(t)$ with density $f(t)$. The sampling rule is such that *individuals* are sampled at random. Data are recorded on a completed spell *provided that at the time of the interview the individual is experiencing the event*. Such sampling rules are in wide use in many national surveys of employment and unemployment.

In order to have a sampled completed spell, a person must be in the state at the time of the interview. Let '0' be the date of the survey. Decompose any completed spell T into a component that occurs before the survey T_b and a component that occurs after the survey T_a. Then $T = T_a + T_b$. For a person to be sampled, $T_b > 0$. The density of T given $T_b = t_b$ is

$$f(t|t_b) = \frac{f(t)}{1 - F(t_b)}, \qquad t \geq t_b. \tag{1.25}$$

Suppose that the environment is stationary. The population entry rate into the state at each instant of time is k. From each vintage of entrants into the state distinguished by their distance from the survey date t_b, only $1 - F(t_b) = \Pr(T > t_b)$

survive. Aggregating over all cohorts of entrants, the population proportion in the state at the date of the interview is P where

$$P = \int_0^\infty k(1 - F(t_b))dt_b \qquad (1.26)$$

which is assumed to exist. The density of T_b^*, sampled pre-survey duration, is

$$g(t_b^* | t_b^* > 0) = \frac{k(1 - F(t_b^*))}{P}. \qquad (1.27)$$

The density of sampled completed durations is thus

$$g(t^*) = \int_0^{t^*} f(t^* | t_b^*)g(t_b^* | t_b^* > 0)dt_b^* = k \frac{f(t^*)}{1 - F(t_b^*)} \frac{1 - F(t_b^*)}{P} \int_0^{t^*} dt_b^* = k \frac{t^* f(t^*)}{P}.$$

Observe from (1.26) that by a standard integration by parts argument

$$P = k \int_0^\infty (1 - F(z))dz = k \int_0^\infty z\, dF(z) = kE(T).$$

Note that

$$g(t^*) = \frac{t^* f(t^*)}{E(T)}. \qquad (1.28)$$

In this form (1.28) is equivalent to (1.1) with $\omega(t) = t$. Hence the term 'length biased sampling'. Intuitively, longer spells are oversampled when the requirement is imposed that a spell be in progress at the time the survey is conducted ($T_b > 0$). Suppose, instead, that individuals are randomly sampled and data are recorded on the *next* spell of the event (after the survey date). As long as successive spells are independent, such a sampling frame does not distort the sampled distribution because no requirement is imposed that the sampled spell be in progress at the date of the interview. It is important to notice that the source of the bias is the requirement that $T_b > 0$, not that only a fraction of the population experiences the event ($P < 1$).

The simple length weight ($\omega(t) = t$) that produces (1.28) is an artefact of the stationarity assumption. Heckman and Singer (1985) consider the consequences of non-stationarity and unobservables when there is selection on the event that a person be in the state at the time of the interview. They also demonstrate the bias that results from estimating parametric models on samples generated by length biased sampling rules when inadequate account is taken of the sampling plan. Vardi (1983, 1985) and Gill and Wellner (1985) consider nonparametric identification and estimation of models with densities of the form (1.28).

It is unfortunate that the lessons of length biased sampling are not adequately appreciated in economics. Two widely cited studies by Clark and Summers (1979) and Hall (1982) use length biased data to prove, respectively, that unemployment and employment spells are 'surprisingly long'. Whether their findings are artefacts of sampling plans remains to be determined.

Example 7. Choice based sampling. Let D be a discrete valued random variable which assumes a finite number of values I. $D = i$, $i = 1, \ldots, I$ corresponds to the occurrence of state i. States are mutually exclusive. In the literature the states may be modes of transportation choice for commuters (Domencich and McFadden, 1975), occupations, migration destinations, financial solvency status of firms, schooling choices of students, etc. Interest centres on estimating a population choice model

$$\Pr(D = i | \mathbf{X} = \mathbf{x}), \qquad i = 1, \ldots, I. \tag{1.29}$$

The population density of $(D, \mathbf{X})$ is

$$f(d, \mathbf{x}) = \Pr(D = d | \mathbf{X} = \mathbf{x}) h(\mathbf{x}), \tag{1.30}$$

where $h(\mathbf{x})$ is the density of the data.

In many problems, plentiful data are available on certain outcomes while data are scarce for other outcomes. For example, interviews about transportation preferences conducted at train stations tend to over-sample train riders and under-sample bus riders. Interviews about occupational choice preferences conducted at leading universities over-sample those who select professional occupations.

In choice based sampling, selection occurs solely on the D coordinate of $(D, \mathbf{X})$. In terms of (1.1) (extended to allow for discrete random variables), $\omega(d, \mathbf{X}) = \omega(d)$. Then sampled $(D^*, \mathbf{X}^*)$ has density

$$g(d^*, \mathbf{x}^*) = \frac{\omega(d^*) f(d^*, \mathbf{x}^*)}{\sum\limits_{i=1}^{I} \int \omega(i) f(i, x^*) \mathrm{d}x^*}. \tag{1.31}$$

Notice that the denominator can be simplified to

$$\sum_{i=1}^{I} \omega(i) f(i),$$

where $f(d^*)$ is the marginal distribution of D^* so that

$$g(d^*, \mathbf{x}^*) = \frac{\omega(d^*) f(d^*, \mathbf{x}^*)}{\sum\limits_{i=1}^{I} \omega(i) f(i)}. \tag{1.32}$$

Also, integrating (1.31) with respect to $\mathbf{x}$ using (1.32) we obtain

$$g(d^*) = \frac{\omega(d^*) f(d^*)}{\sum\limits_{i=1}^{I} \omega(i) f(i)} \tag{1.33}$$

which makes transparent how the sampling rule causes the sampled proportions to deviate from the population proportions. Note further that as a consequence of sampling only on D, the population conditional density

$$h(\mathbf{x}^*|d^*) = \frac{f(d^*, x^*)}{f(d^*)} \quad (1.34)$$

can be recovered from the choice based sample. The density of $\mathbf{x}$ in the sample is thus

$$g(\mathbf{x}^*) = \sum_{i=1}^{l} h(x^*|i)g(i). \quad (1.35)$$

Then using (1.32)–(1.35) we reach

$$g(d^*|\mathbf{x}^*) = f(d^*|\mathbf{x}^*)$$
$$\times \left\{ \left[\frac{\omega(d^*)}{\sum_{i=1}^{l} \omega(i)f(i)} \right] \left[\frac{1}{\sum_{i=1}^{l} f(i|\mathbf{x}^*)\frac{g(i)}{f(i)}} \right] \right\} \quad (1.36)$$

The bias that results from using choice based samples to make inference about $f(d^*|x^*)$ is a consequence of neglecting the terms in braces on the right-hand side of (1.36). Notice that if the data are generated by a random sampling rule, $\omega(d^*) = 1$, $g(d^*) = f(d^*)$ and the term in braces is one.

Manski and Lerman (1977), Manski and McFadden (1981) and Cosslett (1981) provide illuminating discussions of choice based sampling.

Example 8. Size biased sampling. Let N be the number of children in a family. $f(N)$ is the density of discrete random variable N. Suppose that family size is recorded only when at least one child is interviewed. Suppose further that each child has an independent and identical chance β of being interviewed. The probability of sampled family size of $N^* = n^*$ is

$$g(n^*) = \frac{\omega(n^*)f(n^*)}{E[\omega(N^*)]}, \quad (1.37)$$

where $\omega(n^*) = 1 - (1 - \beta)^{n^*}$ (the probability that at least one child from a family of size n^* will be sampled) and

$$E[\omega(N^*)] = \sum_{n^*} (1 - (1 - \beta)^{n^*})f(n^*)$$

is the probability of observing a family. In a large population $\beta \to 0$ with increasing population size. Using l'Hospital's rule, and assuming that passage to the limit under the summation sign is valid

$$\lim_{\beta \to 0} g(n^*) = \frac{n^* f(n^*)}{E(N^*)}. \quad (1.38)$$

Thus the limit form of (1.37) is identical to (1.28). Larger families tend to be oversampled and hence a misleading estimate of family size will be produced from such samples. Since the model is formally equivalent to the length biased sampling model, all references and statements about identification given in example 6 apply with full force to this example. See the discussion in Rao (1965).

2. ECONOMIC MODELS OF SELF-SELECTION

We begin our analysis by expositing the Roy model of self-selection for workers with heterogeneous skills. The statistical framework for this model has been outlined in examples 3 and 4. Following Roy, we assume that there are two market sectors in which income-maximizing agents can work. Agents are free to enter the sector that gives them the highest income. However, they can work in only one sector at a time.

Each sector requires a unique sector-specific task. Each agent has two skills, T_1 and T_2 which he cannot use simultaneously. The model is short run in that aggregate skill distributions are assumed to be given. There are no costs of changing sectors, and investment is ignored. Because of this assumption, the model presented here applies to environments with certain or uncertain prices for sector-specific tasks. For simplicity and without any loss of generality (given the preceding assumptions), we assume an environment of perfect certainty.

Let T_i be the amount of sector i specific task a worker can perform. The price of task i is π_i. An agent works in sector 1 if his income is higher there, that is

$$\pi_1 T_1 > \pi_2 T_2. \tag{2.1}$$

Indifference between sectors is a negligible probability event if the $T_i = 1, 2$ are assumed to be continuous nondegenerate random variables. Throughout we assume that prices are positive ($\pi_i > 0$).

The log wage in task i of an individual with endowment T_i is

$$\ln W_i = \ln \pi_i + \ln T_i. \tag{2.2}$$

The proportion of the population working at task i is the proportion of the population for whom

$$T_1 > \frac{\pi_2}{\pi_1} T_2.$$

Roy assumes that $(\ln T_1, \ln T_2)$ is normally distributed with mean (μ_1, μ_2) and covariance matrix Σ. Letting (U_1, U_2) be a mean zero normal vector, agents in the Roy model choose between two possible wages:

$$\ln W_1 = \ln \pi_1 + \mu_1 + U_1$$

or

$$\ln W_2 = \ln \pi_2 + \mu_2 + U_2.$$

Workers enter sector 1 if $\ln W_1 > \ln W_2$. Otherwise they enter sector 2.

Letting

$$\sigma^* = \sqrt{\mathrm{var}(U_1 - U_2)}$$

and

$$c_i = (\ln(\pi_i/\pi_j) + \mu_i - \mu_j)/\sigma^*, \quad i \neq j,$$

$$\Pr(i) = P(\ln W_i > \ln W_j) = \Phi(c_i), \quad i \neq j, \quad i,j = 1,2$$

where $\Phi(\ )$ is the cumulative distribution function of a standard normal variable. When standard sample selection bias formulae are used (see, e.g. Heckman, 1976), the mean of log wages observed in sector i is

$$E(\ln W_i | \ln W_i > \ln W_j) = \ln \pi_i + \mu_i + \frac{\sigma_{ii} - \sigma_{ij}}{\sigma^*} \lambda(c_i), \quad i,j = 1,2, \quad i \neq j, \quad (2.3)$$

where

$$\lambda(c) = \frac{\dfrac{1}{\sqrt{2\pi}} \exp(-\tfrac{1}{2}c^2)}{\Phi(c)}$$

is a convex monotone decreasing function of c with $\lambda(c) \geqslant 0$, and

$$\lim_{c \to \infty} \lambda(c) = 0, \qquad \lim_{c \to -\infty} \lambda(c) = \infty.$$

Convexity is proved in Heckman and Honoré (1986).

The variance of log wages observed in sector i

$$\text{var}(\ln W_i | \ln W_i > \ln W_j) = \sigma_{ii}\{\rho_i^2[1 - c_i\lambda(c_i) - \lambda^2(c_i)] + (1 - \rho_i^2)\}, \quad i \neq j \tag{2.4}$$

where $\rho_i = \text{correl}(U_i, U_i - U_j), i \neq j = 1,2$. The variance of the log of observed wages never exceeds σ_{ii}, the population variance, because the term in braces in (2.4) is never greater than unity. In general, sectoral variances decrease with increased selection. For example, if ρ_1 and ρ_2 do not equal zero, as π_1 increases with π_2 held fixed so that people shift from sector 2 to sector 1, the variance in the log of wages in sector 1 increases while the variance in the log of wages in sector 2 decreases.

Using the fact that $W_i = \pi_i T_i$, we may use (2.3) to write

$$E(\ln T_1 | \ln W_1 > \ln W_2) = \mu_1 + \frac{\sigma_{11} - \sigma_{12}}{\sigma^*} \lambda(c_1), \tag{2.5a}$$

$$E(\ln T_2 | \ln W_1 > \ln W_2) = \mu_2 + \frac{\sigma_{22} - \sigma_{12}}{\sigma^*} \lambda(c_2). \tag{2.5b}$$

Focusing on (2.5a) and noting that λ is positive for all values of c_1 (except $c_1 = \infty$), the mean of log task 1 used in sector 1 exceeds, equals, or falls short of the population mean endowment of log task 1 as $\sigma_{11} - \sigma_{12}$ is greater than, equal to, or less than zero. If endowments of tasks are uncorrelated ($\sigma_{12} = 0$), self-selection always causes the mean of $\ln T_1$ employed in sector 1 to be above the population mean μ_1. The opposite case occurs when $\sigma_{11} - \sigma_{12}$ is negative.

This case can arise only when values of $\ln T_1$ and $\ln T_2$ are sufficiently positively correlated. If this occurs, the mean of log task 1 used in sector 1 falls below the population mean μ_1. Since covariance matrices must be positive semidefinite, $\sigma_{11} + \sigma_{22} - 2\sigma_{12} \geqslant 0$. Thus if $\sigma_{11} - \sigma_{12} < 0$, $\sigma_{22} - \sigma_{12} > 0$ so the mean of log task 2 employed in sector 2 necessarily lies above the population mean μ_2. In the Roy model the unusual case can arise in at most one sector. Notice from (2.5) that only if $\sigma_{11} - \sigma_{12} = 0$ (so $\rho_1^2 = 0$) is the variance of log task 1 employed in sector 1 identical to the variance of log task 1 in the population. Otherwise, the sectoral variance of observed log task 1 is less than the population variance of log task 1.

To gain further insight into the effect of self-selection on the distribution of earnings for workers in sector 1, it is helpful to draw on some results from normal regression theory. The regression equation for $\ln T_2$ conditional on $\ln T_1$ is

$$\ln T_2 = \mu_2 + \frac{\sigma_{12}}{\sigma_{12}}(\ln T_1 - \mu_1) + \varepsilon_2, \tag{2.6}$$

where $E(\varepsilon_2) = 0$ and $\mathrm{var}(\varepsilon_2) = \sigma_{22}[1 - (\sigma_{12}^2/\sigma_{11}\sigma_{22})]$.

Figure 2 plots regression function (2.6) for the case $\sigma_{12} = \sigma_{11}$ and $\mu_2 > \mu_1 > 0$. For each value of $\ln T_1$, the population values of $\ln T_2$ are normally distributed around the regression line. Individuals with high values of $\ln T_1$ also tend to have a high value of $\ln T_2$. Assuming $\pi_1 = \pi_2$, individuals with $(\ln T_1, \ln T_2)$ endowments above the 45° line of equal income shown in Figure 1 choose to work in sector 2,

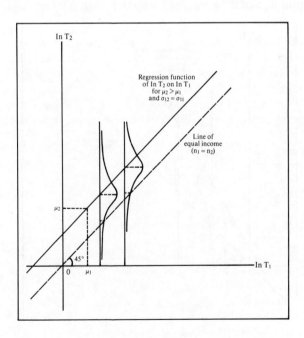

Figure 2

while those individuals with endowments below this line work in sector 1. Because $\sigma_{12} = \sigma_{11}$, the regression function is parallel to the line of equal income.

The distribution of ε_2 about the regression line is the same for all values of $\ln T_1$. When individuals are classified on the basis of their $\ln T_1$ values the same proportion of individuals work in sector 1 at all values of $\ln T_1$. For this reason the distribution of $\ln T_1$ employed in sector 1 is the same as the latent population distribution. If π_1 is raised (or π_2 is lowered) so that the $45°$ equal income line is shifted upward, the same proportion of people enter sector 1 at each value of $T_1 = t_1$. Figure 3 plots regression function (2.6) for the case $\sigma_{12} > \sigma_{11}$ and $\mu_2 > \mu_1 > 0$. As before we set $\pi_1 = \pi_2$. Individuals with endowments above the $45°$ line choose to work in sector 2, while those with endowments below this line work in sector 1. When individuals are classified on the basis of their T_1 values, the fraction of people working in sector 1 decreases the higher the value of T_1. Self-selection causes the mean of log task 1 employed in sector 1 to be less than the mean of log task 1 in the total population. People with high values of T_1 are under-represented in sector 1 and low T_1 values are over-represented. In the extreme, when $\ln T_1$ and $\ln T_2$ are perfectly positively correlated, all high-income individuals are in sector 2, while all the low-income individuals are in sector 1. The highest-paid sector 1 worker earns the same as the lowest-paid sector 2 worker (Roy, 1951; Willis and Rosen, 1979). In this case there is really only one skill dimension and individuals can be unambiguously ranked along this scale.

If π_1 is raised (or π_2 is lowered) so that the line of equal income is shifted

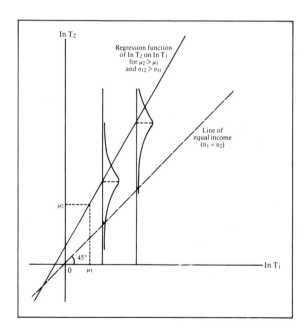

Figure 3

upward, the mean of $\ln T_1$ employed in sector 1 must rise. The only place left to get T_1 is from the high end of the T_1 distribution. Unlike the case of $\sigma_{12} = \sigma_{11}$, in which a 10 per cent increase in π_1 results in a 10 per cent increase in measured average earnings in sector 1, when $\sigma_{12} > \sigma_{11}$, a 10 per cent increase in π_1 results in a greater than 10 per cent increase in the measured average earnings in sector 1 as the average quality of the sector 1 work-force increases. The variance of log wages in sector 1 increases.

If $\sigma_{11} < \sigma_{12}$, then $\sigma_{12} < \sigma_{22}$ in order for Σ to be a covariance matrix. In the population, log task 2 must have greater variability than log task 1. Individuals with high T_1 values tend to have high T_2 values. But the population distribution of log task 2 has more mass in the tails. The higher an agent's value of T_1, the more likely it is that he will be able to get higher income in sector 2. At the lower end of the distribution, the process works in reverse: lower T_1 individuals on average have poor T_2 values. Self-selection causes the $\ln T_1$ distribution in sector 1 to have an evacuated right tail, an exaggerated left tail, and a lower mean than the population mean of $\ln T_1$.

If $\sigma_{12} < \sigma_{11}$ (a case not depicted graphically), the proportion of each T_1 group working in sector 1 increases, the higher the value of T_1. The mean of the log task employed in sector 1 exceeds μ_1. A 10 per cent increase in π_1 produces an increase of less than 10 per cent in the average earnings of workers in sector 1 as the mean of $\ln T_1$ employed in sector 1 declines. In fact if $\sigma_{12} > \sigma_{22}$ it is possible for an increase in π_1 to cause measured sector 1 wages to decline. Thus through a selection phenomenon it is possible for the average wage of people working in sector 1 to decline even though the price per unit skill increases there.

How robust are these conclusions if the normality assumption is relaxed? Heckman and Sedlacek (1985) show that many propositions derived from assumed normality of skills do not hold up for more general distributions. For example, increasing selection need not decrease sectoral variances. The effects of selection on mean employed skill levels are ambiguous. Heckman and Honoré (1986) demonstrate that in a single cross-section of data, it is possible to identify all of the parameters of the model from the data if the normality assumption is invoked. However, in a single cross-section many other models can explain the data equally well. In particular, intuitive notions about the degree of correlation or dependence among skills have no empirical content and so models of skill 'hierarchies' based on the extent of such dependence have no content for single cross-sections of data with all individuals facing common prices.

To show this, write the density of skills as $f(t_1, t_2)$. Let

$$Z = \begin{cases} T_1 & \text{if } T_1 > T_2 \\ 0 & \text{otherwise} \end{cases}$$

$$Z_2 = \begin{cases} T_2 & \text{if } T_2 > T_1 \\ 0 & \text{otherwise} \end{cases}.$$

Prices are normalized to unity ($\pi_1 = \pi_2 = 1$). Then the density of Z_1 is

$$Q'_1(z_1) = \int_{\{t_2 | t_2 < z_1\}} f(z_1, t_2) dt_2 = \int_0^{z_1} f(z_1, t_2) dt_2.$$

The density of z_2 is

$$Q'_2(z_2) = \int_0^{z_2} f(t_1, z_2) dt_1.$$

Note that $Q'_1(n)$ and $Q'_2(n)$ summarize all of the available data on observed earnings.

Now if T_1, T_2 are independent with cdf's F_1^* and F_2^* respectively

$$Q'_1(n) = f_1^*(n) F_2^*(n)$$

$$Q'_2(n) = F_1^*(n) f_2^*(n).$$

Define

$$\bar{Q}(n) = \int_0^n [Q'_1(l) + Q'_2(l)] dt = F_1^*(n) F_2^*(n).$$

Then

$$\int_\phi^\infty \frac{Q'_1(n)}{\bar{Q}(n)} dn = \int_\phi^\infty \frac{f_1^*(n)}{F_1^*(n)} dn = -\ln F_1^*(\phi).$$

Thus we can write

$$F_i^*(\phi) = \exp - \left(\int_\phi^\infty \left[\frac{Q'_i(n)}{\bar{Q}(n)} \right] dn \right) \qquad i = 1, 2$$

so that we can always rationalize the data on wages in a single cross-section by a model of skill independence, and economic models of skill hierarchies have no empirical content for a single cross-section of data.

Suppose, however, that the observing economist has access to data on skill distributions in different market settings i.e. settings in which relative skill prices vary. To take an extreme case, suppose that we observe a continuum of values of π_1/π_2 ranging from zero to infinity. Then it is possible to identify $F(t_1, t_2)$ and it is possible to give empirical content to models based on the degrees of dependence among latent skills.

This point is made most simply in a situation in which Z is observed but the analyst does not know Z_1 or Z_2 (i.e. which occupation is chosen). When $\pi_1/\pi_2 = 0$, everyone works in occupation two. Thus we can observe the marginal density of t_2. When $\pi_1/\pi_2 = \infty$, everyone works in occupation one. As π_1/π_2 pivots from zero to infinity it is thus possible to trace out the full joint distribution of (T_1, T_2).

To establish the general result, set $\sigma = \pi_2/\pi_1$. Let $F(t_1, t_2)$ be the distribution function of T_1, T_2. Then

$$\Pr(Z \leqslant n) = \Pr(\max(T_1, \sigma T_2) \leqslant n) = \Pr\left(T_1 \leqslant n, T_2 \leqslant \frac{1}{\sigma}n \right) = F\left(n, \frac{n}{\sigma} \right).$$

As σ varies between 0 and ∞, the entire distribution can be recovered since N is observed for all values in $(0, \infty)$. Note that it is not necessary to know which sector the agent selects.

This proposition establishes the benefit of having access to data from more than one market. Heckman and Honoré (1986) show how access to data from various market settings and information about the choices of agents aids in the identification of the latent skill distributions.

The Roy model is the prototype for many models of self-selection in economics. If T_1 is potential market productivity and T_2 is non-market productivity (or the reservation wage) for housewives or unemployed individuals, precisely the same model can be used to explore the effects of self-selection on measured productivity. In such a model, T_2 is never observed. This creates certain problems of identification discussed in Heckman and Honoré (1986). The model has been extended to allow for more general choice mechanisms. In particular, selection may occur as a function of variables other than or in addition to T_1 and T_2. Applications of the Roy model include studies of the union–non-union wage differential (Lee, 1978), the returns to schooling (Willis and Rosen, 1979), and the returns to training (Bjorklund and Moffitt, 1986) and Heckman and Robb (1985). Amemiya (1984) and Heckman and Honoré (1986) present comprehensive surveys of empirical studies based on the Roy model and its extensions.

BIBLIOGRAPHY

Amemiya, T. 1984. Tobit models: a survey. *Journal of Econometrics* 24, 3–61.

Bjorklund, A. and Moffitt, R. 1986. Estimation of wage gains and welfare gains from self selection models. *Review of Economics and Statistics* 24, 1–63.

Cain, G. and Watts, H. 1973. Toward a summary and synthesis of the evidence. In *Income Maintenance and Labor Supply*, ed. G. Cain and H. Watts, Madison: University of Wisconsin Press.

Clark, K. and Summers, L. 1979. Labor market dynamics and unemployment: a reconsideration. *Brookings Papers on Economic Activity*, 13–60.

Cosslett, S. 1981. Maximum likelihood estimation from choice based samples. *Econometrica*.

Cosslett, S. 1984. Distribution free estimator of regression model with sample selectivity. Unpublished manuscript, University of Florida.

Domencich, T. and McFadden, D. 1975. *Urban Travel Demand*. Amsterdam: North-Holland.

Flinn, C. and Heckman, J. 1982. New methods for analyzing structural models of labor force dynamics. *Journal of Econometrics* 18, 5–168.

Gallant, R. and Nychka, R. 1984. Consistent estimation of the censored regression model. Unpublished manuscript, North Carolina State.

Gill, R. and Wellner, J. 1985. Large sample theory of empirical distributions in biased sampling models. Unpublished manuscript, University of Washington.

Goldberger, A. 1983. Abnormal selection bias. In *Studies in Econometrics, Time Series and Multivariate Statistics*, ed. S. Karlin, T. Amemiya and L. Goodman, Wiley, NY.

Gronau, R. 1974. Wage comparisons – a selectivity bias. *Journal of Political Economy* 82 (6), 1119–1144.

Hall, R. 1982. The importance of lifetime jobs in the U.S. economy. *American Economic Review* 72, September, 716–724.

Heckman, J. 1974. Shadow prices, market wages and labor supply. *Econometrica* 42(4), 679–94.

Heckman, J. 1976. The common structure of statistical models of truncation, sample selection and limited dependent variables and a simple estimator for such models. *Annals of Economic and Social Measurement* 5(4), 475–92.

Heckman, J. 1977. Sample selection bias as a specification error. *Econometrica* 47(1), 153–62.

Heckman, J. and Honoré, B. 1986. The empirical content of the Roy model. Unpublished manuscript, University of Chicago.

Heckman, J. and MaCurdy, T. 1981. New methods for estimating labor supply functions. In *Research in Labor Economics*, Vol. 4, ed. R. Ehrenberg, Greenwich, Conn.: JAI Press.

Heckman, J. and Robb, R. 1985. Alternative methods for evaluating the effect of training on earnings. in *Longitudinal Analysis of Labor Market Data*, ed. J. Heckman and B. Singer, Cambridge: Cambridge University Press.

Heckman, J. and Sedlacek, G. 1985. Heterogeneity, aggregation and market wage functions. *Journal of Political Economy* 93, December, 1077–125.

Heckman, J. and Singer, B. 1985. Econometric analysis of longitudinal data. In *Handbook of Econometrics*, Vol. III, ed. Z. Griliches and M. Intriligator, Amsterdam: North-Holland.

Lee, L.F. 1978. Unionism and wage rates: a simultaneous equations model with qualitative and limited dependent variables. *International Economic Review* 19, 415–33.

Manski, C. and Lerman, S. 1977. The estimation of choice probabilities from choice based samples. *Econometrica* 45, 1977–88.

Manski, C. and McFadden, D. 1981. Alternative estimates and sample designs for discrete choice analysis. In *Structural Analysis of Discrete Data with Econometric Applications*, ed. C. Manski and D. McFadden, Cambridge: MIT Press.

Pearson, K. 1901. Mathematical contributions to the theory of evolution. *Philosophical Transactions*, 195, 1–47.

Rao, C.R. 1965. On discrete distributions arising out of methods of ascertainment. In *Classical and Contagious Distributions*, ed. G. Patil, Calcutta: Pergamon Press.

Roy, A.D. 1951. Some thoughts on the distribution of earnings. *Oxford Economic Papers*, 3, 135–46.

Vardi, Y. 1983. Nonparametric estimation in the presence of length bias. *Annals of Statistics* 10, 616–20.

Vardi, Y. 1985. Empirical distributions in selection bias models. *Annals of Statistics* 13, 178–203.

Willis, R. and Rosen, S. 1979. Education and self selection. *Journal of Political Economy* 87, S7–S36.

Simulation Models

IRMA ADELMAN

To clarify the concept of simulation requires placing simulation models in the context of available modelling approaches. One can distinguish models by their structure, size, complexity, purpose, solution technique and probabilistic specification. Generally, the purpose for which a model is specified, the state of knowledge in the area, and the relative importance of indirect effects should guide model specification (Robinson, 1987).

Analytic models aim at capturing some key feature(s) of the economy and then doing some comparative statics by differentiating key structural or reduced form relationships with respect to key parameters or variables. Their use is in qualitative economics, to 'sign' some effects, or to compare orders of magnitude.

Stylized numerical models, in which the parameters are specified numerically and parametrized, are used for strategic analysis of policy postures (e.g. import substitution vs. export-led growth) since they highlight some specific casual mechanisms. Numerical models can be more complex than analytic models, may require the use of computers for solution, and incorporate more structural features of the economy. They generally tend to be deterministic and static and stay rather close to analytic models in their transparency.

Applied models are used for policy analysis. They aim at realism. They are institutionally and situationally more specific and more disaggregated in terms of factors and activities. They are usually dynamic and may be stochastic. They may or may not be optimizing. They are numerical and solved by computer. The analytic structure of applied models is not transparent, since they usually incorporate many countervailing processes, but stylized versions of analytic models, which capture some of their essential features, can sometimes be formulated. The stylized versions are either analytic models or numerical models. Applied models are solved numerically under various policy-regime scenarios to derive specific policy recommendations for managers or policymakers.

Applied models are simulation models. Stylized numerical models that are

225

stochastic and require computers for their solution are also generally referred to as simulation models. Policy analysis thus always requires simulation models; strategic analysis sometimes does.

Following Naylor et al. (1966), we define model A to be a simulator of real system B if: (1) A is a close representation of B: (2) A is used to perform 'experiments' that are intended to represent how B would react under the experimental conditions applied to A; and (3) digital or analog computers are used to perform the experiments. The condition that A represents B only in its stochastic distribution is usually added to the theoretical definition of simulation models, but, in practice, many simulation models are treated as deterministic. (General discussions of simulation models are given in Adelman, 1982; Balderston and Hoggatt, 1963; Orcutt et al., 1961; and Naylor et al., 1966.)

Simulation models are fully accepted in engineering, where they are used for design purposes, in management, where they are used for corporate decision making, and in economic planning, where they are used in plan formulation. But simulation models are only partially accepted in economics proper as a tool for understanding the properties of an 'economy' that is too complex, either mathematically or structurally, for analytic solution. The closer a given model is to a numerical model, the more acceptable it is to economists. Nevertheless, simulation models are in wide use in practice. For example, four out of six articles in the Fall, 1985 issue of the *Journal of Policy Modelling* contained simulation models.

The formulation of a simulation model involves the following steps: (1) Specification and estimation of applied model A; (2) writing of a computer program that solves for the endogenous variables of A under particular stochastic specifications of the distributions of the exogenous variables; (3) validation of the model; (4) design of the experiments to be performed with the model; and (5) analysis of the results of the experiments. Step 1 is common to both simulation and numerical models. It requires defining the objectives of the analysis (what questions must be answered, what hypotheses tested, what effects estimated), formulating the model, estimating its parameters and forecasting its exogenous variables. Particularly critical questions in choosing a model specification are: How situation-specific should the model be, how realistic, and how transparent in structure? Answers to these questions will require compromise among conflicting criteria, as well as insights into system B and into the phenomena relevant to the objectives of the analysis.

While steps (3)–(5) are not specific to simulation models, the amount of output generated requires that one pay more attention to these steps in simulation models than with other model types. Model validation (step 3) is particularly important, since it tests the assertion that A is a close representation of B. Usually, the validation is based on the comparison of some quantitative and qualitative aspect of the standard record with the historical record. The procedure is also central to the validation of econometric models, but it has methodological problems which stem from the fact that the information used to estimate the model is reused to test it. Comparisons involve qualitative tests: Are the dynamic features of A – turning points, amplitudes, timing and duration – similar to those of system B (Adelman and Adelman, 1959)? Does a graphic representation of the simulated output of A over the historical period look like that of B (Cyert and March, 1963)? Do the multipliers of A look sensible? Statistical tests of goodness of fit are also useful in model validation. These include regressions of relations simulated on historical time series, analysis of variance techniques, multiple ranking procedures, and nonparametric tests.

The design of experiments to be performed with the simulation models (step 4) poses difficulties which arise from the virtually infinite number of experiments which could be performed. One can narrow down the number of actual experiments by using the statistical principles of experimental design. This entails equating the 'factors' or 'treatments' in experimental design to the exogenous, controlled or uncontrolled, variables of A and setting the 'responses' in factorial design equal to the endogenous, target or irrelevant variables of A. The multiplicity of such experiments usually limits the investigator to 'main effects' or to a few combinations of treatments, called scenarios. One can also use regression techniques to estimate the functional relationships between the response variables and the exogenous variables to generate a 'response surface'. Optimal experimental designs for the fitting of response surfaces have been suggested by Box (1954).

Analysis of the results of experiments (step 5) can be of two types: (1) Summarizing the 'story' told by the experiment by tracing through the causal chains giving rise to a set of simulation results. At this point resort to smaller numerical models or analytic models may be helpful. (2) Analysing the results statistically, by methods similar to those used in step 3.

Simulation has had wide application in economics. The earliest applications were to business cycle analysis and used both analog and digital computers (Phillips, 1957; Adelman and Adelman, 1959; Duesenberry et al., 1960) to study the cyclical characteristics of economic systems. Microsimulations of macroeconomic systems have been important in tax and social security analysis (Orcutt et al., 1961; Pechman and Okner, 1974) and in forecasting (Bergmann, 1974; Fair, 1974–6). The major current uses are in business management and in economic planning. In business, simulation models are used to aid corporate decision making and to study corporate behaviour (Balderston and Hoggatt, 1963; Bonini, 1963; Cyert and March, 1963). In economy-wide planning, simulation models are used by planning agencies and international organizations to analyse issues such as what development strategy is optimal for a given country during a particular period (Dervis, de Melo and Robinson, 1982), how one might increase economic equality and reduce poverty in a particular country (Adelman and Robinson, 1978), what effects changes in population growth might have (Rodger, Hopkins and Wery, 1978), or how best to adjust to heavy foreign indebtedness burdens.

The construction of a 'good' simulation model is an art. It requires striking appropriate compromises between realism, on the one hand, and the generality of the conclusions and the transparency of the model, on the other. As far as possible, the behavioural descriptions and the choice of variables and functional forms should be anchored in theory and estimated econometrically. This is especially important for specifications that drive the results of a given model (for example, the coupling of exponential resource exhaustion with arithmetic growth in technology in Forrester (1973), for which there is almost no empirical justification). Where theory is lacking, however, the only alternative to ad hoc specification based on descriptive information is to omit a potentially important factor, building block, or interaction altogether – in itself a misspecification. Finally, a good simulation model is one that replicates history well and whose major results can be explained *ex post*, though not divined *ex ante*, in terms which are consistent with available theory and relevant stylized facts.

BIBLIOGRAPHY

Adelman, I. 1982. Simulation of economic processes. In *International Encyclopaedia of Statistics*, London: Macmillan.

Adelman, I. and Adelman, F.L. 1959. The dynamic properties of the Klein-Goldberger Model. *Econometrica* 27, 596–625.

Adelman, I. and Robinson, S. 1978. *Income Distribution Policy in Developing Countries*. Stanford: Stanford University Press.

Balderston, F.E. and Hoggatt, A. 1963. *Symposium on Simulation Models*. Cincinnati: Southwest Publishing.

Bergmann, B. 1974. A microsimulation of the macroeconomy with explicitly represented money flows. *Annals of Economic and Social Measurement* 3, 457–89.

Bonini, C.P. 1963. *Simulation of Information and Decision Systems in the Firm*. Englewood Cliffs, NJ: Prentice-Hall.

Box, G.E.P. 1954. The exploration and exploitation of response surfaces. *Biometrics* 10, 16–60.

Cyert, R.M. and March, J.G. 1963. *A Behavioral Theory of the Firm*. Englewood Cliffs, NJ: Prentice-Hall.

Dervis, K., de Melo, J. and Robinson, S. 1982. *General Equilibrium Models for Development Planning*. Cambridge: Cambridge University Press.

Duesenberry, J.S., Eckstein, O. and Fromm, G. 1960. A simulation model of the United States economy in recession. *Econometrica* 28, 749–809.

Fair, R.C. 1974–6. *A Model of Macroeconomic Activity*. 2 vols, Cambridge, Mass.: Ballinger.

Forrester, J.W. 1973. *World Dynamics*. 2nd edn, Cambridge, Mass.: Wright Allen.

Naylor, T.H., Balinfy, J.L., Burdick, D.S. and Chu, K. 1966. *Computer Simulation Techniques*. New York: Wiley.

Orcutt, G.H. et al. 1961. *Microanalysis of Socioeconomic Systems: a Simulation Study*. New York: Harper.

Pechman, J.A. and Okner, B.A. 1974. *Who Bears the Tax Burden?* Washington, DC.: Brookings.

Phillips, A.W. 1957. Mechanical models in economic dynamics. *Economica*, NS 17, 283–305.

Robinson, S. 1987. Multisectoral models of developing countries. In *Handbook of Development Economics*, ed. H.B. Chenery and T.N. Srinivasan, Amsterdam: North-Holland.

Rodgers, G.B. and Hopkins, M.J.D. and Wery, R. 1978. *Population, Employment and Inequality, Bachue-Philippines*. Farnborough: Saxon House.

Simultaneous Equations Models

THOMAS J. ROTHENBERG

Models that attempt to explain the workings of the economy typically are written as interdependent systems of equations describing some hypothesized technological and behavioural relationships among economic variables. Supply and demand models, Walrasian general equilibrium models, and Keynesian macromodels are common examples. A large part of econometrics is concerned with specifying, testing, and estimating the parameters of such systems. Despite their common use, simultaneous equations models still generate controversy. In practice there is often considerable disagreement over their proper use and interpretation.

In building models economists distinguish between *endogenous* variables which are determined by the system being postulated and *exogenous* variables which are determined outside the system. Movements in the exogenous variables are viewed as autonomous, unexplained causes of movements in the endogenous variables. In the simplest systems, each of the endogenous variables is expressed as a function of the exogenous variables. These so-called 'reduced-form' equations are often interpreted as causal, stimulus-response relations. A hypothetical experiment is envisaged where conditions are set and an outcome occurs. As the conditions are varied, the outcome also varies. If the outcome is described by the scalar endogenous variable y and the conditions by the vector of exogenous variables x, then the rule describing the causal mechanism can be written as $y = f(x)$. If there are many outcomes of the experiment, y and f are interpreted as vectors; the rule describing how the ith outcome is determined can be written as $y_i = f_i(x)$.

Most equations arising in competitive equilibrium theory are motivated by hypothetical stimulus-response experiments. Demand curves, for example, represent the quantity people will purchase when put in a price-taking market situation. The conditions of the experiment are, in addition to price, all the other determinants of demand. In any given application, most of these determinants

229

are viewed as fixed as the experiment is repeated; attention is directed at the handful of exogenous variables whose effects are being analysed. In an n good world, there are n such equations, each determining the demand for one of the goods as a function of the exogenous variables.

Reduced-form models where each equation contains only one endogenous variable are rather special. Typically, economists propose interdependent systems where at least some of the equations contain two or more endogenous variables. Such models have a more complex causal interpretation since each endogenous variable is determined not by a single equation but *simultaneously* by the entire system. Moreover, in the presence of simultaneity, the usual least-squares techniques for estimating parameters often turn out to have poor statistical properties.

WHY SIMULTANEITY? Given the obvious asymmetry between cause and effect, it would at first thought appear unnatural to specify a behavioural economic model as an interdependent, simultaneous system. Although equations with more than one endogenous variable can always be produced artificially by algebraic manipulation of a reduced-form system, such equations have no independent interpretation and are unlikely to be interesting. It turns out, however, that there are many situations where equations containing more than one endogenous variable arise quite naturally in the process of modelling economic behaviour. These so-called 'structural' equations have interesting causal interpretations and form the basis for policy analysis. Four general classes of examples can be distinguished.

1. Suppose two experiments are performed, the outcome of the first being one of the conditions of the second. This might be represented by the two equations $y_1 = f_1(x)$ and $y_2 = f_2(x, y_1)$. In this two-step causal chain, both equations have simple stimulus-response interpretations. Implicit, of course, is the assumption that the experiment described by the first equation takes place before the experiment described by the second equation. Sequential models where, for example, people choose levels of schooling and later the market responds by offering a wage are of this type. Such *recursive* models are only trivially simultaneous and raise no conceptual problems although they may lead to estimation difficulties.

2. Nontrivial simultaneous equations systems commonly arise in multi-agent models where each individual equation represents a separate hypothetical stimulus-response relation for some group of agents, but the outcomes are constrained by equilibrium conditions. The simple competitive supply-demand model illustrates this case. Each consumer and producer behaves as though it has no influence over price or over the behaviour of other agents. Market demand is the sum of each consumer's demand and market supply is the sum of each producer's supply, with all agents facing the same price. Although the market supply and demand functions taken separately represent hypothetical stimulus-response situations where quantity is endogenous and price is exogenous, in the

combined equilibrium model both price and quantity are endogenous and determined so that supply equals demand.

Most competitive equilibrium models can be viewed as (possibly very complicated) variants of this supply–demand example. The individual equations, when considered in isolation, have straightforward causal interpretations. Groups of agents respond to changes in their environment. Simultaneity results from market clearing equilibrium conditions that make the environments endogenous. Keynesian macromodels have a similar structure. The consumption function, for example, represents consumers' response to their (seemingly) exogenous wage income – income that in fact is determined by the condition that aggregate demand equal aggregate supply.

3. Models describing optimizing behaviour constitute a third class of examples. Suppose an economic agent is faced with the problem of choosing some vector y in order to maximize the function $F(y, x)$, where x is a vector of exogenous variables outside the agent's control. The optimum value, denoted by y^*, will depend on x. If there are G choice variables, the solution can be written as a system of G equations, $y^* = g(x)$. If F is differentiable and globally concave in y, the solution can be obtained from the first-order conditions $f(y^*, x) = 0$, where f is the G-dimensional vector of partial derivatives of F with respect to y. The two sets of equations are equivalent representations of the causal mechanism. The first is a reduced-form system with each endogenous variable expressed as a function of exogenous variables alone. The second representation consists of a system of simultaneous equations in the endogenous variables. These latter equations often have simple economic interpretations such as, for example, setting marginal product equal to real input price.

4. Models obtained by simplifying a larger reduced-form system are a fourth source of simultaneous equations. The Marshallian long-run supply curve, for example, is often thought of as the locus of price–quantity pairs that are consistent with the marginal firm having zero excess profit. Both price and quantity are outcomes of a complex dynamic process involving the entry and exit of firms in response to profitable opportunities. If, for the data at hand, entry and exit are in approximate balance, the reduced-form dynamic model may well be replaced by a static interdependent equilibrium model.

This last example suggests a possible re-interpretation of the equilibrium systems given earlier. It can be argued (see, for example, Wold, 1954) that multi-agent models are necessarily recursive rather than simultaneous because it takes time for agents to respond to their environments. From this point of view, the usual supply–demand model is a simplification of a considerably more complex dynamic process. Demand and supply in fact depend on *lagged* prices; hence current price need not actually clear markets. However, the existence of excess supply or demand will result in price movement which in turn results in a change in consumer and producer behaviour next period. When time is explicitly introduced into the model, simultaneity disappears and the equations have simple causal interpretations. But, if response time is short and the available data are averages over a long period, excess demand may be close to zero for the available data. The static model with its simultaneity may be viewed as a limiting case, approximating a considerably more complex dynamic world. This interpretation of simultaneity as a limiting approximation is implicit in much of the applied literature and is developed formally in Strotz (1960).

THE NEED FOR STRUCTURAL ANALYSIS. These examples suggest that systems of simultaneous equations appear quite naturally when constructing economic models. Before discussing further their logic and interpretation, it will be useful to develop some notation. Let y be a vector of G endogenous variables describing the outcome of some economic process; let x be a vector of K 'predetermined' variables describing the conditions that determine those outcomes. (In dynamic models, lagged endogenous variables as well as the exogenous variables will be considered as conditions and included in x.) By a simultaneous equations model we mean a system of m equations relating y and x:

$$g_i(y, x) = 0 \qquad (i = 1, \ldots, m).$$

In the important special case where the functions are linear, the system can be written as the vector equation

$$By + \Gamma x = 0, \tag{1}$$

where B is an $m \times G$ matrix of coefficients, Γ is an $m \times K$ matrix of coefficients, and 0 is an m-dimensional vector of zeros. (The intercepts can be captured in the matrix Γ if we follow the convention that the first component of x is a 'variable' that always takes the value one.) A complete system occurs when $m = G$ and B is non-singular. Then the vector of outcome variables can be expressed as a linear function of the condition variables

$$y = -B^{-1}\Gamma x = \Pi x. \tag{2}$$

Although the logic of the analysis applies for arbitrary models, the main issues can most easily be illustrated in this case of a complete linear system.

If both sides of the vector equation (1) are premultiplied by any $G \times G$ nonsingular matrix F, a new representation of the model is obtained, say

$$B^*y + \Gamma^*x = 0, \tag{3}$$

where $B^* = FB$ and $\Gamma^* = F\Gamma$. If F is not the identity matrix, the systems (1) and (3) are not identical. Yet if one representation is 'true' (that is, the real world observations satisfy the equation system) then the other is also 'true'. Which of the infinity of possible representations should we select? The obvious answer is that it does not matter. Any linear combination of equations is another valid equation. Any nonsingular transformation is as good as any other. For simplicity, one might as well choose the solved reduced form given by equation (2).

In practice, however, we are not indifferent between the various equivalent representations. There are a number of reasons for that. First, it may be that some representations are easier to interpret or easier to estimate. The first-order

232

conditions for a profit maximizing firm facing fixed prices may, depending on the production function, be much simpler than the reduced form. Secondly, if we contemplate using the model to help analyse a changed regime, it is useful to have a representation in which the postulated changes are easily described. This latter concern leads to the concept of the degree of *autonomy* of an equation.

In the supply–demand model, it is easy to contemplate changes in the behaviour of consumers that leave the supply curve unchanged. For example, a shift in tastes may modify demand elasticities but have no effect on the cost conditions of firms. In that case, the supply curve is said to be autonomous with respect to this intervention in the causal mechanism. Equations that combine supply and demand factors (like the reduced form relating quantity traded to the exogenous variables) are not autonomous. The analysis of policy change is greatly simplified in models where the equations possess considerable autonomy. If policy changes one equation and leaves the other equations unchanged, its effects on the endogenous variables are easily worked out. Comparative static analysis as elucidated for example, by Samuelson (1947) is based on this idea. Indeed, the power of the general equilibrium approach to economic analysis lies largely in its separation of the behaviour of numerous economic agents into autonomous equations.

As emphasized by the pioneers in the development of econometrics, it is not enough to construct models that fit a given body of facts. The task of the economist is to find models that successfully predict how the facts will change under specified new conditions. This requires knowing which relationships will remain stable after the intervention and which will not. It requires the model builder to express for every equation postulated the class of situations under which it will remain valid. The concept of autonomy and its importance in econometric model construction is emphasized in the classic paper by Haavelmo (1944) and in the expository paper by Marschak (1953). Sadly, it seems often to be ignored in applied work.

The autonomy of the equations appearing in commonly proposed models is often questionable. Lucas (1976) raises some important issues in his critique of traditional Keynesian macromodels. These simultaneous equations systems typically contain distributed lag relations which are interpreted as proxies for expectations. Suppose, for example, consumption really depends on expected future income. If people forecast the future based on the past, the unobserved expectation variable can be replaced by some function of past incomes. However, since income is endogenous, the actual time path of income depends on all the equations of the model. Under rational expectations, any change in the behaviour of other agents or in technology that affects the time path of income will also change the way people forecast and hence the distributed lag. Thus it can be argued that the traditional consumption function is not an autonomous relation with respect to most interesting policy interventions. Sims (1980) pursues this type of argument further, finding other reasons for doubting the autonomy of the equations in traditional macroeconomic models and concluding that policy analysis based on such models is highly suspect. Although one may perhaps disagree with Sims's conclusion, the methodological questions he raises cannot be ignored.

Even if one accepts the view that structural equations actually proposed in practice often possess limited autonomy and are not likely to be invariant to many interesting interventions, it may still be the case that these equations are useful. A typical reduced-form equation contains all the predetermined variables in the system. Given the existence of feedback, it is hard to argue a priori about the numerical values of the various elements of Π. It may be much easier to think about orders of magnitude for the structural coefficients. Our intuition about the behaviour of individual sectors of the economy is likely to be considerably better than our intuition about the general equilibrium solution. As long as there are no substantial structural changes, specification in terms of structural equations may be appropriate even if some of the equations lack autonomy.

SOME ECONOMETRIC ISSUES. The discussion up to now has been in terms of exact relationships among economic variables. Of course, actual data do not lie on smooth monotonic curves of the type used in our theories. This is partially due to the fact that the experiments we have in the back of our mind when we postulate an economic model do not correspond exactly to any experiment actually performed in the world. Changing price, but holding everything else constant, is hypothetical and never observed in practice. Other factors, which we choose not to model, do in fact vary across our sample observations. Furthermore, we rarely pretend to know the true equations that relate the variables and instead postulate some approximate parametric family. In practice we work with models of the form

$$g_i(x, y, \theta, u_i) = 0 \qquad (i = 1, \ldots, m)$$

where the g's are known functions, θ is a vector of unknown parameters, and the u's are unobserved error terms reflecting the omitted variables and the misspecification of functional form. In the special case where the functions are linear in x and y with an additive error, the system can be written as

$$By + \Gamma x = u, \tag{4}$$

where u is a m-dimensional vector of errors. If B is non-singular, the reduced form is also linear and can be written as

$$y = -B^{-1}\Gamma x + B^{-1}u = \Pi x + v. \tag{5}$$

Equation system (4) as it stands is empty of content since, for any value of x and y, there always exists a value of u producing equality. Some restrictions on the error term are needed to make the system interesting. One common approach is to treat the errors as though they were draws from a probability distribution centred at the origin and unrelated to the predetermined variables. Suppose we have T observations on each of the $G + K$ variables, say, from T time periods or from T firms. We postulate that, for each observation, the data satisfy equation

(4) where the parameters B and Γ are constant but the n error vectors $u_1, \ldots, u_T$ are independent random variables with zero means. Furthermore, we assume that the conditional distribution of u_t given the predetermined variables x_t for observation t is independent of x_i. A least-squares regression of each endogenous variable on the set of predetermined variables should then give good estimates of Π if the sample size is large and there is sufficient variability in the regressors. However, unless the inverse of B contains blocks of zeros, equation (5) implies that each of the endogenous variables is a function of all the components of u. In general, every element of y will be correlated with every element of u. Least squares applied to more than one endogenous variable will result in biased parameter estimates.

The conclusion that structural parameters in interdependent systems can not be well estimated using least squares is widely believed by econometric theorists and widely ignored by empirical workers. There are probably two reasons for this discrepancy. First, although the logic of interdependent systems suggests that structural errors are likely to be correlated with all the endogenous variation, if the correlation is small compared with the sample variable in those variables, least squares bias will also be small. Given all the other problems facing the applied econometrician, this bias may be of little concern. Secondly, alternative estimation methods that have been developed often produce terrible estimates. Sometimes the only practical alternative to least squares is no estimate at all – a solution that is rarely chosen.

In some applications, the reduced form parameters Π are of primary concern. The structural parameters B and Γ are of interest only to the extent they help us learn about Π. For example, in a supply–demand model, we may wish to know the effect on price of changes in the weather. Price elasticities of supply and demand are not needed to answer that question. On the other hand, if we wish to know the effect of a sales tax on quantity produced, knowledge of the price elasticities might be essential. Although least squares is generally available for reduced form estimation (at least if the sample is large), it is not obvious that, without further assumptions, good structural estimates are ever attainable. The key assumption of the model is that the G structural errors are uncorrelated with the K predetermined variables. These GK orthogonality assumptions are just enough to determine (say by equating sample moments to population moments) the GK parameters in Π. But the structural coefficient matrices B and Γ contain $G^2 + GK$ elements. Even with G normalization rules that set the units in which the parameters of each question will be measured, there are more coefficients than orthogonality conditions. It turns out that structural estimation is possible only if additional assumptions (e.g., that some elements of B and Γ are known a priori) are made. These considerations lead to three general classes of questions that have been addressed by theoretical econometricians: (1) When, in principle, can good structural estimates be found? (2) What are the best ways of actually estimating the structural parameters, given that it is possible? (3) Are there better ways of estimating the reduced-form parameters than by least squares?

These questions are studied in depth in standard econometrics textbooks and will not be examined here. The answers, however, do have a common thread. If each structural equation has more than K unknown parameters, structural estimation is generally impossible and least squares applied to the reduced form is optimal in large samples. If, on the other hand, each structural equation has fewer than K unknown coefficients, structural estimation generally is possible and least squares applied to the reduced form is no longer optimal. In this latter situation, various estimation procedures are available, some requiring little computational effort. However, the sample size may need to be quite large before these procedures are likely to give good estimates.

The assumption that the errors are independent from trial to trial is obviously very strong and quite implausible in time-series analysis. If the nature of the error dependence can be modelled and if the lag structure of the dynamic behavioural equations is correctly specified, most of the estimation results that follow under independence carry over. Unfortunately, with small samples, it is usually necessary to make crude (and rather arbitrary) specifications that may result in very poor estimates. Despite the fact that simultaneous equations analysis in practice is mostly applied to time series data, it can be argued that the statistical basis is much more convincing for cross-section analysis where samples are large and dependency across observations minimal. Even there, the assumption that the errors are unrelated to the predetermined variables must be justified before simultaneous equations estimation techniques can be applied.

THE ROLE OF SIMULTANEOUS EQUATIONS. Many applied economists seem to view the simultaneous equations model as having limited applicability, appropriate only for a very small subset of the problems actually met in practice. This is probably unwise. Estimated regression coefficients are commonly used to explain how an intervention which changes one explanatory variable will affect the dependent variable. Except for very special cases, this interpretation requires us to believe that the proposed intervention will not affect any of the other explanatory variables and that, in the sample, the errors were unrelated to the variation in the regressors. That is, the mechanism that determines the explanatory variables must be unrelated to the causal mechanism described by the equation under consideration. Unless the explanatory variables were in fact set in a carefully designed controlled experiment, viewing the explanatory variables as endogenous and possibly determined simultaneously with the dependent variable is a natural way to start thinking about the plausibility of the required assumptions.

In a sense, the simultaneous equations model is an attempt by economists to come to grips with the old truism that correlation is not the same as causation. In complex processes involving many decision-makers and many decision variables, we wish to discover stable relations that will persist over time and in response to changes in economic policy. We need to distinguish those equations that are autonomous with respect to the interventions we have in mind and those that are not. The methodology of the simultaneous equations model forces us to think about the experimental conditions that are envisaged when we write down an equation. It will not necessarily lead us to good parameter estimates. but it may help us to avoid errors.

BIBLIOGRAPHY

Haavelmo, T. 1944. The probability approach in econometrics. *Econometrica* 12, Supplement, July, 1–115.

Lucas, R. 1976. Econometric policy evaluation: a critique. In *The Phillips Curve and Labor Markets*, ed. K. Brunner and A. Meltzer, Carnegie-Rochester Conferences Series on Public Policy No. 1, Amsterdam: North-Holland.

Marschak, J. 1953. Economic measurement for policy and prediction. In *Studies in Econometric Method*, ed. W. Hood and T. Koopmans, New York: Wiley.

Samuelson, P. 1947. *Foundations of Economic Analysis*. Cambridge, Mass.: Harvard University Press.

Sims, C. 1980. Macroeconomics and reality. *Econometrica* 48(1), January, 1–48.

Strotz, R. 1960. Interdependence as a specification error. *Econometrica* 28, April, 428–42.

Wold, H. 1954. Causality and econometrics. *Econometrica* 22, April, 162–77.

Specification Problems in Econometrics

EDWARD E. LEAMER

A lengthy list of implicit and explicit assumptions is required to draw inferences from a data set. Substantial doubt about these assumptions is a characteristic of the analysis of non-experimental data and much experimental data as well. If this doubt is left unattended, it can cause serious doubt about the corresponding inferences.

The set of assumptions used to draw inferences from a data set is called a 'specification'. The treatment of doubt about the specification is called 'specification analysis'. The research strategy of trying many different specifications is called a 'specification search'.

When an inference is suspected to depend crucially on a doubtful assumption, two kinds of actions can be taken to alleviate the consequent doubt about the inferences. Both require a list of alternative assumptions. The first approach is statistical estimation which uses the data to select from the list of alternative assumptions and then makes suitable adjustments to the inferences to allow for doubt about the assumptions. The second approach is a sensitivity analysis that uses the alternative assumptions one at a time, thereby demonstrating either that all the alternatives lead to essentially the same inferences or that minor changes in the assumptions make major changes in the inferences. For example, a doubtful variable can simply be included in the equation (estimation), or two different equations can be estimated, one with and one without the doubtful variable (sensitivity analysis).

The borderline between the techniques of estimation and sensitivity analysis is not always clear since a specification search can be either a method of estimation of a general model or a method of studying the sensitivity of an inference to choice of model. Stepwise regression, for example, which involves the sequential deletion of 'insignificant' variables and insertion of 'significant' variables is best thought to be a method of estimation of a general model rather than a study of

238

the sensitivity of estimates to choice of variables, since no attempt is generally made to communicate how the results change as different subsets of variables are included.

When the data evidence is very informative, estimation is the preferred approach. But parameter spaces can always be enlarged beyond the point where data can be helpful in distinguishing alternatives. In fact, parameter spaces in economics are typically large enough to overwhelm our data sets, and when abbreviated parameter spaces appear to be used, there usually lurks behind the scene a much larger space of assumptions that ought to be explored. If this larger space has been explored through a pretesting procedure and if the data are sufficiently informative that estimation is the preferred approach, then adjustments to the inferences are in order to account for the pretesting bias. If the data are not adequately informative about the parameters of the larger space, we need to have answers to the sensitivity question whether ambiguity about the best method of estimation implies consequential ambiguity about the inferences. A data analysis should therefore combine estimation with sensitivity analysis, and only those inferences that are clearly favoured by the data or are sturdy enough to withstand minor changes in the assumptions should be retained.

Estimation and sensitivity analyses are two phases of a data analysis. Simplification is a third. The intent of simplification is to find a simple model that works well for a class of decisions. A specification search can be used for simplification, as well as for estimation and sensitivity analysis. The very prevalent confusion among these three kinds of searches ought to be eliminated since the rules for a search and measures of its success will properly depend on its intent.

The function of econometric theory is to plan responses to data. A response may be an action (e.g. the choice of an hypothesis) or a feeling (e.g. a confidence interval). In settings in which the theory and the method of measurement are clear, responses can be conveniently planned in advance. In practice, however, most analysers of economic data have very low levels of commitment to whatever plans they may have formulated before reviewing the data. Even when planning is extensive, most analysts reserve the right to alter the plans if the data are judged 'unusual'. A review of the planned responses to the data after the data are actually observed can be called criticism, the function of which is either to detect deficiencies in the original family of models that ought to be remedied by enhancements of the parameter space or to detect inaccuracies in the original approximation of prior information. When either the model or the prior information is revised, the planned responses are discarded in favour of what at the time seem to be better responses.

The form that criticism should take is not clear cut. Much of what appears to be criticism is in fact a step in a process of estimation, since the enhancement of the model is completely predictable. An example of an estimation method masquerading as criticism is a t-test to determine if a specific variable should be added to the regression. In this case the response to the data is planned in advance and undergoes no revision once the data are observed.

Criticism and the prospect of the revision of planned responses create a crippling dilemma for classical inference since, according to that theory, the choice of response should be based entirely on sampling properties, which are impossible to compute unless the response to every conceivable data set is planned and fully committed. When a criticism is successful, that is to say when the family of models is enhanced or the prior distribution is altered in response to anomalies in the data, there is a severe double counting problem if estimation then proceeds as if the model and prior distribution were not data-instigated. Even if criticism is not successful, the prospect of successful criticism makes the inferences from the data weaker than conventionally reported because the commitment to the model and the prior is weaker than is admitted.

CHOICE OF VARIABLES FOR LINEAR REGRESSION. Specification problems are not limited to but are often discussed within the context of the linear regression model, probably because the most common problem facing analysers of economic data is doubt about the exact list of explanatory variables. The first results in this literature addressed the effect of excluding variables that belong in the equation, and including variables that do not. Let y represent the dependent variable, x an included explanatory variable, and z a doubtful explanatory variable. Assume that:

$$E(y \mid x, z) = \alpha + x\beta + z\theta.$$

$$\mathrm{Var}(y \mid x) = \sigma^2,$$

$$E(z \mid x) = c + xr$$

$$\mathrm{Var}(z \mid x) = s^2,$$

where α, β, θ, c, r, σ^2, and s^2 are unknown parameters, and y, x, and z are observable vectors. Then β can be estimated with z included in the equation:

$$b_{.z} = (x'M_z x)^{-1}(x'M_z y),$$

or with z excluded:

$$b = (x'x)^{-1}x'y,$$

where

$$M_z = I - z(z'z)^{-1}z'.$$

The first two moments of these estimators are straightforwardly computed:

$$E(b_{.z}) = \beta, \qquad\qquad E(b) = \beta + r\theta$$

$$\mathrm{Bias}(b_{.z}) = 0 \qquad\qquad \mathrm{Bias}(b) = r\theta$$

$$\mathrm{Var}(b_{.z}) = \sigma^2(x'M_z x)^{-1} \quad \mathrm{Var}(b) = \sigma^2(x'x)^{-1},$$

where

$$\mathrm{Bias}(b) = E(b) - \beta.$$

A bit of algebra reveals that $\text{Var}(b_{.z}) \geqslant \text{Var}(b)$. These moments form two basic results in 'specification analysis' made popular by Theil (1957): (1) If a relevant variable is excluded ($\theta \neq 0$), the estimator is biased by an amount that is the product of the coefficient of the excluded variable times the regression coefficient from the regression of the included on the excluded variable. (2) If an irrelevant variable is included ($\theta = 0$), the estimator remains unbiased, but has an inflated variance.

This bias result can be useful when the variable z is unobservable and information is available on the probable values of θ and r, since then the bias in b can be corrected. But if both x and z are observable, these results are not useful by themselves because they do not unambiguously select between the estimators, one doing well in terms of bias but the other doing well in terms of variance. The choice will obviously depend on information about the value of $r\theta$, since a small value of $r\theta$ implies a small value for the bias of b. The choice will also depend on the loss function that determines the tradeoff between bias and variance.

For mathematical convenience, the loss function is usually assumed to be quadratic:

$$L(\beta^*, \beta) = (\beta^* - \beta)^2,$$

where β^* is an estimator of β. The expected value of this loss function is known as the mean squared error of the estimator, which can be written as the variance plus the square of the bias:

$$\text{MSE}(b_{.z}, \beta) - \text{MSE}(b, \beta) = r(\text{Var}(\theta^*_{.x}) - \theta\theta')r',$$

where $\theta^*_{.x}$ is the least squares estimator of θ controlling for x, and where the notation allows x and z to represent collections of variables as well as singlets. By inspection of this formula we can derive the fundamental result in this literature. The estimator based on the restricted model is better in the mean squared error sense than the unrestricted estimator if and only if θ is small enough that $\text{Var}(\theta^*_{.x}) - \theta\theta'$ is positive definite. If θ is a scalar, this condition can be described as 'a true t less than one', $\theta^2/\text{Var}(\theta^*_{.x}) < 1$.

This result is also of limited use since its answer to the question 'Which estimator is better?' is another question 'How big is θ?' A clever suggestion is to let the data provide the answer, and to omit z if its estimated t value is less than one. Unfortunately, because the estimated t is not exactly equal to the true t, this two-step procedure does not yield an estimator that guarantees a lower mean squared error than unconstrained least squares. Thus the question remains: how big is θ? For more discussion consult Judge and Bock (1983).

A Bayesian analysis allows the construction of estimators that make explicit use of information about θ. It is convenient to assume that the information about θ takes the form of a preliminary data set in which the estimate of θ is zero (or some other number, if you prefer). Then the Bayes estimate of β is a weighted average of the constrained and unconstrained estimators:

$$b_\text{B} = (v^{-1} + v'^{-1})^{-1} (v^{-1}b_{.z} + v'^{-1}b),$$

241

where v' is the prior variance for h, and v is the sampling variance for $\theta^*_{.x}$. Instinct might suggest that this compromise between the two estimators would depend on the variances of $b_{.z}$ and b, but the correct weights are inversely proportional to prior variance and the sample variances for θ.

A card-carrying Bayesian regards this to be the solution to the problem. Others will have a different reaction. What the Bayesian has done is only to enlarge the family of estimators. The two extremes are still possible since we may have $v' = 0$ or $v' \to \infty$, but in addition there are the intermediate values $v' > 0$. Thus the Bayesian answer to the question is another question: 'What is the value of v'?'

SENSITIVITY ANALYSIS. At this point we have to switch from the estimation mode to the sensitivity mode, since precise values of v' will be hard to come by on a purely *a priori* basis and since the data usually will be of little help in selecting v' with great accuracy. A sensitivity analysis can be done from a classical point of view simply by contrasting the two extreme estimates, $b_{.z}$ and b, corresponding to the extreme values of v'. A Bayesian approach allows a much richer set of sensitivity studies. A mathematically convenient analysis begins with a hypothetical value for v', say v'_0, which is selected to represent as accurately as possible the prior information that may be available. A neighbourhood around this point is selected to reflect the accuracy with which v'_0 can be chosen. For example, v' might be restricted to lie in the interval

$$v'_0/(1 + c) < v' < v'_0(1 + c),$$

where c measures the accuracy of v'_0. The corresponding interval of Bayes' estimates b_B is

$$1/(v'_0(1 + c) + v) < (b_B - b_{.z})/v(b - b_{.z})$$
$$< (1 + c)/(v'_0 + v(1 + c)),$$

where it is assumed that $(b - b_{.z}) > 0$. If this interval is large for small values of c, then the estimate is very sensitive to the definition of the prior information. For example, suppose that interest focuses on the sign of β. Issues of standard errors aside, if $b_{.z}$ and b are the same sign, then the inference can be said to be sturdy since no value of c can change the sign of the estimate b_B. But if $b > 0 > b_{.z}$, then the values of c in excess of the following will cause the interval of estimates to overlap the origin:

$$c^* = \max[u - 1, u^{-1} - 1],$$

where $u = -(v/v'_0)(b/b_{.z})$. Thus if u is close to one, the inference is fragile. This occurs if differences in the absolute size of the two estimates are offset by differences in the variances applicable to the coefficient of the doubtful variable. Measures like these can be found in Leamer (1978, 1982, 1983b).

ROBUSTNESS. When a set of acceptable assumptions does not map into a specific decision, the inference is said to be fragile. A decision can then sensibly be based on a minimax criterion that selects a 'robust' procedure that works well regardless of the assumption. The literature on 'robustness' such as that reviewed by Krasker et al. (1983) has concentrated on issues relating to the choice of sampling distribution, but could be extended to choice of prior distribution.

SIMPLIFICATION, PROXY SELECTION AND DATA SELECTION. A specification search involving the estimation of many different models can be a method of estimation or a method of sensitivity analysis. Simplification searches are also common, the goal of which is to find a simple quantitative facsimile that can be used as a decision-making tool. For example, a model with a high R^2 can be expected to provide accurate forecasts in a stable environment, whether or not the coefficients can be given a causal interpretation. In particular, if two explanatory variables are highly correlated, then one can be excluded from the equation without greatly reducing the overall fit since the included variable will take over the role of the excluded variable. No causal significance necessarily attaches to the coefficient of the retained variable.

A specification search can also be used to select the best from a set of alternative proxy variables, or to select a data subset. These problems can be dealt with by enlarging the parameter space to allow for multiple proxy variables or unusual data points. Once the space is properly enlarged, the problems that remain are exactly the same as the problems encountered when the parameters are coefficients in a linear regression, namely estimation and sensitivity analysis.

DATA-INSTIGATED MODELS. The subjects of estimation, sensitivity analysis and simplification deal with concerns that arise during the planning phase of a statistical analysis when alternative responses to hypothetical data sets are under consideration. A distinctly different kind of specification search occurs when anomalies in the actual data suggest a revision in a planned response, for example, the inclusion of a variable that was not originally identified. This is implicitly disallowed by formal statistical theories which presuppose the existence of a response to the data that is planned and fully committed. I like to refer to a search for anomalies as 'Sherlock Holmes inference', since when asked who might have committed the crime, Holmes replied, 'No data yet.... It is a capital mistake to theorize before you have all the evidence. It biases the judgements'. This contrasts with the typical advice of theoretical econometricians: 'No theory yet. It is a capital mistake to look at the data before you have identified all the theories'.

Holmes is properly concerned that an excessive degree of theorizing will make it psychologically difficult to see anomalies in the data that might, if recognized, point sharply to a theory that was not originally identified. On the other hand, the econometrician is worried that data evidence may be double counted, once in the Holmesian mode to instigate models that seem favoured by the data and again in the estimation mode to select the instigated models over original models. Holmes is properly unconcerned about the double counting problem, since he has the ultimate extra bit of data: the confession. We do not have the luxury of running additional experiments and the closest that we can come to the Holmesian procedure is to set aside a part of the data set in hopes of squeezing a confession after we have finished identifying a set of models with a Holmesian analysis of the first part of the data. Unfortunately, our data sets never do confess, and the ambiguity of the inferences that is clearly present after the Holmesian phase lingers on with very little attenuation after the estimation phase. Thus we are forced to find a solution to the Holmesian conundrum of how properly to characterize the data evidence when models are instigated by the data, that is to say, how to avoid the double counting problem. Clearly, what is required is some kind of penalty that discourages but does not preclude Holmesian discoveries. Leamer (1978) proposes one penalty that rests on the assumption that Holmesian analysis mimics the solution to a formal presimplification problem in which models are explicitly simplified before the data are observed in order to avoid observation and processing costs that are associated with the larger model. Anomalies in the data set can then suggest a revision of this decision. Of course real Holmesian analysis cannot actually solve this sequential decision problem since in order to solve it one has to identify the complete structure that is simplified before observation. But we can nonetheless act as if we were solving this problem, since by doing so we can compute a very sensible kind of penalty for Holmesian discoveries (Leamer, 1978).

CRITICISM. Estimation and sensitivity analysis are two important phases of a data analysis. The third is criticism. The function of criticism is to highlight anomalies in a data set that might lead to Holmesian revisions in the model. Criticism and data instigated models are not as frequent as they may appear. As remarked before, much of what is said to be criticism is only a step in a method of estimation, and many models that seem to be data-instigated are in fact explicitly identified in advance of the data analysis. For example, forward stepwise regression, which adds statistically significant variables to a regression equation, cannot be said to be producing data-instigated models because the set of alternative models is explicitly identified before the data analysis commences and the response to the data is fully planned in advance. Stepwise regression is thus only a method of estimation of a general model. Likewise, various diagnostic tests which lead necessarily to a particular enhancement of the model, such as a Durbin–Watson test for first order autocorrelation, select but do not instigate a model.

'Goodness of fit' tests which do not have explicit alternatives are sometimes used to criticize a model. However, the Holmesian question is not whether the data appear to be anomalous with respect to a given model but rather whether there is a plausible alternative that makes them appear less anomalous. In large samples, all models have large goodness of fit statistics, and the size of the statistic is no guarantee, or even a strong suggestion, that there exists a plausible alternative model that is substantially better than the one being used. Still, I admit that there are examples in which a goodness-of-fit statistic can be suggestive, probably because the set of alternative hypotheses, though not explicitly stated, is nonetheless 'intuitive'.

Unexpected parameter estimates are probably the most effective criticisms of a model. A Durbin–Watson statistic that indicates a substantial amount of autocorrelation can be used legitimately to signal the existence of left-out variables in settings in which there is strong prior information that the residuals are white noise. Aside from unexpected estimates, graphical displays and the study of influential data points may stimulate thinking about the inadequacies in a model.

BIBLIOGRAPHY

Box, G.E.P. 1980. Sampling and Bayes' inference in scientific modelling and robustness. *Journal of the Royal Statistical Society*, Series A, Pt 4, 383–430.

Judge, G.G. and Bock, M.E. 1983. Biased estimation. In *Handbook of Econometrics*, Vol. 1, ed. Z. Griliches and M. Intriligator, Amsterdam: North-Holland.

Krasker, W.S., Kuh, E. and Welsch, R.E. 1983. Estimation for dirty data and flawed models. In *Handbook of Econometrics*, Vol. 1, ed. Z. Griliches and M. Intriligator, Amsterdam: North-Holland.

Leamer, E.E. 1978. *Specification Searches*. New York: Wiley.

Leamer, E.E. 1982. Sets of posterior means with bounded variance priors. *Econometrica* 50, May, 725–36.

Leamer, E.E. 1983a. Let's take the con out of econometrics. *American Economic Review* 73, March, 31–43.

Leamer, E.E. 1983b. Model choice and specification analysis. In *Handbook of Econometrics*, Vol. 1, ed. Z. Griliches and M. Intriligator, Amsterdam: North-Holland.

Theil, H. 1957. Specification errors and the estimation of economic relationships. *Review of the International Statistical Institute* 25, 41–51.

Spurious Regression

C.W.J. GRANGER

If a theory suggests that there is a linear relationship between a pair of random variables X and Y, then an obvious way to test the theory is to estimate a regression equation of form

$$Y = \alpha + \beta X + e.$$

Estimation could be by least-squares and the standard diagnostic statistics would be a t-statistic on β, the R^2 value and possibly the Durbin–Watson statistic d. With such a procedure there is always the possibility of a type II error, that is accepting the relationship as significant when, in fact, X and Y are uncorrelated. This possibility increases if the error term e is autocorrelated, as first pointed out by Yule (1926). As the autocorrelation structure of e is the same as that for Y, when the true $\beta = 0$, this problem of 'nonsense correlations' or 'spurious regressions' is most likely to occur when testing relationships between highly autocorrelated series.

If X_t, Y_t are a pair of independent non-drifting random walks given by

$$X_t - X_{t-1} = \varepsilon_{1t}$$
$$Y_t - Y_{t-1} = \varepsilon_{2t},$$

where ε_{1t}, ε_{2t} are independent zero-mean white-noise (uncorrelated) series, then it was shown by Granger and Newbold (1974) by simulation that high R^2 values can occur together with apparently significant t-values. For example, using samples of length 50, 100 simulations produced 87 t-values greater than 2 in magnitude, including 53 greater than 4 and 27 greater than 6. Thus, the majority of these regressions between a pair of independent series would have produced relationships that appear to be significant under the standard classical test. The problem, of course, is that the t-statistic does not have the standard distribution if the error term in the regression is not white noise, and this problem is particularly

246

important when the error-term is strongly autocorrelated. Thus, a high value for t or for R^2, when combined with a low d-value is no indication of a true relationship. That this finding is not just a small-sample problem has been proved by some asymptotic theory results of Phillips (1985). He found that when non-drifting random walks are regressed using a least-squares procedure, then asymptotically the distribution of R^2 is non-degenerate so that a positive R^2 value can occur, d tends to zero in probability and the t-statistic when divided by the square root of the sample size tends to a non-degenerate, finite variance distribution, but not the t-distribution. He further finds that the estimate of α has variance proportional to the sample size, so that this estimate divided by the square root of sample size tends to a random variable with finite variance.

These results, plus simulations by Granger and Newbold (1974), suggest that similar problems will occur if any pair of independent series that are integrated of order one are analysed by a simple least-squares regression. (A series is said to be integrated of order one (I(1)) if the differenced series is stationary with positive spectrum at zero frequency.) This result is of some practical importance because many macroeconomic series appear to be I(1), and so spurious regressions can easily occur if care is not taken in the model specification. It is, in fact, rather easy to find examples in early applied economic literature of regressions with large R^2 values but low d-values. Sometimes, when the regression is repeated using changes of the variables, a very low R^2 value is achieved, but a satisfactory d-value, suggesting that the regression in levels was probably spurious.

If more than two independent I(1) series are used in a regression, the possibility of a spurious relationship increases further. For example, a simulation by Granger and Newbold (1974) where one random walk was 'explained' by five other independent random walks found in 100 cases that a t-value of 2 or more in magnitude occurred in 96 occasions, with an average corrected R^2 of 0.59, and with 37 corrected R^2 values over 0.7 and an average d-value of 0.88. When the same regression was run on changes, only six t-values were over 2 in size, the average corrected R^2 was 0.012 with none over 0.7 and the average d-value was 1.99.

The possibility of a spurious relationship also increases further if the random walks contain drift, and if no trend term is included in the regression. A simulation by Newbold and Davies (1975) found that a Cochran–Orcutt correction to the estimation procedure did not completely remove the problem if residuals are not actually autoregressive of order one.

The obvious difficulty with the likelihood of spurious regression is to know when a regression is spurious or not. A simple cure with I(1) series is to perform the regression on differenced series, but this is not completely recommended as important parts of the potential relationship can be lost. A better approach is to embed the relationship being investigated within a sufficiently complex dynamic specification, including lagged dependent and independent variables, so that the truth might be discovered. An obvious objective is to make the residuals stationary, as discussed, for example, by Hendry et al. (1985).

BIBLIOGRAPHY

Granger, C.W.J. and Newbold, P. 1974. Spurious regressions in econometrics. *Journal of Econometrics* 2(2), July, 111–20.

Hendry, D.F., Pagan, A. and Sargan, J.D. 1985. Dynamic specification. In *Handbook of Econometrics*, Vol. 2, ed. Z. Griliches and M.D. Intriligator, Amsterdam: North-Holland.

Newbold, P. and Davies, N. 1975. Error mis-specification and spurious regressions. Department of Mathematics, University of Nottingham.

Phillips, P.C.B. 1985. Understanding spurious regressions in econometrics. Working paper, Cowles Foundation, Yale University.

Yule, G.U. 1926. Why do we sometimes get nonsense correlations between time-series? *Journal of the Royal Statistical Society* 89, 1–64.

Survey Research

JAMES N. MORGAN

Getting facts, expectations, reasons or attitudes by interviewing people has a long history, but scientific survey research required three innovations which only came in the 20th century – scientific probability sampling, controlled question stimuli and answer categorization, and multivariate analysis of the rich resulting data sets. Textbooks abound (Moser and Kalton, 1971; Lansing and Morgan, 1971; Sonquist and Dunkelberg, 1977; Rossi et al., 1983).

Interview surveys were conducted in Germany in the last century on such things as the attitudes of workers in factories (Oberschall, 1964). But political concerns overwhelmed scientific interests, and objectivity was soon lost. Later, mostly early in this century, surveys in England and France documented the plight of the poor, usually those in urban slums as a result of the industrial revolution. Soon after that, surveys of income and expenditures started appearing, and by 1935 it was possible to produce an annotated list of 1500 family living studies in 52 countries (Williams and Zimmerman, 1935). Starting in the 1940s a rapid expansion of surveys was driven by concerns about measuring unemployment, establishing weights for cost-of-living indexes, estimating income elasticities for various expenditure types, studying saving and wealth, and investigating markets for consumer goods (International Labour Office, 1961; Glock, 1967).

SAMPLING. Inferring anything about some population requires some kind of unbiased sampling, not necessarily random, but surely with a known probability of selection of every eligible unit. Since people do not stay in one spot, and there are seldom complete lists than can serve as a 'sampling frame', the innovation that allowed progress was the notion of sampling geography – occupied dwellings – and trying to associate everyone with some place where he or she lived during most of the interviewing period. Since it is expensive to travel, or even get detailed sampling materials for every place, clustering of samples reduced the information per interview, but increased it per dollar. Clustering usually means multi-stage

249

selection of increasingly smaller chunks of space, ending with a dwelling where all occupying families may be included (Kish, 1965). But areas are not selected at random. One can do better than random by arranging areas at each stage in systematic order and using a random start and an interval – a process called stratification, which gains precision at no cost and with no bias. A final sophistication and improvement involves controls beyond simple stratification which can further reduce the probability of inadvertent concentrations.

Even the use of telephone for sampling involves innovation. Random digit dialling allows the inclusion of unlisted numbers, but requires stepwise procedures for avoiding ranges of numbers with few or no operating telephones in private households. And adjustments for or separate inclusion of those without telephones may be called for. There is less final clustering at the block level, but otherwise clustering and stratification is possible.

INTERVIEWING. The second breakthrough after sampling was careful, reproducible procedures for uniform stimuli (questions and introductions) and controlled categorization of responses (Kahn and Cannell, 1965; Oppenheim, 1966; Turner and Martin, 1984). The development of fixed questions, asked word for word, and central office coding of verbatim answers allows potentially reproducible results, and studies of change unsullied by changes in categorization procedures. (One can recode a sample of the earlier protocols with the new coding staff to be sure.) Of course, this requires careful pre-testing and development, and there is an extensive body of research literature on the differences in responses one gets with different question wording, question order, interviewer training or even different survey organizations. Furthermore, once questions have been tested and used, and codes established it is tempting, particularly with the more factual items, to allow the interviewer or respondent to check boxes. With mail questionnaires the pressure to use precoded categories and check boxes is ever greater. The cost is, of course, lack of control over the coding process, since it is being done by many different interviewers or still more varied respondents, with no chance to review or re-do it. A quality-control process for check coding is customary in survey organizations, even for check boxes where it only picks up mechanical errors (Zarkovich, 1966).

COMPUTERS. The third and final crucial breakthrough was of course the computer, which allows the rich complex matrix of information elicited in an interview to be analysed. Parallel with the explosion of computer capability has been development of statistical analysis procedures to take advantage of the many more degrees of freedom with thousands of interviews rather than a few years of a time series (O'Muircheartaigh and Payne, 1977). There was a relatively rapid movement from tables to multiple regression to recursive path models (though little use of structural equation systems). Categorical predictors were handled without elaborate scaling analysis by the use of dichotomous (dummy) variables, and categorical dependent variables by log linear analysis. The basic impossibility of separating the effects of age, year of birth and year of history for their effects led to various (imperfect) 'solutions'. The need to estimate things when not all the relevant group was measured (selection bias) led to (again imperfect) adjustments for (and estimates of) the selection bias.

The computer also allowed improvements in processing and even in interviewing. Direct data entry allows checking for inconsistencies and wild codes immediately, reduces transcription errors and allows long records immediately without merging decks of IBM cards. Computer-assisted telephone interviewing goes even further and helps the interviewer to move properly through complex sequences and can also catch inconsistencies and wild codes instantly. It opens up possibilities for complex interactive interviews which can cycle back when necessary, or introduce information or insights to elicit reactions to them.

Computer data files are also increasingly transferrable and usable by researchers for secondary analysis. The Interuniversity Consortium for Political and Social Research at the University of Michigan distributes free to its member institutions a vast archive of survey data in the social sciences, and the Census has vastly expanded its facilities for distributing data from its collections. The Roper Collection at Williams is largely attitudinal surveys. Procedures for transferring data files and dictionaries from one software to another are appearing; for example, between SPSS and OSIRIS.

PROGRESS AND PROBLEMS IN ANALYSIS. Survey data by age groups (and hence birth cohorts), repeated in later surveys, and even enriched by panels following the same individuals as they aged, did not solve the problem of disentangling the effects of age, year of birth and period of history, since any one is a linear function of the other two. Better data plus some assumptions helped, but the results proved sensitive to which assumptions, and the solution probably lies in direct measurement of the various things thought to be represented by age, or year of birth, or year of history.

Another analysis problem was generically called 'selection bias'. Any sampling statistician knows that if a sample uses different probabilities of selection for different people, unweighted estimates can have bias except when a model happens to be perfectly specified. If the probabilities are known, that bias can be eliminated simply and for all problems by weighting each case by the inverse of its probability of falling into the sample. If some individuals have no chance of inclusion, then in principle they would have infinite weights (we can say nothing about them). But in intermediate cases where there is some stochastic selection process, various methods have been proposed for estimating the probability of inclusion and (with proper attention to distributions of the errors) introducing it into the model, both to reduce bias and to test for the significance of the selection bias (Chamberlain, 1978; Heckman, 1979).

The problem, of course, is to find predictors of inclusion in the sample that are not also the variables in the explanatory model. And if the selection bias adjustments are small and insignificant, that may only mean that we were not able to model the selection process well. Sometimes selection is clearly endogenous, as when some women, presumably different from others, decide not to work for pay.

A third and perhaps most crucial problem of all arose, interestingly enough, only when we had dynamic panel data and sought to untangle causal effects across time. It seemed tempting to think that looking at change over time for each individual would allow us to eliminate many interpersonal differences that plagued cross-section analysis. We could then ask what the effect of events or conditions at one point in time was on subsequent changes, events or conditions.

The introduction of panel (reinterview) data seemed to open up vast new possibilities for analysis, reducing the amount of interpersonal difference to be accounted for, but it did not really allow clean and simple estimation of effects across time. As soon as we pooled observations in order to estimate effects for populations, we found that persistent interpersonal differences confounded our interpretation of the effects.

Relations between a state or event at one time and a state or event at a later time could occur in four ways: 1. Negatively, but with no causal implications, if there were measurement errors or random shocks. 2. Positively, also without causal inference, if there were persistent interpersonal differences. Moving is correlated with moving again later, because some people just like to move, and just adjusting for age doesn't account for all the differences in propensity to move. 3. Negatively, with causal implications, if an adaptive act reduced the need for further action. A better job may reduce the likelihood of changing again. 4. Positively, showing real effects, if scarring of unemployment or seniority in job tenure made the same state (unemployed or employed) more likely later on.

Sophisticated procedures for attempting to sort out the reasons behind intertemporal relations have been proposed by Heckman and by Chamberlain, both methods requiring multiple waves of data (Heckman, 1981; Chamberlain, 1984).

Elsewhere you can read about selection bias, about state-dependence and heterogeneity (true and false autocorrelation), about log-linear models and path analysis and age–period–cohort problems. A combination of computer power to make estimates iteratively when there is no analytic solution, and of models which call for the simultaneous combination of multiple measures (confirmatory factor analysis) with estimation of relationships and of error components has led to increasingly complex models and directed attention to issues of robustness and to the importance of better data.

SUBSTANTIVE CONTRIBUTIONS. What are surveys good for substantively, and why not just use available micro data from files and records?

Records tend to be narrow, limited, often inaccessible. Only an individual can provide a coherent picture of the various connections with other individuals, employers, financial institutions, a dwelling and its environment, as well as interpretations of the past, expectations about the future and reasons (however biased or defensive) for decisions. People can move in and out of records, so that longer-term analysis of change using records is often difficult. Even Social Security records omit some income, deal with individuals not their families and provide little related information. Much of the early development of surveys was by sociologists and involved an extensive concern with attitudes and perceptions. Economists, with a much larger set of data from other sources, were slower to come to the conviction that better data would be worth the cost.

Economic surveys tend to focus on what appear at first to be hard data, but soon turn out to have many of the same conceptual and measurement problems. For example, an early driving concern as the United States was going through the great depression of the 1930s and its aftermath, was the measurement of unemployment. But this turned out to require measuring just who was really in the labour force, and deciding what to do about people on temporary layoff, or who wanted more work than they could get, or who, like teachers, had the summer off. It also led to a complex sample design with overlapping reinterviews which eliminated or at least averaged out a curious tendency for people on subsequent reinterviews to be less and less likely to call themselves unemployed. The Census uses a very narrow and explicit set of questions about employment status in order to minimize the measurement error.

Even such apparently simple facts as home ownership turn out to be frequently ambiguous, with titles tied up in probate, mixed with a cooperative or condominium arrangement, owned by a temporarily absent family member.

Survey data are used in the first instance for descriptive purposes, then to estimate static relationships, but finally to attempt to estimate more dynamic relationships starting with initial state-subsequent change relations. The ultimate payoff from the availability of such data would appear to be from using them in simulation models to spell out the system-dynamics of socio-economic systems, So far the quantity and quality of behavioural data and of the funding and development of simulation capacities have restricted this development. But it seems likely that ultimately a coherent and cooperative programme will develop in which the needs of the system analysts will help set the agenda for empirical survey research on behaviour, and the kinds of analysis done on those data, while the data people will advise on revisions of the system models.

SOME HISTORY. National sample surveys in economics got their first impetus, funding and concerns with accuracy from issues of unemployment and inflation. The range of uncertainty before World War II about the percentage unemployed was substantial. Inflation raises questions of proper weighting of the different prices, in proportion to the fraction of family incomes spent on each item, and hence calls for expenditure surveys. And economists have always been interested in saving because it can reduce inflation and encourage investment and progress. It was partly concern over what people would do with their accumulated war bonds after World War II that led to the annual surveys of consumer finances, conducted by The Institute for Social Research at the University of Michigan for the Board of Governors of the Federal Reserve System. Surveys made it quite clear that there would be no mass attempt to cash the bonds when the war was over.

Repeated cross-sections can reveal trends and change, but with higher sampling variances than the more dynamic micro data available from retrospective (memory) or from reinterviews and panel studies. Measurement of saving adequately probably requires reinterviews. Some reinterviews were built into the Surveys of Consumer Finances. The Current Population Surveys have a pattern of overlapping reinterviews, used not to produce change data for individuals but to reduce the sampling variances of estimates of change without the need to follow movers.

Starting around 1968, however, a number of panel studies following people for extended periods, were started. The Longitudinal Retirement History Study of the Social Security Administration interviewed a cohort of people close to retirement age six times over ten years. The National Longitudinal Surveys started with three cohorts; young men and women expected to make the transition from school to work, middle-aged women expected to re-enter the labour market and mature men expected to retire. Later two new cohorts of young men and of young women were added. The Panel Study of Income Dynamics started in 1968 with a combined sample – a low-income, heavily minority sample subselected from the Survey of Economic Opportunity (Census for Office of Economic Opportunity) and a fresh cross-section sample from the Institute for Social Research national sample frame. Weights allow proper merging of the two samples and allowance for the widely different sampling fractions. More recently, out of a concern both for more precise information about income and its short-run fluctuations, and about the impact of government programmes, the Survey of Income and Program Participation (Census) was started, with overlapping panels each interviewed three times a year over a two-and-a-half-year period.

Panels similiar to the Panel Study of Income Dynamics have been started in West Germany, Sweden, the Netherlands, Luxembourg and Belgium, and attempts are being made to increase the comparability of these data sets in order to facilitate international comparisons not just of overall measures but of relationships and dynamics.

Starting right after World War II there were repeated surveys of expectations and intentions of both businessmen and consumers. In the case of consumers there was a theoretical base provided by George Katona which affected the nature of the data collected and made them useful both for short-term forecasting and for studying the impact of national events on consumer optimism and confidence and thereby on their willingness to spend and make commitments to future standards of living (and repayments) (Katona, 1975).

There are, of course, many other data collections, some involving reinterviews, some involving repeated cross-sections but with enough consistency to facilitate studies of change in subgroups. The annual Housing Survey and the various health surveys are examples. Numerous Presidential Commissions have in the course of their short lives managed to commission surveys on such things as pensions, impact of minimum-wage laws on employers, and bankruptcy. Finally, the occasional large-scale consumer expenditure survey has been replaced by more regular ongoing expenditure surveys combining diaries for small frequent items with interviews to cover the large less frequent ones.

The Commission on National Statistics of the National Research Council,

National Academy of Sciences, has, among others, been concerned with the quality of survey data and problems of proper revelation of essential procedures. We have mentioned the Interuniversity Consortium for Political and Social Research at the University of Michigan, which documents archives and distributes to its member universities and other organizations a wide range of survey and other data and has vastly improved the access to survey data for secondary analysis.

FUTURE PROMISE. While survey data, particularly panel data, have vastly expanded the possibilities for studying behaviour and testing theories about behavioural responses, particularly to policy-relevant variables, there are still untapped possibilities both for analysis and use of existing survey data and for specifying better data tailored to the important issues. Little has been done with the data to study lagged responses to exogenous changes nor untangle joint-decision processes. Nor, as we have said, has there been an adequate effort to have the data collected, analysed and used in simulation models to spell out the aggregate dynamic implications in socio-economic systems of the behavioural responses. Much of what is called simulation is static use of survey data to spell out the impact of proposed new taxes or subsidies on various subsets of the population. Dynamic microsimulation is both more difficult and more promising.

More promising still is the specification of data that would allow bypassing presently difficult or intractable problems. One can disentangle age, period and cohort effects by imposing constraints, such as assuming that one of them has only a linear effect, but the results are highly sensitive to the particular constraint chosen. Collecting more information about the specific things that are supposed to be affected by age, year or year of birth would appear more promising. Joint and related decisions cannot really be untangled by looking at sequence, nor easily inferred statistically, but people might well be able to provide direct evidence about what was related to what and how one choice influenced or was influenced by or was made jointly with some other choice. Persistent interpersonal differences which pollute attempts to estimate effects across time, or the differences associated with selection biases, might be investigated directly. Even the rational expectations or the implicit contracts so favoured in economic theory might be asked about in interviews in various indirect or direct ways.

The ultimate coherent development of economics might be seen as cooperative efforts in three related domains: designing and collecting information about human behaviour, analysing survey and other data to estimate dynamic behavioural responses, particularly responses to crucial policy parameters (manipulable?) and using those estimates in simulation models to spell out the aggregate dynamic implications, the sensitivity of the system to changes in rules or behaviour, and the impact of changes on subgroups in society. Such an articulated programme would allow the modellers to specify which behavioural parameters are needed with the most precision and the statistical analysts to specify what survey data they need for making such estimates. The influence might also go the other way, with empirical survey researchers helping make the models more realistic and more parsimonious, omitting relationships known to be trivial or weak. The result should be a unified science of economics that was both behavioural and analytical, micro and macro, equilibrium and dynamic.

BIBLIOGRAPHY

Chamberlain, G. 1978. Omitted variable bias in panel data: estimating the returns to schooling. In *The Econometrics of Panel Data*. Colloque International ce CNRS, *Annales de l'INSEE*, 50–82.

Chamberlain, G. 1984. Heterogeneity, omitted variable bias and duration dependence. In *Longitudinal Analyses of Labor Market Data*, ed. J. Heckman and B. Singer, New York: Academic Press.

Federal Reserve System, Board of Governors. 1950–60. Surveys of consumer finances. In various issues of the *Federal Reserve Bulletin*.

Glock, C.Y. 1967. *Survey Research in the Social Sciences*. New York: Russell Sage.

Heckman, J.J. 1979. Sample selection bias as a specification error. *Econometrica* 47(1), 153–61.

Heckman, J. 1981. Heterogeneity and state dependence. In *Studies in Labor Markets*, ed. S. Rosen, Chicago: University of Chicago Press.

Heckman, J. and Borgas, J. 1980. Does unemployment cause future unemployment? Definitions, questions and answers from a continuous time model of heterogeneity and state dependence. *Economica* 47, August, 247–83.

International Labour Office. 1961. *Family Living Studies: A Symposium*. Geneva: ILO.

Kahn, R. and Cannell, C. 1965. *Dynamics of Interviewing*. New York: Wiley.

Kalton, G. 1983. *Introduction to Survey Sampling*. Beverly Hills: Sage.

Katona, G. 1975. *Psychological Economics*. New York: Elsevier.

Kish, L. 1965. *Survey Sampling*. New York: Wiley.

Lansing, J.D. and Morgan, J.N. 1971. *Economic Survey Methods*. Ann Arbor: Institute for Social Research.

Moser, C.A. and Kalton, G. 1971. *Survey Methods in Social Investigation*. London and New York: Basic Books.

Oberschall, A. 1964. *Empirical Social Research In Germany*. Paris: Mouton & Co.

O'Muircheartaigh, C.A. and Payne, C. 1977. *The Analysis of Survey Data*. Vol. I, *Exploring Data Structures*; Vol. II, *Model Fitting*. London: Wiley.

Oppenheim, A.N. 1966. *Questionnaire Design and Attitude Measurement*. New York: Basic Books.

Rossi, P.A., Wright, J.D. and Anderson, A.B. 1983. *Handbook of Survey Research*. New York: Academic Press.

Sonquist, J.A. and Dunkelberg, W.C. 1977. *Survey and Opinion Research*. Englewood Cliffs, NJ: Prentice-Hall.

Sudman, S. 1976. *Applied Sampling*. New York: Academic Press.

Turner, C.F. and Martin, E. (eds) 1984. *Surveying Subjective Phenomena*. 2 vols, New York: Russell Sage.

Williams, F.M. and Zimmerman, C.C. 1935. *Studies of Family Living in the United States and Other Countries: An Analysis of Materials and Method*. USDA Miscellaneous Publication 223, Washington, DC: USGPO.

Zarkovic, S.S. 1966. *Quality of Statistical Data*. Rome: Food and Agriculture Organization of the United Nations.

Transformation of Statistical Variables

D. R. COX

Transformations of many kinds are used in statistical method and theory including simple changes of unit of measurement to facilitate computation or understanding, and the linear transformations underlying the application and theory of multiple regression and the techniques of classical multivariate analysis. Nevertheless the word transformation in a statistical context normally brings to mind a non-linear transformation (to logs, square roots, etc.) of basic observations done with the objective of simplifying analysis and interpretation. This essay focuses on that aspect.

Mostly we discuss problems in which variation in a univariate response variable, y, is to be explained in terms of explanatory variables $x_1, \ldots, x_p$; the terminology here is self-explanatory and avoids overuse of the words dependent and independent! We consider transformations of y and/or some or all of the explanatory variables. Note that where a number of variables are of very similar kinds, it may be sensible to insist on transforming them in the same way.

A brief historical note is desirable. Until the wide availability of computers, the majority of relatively complicated statistical analyses used the method of least squares or fairly direct elaborations thereof. Particular requirements of these methods are linear representations of the expected response, constancy of variance and normality of distribution of errors. When the data manifestly do not obey one or more of these conditions, transformation of variables provides a flexible and powerful technique for recovering a situation to which well-understood methods of analysis are reasonably applicable and thus greatly extends the range of applicability of those methods. With powerful and sometimes even flexible computing facilities now commonplace, such transformations, while remaining important, are less so than they used to be, because it is now feasible to develop special models for each specific application and to implement an appropriate analysis from first principles.

257

PURPOSE OF TRANSFORMATIONS. The key assumptions of the 'classical' methods mentioned above are (a) simplicity of structure, additivity, linearity, absence of interaction; (b) constancy of variance; (c) normality of error distribution. Independence of errors is another very important assumption, needing especially careful consideration in the case of time series data, but is not particularly relevant in the present discussion.

While the relative importance of (a)–(c) depends on the context, they are listed in broadly decreasing order of importance. Linear relations are easy to specify and understand; absence of interaction, for example that important relations retain their form for different groups of data, is important not only for understanding but also as a basis for extrapolation to new groups of data.

Constancy of variance has a triple role. If the pattern of variance is of intrinsic interest, constancy of variance is a reference level for interpretation. If the effect of explanatory variables on whole distributions is of interest, constancy of variance suggests that only changes in location need be studied. Finally constancy of variance is required for various technical statistical reasons. Appreciable changes in variance vitiate standard errors and tests of significance and will lead to a general loss of efficiency; the method of weighted least squares can be used when the nature of the changes in variance is at least roughly known.

The assumption of normality of error distributions is particularly important if the ultimate objective is prediction in the tails of a distribution. Otherwise appreciable non-normality is sometimes an indication that a quite different distributional formulation is called for, sometimes a warning about the occurrence of aberrant values in the data and more broadly is a sign of potential loss of efficiency and possible failure of tests of significance.

The possibility of approximately satisfying all three requirements simultaneously is often an expression of rational optimism, to be assumed although not taken for granted.

An important aspect of any statistical analysis is the presentation of conclusions in a single form and this may demand reinterpretation of conclusions on to the original scale of measurement.

CONSTRUCTION OF TRANSFORMATIONS. We now discuss in outline a number of techniques for choosing a suitable transformation.

The two most important techniques are probably previous experience of similar data, and the application of diagnostic checks to the analysis of untransformed data. In the latter case it may be clear that 'pulling in' either of the upper tail or of the lower tail of the data would be helpful.

To stabilize variance, a widely used technique is to establish either empirically or theoretically a relation between variance and mean. If for observations of true mean μ the variance is $v(\mu)$, then it is easy to show by local linearization that the transformation

$$y \to \int_0^y dx/\sqrt{v(x)}$$

will induce observations of approximately unit variance. A common possibility is to find $v(\mu)$ approximately of the form $a\mu^b$, often established by plotting log sample variance against log sample mean, when a line of slope b should result. This leads to a power transformation except for $b = 2$, when a log transformation is indicated. The z transformation of correlation coefficients, r,

$$r \to \tfrac{1}{2} \log\{(1 + r)/(1 - r)\}$$

is historically the first example of this argument, the relation between mean and variance being obtained theoretically.

Some simple equations expressing non-linear relations have simple linearizing transformations, of which the most common and important is the relation

$$y = \alpha x_1^{\beta_1} x_2^{\beta_2},$$

which is linearized by taking logs of all variables. A more empirical approach, not in fact much used in practice, is to search within some family of possible transformations for one which minimizes a measure of non-linearity or interaction.

A much more formal approach to the choice of a transformation is to start with some parametric family of transformations $y \to y^{(\lambda)}$ of which the most important is normally the family of power transformations, including as a limiting case the log transformation. The unknown parameter λ indexes the transformation that is appropriate. If now it is assumed that for some unknown λ the transformed values satisfy all the standard assumptions of some special convenient model, such as the normal theory general linear model, formal methods of estimation, in particular the method of maximum likelihood, can be applied to estimate λ, to see whether there is evidence that a transformation really does improve fit, to compare the values of λ in several unrelated sets of data, and so on. The calculations are relatively simple and straightforward. The usual procedure is to choose as a scale for analysis that corresponding to a simple value of λ reasonably consistent with the data.

Transformations to normality are always possible for a single continuous distribution, because any continuous distribution can be transformed into any other. Normalizing transformations are quite widely used in theoretical arguments; their direct use in the analysis of empirical data is on the whole rather less common, essentially for the reasons outlined above.

SOME FURTHER DEVELOPMENTS. The topics outlined above have an extensive literature. Some recent points of discussion and open issues are as follows:

(i) There are no good techniques for the transformation of multivariate distributions other than component by component.

(ii) Transformation selection by methods that are robust to outliers have been discussed, although in many practical situations it is the extreme observations that carry the most information about the appropriateness of transformations and whose accommodation is particularly important.

(iii) Following the choice of a transformation estimation an interpretation of effects is usually carried out on the transformed scale as if this had been given a priori. The appropriateness and justification of this has been the subject of lively discussion.

(iv) It is possible to transform to simple models other than the standard normal ones, for example to the exponential based models so useful in the analysis of duration data.

(v) The main procedures discussed above involve an interpretation essentially in terms of the expected response on the transformed scale. An alternative approach postulates that the expected value of the response on the original scale is a suitable non-linear function of a linear combination of explanatory variables. To distinguish empirically between these formulations is likely to require a large amount of high quality data.

(vi) Methods can be developed for estimating transforming functions totally non-parametrically. Such an approach uses a great deal of computer time.

BIBLIOGRAPHY

Bartlett (1943) gives an excellent account of the early work; Box and Cox (1964) discuss the estimation of transformations via the likelihood and Bayesian methods. Butter and Verbon (1982) describe economic applications in some depth. Bickel and Doksum (1981) and Box and Cox (1982) give opposing views of estimation following a transformation.

Bartlett, M.S. 1947. The use of transformations. *Biometrics* 3, 39–52.

Bickel, P.J. and Doksum, K.A. 1981. An analysis of transformations revisited. *Journal of the American Statistical Association* 76, 296–311.

Box, G.E.P. and Cox, D.R. 1964. An analysis of transformations. *Journal of the Royal Statistical Society*, Series B 26, 211–43.

Box, G.E.P. and Cox, D.R. 1982. An analysis of transformations revisited, rebutted. *Journal of the American Statistical Association* 77, 209–10.

den Butter, F.A.G. and Verbon, H.A.A. 1982. The specification problem in regression analysis. *International Statistical Review* 50, 267–83.

Transformation of Variables in Econometrics

PAUL ZAREMBKA

Economic theory usually fails to describe the functional relationship between variables (the CES production function being an exception). In econometrics, implications of simplistic choice of functional form include the danger of misspecification and its attendant biases in assessing magnitudes of effects and statistical significance of results, It is safe to say that when functional form is specified in a restrictive manner a priori before estimation, most empirical results that have been debated in the professional literature would have had a modified, even opposite, conclusion if the functional relationship had not been restrictive (see Zarembka, 1968, p. 509, for an illustration; also, Spitzer, 1976).

Most econometric research is not based on a large enough sample size for elaborate functional relationships to be meaningful. Therefore, a functional relationship which preserves additivity of effect (as in the linear model), but is more general than the usual choice between linear and linear-in-logarithmic models, ought to be sufficiently general. A transformation of variables in the form

$$y^{(\lambda)} = \begin{cases} (y^\lambda - 1)/\lambda, & \lambda \neq 0 \\ \ln y, & \lambda = 0 \end{cases}$$

offers a solution, where we note that $\lim \lambda \to 0$ in the upper expression is in fact $\ln y$, the lower expression.

Such transformations can be applied both to the dependent and independent variables with additivity of effect preserved on the transformed variable(s). The linear and linear-in-logarithmic models are both special cases ($\lambda = 1$ and $\lambda = 0$ for all variables, respectively). The transformation on the dependent variable may be different from those for the independent variables and different transformations may be applied to different independent variables, with corresponding increases in the parameter space (an obvious extension not elaborated upon here). It is important to note that a constant term must be included as an independent

261

variable in order to preserve invariance of estimates of a transformation on a variable to changes in units of measurement for that variable (Schlesselman, 1971); otherwise the form y^λ or y^λ/λ would have to be used.

Usual econometric practice with a linear model, in this case in transformed variables, is to add an error term with a normal distribution of zero mean and constant variance (actually, here, only approximately normal since negative values on a transformed dependent variable would generally be truncated). Using maximum likelihood estimation, Box and Cox (1964) follow this approach. However, Amemiya and Powell (1981) have questioned such a procedure on grounds that the error distribution must be truncated and they show with the example of a gamma distribution on the dependent variable before transformation that the Box and Cox procedure is inconsistent and typically leads to quite different results than their statistically proper procedure. Nevertheless, Draper and Cox (1969) have shown that, as long as the error term is reasonably symmetric, the Box and Cox procedure is robust. (The apparent discrepancy between Draper and Cox and Amemiya and Powell is presumably that the latters' assumed gamma distribution on the untransformed dependent variable need not imply a 'reasonably' symmetric distribution of the transformed variable. The issue deserves further research.)

Following usual practice in its assumed normality (albeit here truncated) of the error term, along with independent and identically distributed terms, the iterated ordinary least squares is conceptually the simplest procedure for estimation. If σ^2 is the constant variance of the error distribution and N is the number of observations, then the maximized log-likelihood L for given λ is, except for a constant,

$$-\tfrac{1}{2}N \ln \hat{\sigma}^2(\lambda) + (\lambda - 1) \sum_{i=1}^{N} \ln y_i,$$

or, with the specific sample of y scaled by its geometric mean so that the latter term is zero,

$$L_{\max}(\lambda) = -\tfrac{1}{2}N \ln \hat{\sigma}^2(\lambda).$$

To maximize over the whole parameter space, simply take alternative values of λ; the one that minimizes $\hat{\sigma}^2(\lambda)$ maximizes the log likelihood (a procedure almost any simple least squares programme can handle). Estimates of parameters for independent variables are also thus provided, while (as emphasized by Spitzer, 1982a, p. 311) their standard errors should be obtained from the information matrix. An approximate $100(1 - \alpha)$ per cent confidence region for λ can be obtained from

$$L_{\max}(\hat{\lambda}) - L_{\max}(\lambda) < \tfrac{1}{2}\chi_1^2(\alpha).$$

For example, for a 95 per cent confidence interval ($\alpha = 0.05$), the region can be obtained from $L_{\max}(\hat{\lambda}) - L_{\max}(\lambda) < 1.92$. (Beauchamp and Kane (1984), give a survey of other estimation procedures, including Spitzer's (1982b) modified Newton algorithm preferred by him for its greater computational efficiency.)

The above has assumed that the error distribution is homoskedastic across observations on the dependent variable as transformed by the true λ. While such an assumption is relaxingly convenient, there is no obvious justification for it. Zarembka (1974, pp. 87–95) has analysed the circumstance in which hetero-skedasticity of the error term obtains and shows that an incorrect assumption of homoskedasticity implies that the resulting maximum-likelihood procedure is biased asymptotically away from the true λ toward that transformation which more nearly stabilizes the error variance. Other parameters will also fail to be consistently estimated. For example, if the variance of the untransformed dependent variable y_i is constant, the bias is toward $\lambda = 1$; if the coefficient of variation of y_i is constant, the bias is toward $\lambda = 0$.

To estimate consistently the model under heteroskedasticity, some assumption concerning its pattern seems required. Zarembka (1974, pp. 93–5) considers the case where the variance of y_i is related to the power of the expectation of the transformed y_i. Lahiri and Egy (1981) consider the case where the variance of the transformed y_i is related to a power of any exogenous variable while Gaudry and Dagenais (1979) relate that variance to a function of several exogenous variables. Seaks and Layson (1983) consider the case where the variance of the transformed dependent variable is related to the square of one of the independent variables, while they also include autocorrelation in the error terms as an additional possibility (a problem first tackled for such transformation-of-variables models by Savin and White, 1978; see also Gaudry and Dagenais, 1979). Most show through examples the actual importance of confronting the possibility of heteroskedasticity. In the absence of specifying a structure for heteroskedasticity, Tse (1984) suggests a Lagrange multiplier test for its possible presence.

Almost all empirical uses of transformation of variables still use the conventional assumptions of normally and independently distributed error terms of constant variance (with exceptions such as Blaylock and Smallwood, 1982). In econometrics, examples of the wide range of applications of transformations of variables have included the elasticity of factor substitution in neoclassical production economics (and its possible variability), economies of scale in banking, the rate of technical progress represented in the 'Indianapolis 500', willingness to pay for automobile efficiency, economic depreciation of used buildings, capital asset pricing models, elasticities of demand for consumption (and specifically, meat, food, radios, and air quality), elasticities of the demand for money (and a possible 'liquidity trap') and for imports, demand for leisure and non-pecuniary job characteristics, relation of earnings to schooling and cognitive abilities, wage and rent gradients and the price elasticity of demand for urban housing, and elasticities of interstate migration.

BIBLIOGRAPHY

Amemiya, T. and Powell, J.L. 1981. A comparison of the Box–Cox maximum likelihood estimator and the non-linear two-stage least squares estimator. *Journal of Econometrics* 17, 351–81.

Beauchamp, J.J. and Kane, V.E. 1984. Application of the power-shift transformation. *Journal of Statistical Computation and Simulation* 19, 35–58.

Blaylock, J.R. and Smallwood, D.M. 1982. Analysis of income and food expenditure distributions: a flexible approach. *Review of Economics and Statistics* 64, 104–9.

Box, G.E.P. and Cox, D.R. 1964. An analysis of transformations. *Journal of the Royal Statistical Society*, Series B 26, 211–43.

Draper, N.R. and Cox, D.R. 1969. On distributions and their transformation to normality. *Journal of the Royal Statistical Society*, Series B 31, 472–6.

Gaudry, M.J.I. and Dagenais, M.G. 1979. Heteroskedasticity and the use of Box–Cox transformations. *Economics Letters* 2, 225–9.

Lahiri, K. and Egy, D. 1981. Joint estimation and testing for functional form and heteroskedasticity. *Journal of Econometrics* 15, 299–307.

Savin, N.E. and White, K.J. 1978. Estimation and testing for functional form and autocorrelation. *Journal of Econometrics* 8, 1–12.

Schlesselman, J. 1971. Power families: a note on the Box and Cox transformation. *Journal of the Royal Statistical Society*, Series B 33, 307–11.

Seaks, T.G. and Layson, S.K. 1983. Box–Cox estimation with standard econometric problems. *Review of Economics and Statistics* 65, 160–64.

Spitzer, J.J. 1976. The demand for money, the liquidity trap, and functional forms. *International Economic Review* 17, 220–27.

Spitzer, J.J. 1982a. A primer on Box–Cox estimation. *Review of Economics and Statistics* 64, 307–13.

Spitzer, J.J. 1982b. A fast and efficient algorithm for the estimation of parameters in models with the Box–Cox transformation. *Journal of the American Statistical Association* 77, 760–66.

Tse, Y.K. 1984. Testing for linear and log-linear regressions with heteroskedasticity. *Economics Letters* 16, 63–9.

Zarembka, P. 1968. Functional form in the demand for money. *Journal of the American Statistical Association* 63, 502–11.

Zarembka, P. 1974. Transformation of variables in econometrics. In *Frontiers in Econometrics*, ed. P. Zarembka, New York: Academic Press.

Two-stage Least Squares and the *k*-class Estimator

N.E. SAVIN

Two-stage least squares (TSLS) is a method of estimating the parameters of a single structural equation in a system of linear simultaneous equations. The TSLS estimator was proposed by Theil (1953a, 1961) and independently by Basmann (1957). The early work on simultaneous equation estimation was carried out by a group of econometricians at the Cowles Commission. This work was based on the method of maximum likelihood. Anderson and Rubin (1949) proposed the limited information maximum likelihood (LIML) estimator for the parameters of a single structural equation.

Although introduced later, TSLS was by far the most widely used method in the 1960s and the early 1970s. The explanation involves both the state of computer technology and the state of statistical knowledge among applied econometricians. By the end of the 1950s computer programs for ordinary least squares were available. These programs were simpler to use and much less costly to run than the programs for calculating LIML estimates. Among the applied econometricians relatively few had the statistical training to master Cowles Commission Monograph 14 (1953), which is the classic exposition of maximum likelihood methods of simultaneous equations estimation. Owing to advances in computer technology and, perhaps, also better statistical training, the popularity of TSLS started to wane by the end of the 1970s. In particular, the cost of calculating LIML estimates was no longer an important constraint.

There are many structural estimators in addition to TSLS and LIML. The problem is to decide which estimator to use. The presumption is that choice depends on the statistical properties of the estimators and how the estimators compare. The statistical properties have been intensively investigated in the case of a model of a single structural equation with normal errors and no lagged dependent variables. In this case some useful results have been recently established on the comparison of estimators. In order to discuss these results certain statistical concepts have to be introduced. I shall try to present these concepts informally, but with enough rigour so as not to be misleading. More research is required to establish the statistical properties of estimators for models with non-normal error specifications and for models with dynamics.

The model with normal errors and no lagged dependent variables is presented in section 1. Section 2 defines the concept of a consistent estimator and discusses the properties of the least squares method. Section 3 shows that there is an abundance of consistent estimators and section 4 defines the property of asymptotic efficiency. Some interpretations of the TSLS method are given in section 5 and the k-class family of estimators is defined in section 6. The results on the comparison of estimators are reported in section 7 and the concluding comments are in section 8.

1. THE MODEL. Consider the structural equation

$$y = Y\gamma + X_1\beta + u = Z\delta + u, \tag{1.1}$$

where y is a $T \times 1$ vector and Y is a $T \times (L-1)$ matrix of observations on the included endogenous variables and X_1 is a $T \times K_1$ matrix of observations on the included exogenous variables. It is assumed that the system can be solved for y and Y in terms of the exogenous variables and the errors. The solution is called the reduced form of the system. The reduced form can be written as

$$[y, Y] = [X_1, S_2]\begin{bmatrix} \pi_1 & \Pi_1 \\ \pi_2 & \Pi_2 \end{bmatrix} + [v, V]$$
$$= X[\pi, \Pi] + [v, V], \tag{1.2}$$

where X_2 is a $T \times K_2$ matrix of observations on the exogenous variables excluded from (1.1) but appearing elsewhere in the system. It is assumed that $X = [X_1, X_2]$ is a matrix of constants and has full column rank. The rows of $[v, v]$ are assumed to be independent normal vectors with mean zero and positive definite covariance matrix

$$\Omega = \begin{bmatrix} \omega_{11} & \omega_{12}^T \\ \omega_{12} & \Omega_{22} \end{bmatrix}. \tag{1.3}$$

In other words, the rows of $[y, Y]$ are independently normally distributed with conditional means given by the rows of $X[\pi, \Pi]$ and with the same conditional covariance matrix which is given by Ω.

In Tintner's (1952, pp. 176–9) two equation model of the American meat market the endogenous variables are meat consumption and meat price and the exogenous variables are disposable income, the unit cost of meat processing and the cost of agricultural production. The demand equation omits the cost variables.

The relation between the structural parameters and the reduced form parameters is found by post-multiplying the reduced form (1.2) by the vector $[1, \gamma^T]^T$. This gives relations

$$\pi_1 - \Pi_1 \gamma = \beta, \tag{1.4}$$

$$\pi_2 - \Pi_2 \gamma = 0 \tag{1.5}$$

and

$$u = v - V\gamma. \tag{1.6}$$

The coefficients of the structural equation (1.1) are identified if they can be uniquely determined from knowledge of $[\pi, \Pi]$. If rank $\Pi_2 = \text{rank}[\pi_2, \Pi_2] = L - 1$, then (1.5) can be solved for a unique value of γ. Given a value of γ, (1.4) uniquely determines β. Hence, the rank condition for identification is that rank $\Pi_2 = \text{rank}[\pi_2, \Pi_2]$. It is assumed that the rank condition for identification is satisfied and hence that the so-called order condition, $K_2 \geqslant L - 1$, is also satisfied. From (1.6) it follows that the components of u are independently normally distributed with mean zero and variance $\sigma^2 = \omega_{11} - 2\omega_{12}\gamma + \gamma^T W_{22}\gamma$. For an exposition of simultaneous equation models see Hausman (1983).

2. ORDINARY LEAST SQUARES. The problem is to find an estimator of the parameters γ and β which has good statistical properties. An obvious question is whether ordinary least squares (OLS) is a good estimator. The answer depends on whether a certain correlation is zero.

An estimation method defines a random variable for each sample size and hence a sequence of random variables indexed by the sample size. A sequence of random variables $\{X_n\}$ is said to converge to a constant c in probability if

$$\lim_{n \to \infty} P(|X_n - c| > \varepsilon) = 0, \quad \text{for any } \varepsilon > 0.$$

We write p $\lim X_n = c$. A sequence of $n \times m$ random matrices is said to converge in probability if each element converges. Let θ_T be an estimator of the parameter θ which converges to θ_0 in probability where θ_0 denotes the true parameter value. The estimator θ_T is said to be a consistent estimator for θ.

The OLS estimator of δ is

$$d = [Z^T Z]^{-1} Z^T y = \delta + [Z^T Z]^{-1} Z^T u. \tag{2.1}$$

If this estimator converges in probablity to a constant, then that constant is given by

$$\text{p} \lim d = \delta + [\text{p} \lim Z^T Z / T]^{-1} \text{p} \lim Z^T u / T. \tag{2.2}$$

It is conventional to impose assumptions on X such that as the sample size increases the term in square brackets converges in probability to a matrix of constants and the correlation between X and $[v, V]$ and hence between X and

u converges in probability to zero. The OLS estimator is consistent if

$$\text{p lim } Y^T u / T = \text{p lim} [X\Pi + V]^T u / T$$

$$= \text{p lim } V^T u / T = w_{12} - \Omega_{22}\gamma = 0, \qquad (2.3)$$

where (2.3) is the correlation between the tth component of u and the tth row of V. Observe that the correlation between Y and u is zero if

$$\gamma = \Omega_{22}^{-1}\omega_{12}. \qquad (2.4)$$

It is instructive to examine this condition in more detail. The joint normality of y and Y implies that the conditional density of y given Y is normal where the mean of the conditional density is linear in Y:

$$E(y \mid Y) = E(y) + [Y - E(Y)]\Omega_{22}^{-1}\omega_{12} \qquad (2.5)$$

$$= [E(y) - E(Y)\alpha] + Y\alpha,$$

where $\alpha = \Omega_{22}^{-1}\omega_{12}$ is the true slope coefficient in the regression of y on Y. This provides an interpretation for the value of γ which makes the correlation between Y and u equal zero. If $\alpha = \gamma$, then $E(y \mid Y) = Y\gamma + X_1\beta$ which in turn implies that OLS estimator is not only consistent but also unbiased for the structural parameters.

Under the normality assumption, if Y and u are uncorrelated, then Y is said to be weakly exogenous for the structural coefficients γ and β. See Engle, Hendry and Richard (1983). The reason OLS is not used is that the weak exogeneity condition is typically not satisfied. There are a number of different tests for weak exogeneity. Examples are the Revankar and Hartley (1973) test and the Wu (1973) and Hausman (1978) test. For further discussion of weak exogeneity tests see Engle (1984).

3. A PLETHORA OF CONSISTENT ESTIMATORS. When the weak exogeneity condition fails the OLS estimator is not consistent. In fact, there is an abundant supply of consistent estimators. The standard textbook treatment of structural estimation usually begins with the indirect least squares (ILS) method. The starting point for this method is the sample analogue of (1.5):

$$p_2 = P_2 g \qquad (3.1)$$

where $[p_2, P_2]$ is the OLS estimate of the $K_2 \times L$ reduced form coefficient matrix $[\pi_2, \Pi_2]$. The OLS estimator is

$$[p_2, P_2] = [X_2^T M_1 X_2]^{-1} X_2^T M_1 [y, Y], \qquad (3.2)$$

where $M_1 = I - X_1^T [X_1^T X_1]^{-1} X_1$ and $X_2^T M_1 X_2$ is the sum of squared residuals from the OLS regression of X_2 on X_1. Since the reduced form equations satisfy the assumptions of the classical normal linear regression model, the OLS estimator (3.2) is minimum variance unbiased and consistent.

The structural equation (1.1) is defined to be just-identified if $K_2 = L - 1$ and over-identified if $K_2 \geqslant L - 1$. Since it is assumed that the structural equation (1.1) is identified, the rank of Π_2 and of P_2 is $L - 1$. If $K_2 = L - 1$, the rank of $[p_2, P_2]$ is $L - 1$ so that p_2 is in the column space of P_2. Hence, when the equation is just-identified the estimator defined by (3.1) is given by

$$\dot{\gamma} = P_2^{-1} p_2 \qquad\qquad (3.3)$$

since P_2 is square. This is the ILS estimator and it is easy to show that it is consistent since $[p_2, P_2]$ is consistent for $[\pi_2, \Pi_2]$. Once the estimate of γ is uniquely determined, the sample analogue of (1.4) is used to determine the estimate of β. The ILS method is available only in the just-identified case. This is because when $K_2 > L - 1$ the rank of $[p_2, P_2]$ is L with probability one so that (3.1) has no solution.

In the over-identified case there are several possibilities of obtaining a consistent estimator. One is to throw enough rows of $[p_2, P_2]$ to bring its rank down to $L - 1$. As Goldberger (1964, p. 328) remarks, consistent estimates are still obtained, but this procedure is not recommended since it is arbitrary and since discarding information results in a loss of efficiency. A consistent estimator of γ can be obtained by regressing p_2 on P_2. This gives the estimator

$$\gamma^* = [P_2^{\mathsf{T}} P_2]^{-1} P_2^{\mathsf{T}} p_2. \qquad\qquad (3.4)$$

This estimator does not have any of the disadvantages noted above by Goldberger. When the question is just-identified it reduces to the ILS estimator.

If the rank of $[p_2, P_2]$ were always $L - 1$ and if the aim were to obtain an estimator with good large sample properties, then the analysis of structural estimation need go no further. This is because ILS is not only consistent, but asymptotically efficient.

4. A MATTER OF EFFICIENCY. A widely used criterion for choosing among consistent estimators is asymptotic efficiency. Asymptotic efficiency is defined for estimators which have limiting normal distributions. A sequence of random variables $\{X_n\}$ is said to converge to a variable X in distribution if the distribution function F_n of X_n converges to the distribution function F of X at every continuity point of F. The distribution function F is called the limit distribution of $\{X_n\}$. For consistent estimators the limit distribution is simply a point. Under appropriate general conditions TSLS and LIML are consistent and when normalized by multiplying by the square root of the sample size both estimators converge in distribution to the same limiting (asymptotic) normal distribution, where the covariance matrix of the limiting normal distribution is the inverse of the standardized Fisher information matrix. This convariance matrix is also referred to as the Cramer–Rao lower bound.

In the class of consistent and asymptotically normal (CAN) estimators of the parameter θ the mean of the limiting normal distribution is equal to the true parameter value, say θ_0, for all estimators in the class. On the other hand, the covariance matrix of the limiting normal distribution, which is called the asymptotic variance, may be different for different CAN estimators. Hence it is natural to define the best CAN estimator as the one with the smallest asymptotic variance. At one time statisticians believed that the minimum asymptotic variance was given by the Cramer–Rao lower bound. This was proved wrong, but despite this, there are good reasons for continuing the practice of defining a CAN estimator to be asymptotically efficient if it achieves the Cramer–Rao lower bound. An asymptotically efficient estimator is said to be best asymptotically normal or BAN for short. For a discussion of asymptotic efficiency see Amemiya (1985, Ch. 4).

From the point of view of large sample properties the reason TSLS merits attention is that it is a BAN estimator. In the just-identified case ILS is identically equal to the TSLS and the LIML estimators and hence is a BAN estimator. As will become apparent, in the over-identified case there are many BAN estimators in addition to TSLS and LIML.

5. TWO STAGE LEAST SQUARES. The TSLS estimator is defined by

$$\hat{\delta} = [Z^T X (X^T X)^{-1} X^T Z]^{-1} Z^T X (X^T X)^{-1} X^T y. \tag{5.1}$$

Theil (1971, ch. 9.5) gives two interpretations for this formula. In the first the structural equation (1.1) is multiplied by $(X^T X)^{-1} X^T$:

$$(X^T X)^{-1} X^T y = (X^T X)^{-1} X^T Y \gamma + (X^T X)^{-1} X_1 \beta$$
$$+ (X^T X)^{-1} X^T u$$
$$p = P\gamma + (X^T X)^{-1} X^T X_1 \beta + (X^T X)^{-1} X^T u. \tag{5.2}$$

The error term $(X^T X)^{-1} X^T u$ is normally distributed with mean zero and covariance matrix $\sigma^2 (X^T X)^{-1}$ and the correlation between P and $(X^T X)^{-1} X^T u$ converges in probability to zero:

$$\mathrm{p} \lim [(P - \Pi)^T (X^T X/T)^{-1} (X^T u/T)]$$
$$= \mathrm{p} \lim [(V^T X/T)(X^T X/T)^{-1} (X^T X/T)^{-1} (X^T u/T)]$$
$$= 0 \tag{5.3}$$

when assumptions are imposed on X such that $X^T X/T$ converges to a non-singular matrix of constants and $X^T V/T$ and $X^T u/T$ both converge in probability to zero. Since in large samples (5.2) approximately satisfies the assumptions of the generalized normal linear regression model, it is tempting to apply generalized least squares (GLS) to (5.2) to estimate δ. The GLS estimator is obtained by multiplying (5.2) by $(X^T X)^{1/2}$ and applying OLS. This yields the TSLS estimator. The TSLS estimator does not have the finite sample properties of the GLS estimator in the generalized normal linear regression model since (5.2) does not fully satisfy the assumptions of that model. Proofs of the large sample properties of TSLS are given in Theil (1971, ch. 10) and Amemiya (1985, ch. 7).

The second interpretation is the source of the name TSLS. Write the structural equation (1.1) as

$$y = [X\Pi, X_1]\begin{bmatrix} \gamma \\ \beta \end{bmatrix} + u + (Y - X\Pi)\gamma. \tag{5.4}$$

Since the matrix $[X\Pi, X_1]$ is not stochastic, it is not correlated with the compound error term $u + (Y - X\Pi)\pi$. It is easy to show that rows of this error term are independently normally distributed with zero mean and constant variance. Hence, the obvious estimation procedure is to apply OLS to (5.4). The difficult is that Π is unknown. The solution to this difficulty is a two-stage procedure. In the first stage, the portion of the reduced form equation (1.2) which is for Y is estimated by OLS in order to obtain an estimate of Π. The OLS estimator of Π is $P = [X^TX]^{-1}X^TY$. In the second stage XP is substituted for $X\Pi$ in (5.4), or, equivalently, for Y in the structural equation (1.1), and the resulting equation is estimated by OLS. The estimates of γ and β are the TSLS estimates.

The next two interpretations of TSLS use the sample analogue of (1.4) as a starting point. The TSLS estimator of γ is defined by

$$\dot{\gamma} = [P_2^T X_2 M_1 X_2 P_2]^{-1} P_2^T X_2^T M_1 X_2 p_2, \tag{5.5}$$

from which it is easy to verify that TSLS reduces to the ILS in the just-identified case. Anderson and Sawa (1973) provide a motivation for this formula. Premultiplying the structural equation (1.1) by $[X_2^T M_1 X_2]^{-1} X_2^T M_1$ gives

$$p_2 = P_2\gamma + w, \tag{5.6}$$

where w is normally distributed with zero mean and covariance $\omega^2 [X_2^T M_1 X_2]^{-1}$, where ω^2 is Ω pre- and postmultiplied by $[1, -\gamma^T]^T$. Since the correlation between P_2 and w converges in probability to zero, in large samples (5.6) approximately satisfies the assumptions of the generalized linear regression model. Applying generalized least squares (GLS) to (5.6) gives (5.5). Another interpretation of (5.5) is that it is the estimator which minimizes

$$[1, -g^T] W_1 \begin{bmatrix} 1 \\ -g \end{bmatrix} = (p_2 - P_2 g)^T X_2^T M_1 X_2 (p_2 - P_2 g), \tag{5.7}$$

where $W_1 = [y, Y]^T M_1 [y, Y]$ is the matrix of the sum of squared residuals from the OLS regression of $[y, Y]$ on X_1. The expression (5.7) is the GLS criterion function for (5.6) since the GLS estimator minimizes (5.7), that is, the TSLS estimator (5.5) minimizes (5.7).

6. THE *k*-CLASS FAMILY. The *k*-class family of estimators of δ is defined by

$$\hat{\delta}_k = [Z^T(I - kM)Z]^{-1} Z^T(I - kM)y, \tag{6.1}$$

where $M = I - X(X^TX)^{-1}X$. This family was introduced by Theil (1953b, 1961). It includes the OLS estimator ($k = 0$) and the TSLS estimator ($k = 1$).

A remarkable fact is that the *k*-class family also includes LIML. The LIML estimator is obtained by setting $k = \lambda_0$, where λ_0 is the smallest root of

$$| W_1 - \lambda W | = 0. \tag{6.2}$$

In the determinantal equation W_1, which is defined in section 5, is the sum of squared residuals from the OLS regression of $[y, Y]$ on X_1 and

$$W = [y. Y]^T M [y. Y]$$

which is the sum of squared residuals from a regression of $[y, Y]$ on X. The LIML estimator of γ minimizes the variance ratio

$$\frac{[1, -g^T] W_1 \begin{bmatrix} 1 \\ -g \end{bmatrix}}{[1, -g^T] W \begin{bmatrix} 1 \\ -g \end{bmatrix}}. \tag{6.3}$$

Another interpretation of LIML is that it maximizes the likelihood function of $[y, Y]$ subject to the restriction $\pi_2 - \Pi_2 \gamma = 0$.

The k-class estimator $\hat{\delta}_k$ is consistent if p $\lim(k - 1) = 0$ and has the same limiting distribution as TSLS if p $\lim T^{1/2}(k - 1) = 0$. These conditions are clearly not satisfied when $k = 0$ and hence by OLS. The proof that these conditions are satisfied for LIML is based on a result in Anderson and Rubin (1950).

7. EXACT DISTRIBUTIONS AND SECOND ORDER APPROXIMATIONS. The limiting distribution of an estimator is an approximation to the finite sample distribution where the accuracy of the approximation gets better as the sample size increases. The exact finite sample distributions of TSLS and LIML are different. This illustrates the fact that not all the BAN estimators have the same finite sample distribution. The question is whether the differences in the finite sample distributions are important when choosing a BAN estimator. The answer depends on the sample size used in estimation of simultaneous equation models.

The accuracy of the limiting normal approximation to the distributions of the TSLS and LIML estimators has been investigated for the case of two endogenous variables. In these studies the two estimators are normalized such that the limiting distribution is standard normal. From a study of the tables and graphs of the distributions Anderson (1982) concludes:

> For many cases that occur in practice (perhaps most), the standard normal theory is inadequate for the TSLS estimator. Even though the moments of the LIML estimator are not finite, the standard normal distribution is a fairly good approximation to the actual distribution.

This finding implies that in many cases of practical interest the differences between the finite sample distributions of TSLS and LIML are important when deciding which estimator to use.

There are several ways to compare BAN estimators on the basis of finite sample properties. One is to use the exact distributions of the estimators. The exact finite sample distributions of TSLS and LIML have been examined using analytical and Monte Carlo techniques. For a survey of the results see Phillips (1983). The exact distributions are usually very complicated and as a result it is difficult to draw meaningful general conclusions. It is also difficult to draw general conclusions from the Monte Carlo studies.

Another approach is to use an approximation which is closer to the exact distribution. Let θ_T be a BAN estimator of the parameter θ. The procedure is to approximate the distribution of $T^{1/2}(\theta_T - \theta)$ by the first three terms in an asymptotic expansion of the distribution in powers of $T^{-1/2}$: the expansion of the distribution is to terms of order $0(T^{-1})$ where the first term in the expansion is the limiting normal distribution of the BAN estimator. This expansion is described as second-order by some statisticians and third-order by others. We will use the former description and call the distribution based on this expansion the second-order approximate distribution. The first moment of this distribution is the (second-order) approximate bias of the estimator and the mean squared error is the (second-order) approximate mean squared error. For an excellent treatment of second-order asymptotic theory see Rothenberg (1984).

Anderson, Kunitomo and Morimune (1986) compared various single equation estimators on the basis of second-order approximate distributions. One criterion used for comparing alternative estimators was the approximate mean squared error. Another was the probability of concentration of the second-order approximate distribution about the true parameter value. They show that approximate mean squared errors of the fixed k-class estimators are greater than or equal to that of a modified LIML estimator. Similar results are obtained using the probability of concentration. As a consequence, they do not recommend using the fixed k-class estimators including the TSLS estimator.

A BAN estimator can be approximately corrected for bias by subtracting the approximate bias. Since the approximate bias will generally depend on the unknown parameter, this parameter is replaced by its BAN estimator to give an (second-order) approximate unbiased estimator. Under certain regularity conditions on the large sample expansions Takeuchi and Morimune (1985) prove that the approximate unbiased LIML estimator is second-order efficient: in the class of all approximate unbiased BAN estimators the approximate mean squared error of the approximate unbiased LIML estimator is at least as small as that of any other estimator. In this context the approximate mean squared error is equal to the second-order approximate variance. Anderson and his associates (1985) prove that the property of second-order efficiency is shared by other estimators including a Bayes estimator proposed by Dreze (1976) and a modification of LIML proposed by Fuller (1977). The approximate unbiased TSLS estimator is not second-order efficient.

The distribution of an estimator can also be approximated by expanding the distribution in powers of the structural error variance σ and letting σ go to zero. Anderson and his associates also compare the estimators using the small disturbance expansion. This does not alter the recommendations even though the uniform domination by one estimator over others is not necessarily obtainable using small disturbance expansions.

8. CONCLUSION. There is a caveat which must be kept in mind when considering the results reported by Anderson (1982) and Anderson et al. (1986). These results are for the model specified in section 1. The model may not be plausible in many empirical applications owing to the presence of non-stationary and possibly non-normal errors. In particular, the covariance matrix of the errors may be time varying. Most of the models which have been estimated incorporate dynamics. The dynamic specification and the values of the roots of the associated characteristic equation may have an important influence on the finite sample distributions. The next step is to examine the finite sample distributions in models with more general error processes and in models with dynamics. Taking this next step seems to be a difficult one and so the final verdict on TSLS has still to be reached.

BIBLIOGRAPHY

Amemiya, T. 1985. *Advanced Econometrics*. Cambridge, Mass.: Harvard University Press.
Anderson, T.W. 1982. Some recent developments on the distribution of single-equation estimators. In *Advances in Econometrics*, ed. W. Hildenbrand, Cambridge: Cambridge University Press.
Anderson, T.W. and Rubin, H. 1949. Estimator of the parameters of a single equation in a complete system of stochastic equations. *Annals of Mathematical Statistics* 20, 46–63.
Anderson, T.W. and Rubin, H. 1950. The asymptotic properties of estimates of the parameters of a single equation in a complete system of stochastic equations. *Annals of Mathematical Statistics* 21, 570–82.
Anderson, T.W. and Sawa, T. 1973. Distributions of estimates of coefficients of a single equation in a simultaneous system and their asymptotic expansions. *Econometrica* 41, 683–714.
Anderson, T.W., Kunitomo, N. and Morimune, K. 1986. Comparing single equation estimators in a simultaneous equation system. *Econometric Theory* 2, 1–32.
Basmann, R.L. 1957. A generalized classical method of linear estimation of coefficients in a structural equation. *Econometrica* 25, 77–83.
Drèze, J.H. 1976. Bayesian limited information analysis of the simultaneous equations model. *Econometrica* 44, 1045–75.
Engle, R.F. 1984. Wald likelihood ratio and Lagrange multiplier tests. In *Handbook of Econometrics*, ed. Z. Griliches and M.D. Intriligator, Amsterdam: North-Holland.
Engle, R.F., Hendry, D.F. and Richard, J.-F. 1983. Exogeneity, *Econometrica* 51(2), 227–304.
Fuller, W.A. 1977. Some properties of a modification of the limited information estimator. *Econometrica* 45, 939–53.
Goldberger, A.S. 1964. *Econometric Theory*. New York: John Wiley.
Hausman, J. 1978. Specification tests in econometrics. *Econometrica* 46, 1251–71.
Hausman, J. 1983. Specification and estimation of simultaneous equation models. In *Handbook of Econometrics*, ed. Z. Griliches and M.D. Intriligator, Amsterdam: North-Holland.
Koopmans, T.C. and Hood, W.C. 1953. The estimation of simultaneous linear economic

relationships. In *Studies in Econometric Method*, ed. W.C. Hood and T.C. Koopmans, New York: John Wiley.

Phillips, P.C.B. 1983. Exact small sample theory in the simultaneous equation model. In *Handbook of Econometrics*, ed. Z. Griliches and M.D. Intriligator, Amsterdam: North-Holland.

Revankar, H.S. and Hartley, M.J. 1973. An independence test and conditional unbiased predictions in the context of simultaneous equation systems. *International Economic Review* 14, 625–31.

Rothenberg, T.J. 1984. Approximating the distributions of econometric estimators and test statistics. In *Handbook of Econometrics*, ed. Z. Griliches and M.D. Intriligator, Amsterdam: North-Holland.

Takeuchi, K. and Morimune, K. 1985. Third-order efficiency of the extended maximum likelihood estimator in a simultaneous equation system. *Econometrica* 53, 177–200.

Theil, H. 1953a. Repeated least-squares applied to complete equation systems. The Hague: Central Planning Bureau (mimeographed).

Theil, H. 1953b. Estimation and simultaneous correlation in complete equation systems. The Hague: Central Planning Bureau (mimeographed).

Theil, H. 1961. *Economic Forecasts and Policy.* 2nd edn, Amsterdam: North-Holland.

Theil, H. 1971. *Principles of Econometrics.* New York: John Wiley.

Tintner, G. 1952. *Econometrics.* New York: John Wiley.

Wu, De-Min. 1973. Alternative tests of independence between stochastic regressors and disturbances. *Econometrica* 41, 733–50.

Wiener Process

A.G. MALLIARIS

Brownian motion is the most renowned, and historically the first stochastic process that was thoroughly investigated. It is named after the English botanist, Robert Brown who in 1827 observed that small particles immersed in a liquid exhibited ceaseless irregular motion. Brown himself mentions several precursors starting at the beginning with Leeuwenhoek (1632–1723). In 1905 Einstein, unaware of the existence of earlier investigations about Brownian motion, obtained a mathematical derivation of this process from the laws of physics. The theory of Brownian motion was further developed by several distinguished mathematical physicists until Norbert Wiener gave it a rigorous mathematical formulation in his 1918 dissertation and in later papers. This is why the Brownian motion is also called the Wiener process. For a brief history of the scientific developments of the process see Nelson (1967).

Having made these remarks we now define the process. A *Wiener process* or a *Brownian motion process*

$$\{Z(t, \omega): [0, \infty) \times \Omega \to R\}$$

is a stochastic process with index $t \in [0, \infty)$ on a probability space Ω, and mapping to the real line R, with the following properties:

(1) $Z(0, \omega) = 0$ with probability 1, that is by convention we assume that the process starts at zero.

(2) If $0 \leqslant t_0 \leqslant t_1 \leqslant \cdots \leqslant t_n$ are time points then for any real set H_i

$$P[Z(t_i) - Z(t_{i-1}) \in H_i \text{ for } i \leqslant n] = \prod_{i \leqslant n} P[Z(t_i) - Z(t_{i-1}) \in H_i].$$

This means that the increments of the process $Z(t_i) - Z(t_{i-1})$, $i \leqslant n$, are independent variables.

(3) For $0 \leqslant s < t$, the increment $Z(t) - Z(s)$ has distribution

$$P[Z(t) - Z(s) \in H] = (1/\sqrt{2\pi(t-s)}) \int_H \exp[-x^2/2(t-s)] \, dx.$$

This means that every increment $Z(t) - Z(s)$ is normally distributed with mean zero and variance $(t-s)$.

(4) For each $\omega \in \Omega$, $Z(t, \omega)$ is continuous in t, for $t \geqslant 0$.

Note that condition (4) can be proved mathematically using the first three conditions. Here it is added because in many applications such continuity is essential. Although the sample paths of the Wiener process are continuous, we immediately state an important theorem about their differentiability properties.

Theorem. (Non-differentiability of the Wiener process.) Let $\{Z(t), t \geqslant 0\}$ be a Wiener process in a given probability space. Then for ω outside some set of probability 0, the sample path $Z(t, \omega)$, $t \geqslant 0$, is nowhere differentiable.

Intuitively, a nowhere differentiable sample path represents the motion of a particle which at no time has a velocity. Thus, although the sample paths are continuous, this theorem suggests that they are very kinky, and their derivatives exist nowhere. The mathematical theory of the Wiener process is briefly presented in Billingsley (1979) and more extensively in Knight (1981).

The first application of Brownian motion or the Wiener process in economics was made by Louis Bachelier in his dissertation 'Théorie de la spéculation' in 1900. Cootner (1964) collects several papers and cites additional references on the application of the Wiener process in describing the random character of the stock market. In the early 1970s Merton, in a series of papers, established the use of stochastic calculus as a tool in financial economics. The Wiener process is a basic concept in stochastic calculus and its applicability in economics arises from the fact that the Wiener process can be regarded as the limit of a continuous time *random walk* as step sizes become infinitesimally small. In other words, the Wiener process can be used as the cornerstone in modelling *economic uncertainty* in continuous time. For purposes of illustration consider the stochastic differential equation

$$dX(t) = \mu(t, x) \, dt + \sigma(t, x) \, dZ(t) \tag{1}$$

which appears in the economic literature describing asset prices, rate of inflation, quantity of money or other variables. In (1), changes in the variable $X(t)$, denoted as $dX(t)$, are described as a sum of two terms: $\mu(t, x)$ which is the *expected* instantaneous change and $\sigma(t, x) \, dZ(t)$ which is the *unexpected* change. Furthermore, this unexpected change is the product of the instantaneous standard deviation $\sigma(t, x)$ and uncertainty modelled by increments in the Wiener process. See Merton (1975) for a methodological essay on continuous time modelling and Malliaris and Brock (1982) or Harrison (1985) for numerous applications of the Wiener process in economics and business.

Economists have constructed various processes based on the Wiener process. Let $\{Z(t), t \geqslant 0\}$ be a Wiener process and use it to construct a process $\{W(t),$

$t \geqslant 0\}$ defined by $W(t) = Z(t) + \mu t$, $t \geqslant 0$, where μ is a constant. Then we say that $\{W(t), t \geqslant 0\}$ is a *Wiener process* or *Brownian motion process with drift* and μ is called the drift parameter. In this case the only modification that occurs in the definition of a Wiener process is in property (3) where $W(t) - W(s)$ is normally distributed with mean $\mu(t - s)$ and variance $(t - s)$. Finally, let $W(t)$ be a Wiener process with drift as just defined. Consider the new process given by $Y(t) = \exp[W(t)]$, $t \geqslant 0$. Then $\{Y(t), t \geqslant 0\}$ is called a *geometric Brownian motion* or *geometric Wiener process*.

The availability of an extensive mathematical literature on the Wiener process and the economists' fundamental goal to model economic uncertainty in continuous time suggest that this process will continue to be an important tool for economic theorists.

BIBLIOGRAPHY

Billingsley, P. 1979. *Probability and Measure*. New York: John Wiley.

Cootner, P.H. 1964. *The Random Character of Stock Market Prices*, Cambridge, Mass. MIT Press.

Harrison, J.M. 1985. *Brownian Motion and Stochastic Flow Systems*. New York: John Wiley.

Knight, F.B. 1981. *Essentials of Brownian Motion and Diffusion*. Mathematical Surveys, Number 18. The American Mathematical Society, Providence, Rhode Island.

Malliaris, A.G. and Brock, W.A. 1982. *Stochastic Methods in Economics and Finance*. Amsterdam: North-Holland Publishing Company.

Merton, R.C. 1975. Theory of finance from the perspective of continuous time. *Journal of Financial and Quantitative Analysis* 10, 659–74.

Nelson, E. 1967. *Dynamical Theories of Brownian Motion*. Princeton, New Jersey: Princeton University Press.

Contributors

Irma Adelman Professor of Economics, University of California, Berkeley. Fellow, Econometric Society; Member, National Academy of Sciences; Vice President, American Economic Association (1979–80). *Theories of Economic Growth and Development* (1958); *Society, Politics and Economic Development: a quantitative approach* (1967); *Practical Approaches to Development Planning – Korea's second five year plan* (1969); *Economic Growth and Social Equity in Developing Countries* (1973); *Income Distribution Policy in Developing Countries: a case study of Korea* (1978).

Dennis J. Aigher Dean, Graduate School of Management, University of California. Fulbright Scholar (1970–1); Fellow, Econometric Society. 'On estimating the industry production function', *American Economic Review* (with S. Chu, 1968); 'Estimation of Pareto's law from grouped observations', *Journal of the American Statistical Association* (with A.S. Goldberger, 1970); 'Estimation and prediction from aggregate data when aggregates are measured more accurately than their components', *Econometrica* (with S.M. Goldfeld, 1974); 'Formulation and estimation of stochastic frontier production functions', *Journal of Econometrics* (with C.A.K. Lovell and P. Schmidt, 1979); 'Estimation of time-of-use pricing response in the absence of experimental data: an application of the methodology of data transferability', *Journal of Econometrics* (with E. Leamer, 1984); 'Me and my shadow: estimating the size of the U.S. underground economy from time series data' (with F. Schneider and D. Ghosh) in *Dynamic Econometric Modelling* (ed. W. Barnett, 1988).

T. Amemiya Edward Ames Edmonds Professor of Economics, Stanford University. Fellow, American Academy of Arts and Sciences; Guggenheim Fellowship. 'Regression analysis when the dependent variable is truncated normal', *Econometrica* (1973); 'Multivariate regression and simultaneous equation models when the dependent variables are truncated normal', *Econometrica* (1974); 'The nonlinear two stage least squares estimator', *Journal of Econometrics* (1974); 'The maximum likelihood and the nonlinear three-stage least squares estimator in the general nonlinear simultaneous equation model', *Econometrica* (1977); *Advanced Econometrics* (1985).

Pietro Balestra Professor, Department of Economics, University of Geneva. Fellow, Econometric Society, 'Pooling cross-section and time series data in the estimation of dynamic models: the demand for natural gas', *Econometrica* (1966); 'Best quadratic unbiased estimators of the variance–covariance matrix in normal regression', *Journal of Econometrics* (1973); 'Full information estimation of a system of simultaneous equations with error component structure', *Econometric Theory* (with J. Krshnaknmar, 1987); 'Optimal experimental design for error component models', *Econometrica* (with D.J. Aigner, 1988).

James R. Barth Director, Office of Policy and Economic Research, Federal Home Loan Bank. 'The rational expectations approach of economic modelling', *Journal of Economic Dynamics and Control* (with P.A.V.B. Swamy and Peter Tinsley, 1982); 'The effect of government regulations on personal loan markets: a tobit estimation of a microeconomic model', *Journal of Finance* (with P. Gotur, N. Manage and A. Yezer, 1983); 'Benefits and costs of legal restrictions on personal markets', *Journal of Law and Economics* (with J. Cordes and A. Yezer, 1986); 'Government debt, government spending, and private sector behavior: comment', *American Economic Review* (with G. Iden and F. Russek, 1986); 'The evolving role of regulation in the savings and loan industry' (with Martin A. Regalia) in *The Financial Services Revolution: policy directions for the future* (ed. Catherine England and Thomas F. Huertas, 1988); 'On interest rates, inflationary expectations and tax rates', *Journal of Banking and Finance* (with Michael Bradley, forthcoming).

Charles E. Bates Assistant Professor, Johns Hopkins University. 'An asymptotic theory of consistent estimation for parametric models', *Econometric Theory* (with H. White, 1985); 'Efficient instrumental variables estimation of systems of implicit heterogeneous nonlinear dynamic equations with nonspherical errors' (with H. White) in *International Symposia in Economic Theory and Econometrics* (1988).

Olivier J. Blanchard Professor, MIT. Fellow, Econometric Society; Co-editor, *Quarterly Journal of Economics*. 'Speculative bubbles, crashes and rational expectations', *Economic Letters* (1979); 'Output, the stock market and interest rates', *American Economic Review* (1981); 'The production and inventory behaviour of the U.S. automobile industry', *Journal of Political Economy* (1983); 'Deficits, debt and finite horizons', *Journal of Political Economy* (1985); 'Hysteresis and European unemployment' in *Macroeconomics Annual* (ed. Stanley Fischer, 1986); *Lectures on Macroeconomics* (with Stanley Fischer, 1988).

Wilfred Corlett Emeritus Reader in Political Economy, University of London (retired). 'The Influence of price in international trade: a study in method', *Journal of the Royal Statistical Society* (with D.J. Morgan, 1951); 'Complementarity and the excess burden of taxation', *Review of Economic Studies* (1953); *The Economic Development of Detergents* (1958); *Report on the Study of Trends in Building Prices* (with M.E.A. Bowley, 1970).

Ray C. Fair Professor, Cowles Foundation, Department of Economics, Yale University. *The Short-Run Demand for Workers and Hours* (1969); 'The estimation of simultaneous equation models with lagged endogenous variables and first order serially correlated errors', *Econometrica* (1970); 'The optimal distribution of income', *Quarterly Journal of Economics* (1971); 'On the solution of optimal control problems as maximization problems', *Annals of Economic and Social Measurement* (1974); 'The effect of economic events on votes for president', *Review of Economics and Statistics* (1978); *Specification, Estimation and Analysis of Macroeconomic Models* (1984).

Walter D. Fisher Professor Emeritus of Economics, Northwestern University. Fellow, Econometric Society; Guggenheim Fellow (1961–2). 'On grouping for maximum homogeneity', *Journal of the American Statistical Association* (1958); 'Estimation in the linear decision model', *International Economic Review* (1962); *Clustering and Aggregation in Economics* (1969); 'An econometric model of intraurban location', *Journal of Regional Science* (1974); 'A note on aggregation and disaggregation', *Econometrica* (1979); *Statistics Economized* (1981).

A. Ronald Gallant Professor, Department of Statistics and Department of Economics, North Carolina State University. Fellow, Econometric Society; Fellow, American Statistical Association. *Nonlinear Statistical Models* (1987); *A Unified Theory of Estimation and Inference for Nonlinear Dynamic Models* (with Halbert L. White, Jr., 1987); 'Semi-nonparametric maximum likelihood estimation', *Econometrica* (with Douglas W. Nychka, 1987); 'On choosing between two nonlinear models estimated robustly: some Monte Carlo evidence' in *Communications in Statistics, Simulation and Computation* (with Victor Aguiree-Torres and Jorge Cumingez, forthcoming).

Vincent J. Geraci Professor, Department of Economics, University of Texas. Brookings Economic Policy Fellowship (1978–9). 'Identification of simultaneous equation models with measurement error', *Journal of Econometrics* (1976); 'Bilateral trade flows and transport costs', *Review of Economics and Statistics* (with W. Prewo, 1977); 'Measuring the benefits from property tax assessment reform', *National Tax Journal* (1977); 'Estimation of simultaneous equation models with measurement error', *Econometrica* (1977); 'An empirical demand and supply model of multilateral trade', *Review of Economics and Statistics* (with W. Prewo, 1982); 'Errors in variables and the individual structural equation', *International Economic Review* (1983).

John Geweke Director, Institute of Statistics and Decision Sciences, Duke University. Fellow, Econometric Society; Alfred P. Sloan Research Fellow (1982–4). 'The approximate slopes of econometric tests', *Econometrica* (1979); 'The Measurement of linear dependence and feedback between multiple time series', *Journal of the American Statistical Association* (1982); 'Causality, exogeneity and inference' in *Advances in Econometrics* (ed. D. Hildenbrand, 1983); 'Inference and causality in economic time series models', *Handbook of Econometrics* (1984); 'The superneutrality of money in the United States: an interpretation of the evidence', *Econometrica* (1986); 'Bayesian inference in econometric models using Monte Carlo integration', *Econometrica* (forthcoming).

C.W. Granger Professor of Economics, University of California. Fellow, Econometric Society; Guggenheim Fellow (1988). *Spectral Analysis of Economics Time Series* (with M. Hatanaka, 1964); *Predictability of Stock Market Prices* (with O. Morgenstern, 1970); *Forecasting Economic Time Series* (with Paul Newbold, 1977); *Introduction to Bilinear Time Series Models* (with A. Andersen, 1978); *Forecasting in Business and Economics* (1980).

Peter E. Hart Emeritus Professor of Economics, University of Reading. 'Entropy and other measures of concentration', *Journal of the Royal Statistical Society* (1971); 'Population densities and optimal aircraft flight paths', *Regional Studies* (1973); 'Moment distributions in economics: an exposition', *Journal of the Royal Statistical Society* (1975); 'The comparative statics and dynamics of income distributions', *Journal of the Royal Statistical Society* (1976); 'The dynamics of earnings, 1963–73', *Economic Journal* (1976); *Youth Unemployment in Great Britain* (1988).

James Joseph Heckman A. Whitmey Griswuld Professor of Economics, Yale University. Fellow, Econometric Society; Guggenheim Fellow (1977–8). 'Shadow prices, market wages and labour supply', *Econometrica* (1974); 'Sample selection bias as a specification error', *Econometrica* (1979); 'A method for minimizing the impact of distributional assumptions in econometric models for duration data', *Econometrica* (1984); 'Determining the impact of federal antidiscrimination policy on the economic status of blacks: a study of South Carolina', *American Economic Review* (1989).

Cheng Hsiao Department of Economics, University of South California. 'Some estimation methods for a random coefficient model', *Econometrica* (1975); 'Measurement error in a dynamic simultaneous equations model with stationary disturbances', *Econometrica* (1979); 'Estimation of dynamic models with error components', *Journal of the American Statistical Association* (with T.W. Anderson, 1980); 'Autoregressive modelling and causal ordering of economic variables', *Journal of Economic Dynamics and Control* (1982); 'Estimating the short-run income elasticity of demand for electricity using cross-sectional categorized data',

Journal of the American Statistical Association (with Dean Mountain, 1985); *Analysis of Panel Data* (1986).

Edward E. Leamer Department of Economics, University College of Los Angles. *Quantitative International Economics* (with R.M. Stern, 1970); *Specification Searches: ad hoc inference with non experimental data* (1978); 'Let's take the con out of econometrics', *American Economic Review* (1983); *Sources of International Comparative Advantage: theory and evidence* (1984); 'The Leontief paradox, reconsidered' in *International Trade: selected readings* (ed. J. Bhagwati, 1986).

Esfandiar Massoumi Professor of Economics, Indiana University. Editor, *Econometric Reviews*. 'A modified Stein-like estimator for the reduced form coefficients of simultaneous equations', *Econometrica* (1978); 'A ridge-like method for simultaneous estimation of simultaneous equations', *Journal of Econometrics* (1980); 'The measurement and decomposition of multi dimensional inequality', *Econometrica* (1986); *Contributions to Econometrics: J.D. Sargan* (ed., 2 vols., 1988); 'A comparison of GRF and other reduced form estimators in simultaneous equation models', *Journal of Econometrics* (with J.H. Jeong, 1988); 'Transaction costs and the interest parity theorem', *Journal of Political Economy* (with J. Pippenger, forthcoming).

G.S. Maddala Graduate Research Professor, University of Florida. Fellow, Econometric Society. *Econometrics* (1977); *Limited Dependent and Qualitative Variables in Econometrics* (1983); *Introduction to Econometrics* (1988).

James N. Morgan Research Scientist and Professor of Economics Emeritus, Institute for Social Research, University of Michigan. Member, National Academy of Sciences; Fellow, American Academy of Arts and Sciences. *The Economics of Personal Choice* (with Greg Duncan and Ann Arbor, 1980); 'The role of time in the measurement of transfers and well-being' in *Economic Transfer in the United States* (ed. Marilyn Moon, 1984); *1985 Household Survey of Grenada* (with Ann Arbor, 1986); 'Consumer choice is more than search' in *Frontier of Research in Consumer Interest* (ed. E. Scott Maynes, 1988); 'Survey estimates of wealth: an assessment of quality' (with Richard T. Curtin and F. Thomas Juster) in *The Measurement of Saving, Investment, and Wealth* (ed. Robert E. Lipsey and Helen S. Tice, 1988).

Forrest D. Nelson Department of Economics, University of Iowa. 'Maximum likelihood methods for models of markets in disequilibrium', *Econometrica* (1974); 'Censored regression models with unobserved, stochastic censoring thresholds', *Journal of Econometrics* (1977); 'Specification and estimation of a simultaneous equation model with limited dependent variables', *International Economic Review* (with L. Olson, 1978); 'A test for misspecification in the censored-normal model', *Econometrica* (1981); 'Efficiency of the two step estimator for models with endogenous sample selection', *Journal of Econometrics* (1984); 'The Iowa presidential stock market: a field experiment' (with R. Forsythe, G. Neumann and J. Wright) in *Research in Experimental Economics* (ed. M. Isaac, 1989).

M. Hashem Pesaran Professor of Economics, Cambridge University; Fellow, Trinity College, Cambridge. 'On the general problem of model selection', *Review of Economic Studies* (1974); *Dynamic Regression: theory and algorithms* (with L.J. Slater, 1980); 'A critique of the proposed tests of the natural rate/rational expectations hypothesis', *Economic Journal* (1982); 'The system of dependent capitalism in pre- and post-revolutionary Iran', *International Journal of Middle East Studies* (1982); *The Limits to Rational Expectations* (1987); *Data-FIT: an interactive software econometric package* (with B. Pesaran, 1987).

T.J. Rothenberg Professor, Department of Economics, University of California. *Efficient Estimation with A Priori Information* (1973); *Least-Square Autoregression with Near-Unit Roots* (with R. Magnus, 1988).

N.E. Savin Professor of Economics, University of Iowa. Fellow, Econometric Society. 'Conflict among criteria for testing hypotheses in the multivariate linear regression model', *Econometrica* (with E.R. Berndt, 1977); 'Testing for unit roots: 1', *Econometrica* (with G.B.A. Evans, 1981); 'Testing for unit roots: 2', *Econometrica* (with G.B.A. Evans, 1984); 'Rational expectations equilibrium, learning and model specification', *Econometrica* (with M.M. Bray, 1986); 'Finite sample distributions of t and F statistics in an AR(1) model', *Econometric Theory* (with J.C. Nankervis, 1987); 'The student's t approximation in a stationary first order autoregressive model', *Econometrica* (with J.C. Nankervis, 1988).

Herbert A. Simon Professor of Computer Science and Psychology, Carnegie-Mellon University. Nobel Memorial Prize in Economics (1978); Distinguished Fellow, American Economic Association. *Administrative Behaviour* (1947); *Models of Man* (1957); *The Sciences of the Artificial* (1969); *Human Problem Solving* (with A. Newell, 1972); *Models of Discovery* (1977); *Models of Bounded Rationality* (1982).

P.A.V.B Swamy Senior Economist, Federal Reserve Board, Washington. 'Bayesian and non-Bayesian analysis of switching regressions and of random coefficient regression models', *Journal of the American Statistical Association* (with J.S. Mehta, 1975); 'Estimation of common coefficients in two regression equations', *Journal of Econometrics* (with J.S. Mehta, 1979); 'Linear prediction and estimation methods for regression models with stationary stochastic coefficients', *Journal of Econometrics* (with P.A. Tinsley, 1980); 'A comparison of estimators for undersized samples', *Journal of Econometrics* (1980); 'Convergence of the moments of the modified k-class estimators', *Sankhya* (with J.S. Mehta and N.S. Iyengar, 1983); 'Further results on estimating linear regression models with partial prior information', *Economic Modelling* (with A.K. Kashyap, J.S. Mehta and R.D. Porter, 1988).

Insan Tunali Department of Economics, Cornell University and Economics Research Centre, University of Chicago. 'A general structure for models of double-selection and an application to a joint migration/earnings process with re-migration', *Research in Labor Economics* (1986).

Roger N. Waud Professor of Economics, University of California; Research Associate, National Bureau of Economic Research. 'Net outlay uncertainty and liquidity preference as behaviour towards risk', *Journal of Money, Credit and Banking* (1975); 'Asymmetric policy makes utility functions and optimal policy under uncertainty', *Econometrica* (1976); 'An examination of aggregate price uncertainty in four countries and some implications for real output', *International Economic Review* (with R. Friyen, 1987); 'Real business cycles and the Lucas paradigm', *Economic Inquiry* (with R. Froyen, 1988).

Paul Zarembka Professor of Economics, State University of New York at Buffalo. Fulbright-Hayes Lecturer, Academy of Economic Studies, Poznan, Poland. *Towards a Theory of Economic Development* (1972); *Frontiers in Econometrics* (ed., 1974); *Essays in Modern Capital Theory* (ed., with M. Brown and K. Sato, 1976).